Oh My Goddess!

ああっ女神さまっ

12

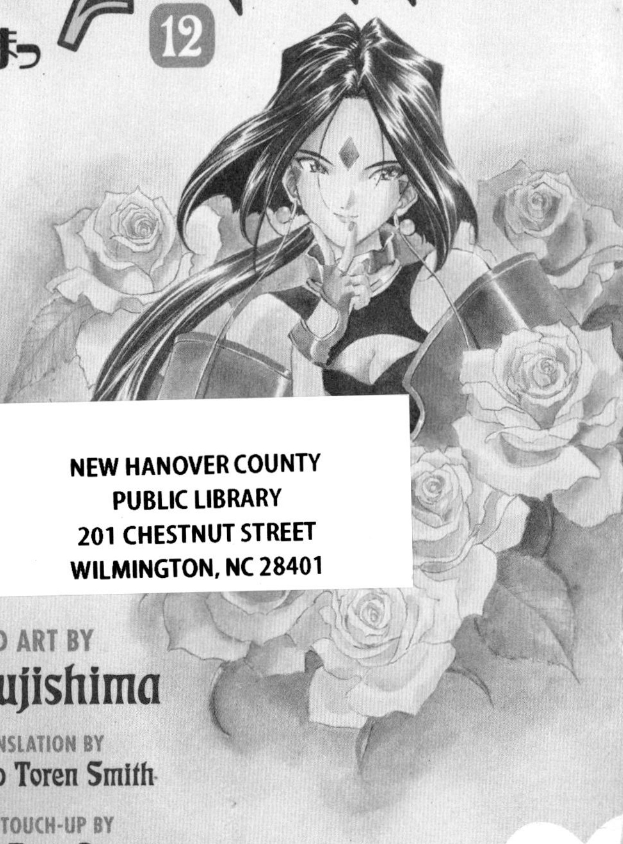

STORY AND ART BY
Kosuke Fujishima

ORIGINAL TRANSLATION BY
Dana Lewis AND Toren Smith

LETTERING AND TOUCH-UP BY
Susie Lee AND Betty Dong
WITH Tom2K, Tom Orzechowski,
L. Lois Buhalis AND Tomoko Saito

DARK HORSE MANGA™

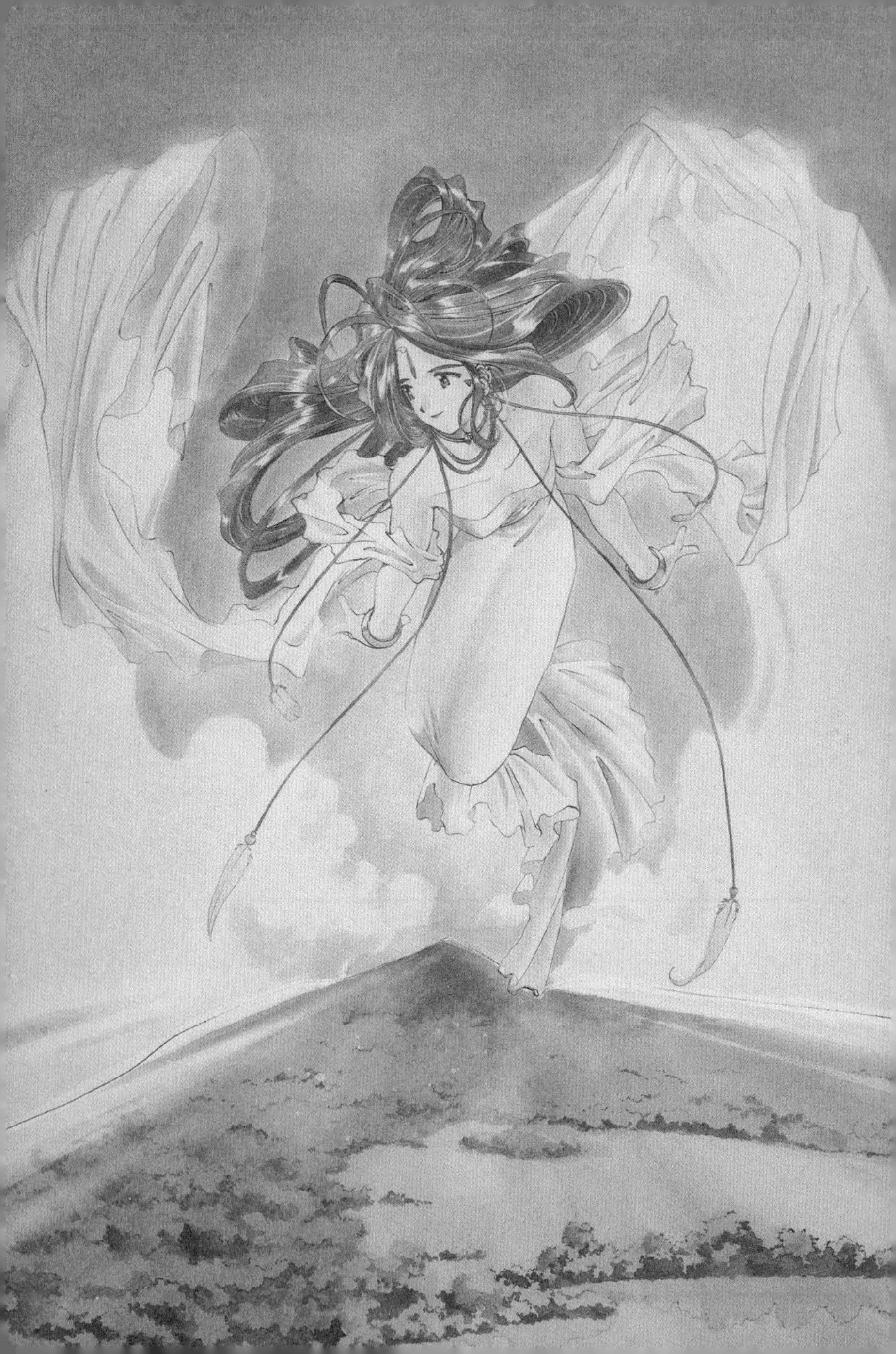

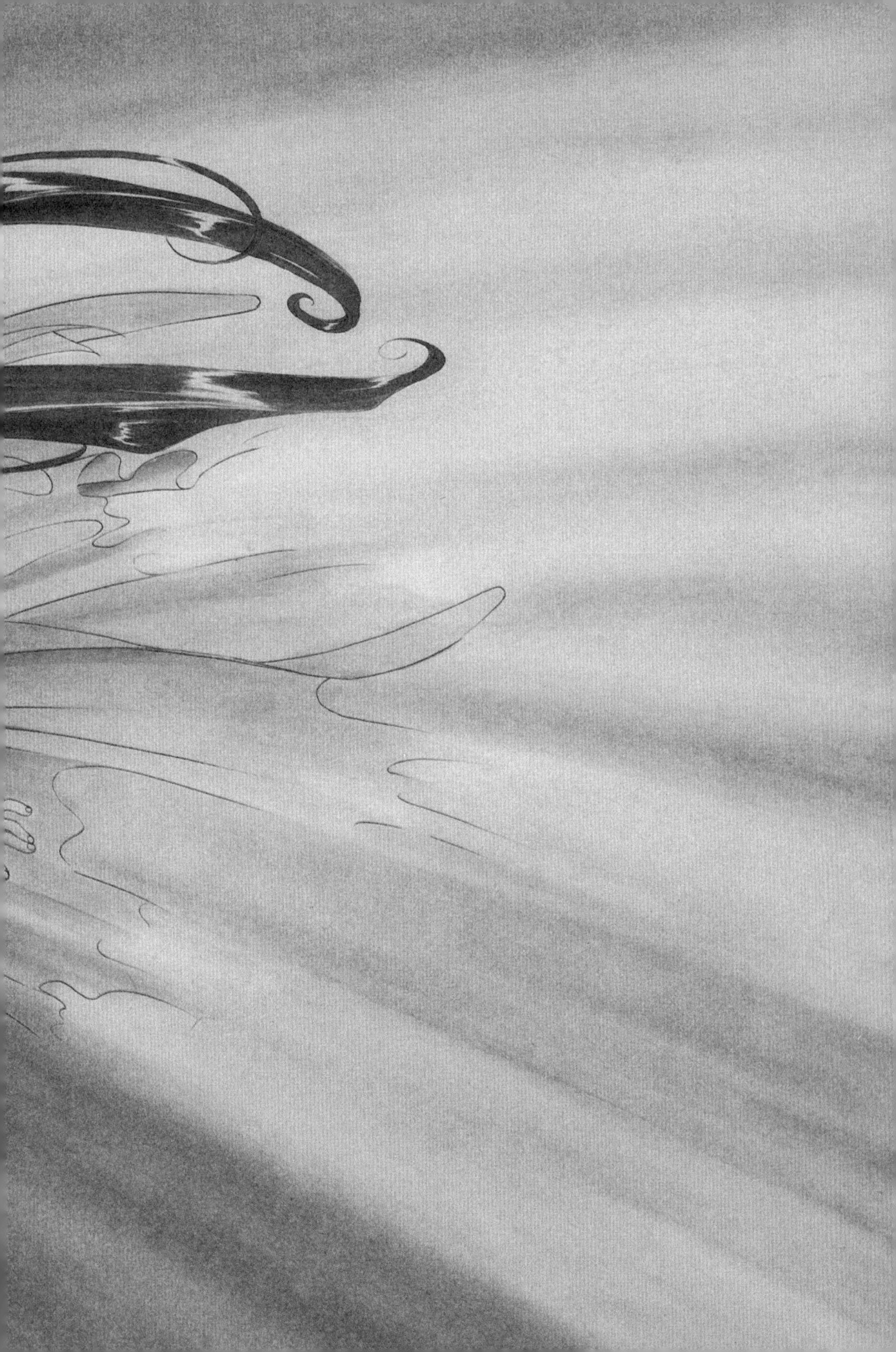

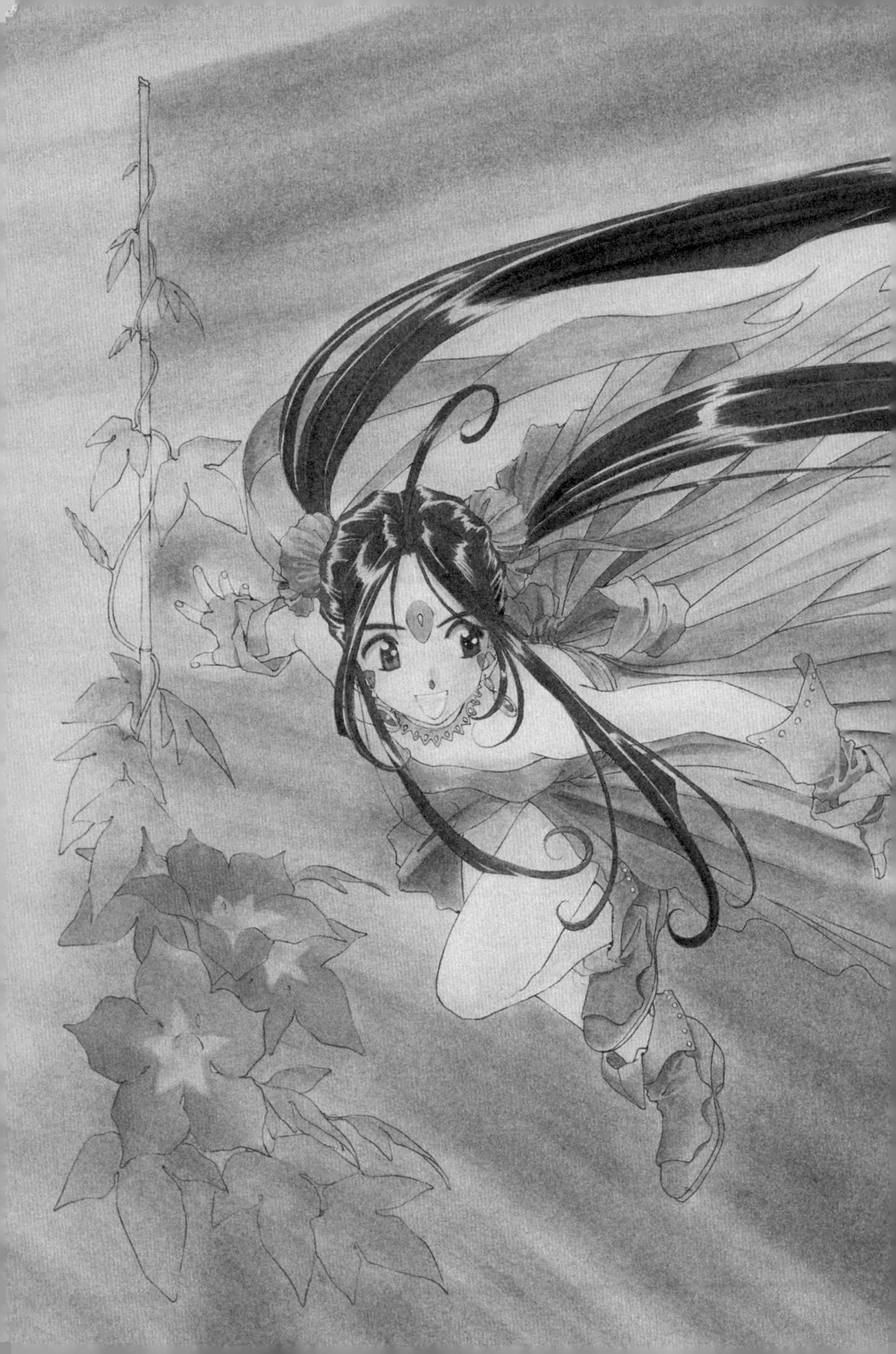

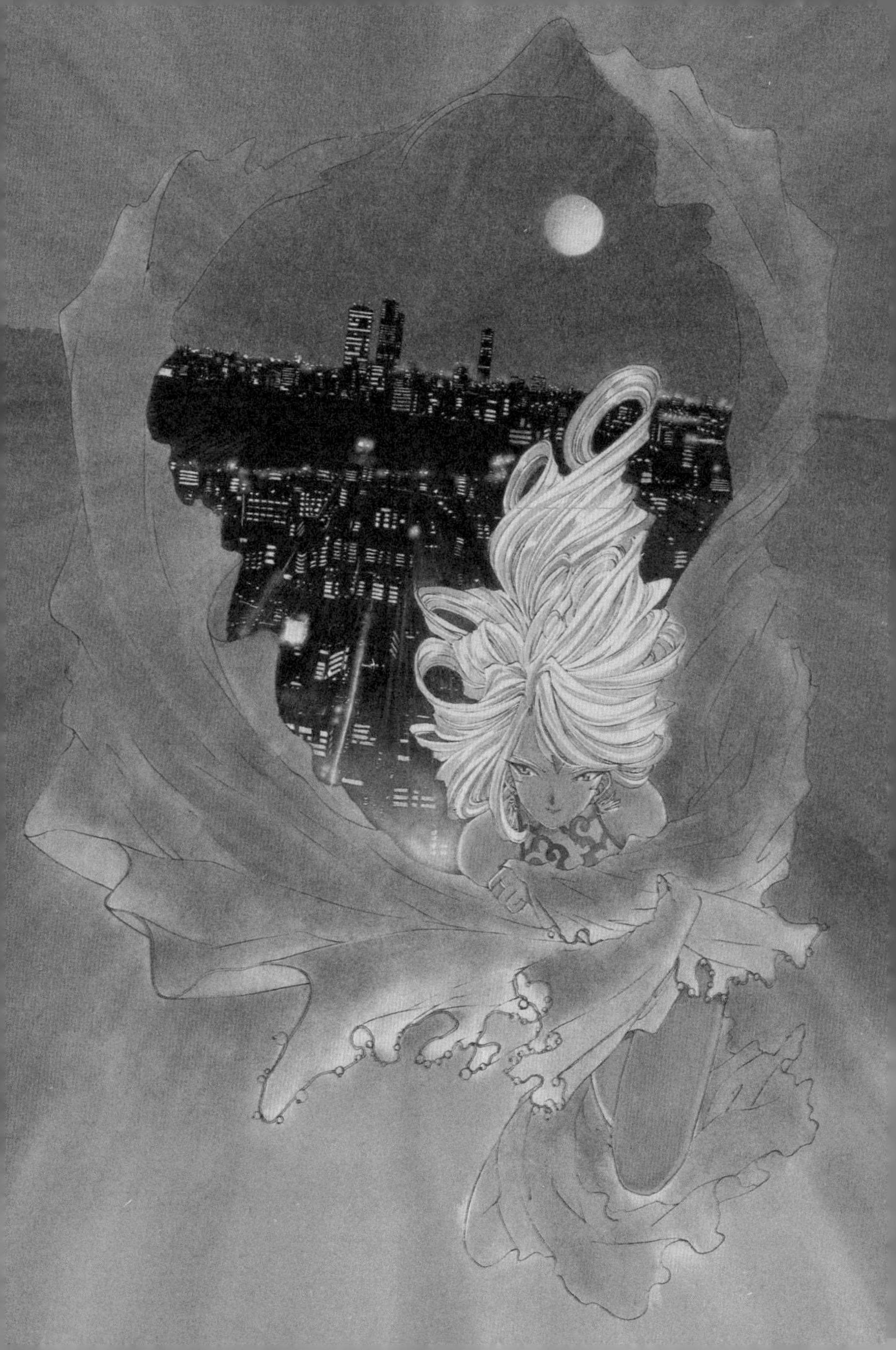

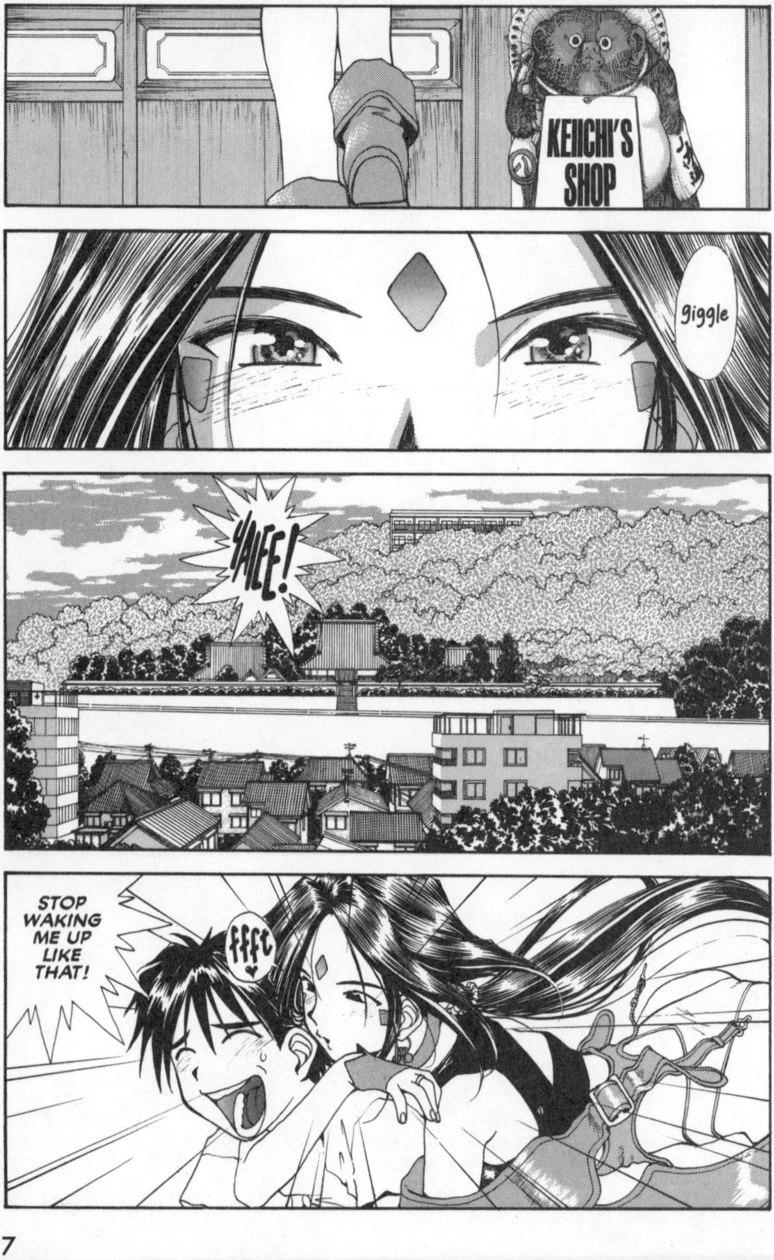
KEIICHI'S SHOP
giggle
YAIEE!
STOP WAKING ME UP LIKE THAT!
ffft

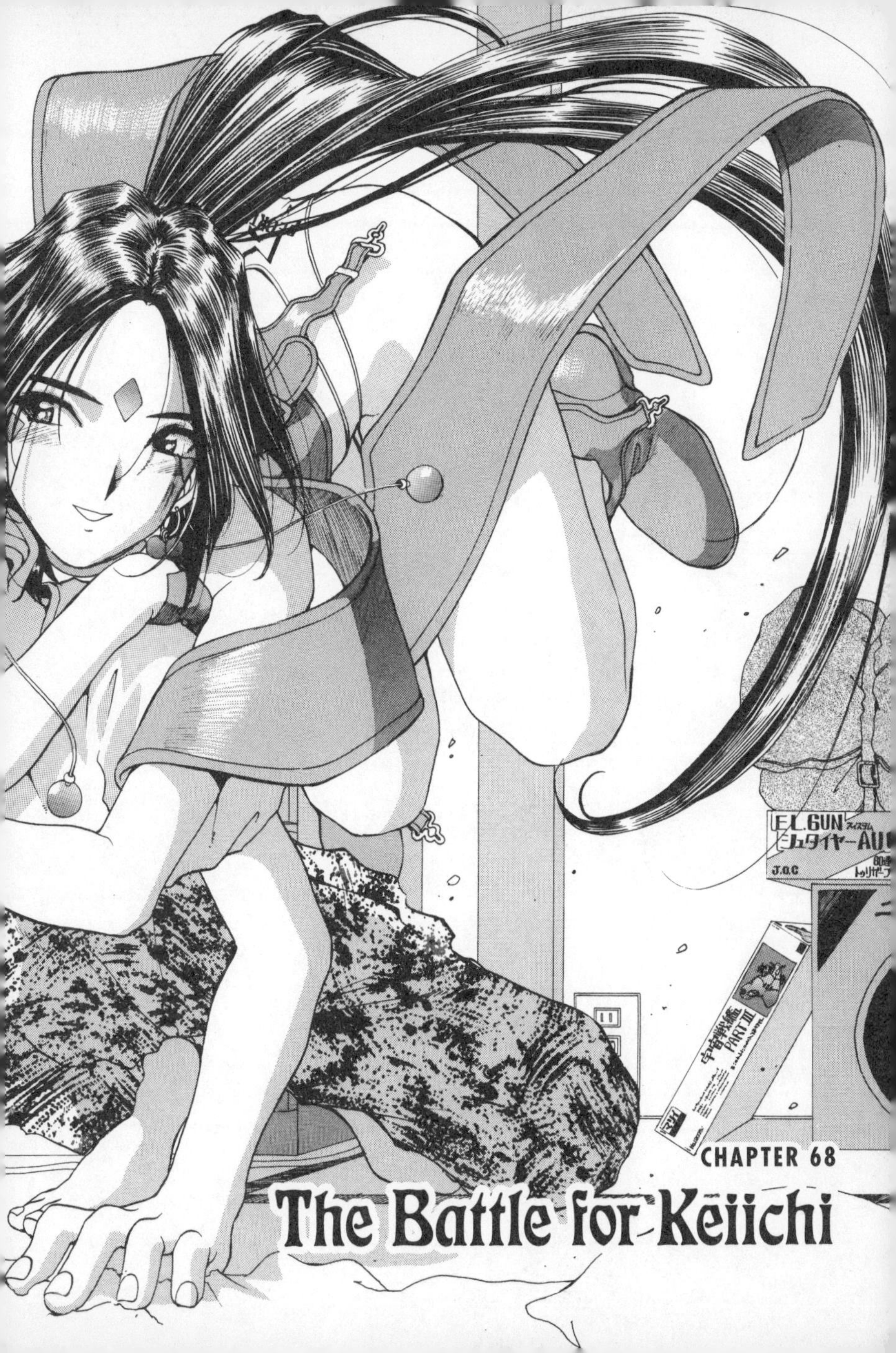
E.L.GUN
J.O.C

CHAPTER 68

The Battle for Keiichi

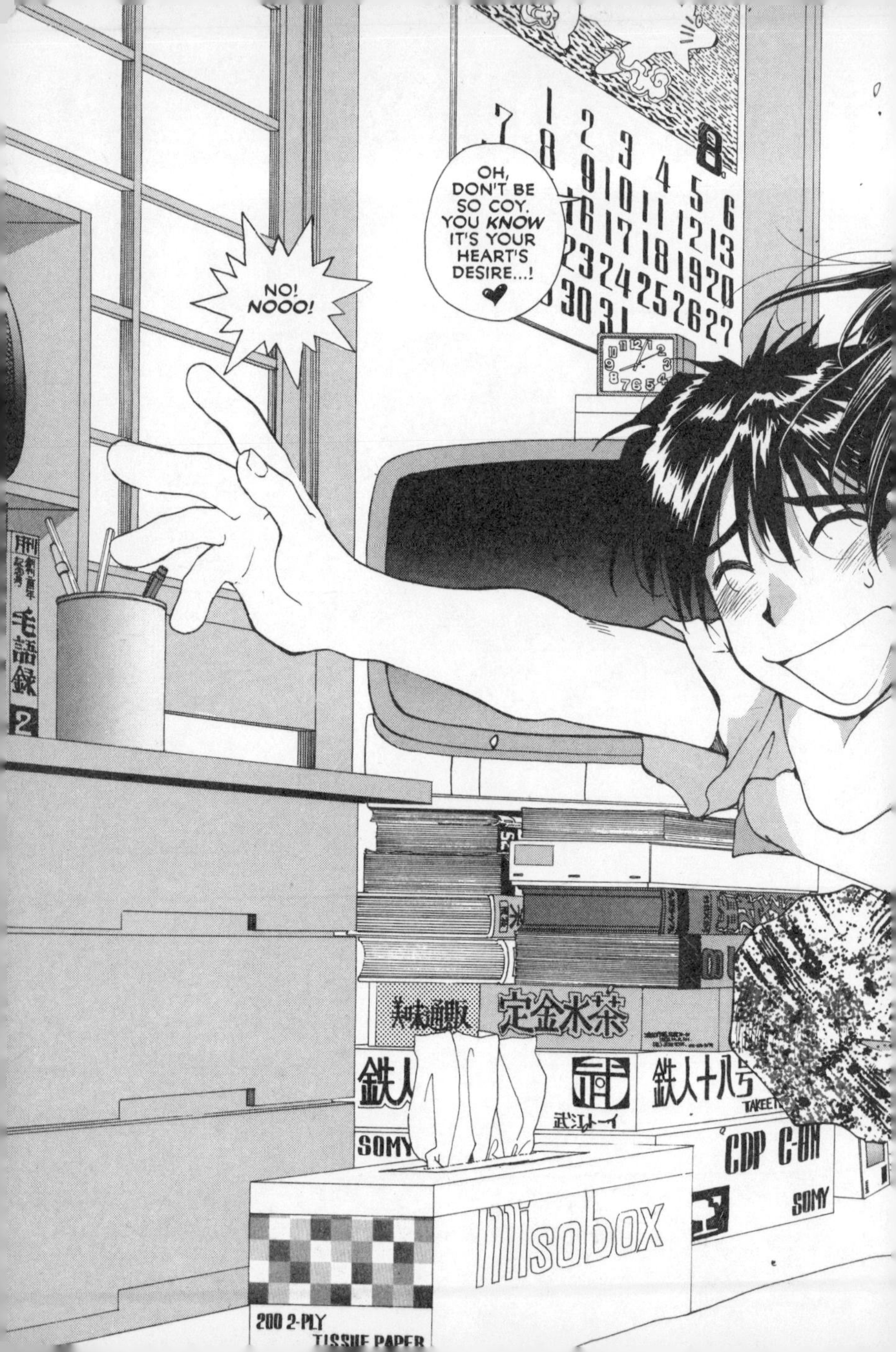
OH, DON'T BE SO COY. YOU *KNOW* IT'S YOUR HEART'S DESIRE...! ♥
NO! *NOOO!*

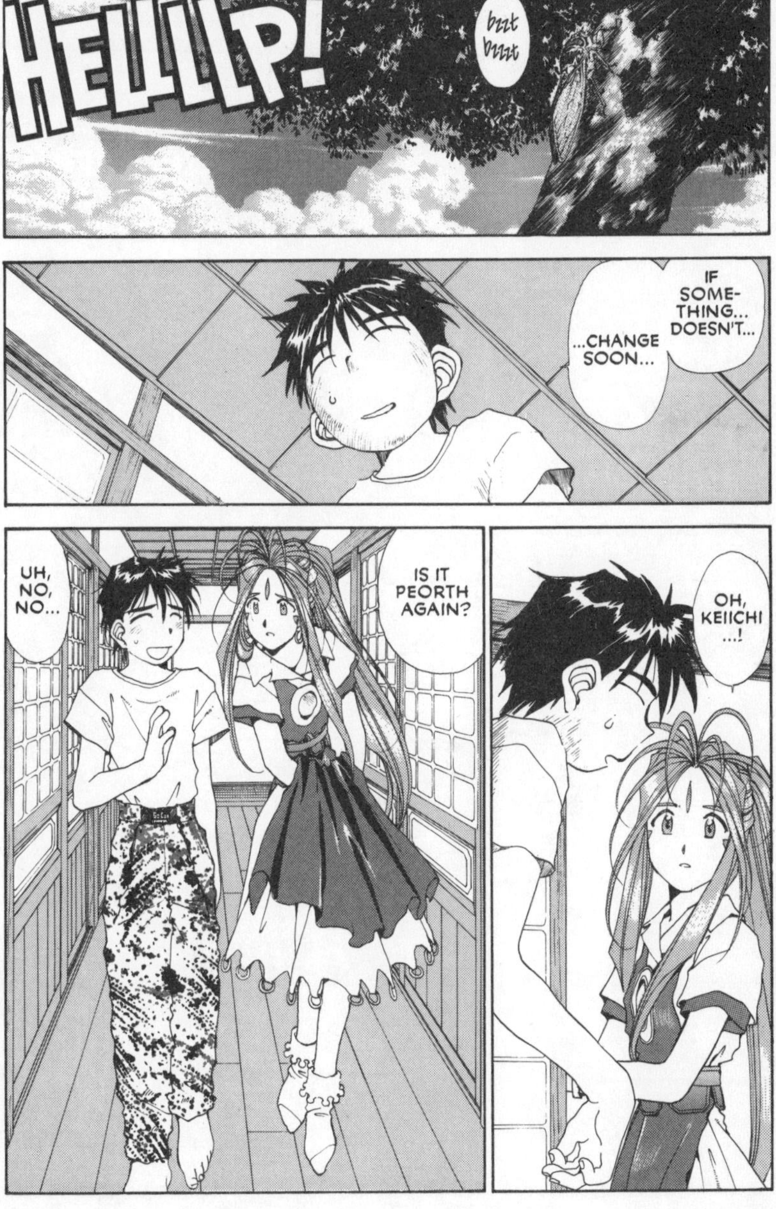
bzzt bzzzt
HELLLP!
IF SOME-THING... DOESN'T...
...CHANGE SOON...
OH, KEIICHI ...!
IS IT PEORTH AGAIN?
UH, NO, NO...

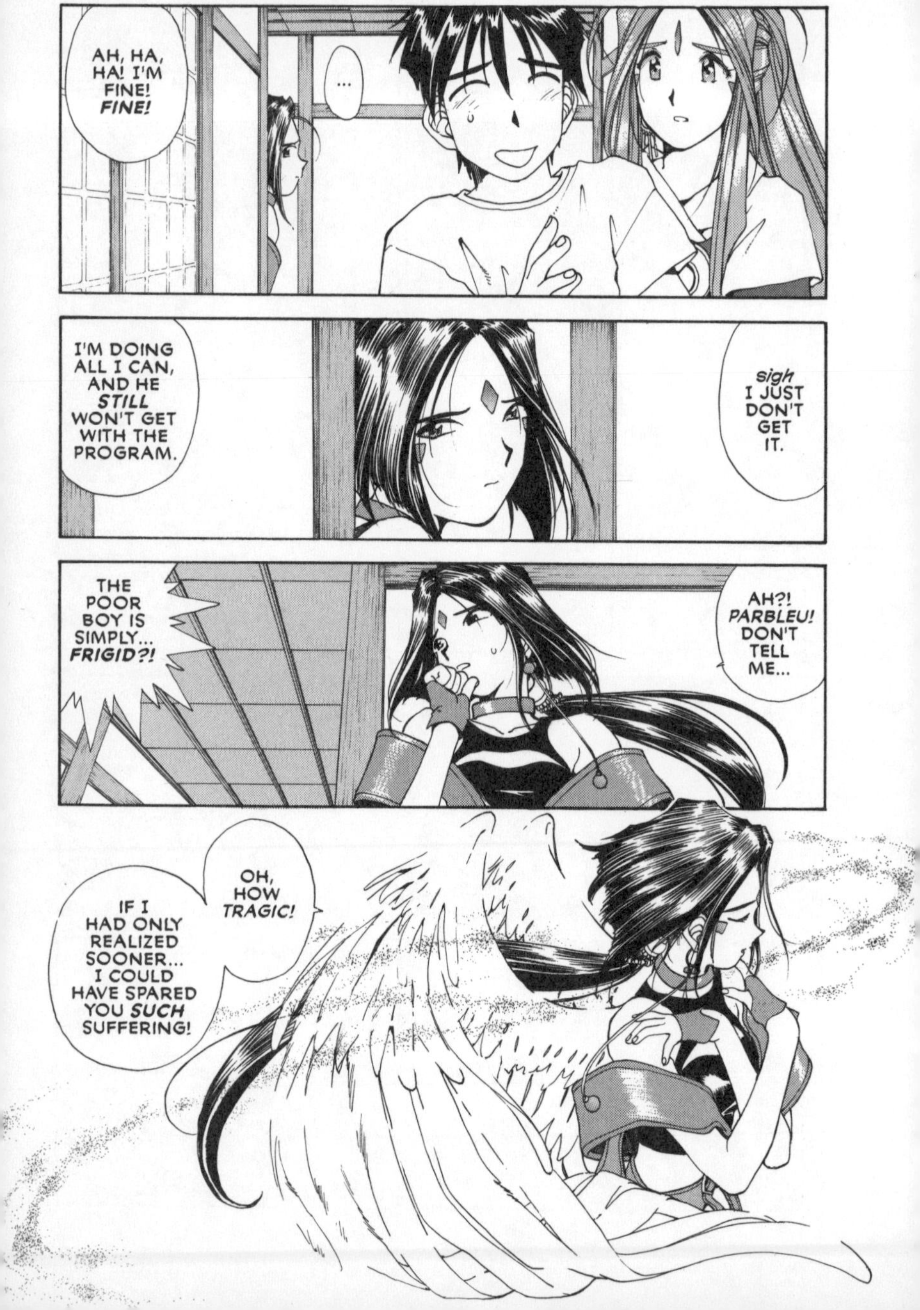
...
AH, HA, HA! I'M FINE! *FINE!*
sigh I JUST DON'T GET IT.
I'M DOING ALL I CAN, AND HE *STILL* WON'T GET WITH THE PROGRAM.
AH?! *PARBLEU!* DON'T TELL ME...
THE POOR BOY IS SIMPLY... *FRIGID?!*
OH, HOW *TRAGIC!*
IF I HAD ONLY REALIZED SOONER... I COULD HAVE SPARED YOU *SUCH* SUFFERING!

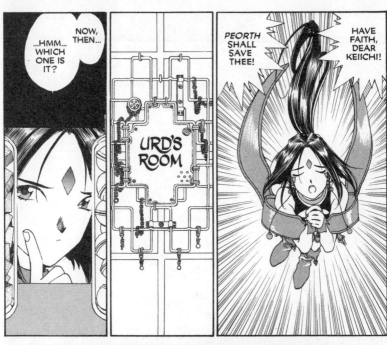

HAVE FAITH, DEAR KEIICHI!
PEORTH SHALL SAVE THEE!
URD'S ROOM
NOW, THEN...
...HMM... WHICH ONE IS IT?
SUPER GROWTH POTION GIANT X...
...M-BOY-TYPE OXYGUM...
THIS IS ALL SO POINTLESS, URD.
WHERE IS THE ONLY ONE THAT MATTERS ...?
AH! HERE WE ARE!
LOVE SEEDS!

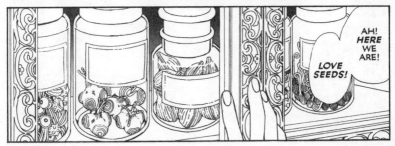

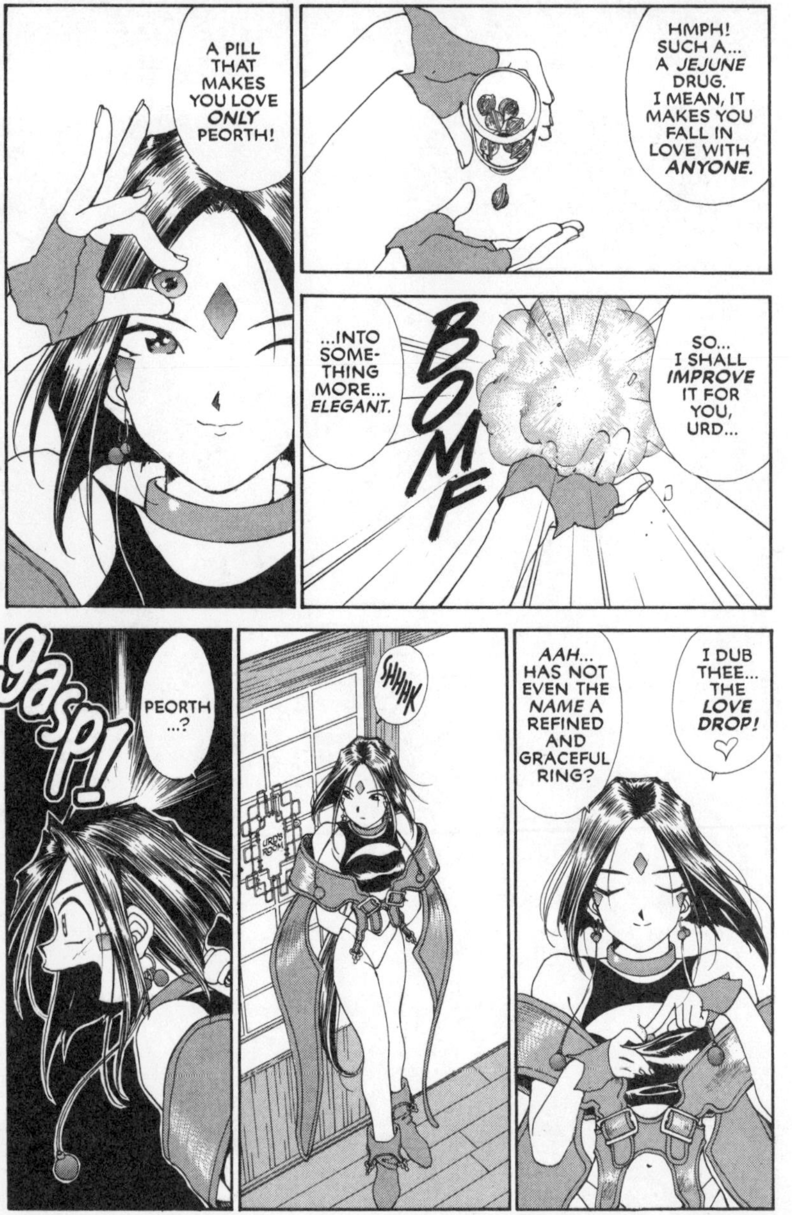
HMPH! SUCH A... A *JEJUNE* DRUG. I MEAN, IT MAKES YOU FALL IN LOVE WITH **ANYONE.**
SO... I SHALL *IMPROVE* IT FOR YOU, URD...
BOMF
...INTO SOMETHING MORE... *ELEGANT.*
A PILL THAT MAKES YOU LOVE *ONLY* PEORTH!
I DUB THEE... THE *LOVE DROP!*
AAH... HAS NOT EVEN THE *NAME* A REFINED AND GRACEFUL RING?
SHHHK
URD'S ROOM
gasp!
PEORTH ...?

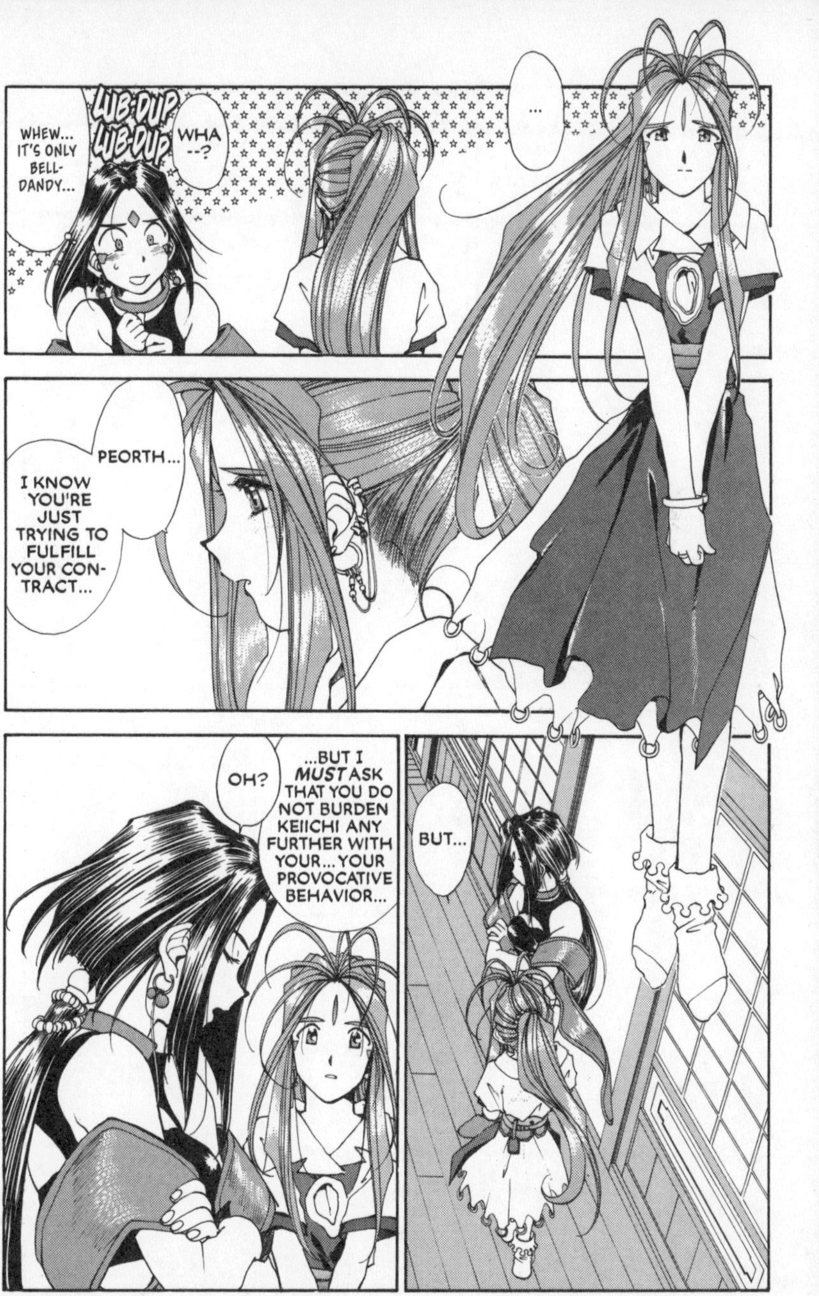
...
WHA --?
LUB-DUP LUB-DUP
WHEW... IT'S ONLY BELL-DANDY...
PEORTH...
I KNOW YOU'RE JUST TRYING TO FULFILL YOUR CON-TRACT...
BUT...
...BUT I *MUST* ASK THAT YOU DO NOT BURDEN KEIICHI ANY FURTHER WITH YOUR... YOUR PROVOCATIVE BEHAVIOR...
OH?

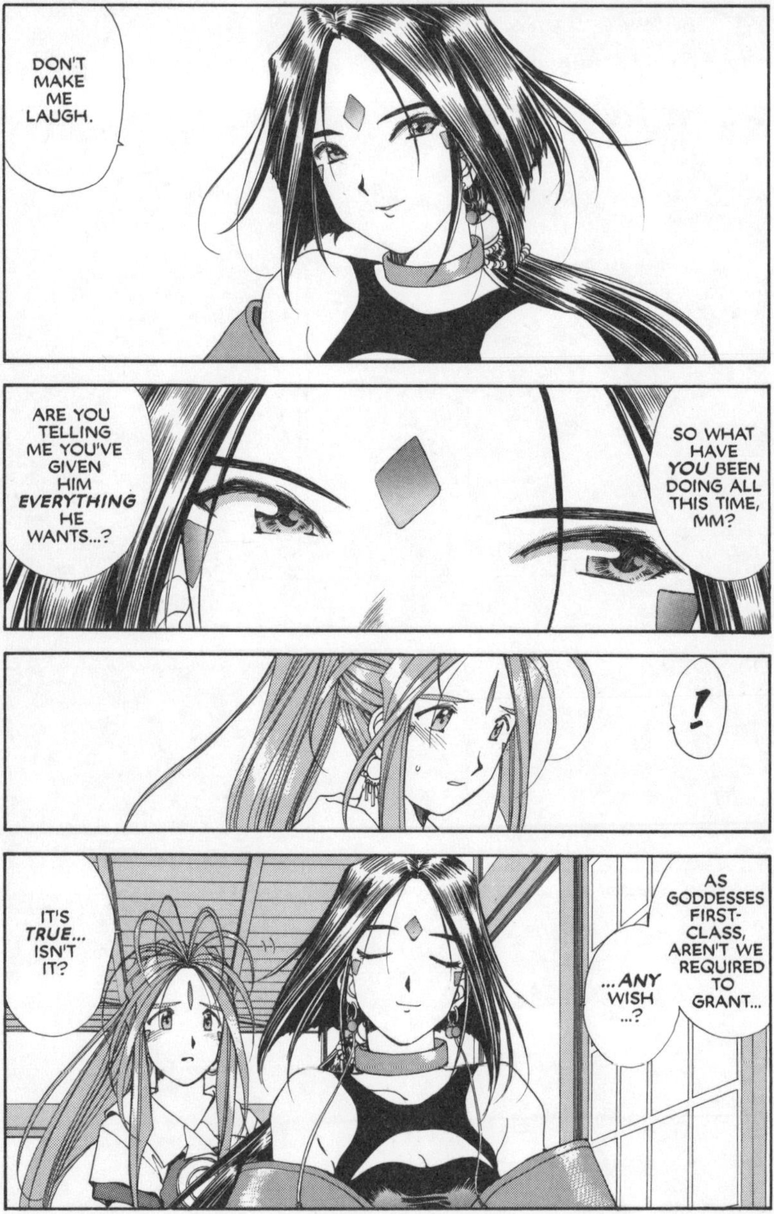
DON'T MAKE ME LAUGH.
SO WHAT HAVE *YOU* BEEN DOING ALL THIS TIME, MM?
ARE YOU TELLING ME YOU'VE GIVEN HIM *EVERYTHING* HE WANTS...?
!
AS GODDESSES FIRST-CLASS, AREN'T WE REQUIRED TO GRANT...
...*ANY* WISH ...?
IT'S *TRUE*... ISN'T IT?

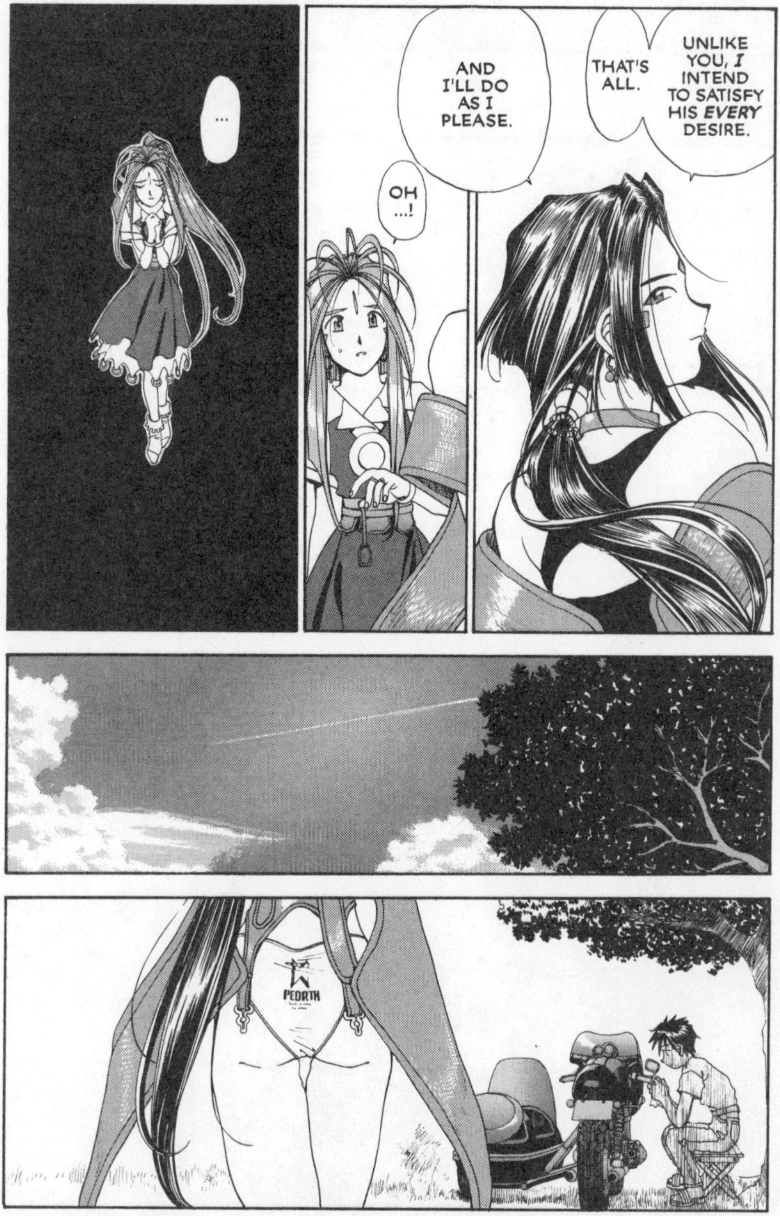
UNLIKE YOU, *I* INTEND TO SATISFY HIS *EVERY* DESIRE.
THAT'S ALL.
AND I'LL DO AS I PLEASE.
OH ...!
...

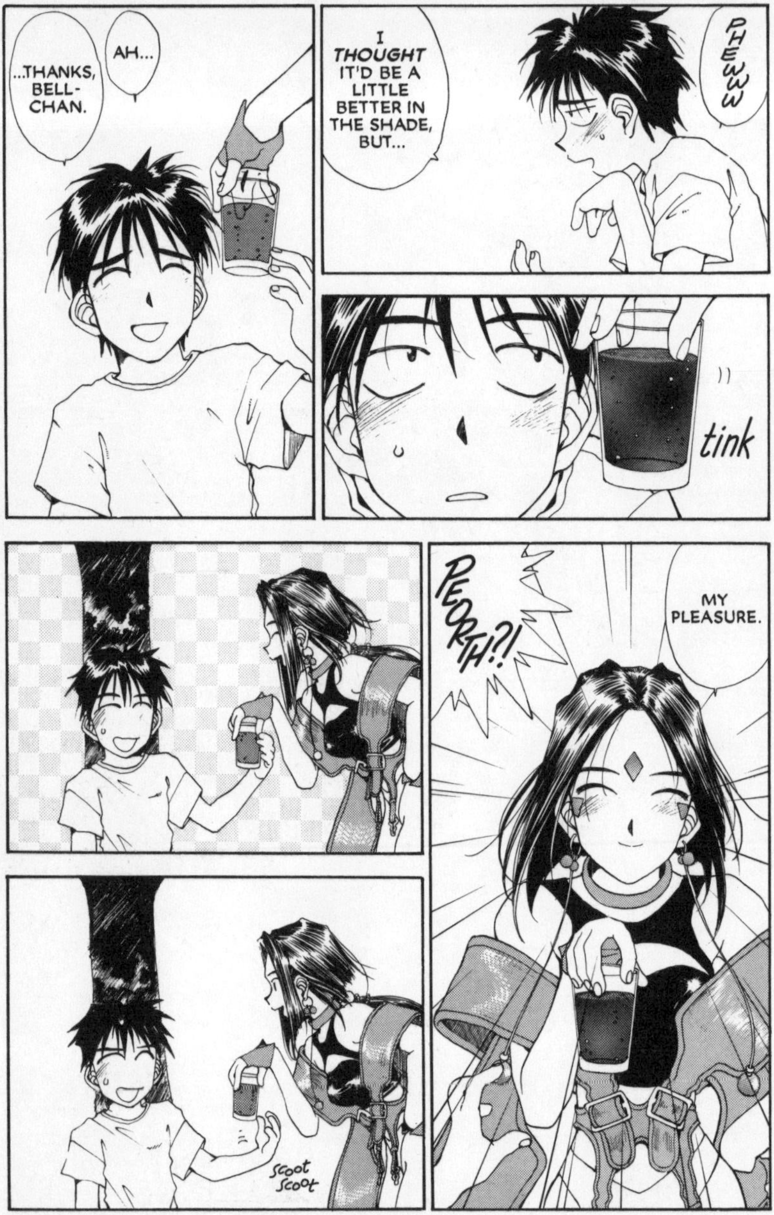
PHEWWW
I THOUGHT IT'D BE A LITTLE BETTER IN THE SHADE, BUT...
tink
AH...
...THANKS, BELL-CHAN.
MY PLEASURE.
PEORTH?!
scoot scoot

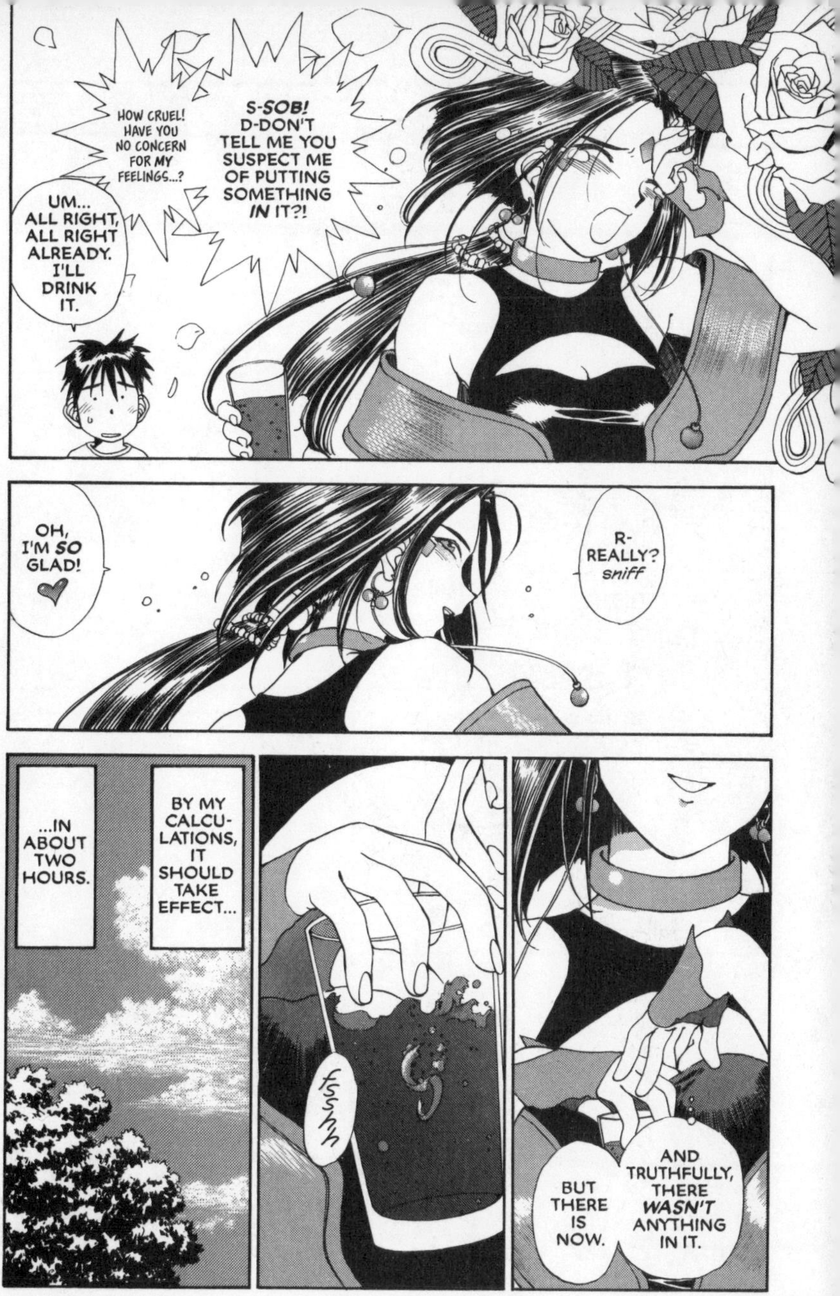

S-SOB! D-DON'T TELL ME YOU SUSPECT ME OF PUTTING SOMETHING IN IT?!
HOW CRUEL! HAVE YOU NO CONCERN FOR MY FEELINGS...?
UM... ALL RIGHT, ALL RIGHT ALREADY. I'LL DRINK IT.
R-REALLY? sniff
OH, I'M SO GLAD! ♥
AND TRUTHFULLY, THERE WASN'T ANYTHING IN IT.
BUT THERE IS NOW.
BY MY CALCULATIONS, IT SHOULD TAKE EFFECT...
...IN ABOUT TWO HOURS.

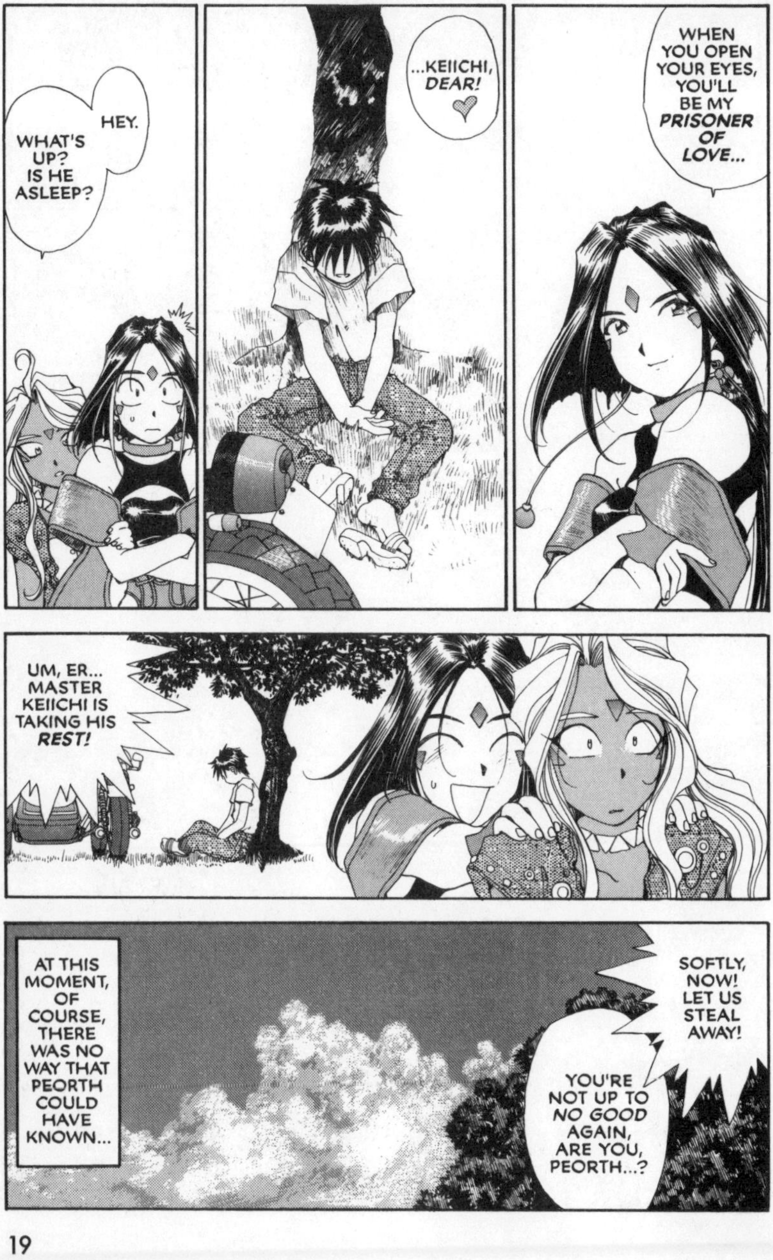
WHEN YOU OPEN YOUR EYES, YOU'LL BE MY *PRISONER OF LOVE*...
...KEIICHI, *DEAR!*
HEY.
WHAT'S UP? IS HE ASLEEP?
UM, ER... MASTER KEIICHI IS TAKING HIS *REST!*
SOFTLY, NOW! LET US STEAL AWAY!
YOU'RE NOT UP TO *NO GOOD* AGAIN, ARE YOU, PEORTH...?
AT THIS MOMENT, OF COURSE, THERE WAS NO WAY THAT PEORTH COULD HAVE KNOWN...

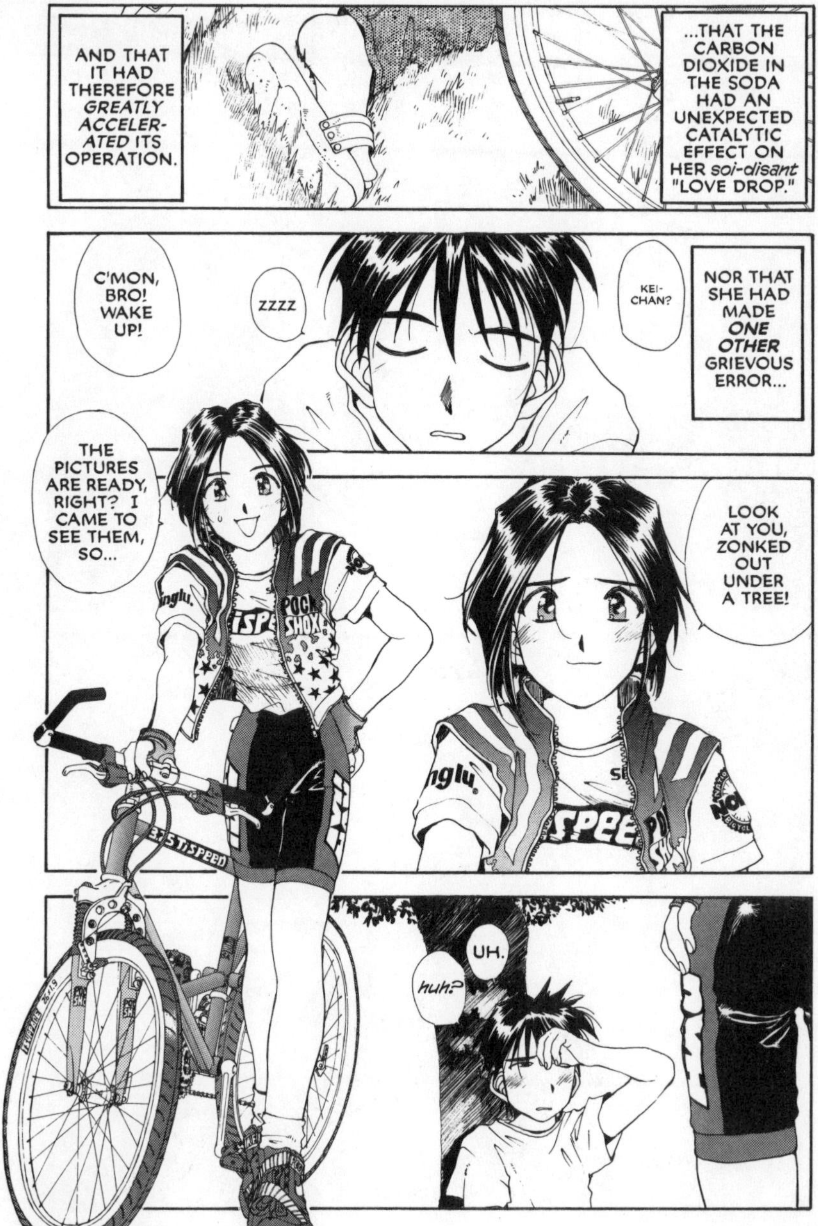
...THAT THE CARBON DIOXIDE IN THE SODA HAD AN UNEXPECTED CATALYTIC EFFECT ON HER *soi-disant* "LOVE DROP."
AND THAT IT HAD THEREFORE *GREATLY ACCELERATED* ITS OPERATION.
NOR THAT SHE HAD MADE ***ONE OTHER*** GRIEVOUS ERROR...
KEI-CHAN?
ZZZZ
C'MON, BRO! WAKE UP!
LOOK AT YOU, ZONKED OUT UNDER A TREE!
THE PICTURES ARE READY, RIGHT? I CAME TO SEE THEM, SO...
UH.
huh?

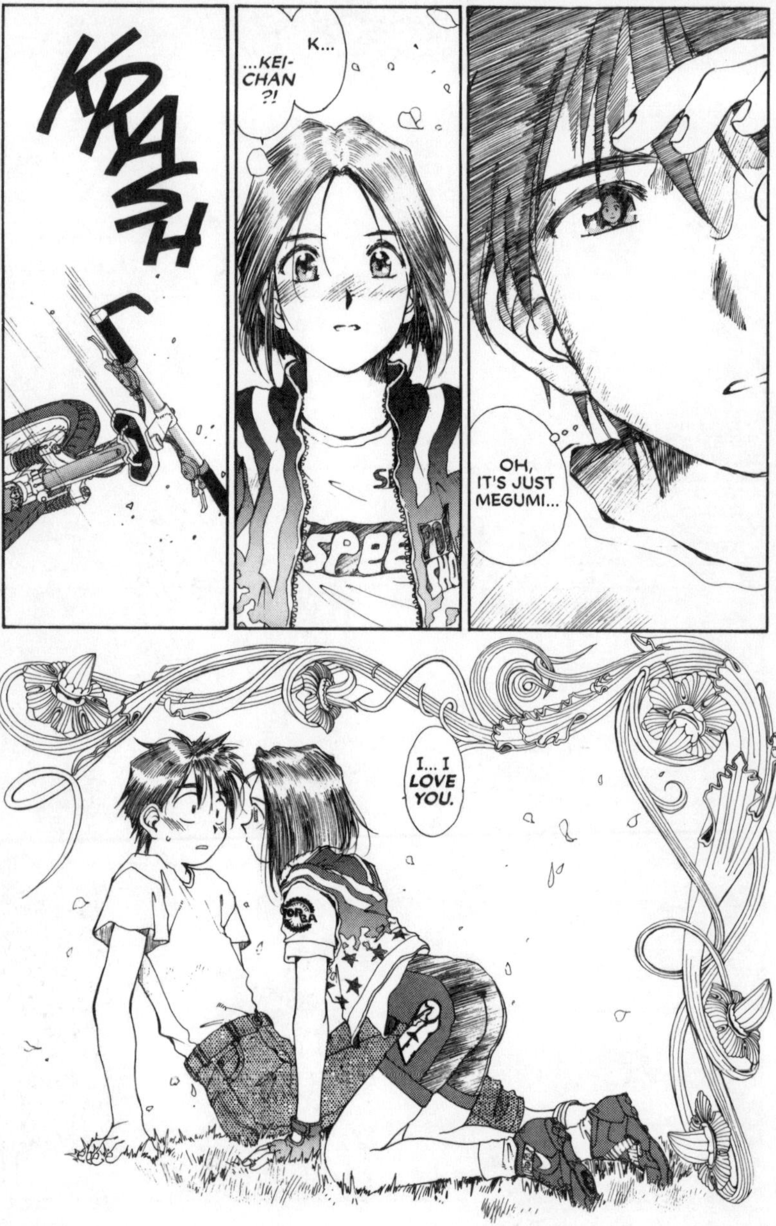
OH, IT'S JUST MEGUMI...
K...
...KEI-CHAN ?!
KRASH
I... I *LOVE* YOU.

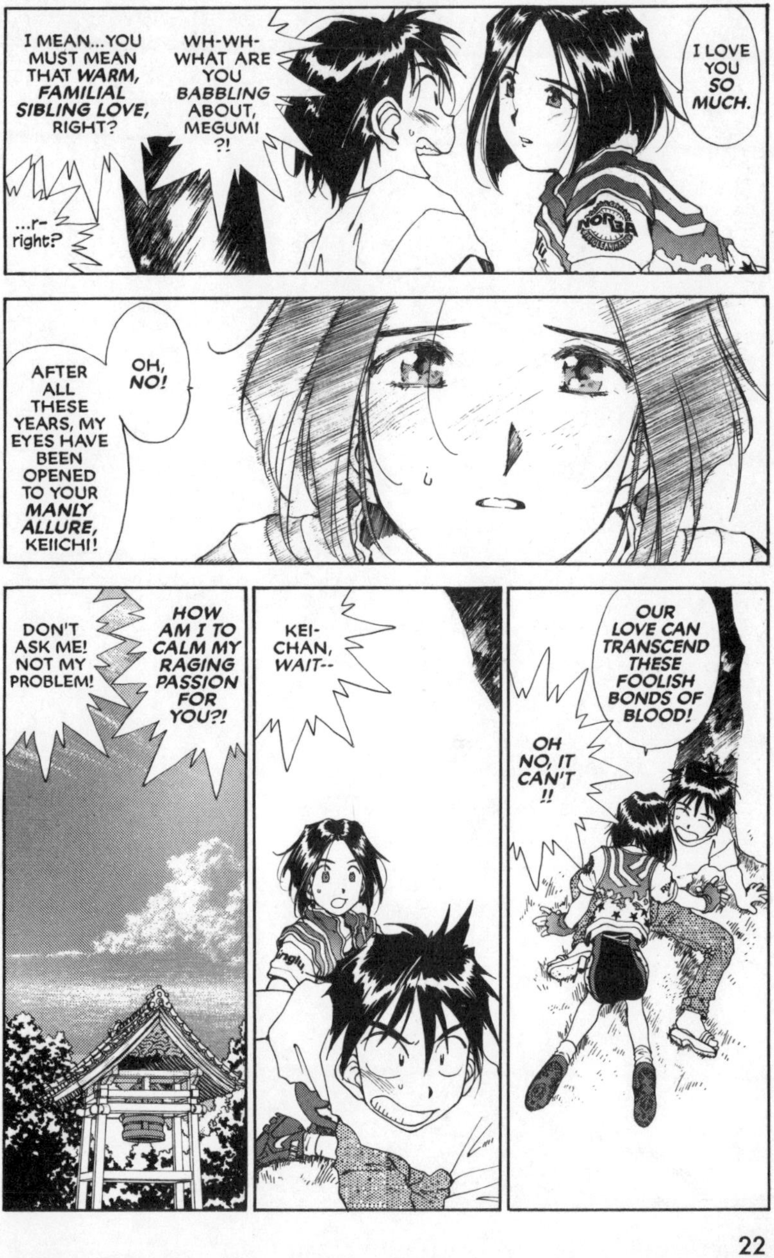
I LOVE YOU SO MUCH.
WH-WH-WHAT ARE YOU BABBLING ABOUT, MEGUMI?!
I MEAN...YOU MUST MEAN THAT WARM, FAMILIAL SIBLING LOVE, RIGHT?
...r-right?
OH, NO!
AFTER ALL THESE YEARS, MY EYES HAVE BEEN OPENED TO YOUR MANLY ALLURE, KEIICHI!
OUR LOVE CAN TRANSCEND THESE FOOLISH BONDS OF BLOOD!
OH NO, IT CAN'T!!
KEI-CHAN, WAIT--
HOW AM I TO CALM MY RAGING PASSION FOR YOU?!
DON'T ASK ME! NOT MY PROBLEM!

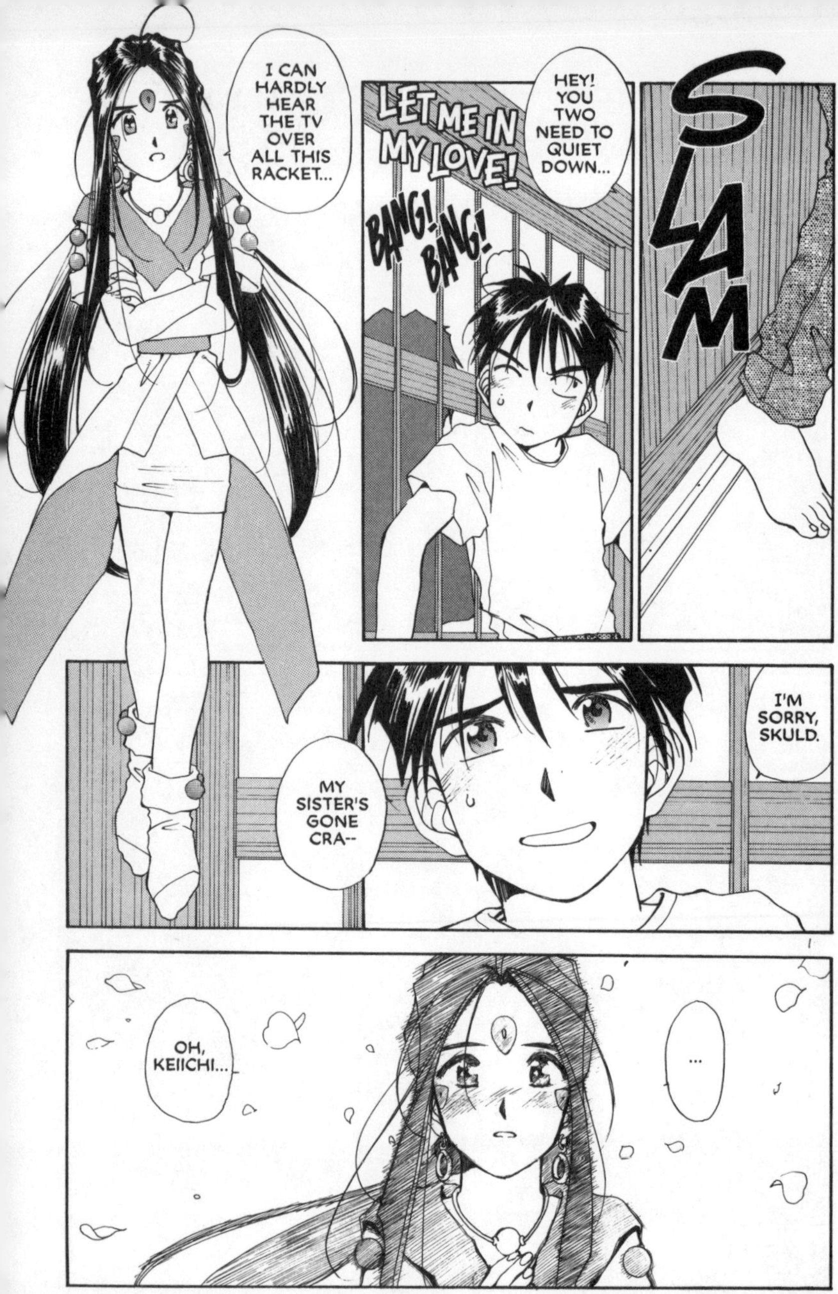
SLAM
LET ME IN MY LOVE!
BANG! BANG!
HEY! YOU TWO NEED TO QUIET DOWN...
I CAN HARDLY HEAR THE TV OVER ALL THIS RACKET...
I'M SORRY, SKULD.
MY SISTER'S GONE CRA--
...
OH, KEIICHI...

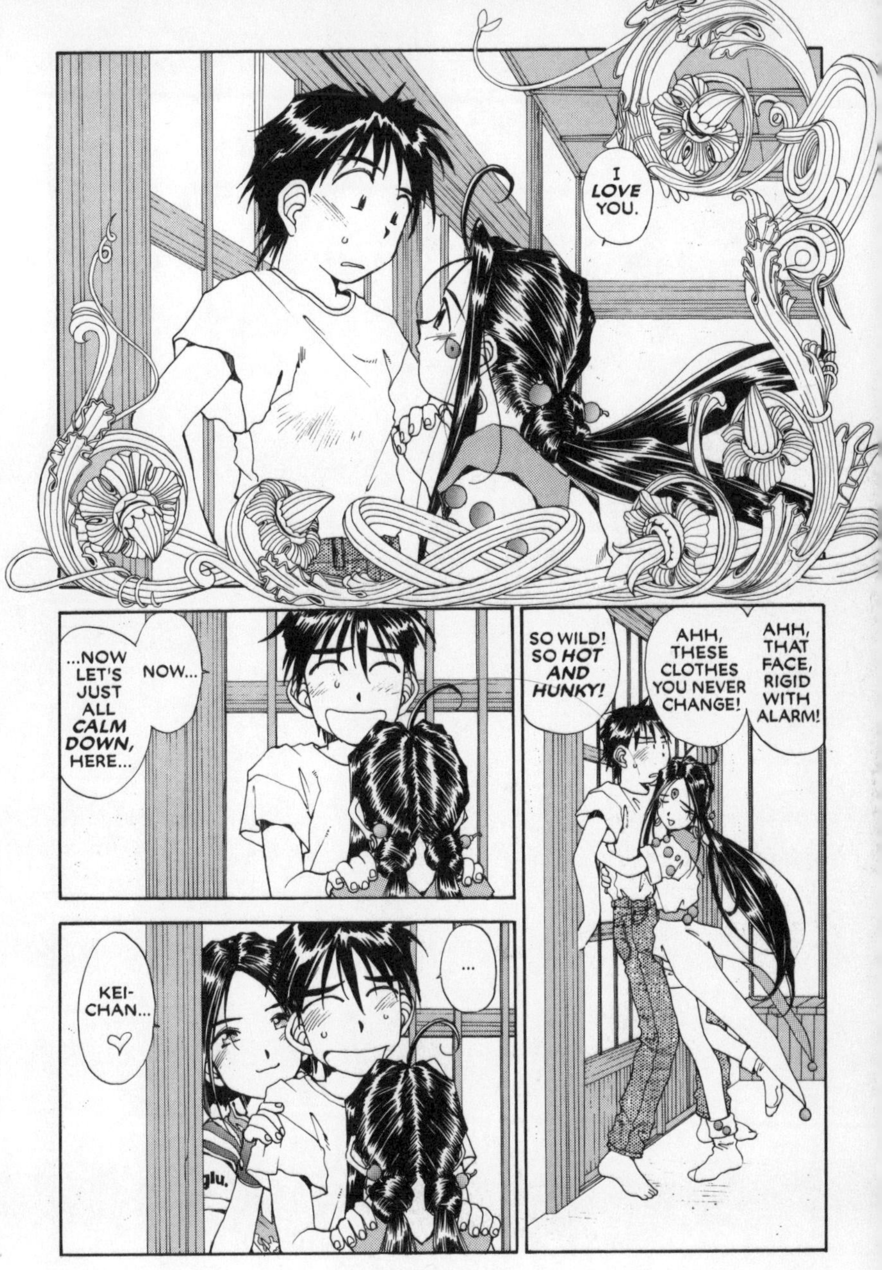
I *LOVE* YOU.
AHH, THAT FACE, RIGID WITH ALARM!
AHH, THESE CLOTHES YOU NEVER CHANGE!
SO WILD! SO *HOT AND HUNKY!*
NOW...
...NOW LET'S JUST ALL *CALM DOWN,* HERE...
...
KEI-CHAN... ♡

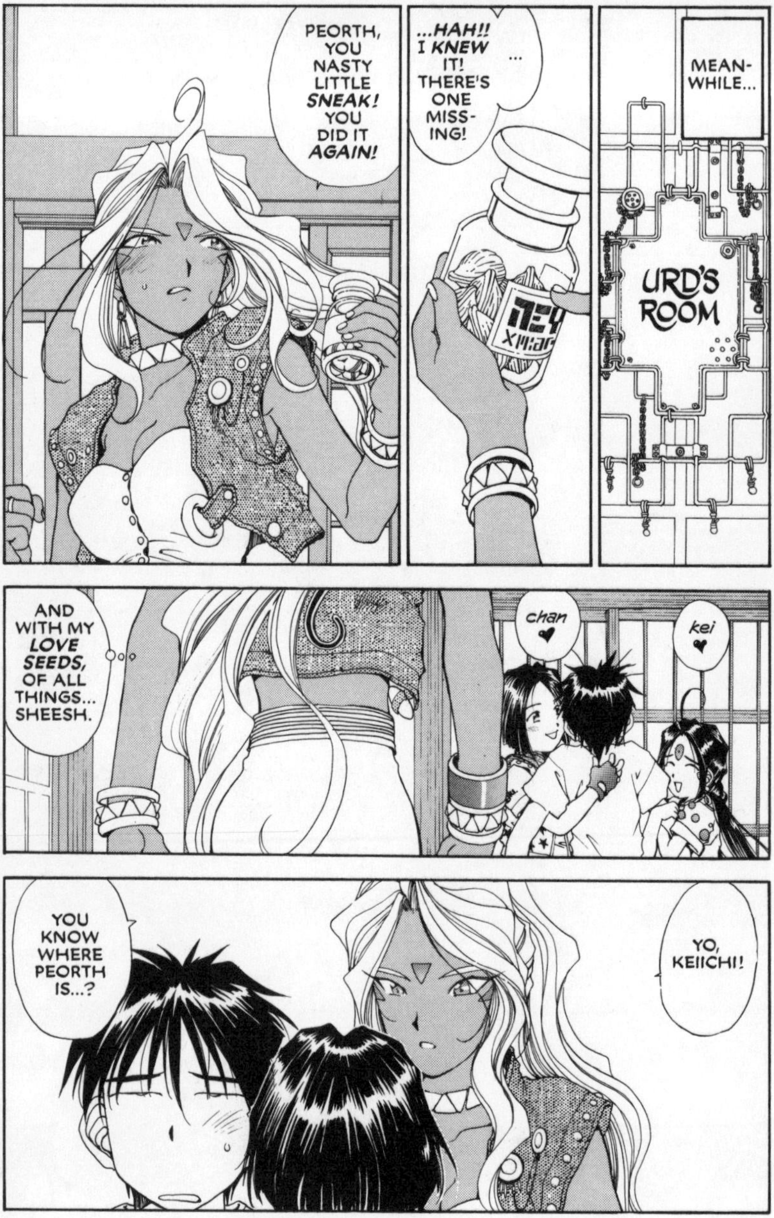
MEAN-WHILE...
URD'S ROOM
...HAH!! I KNEW IT! THERE'S ONE MISSING!
...
PEORTH, YOU NASTY LITTLE SNEAK! YOU DID IT AGAIN!
kei ♥
chan ♥
AND WITH MY LOVE SEEDS, OF ALL THINGS... SHEESH.
YO, KEIICHI!
YOU KNOW WHERE PEORTH IS...?

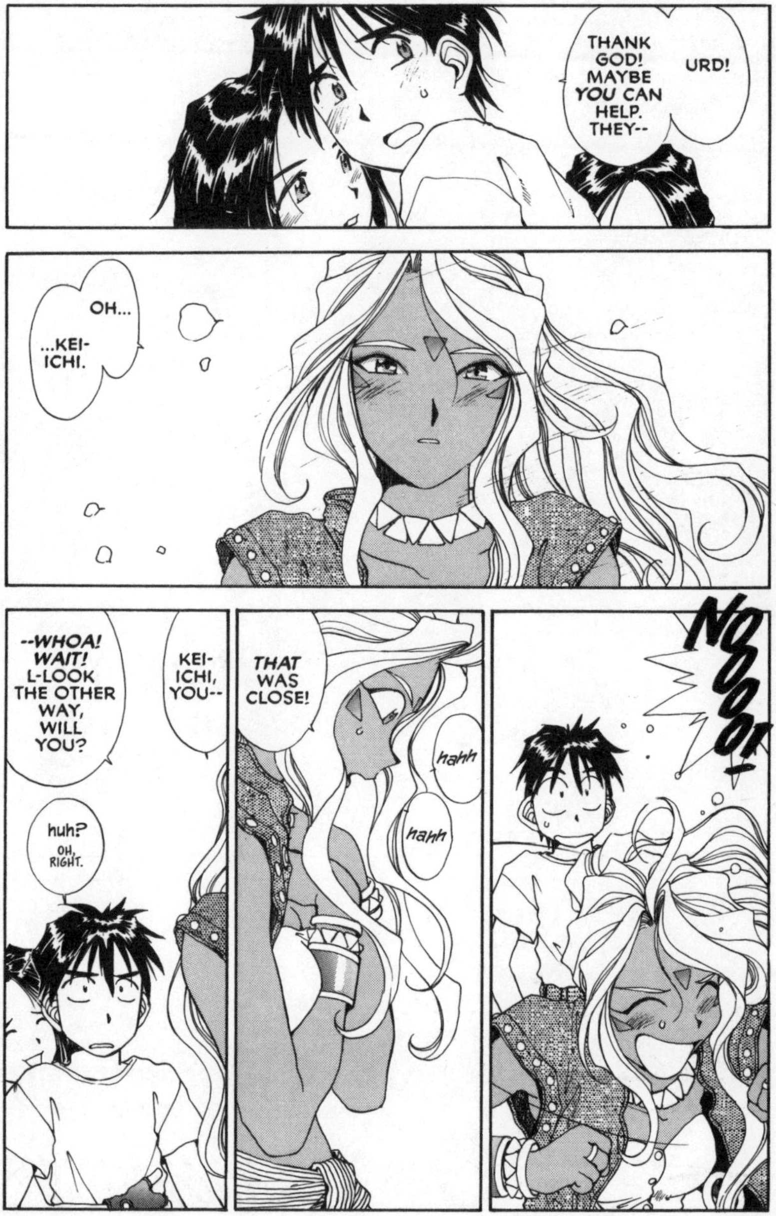
URD!
THANK GOD! MAYBE *YOU* CAN HELP. THEY--
OH...
...KEI-ICHI.
NOOOO!
THAT WAS CLOSE!
hahh
hahh
KEI-ICHI, YOU--
--WHOA! WAIT! L-LOOK THE OTHER WAY, WILL YOU?
huh? OH, RIGHT.

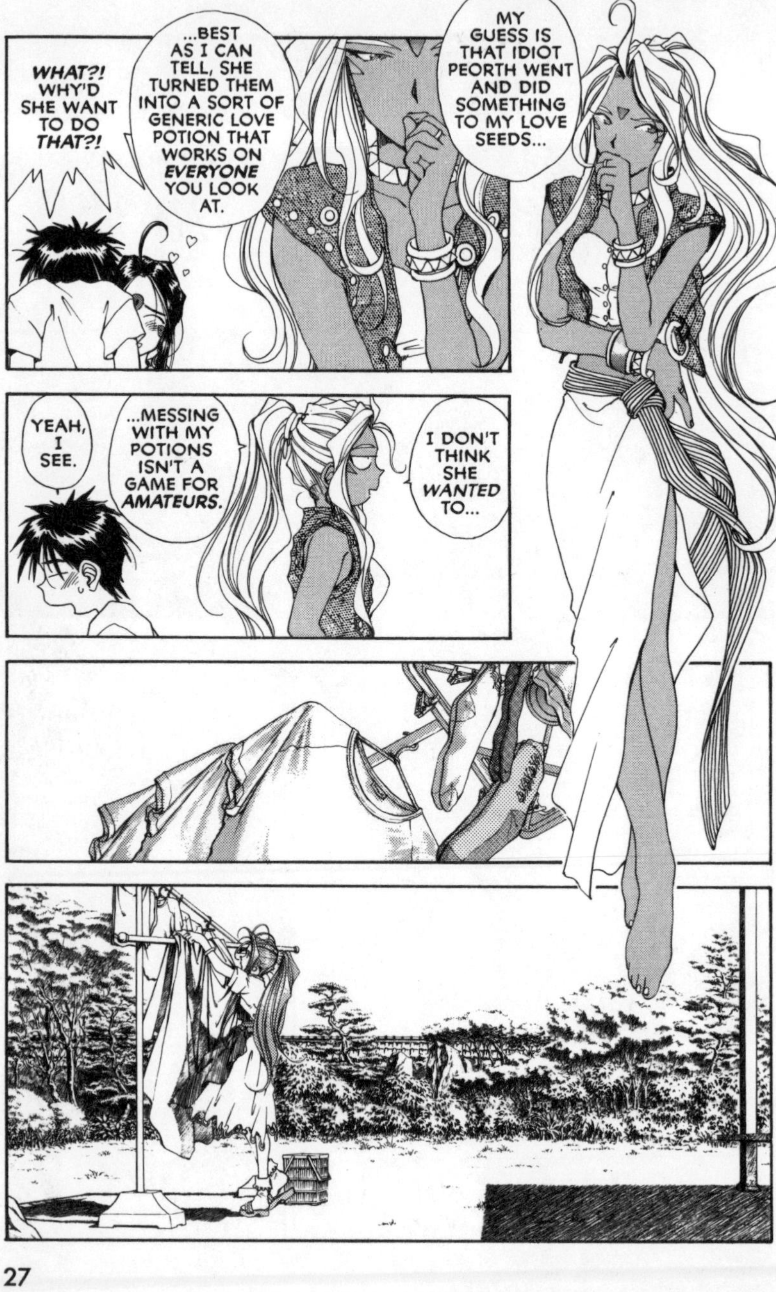
MY GUESS IS THAT IDIOT PEORTH WENT AND DID SOMETHING TO MY LOVE SEEDS...
...BEST AS I CAN TELL, SHE TURNED THEM INTO A SORT OF GENERIC LOVE POTION THAT WORKS ON *EVERYONE* YOU LOOK AT.
WHAT?! WHY'D SHE WANT TO DO *THAT?!*
I DON'T THINK SHE *WANTED* TO...
...MESSING WITH MY POTIONS ISN'T A GAME FOR *AMATEURS*.
YEAH, I SEE.

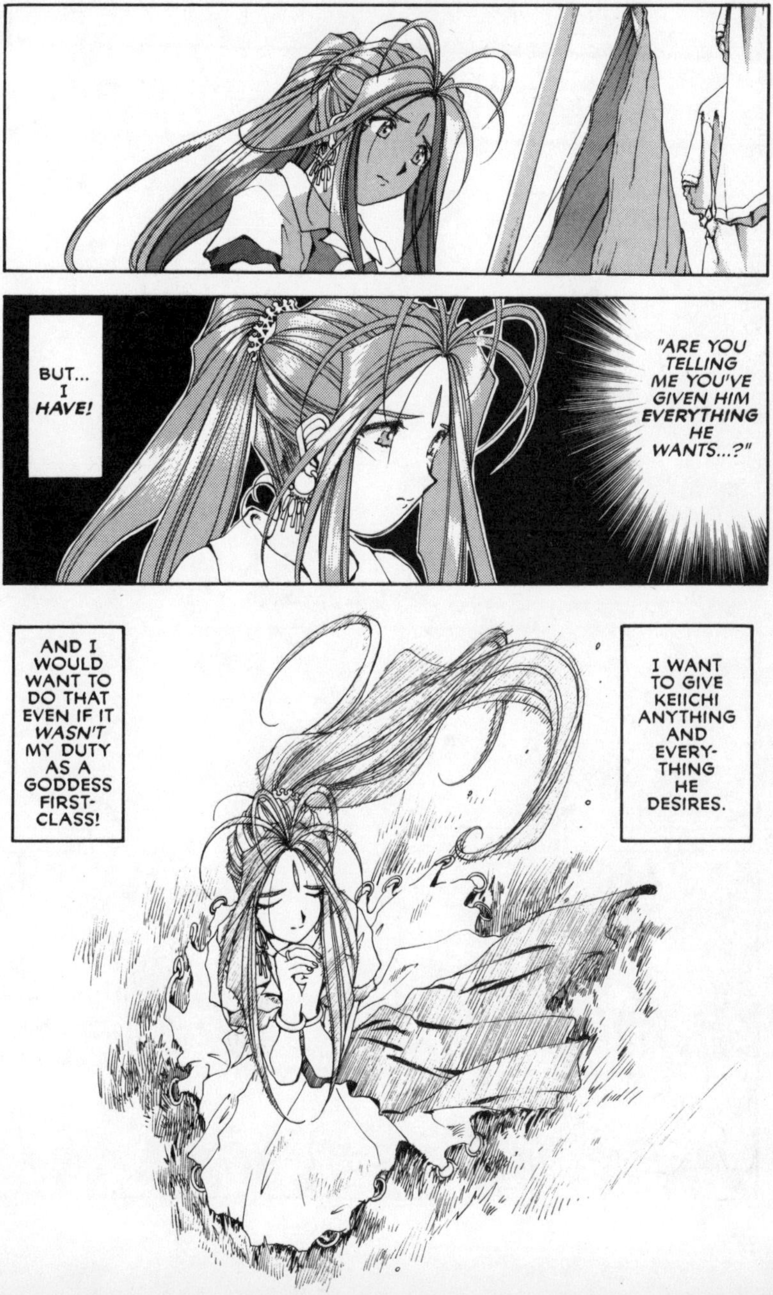
"ARE YOU TELLING ME YOU'VE GIVEN HIM *EVERYTHING* HE WANTS...?"
BUT... I *HAVE!*
I WANT TO GIVE KEIICHI ANYTHING AND EVERY-THING HE DESIRES.
AND I WOULD WANT TO DO THAT EVEN IF IT *WASN'T* MY DUTY AS A GODDESS FIRST-CLASS!

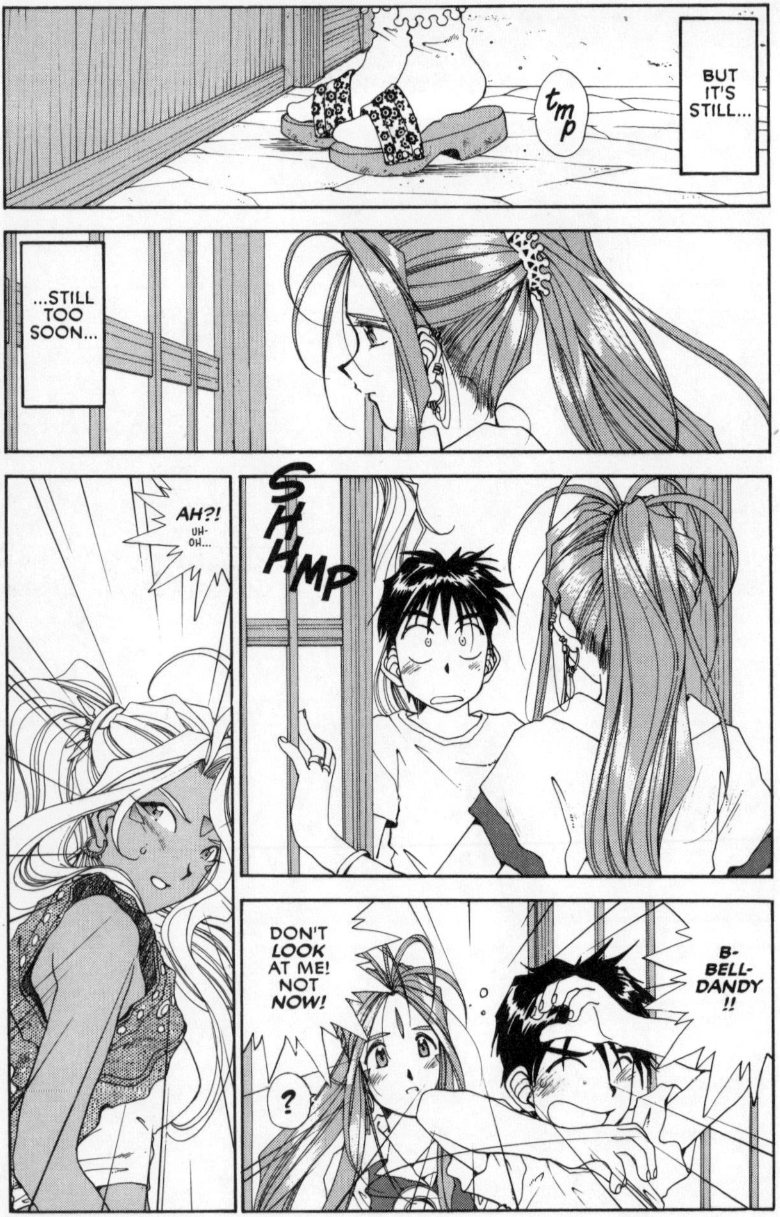

BUT IT'S STILL...
tmp
...STILL TOO SOON...
SHHMP
B-BELL-DANDY!!
DON'T *LOOK* AT ME! NOT *NOW!*
?
AH?!
UH-OH...

oops
I, TOO!
OH...
...NO.
KIND OF HARD WORK, BEING A STUD...
WATCH YOUR MOUTH, SKULD!
BACK OF THE LINE, URD!
HANDS OFF MY BROTHER, SISTERS!
KEIICHI ...?
!
WHOA! I TOLD YOU NOT TO LOOK AT ME!
PEORTH USED SOME DRUG ON ME, AND--
KEIICHI!

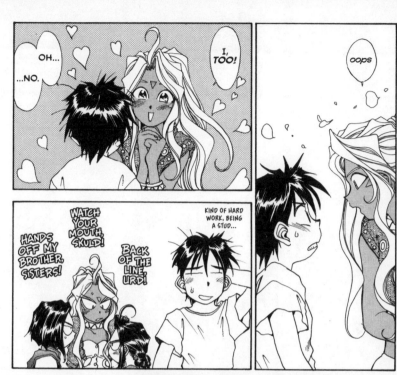

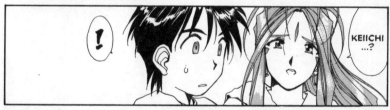

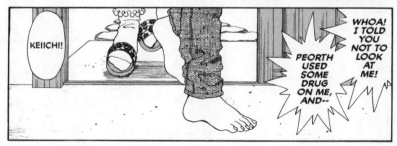

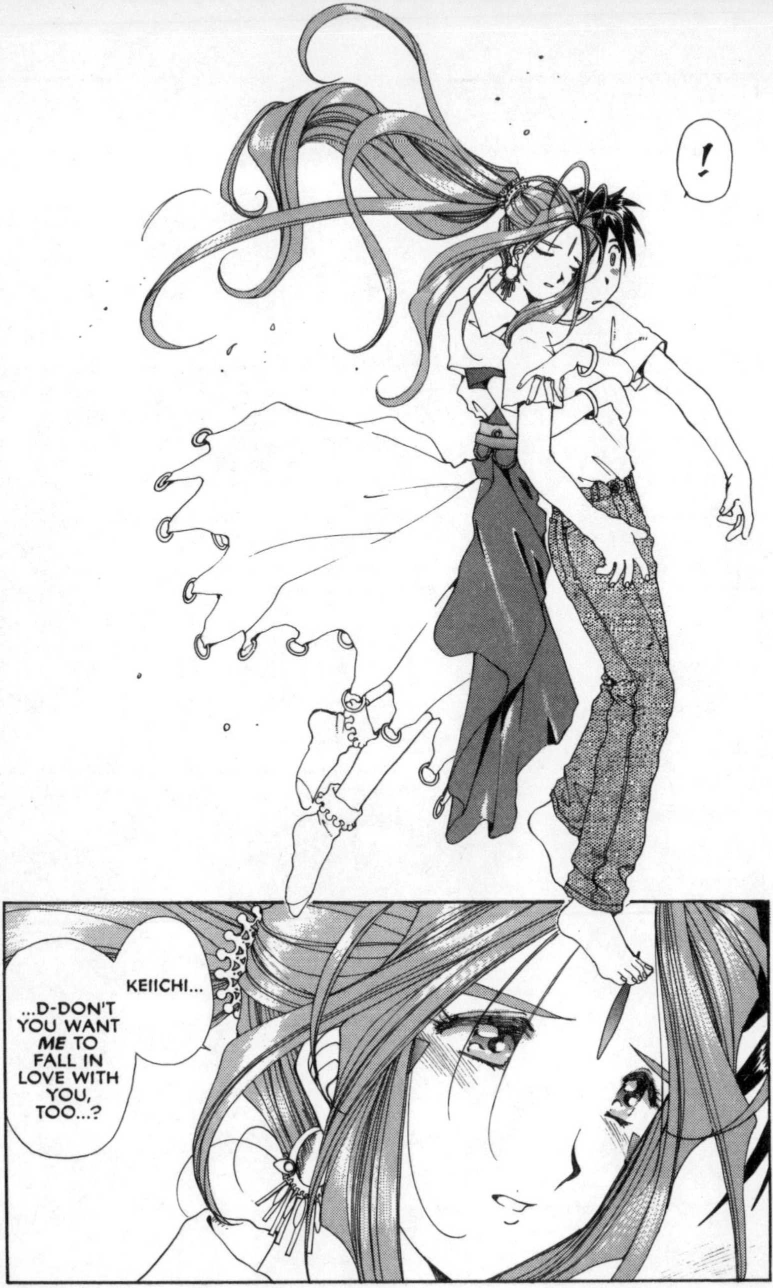
!
KEIICHI...
...D-DON'T YOU WANT *ME* TO FALL IN LOVE WITH YOU, TOO...?

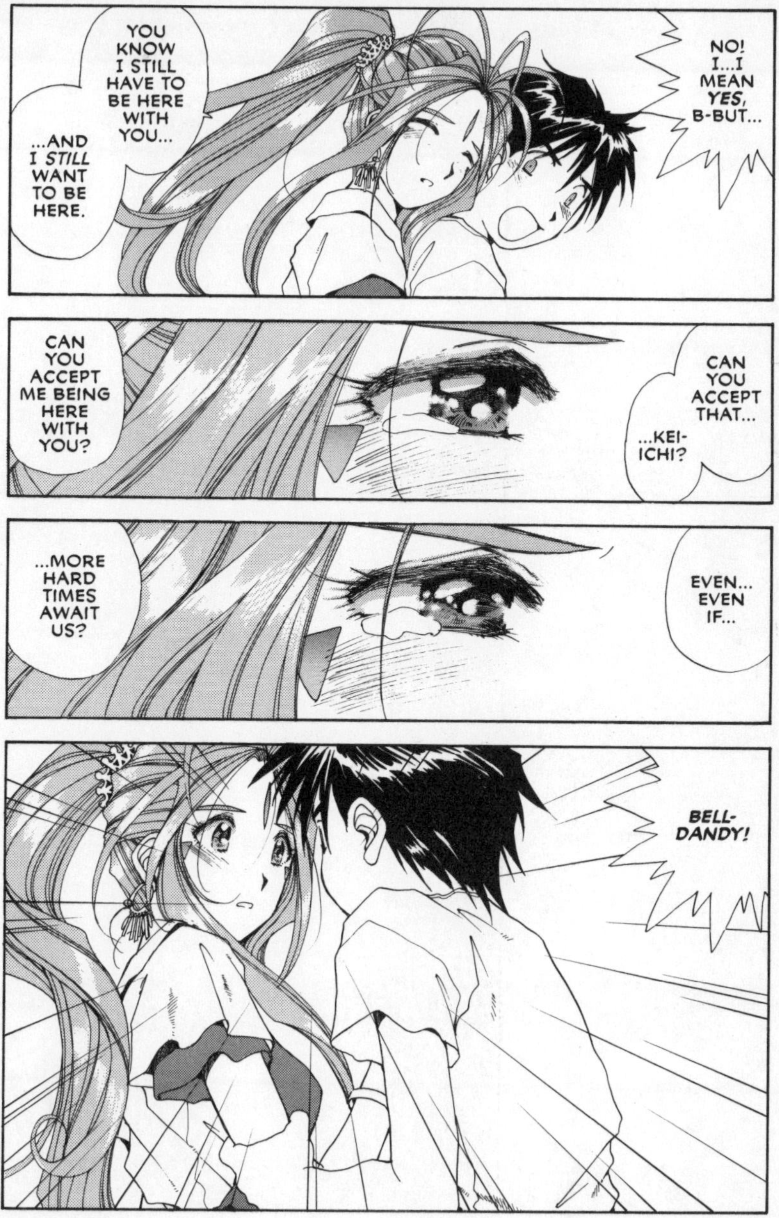
NO! I...I MEAN *YES*, B-BUT...
YOU KNOW I STILL HAVE TO BE HERE WITH YOU...
...AND I *STILL* WANT TO BE HERE.
CAN YOU ACCEPT THAT... ...KEI-ICHI?
CAN YOU ACCEPT ME BEING HERE WITH YOU?
EVEN... EVEN IF...
...MORE HARD TIMES AWAIT US?
BELL-DANDY!

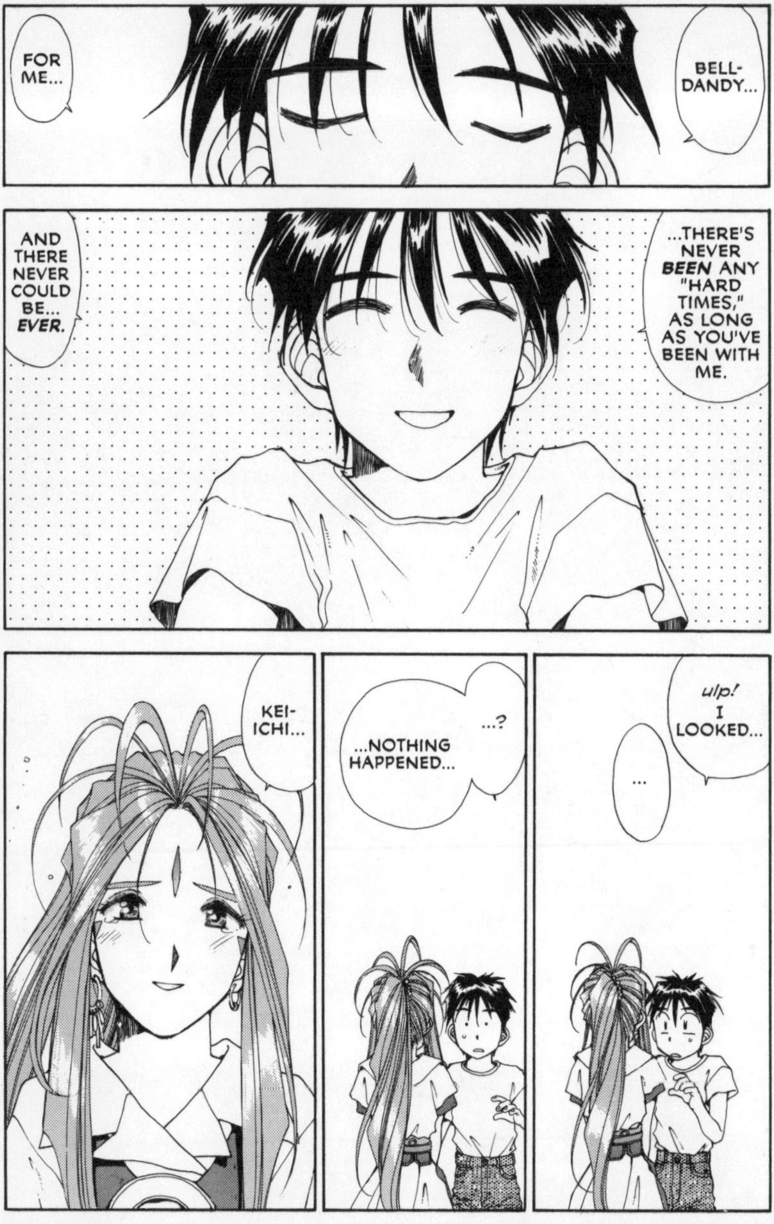
BELL-DANDY...
FOR ME...
...THERE'S NEVER *BEEN* ANY "HARD TIMES," AS LONG AS YOU'VE BEEN WITH ME.
AND THERE NEVER COULD BE... *EVER.*
ulp! I LOOKED...
...
...?
...NOTHING HAPPENED...
KEI-ICHI...

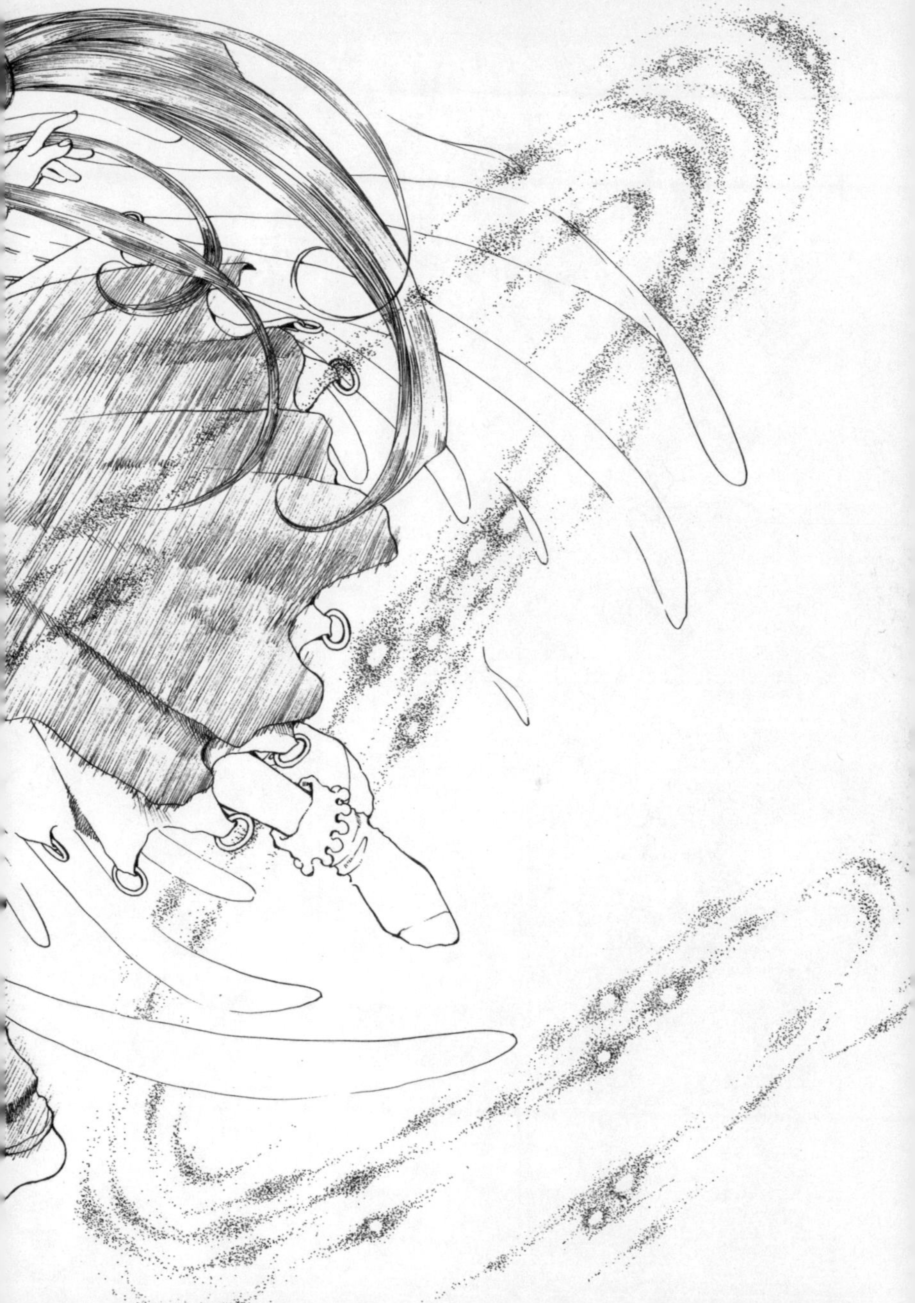

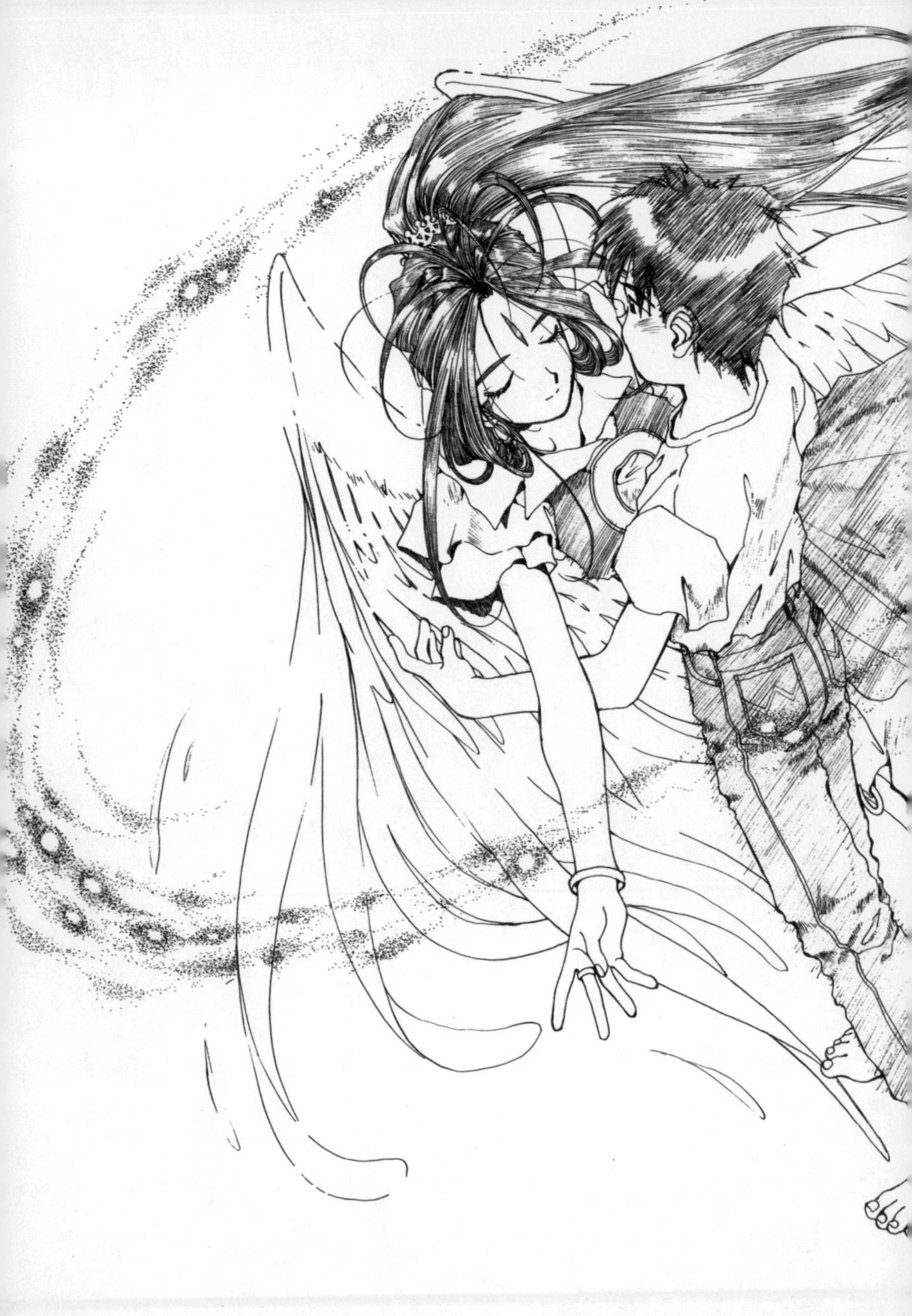

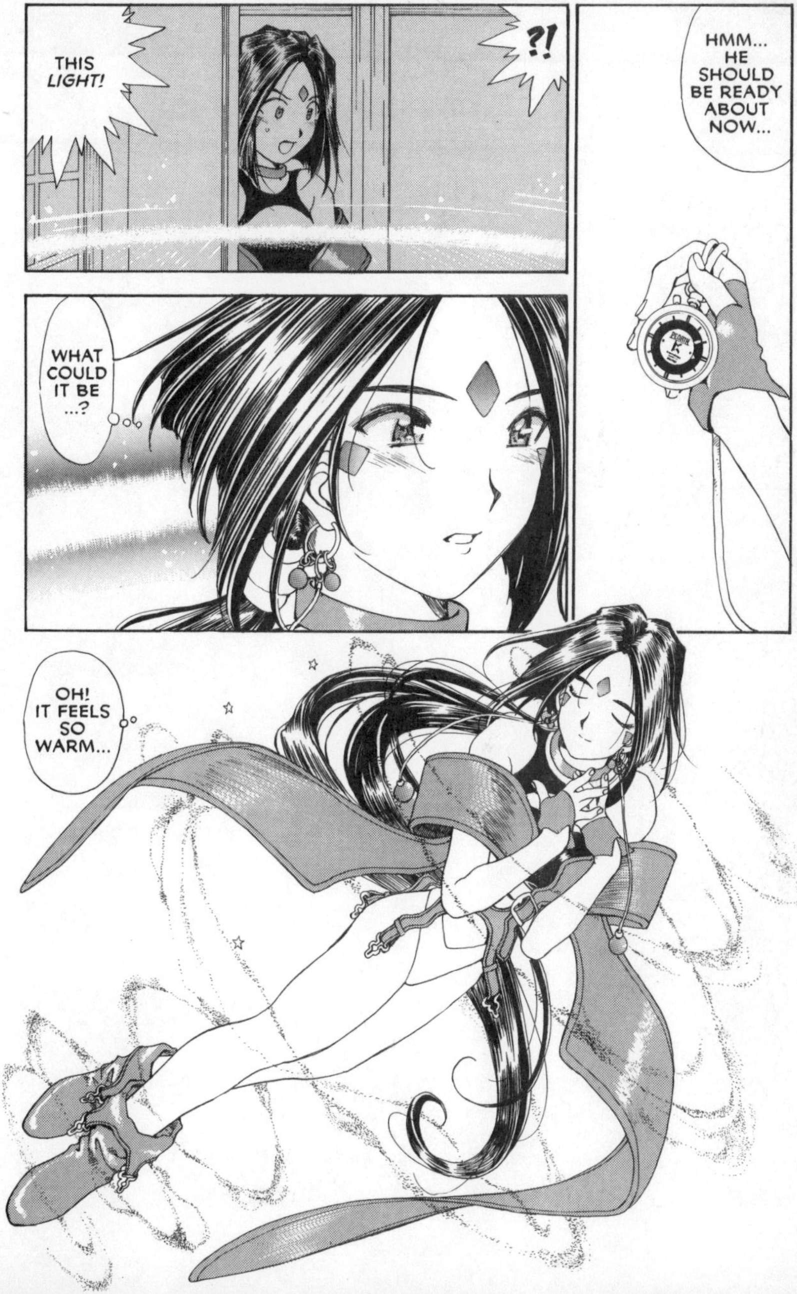
HMM... HE SHOULD BE READY ABOUT NOW...
?!
THIS LIGHT!
WHAT COULD IT BE ...?
OH! IT FEELS SO WARM...

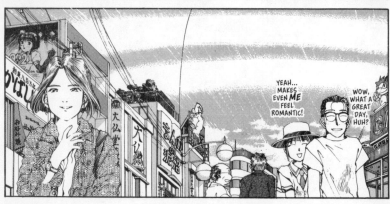

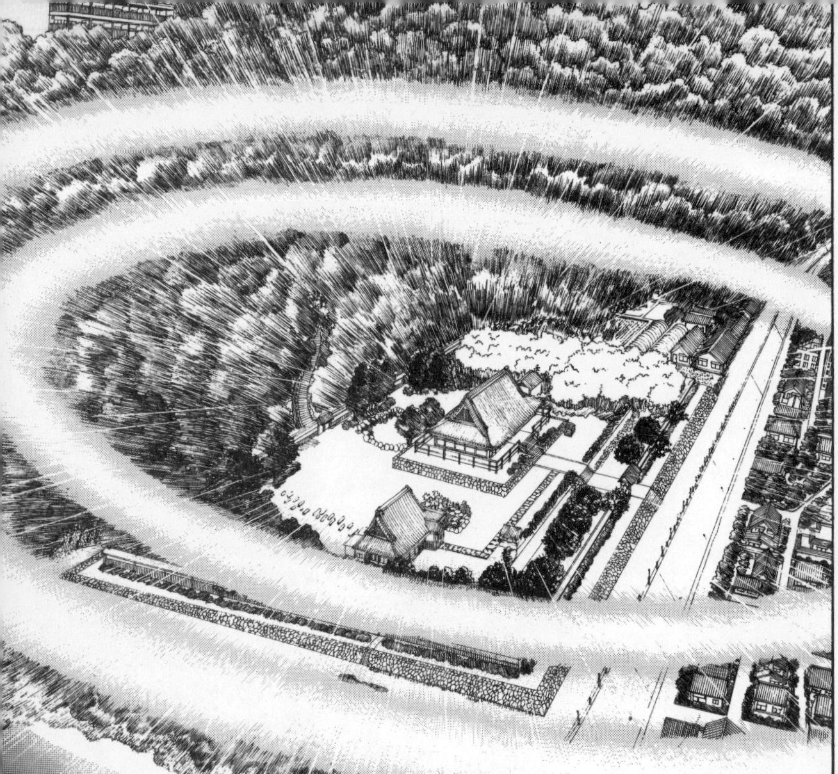
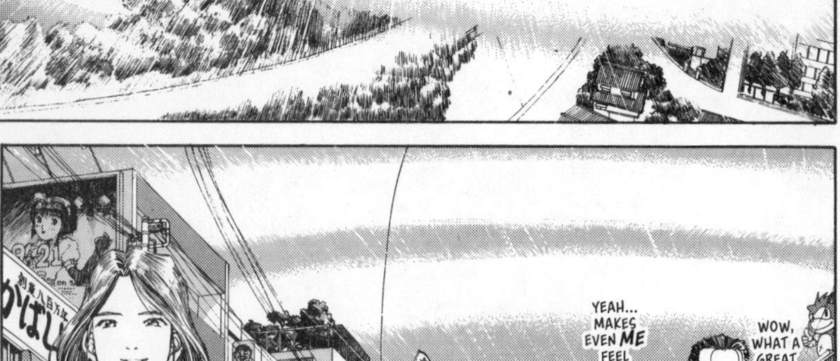
WOW, WHAT A GREAT DAY, HUH?
YEAH... MAKES EVEN **ME** FEEL ROMANTIC!

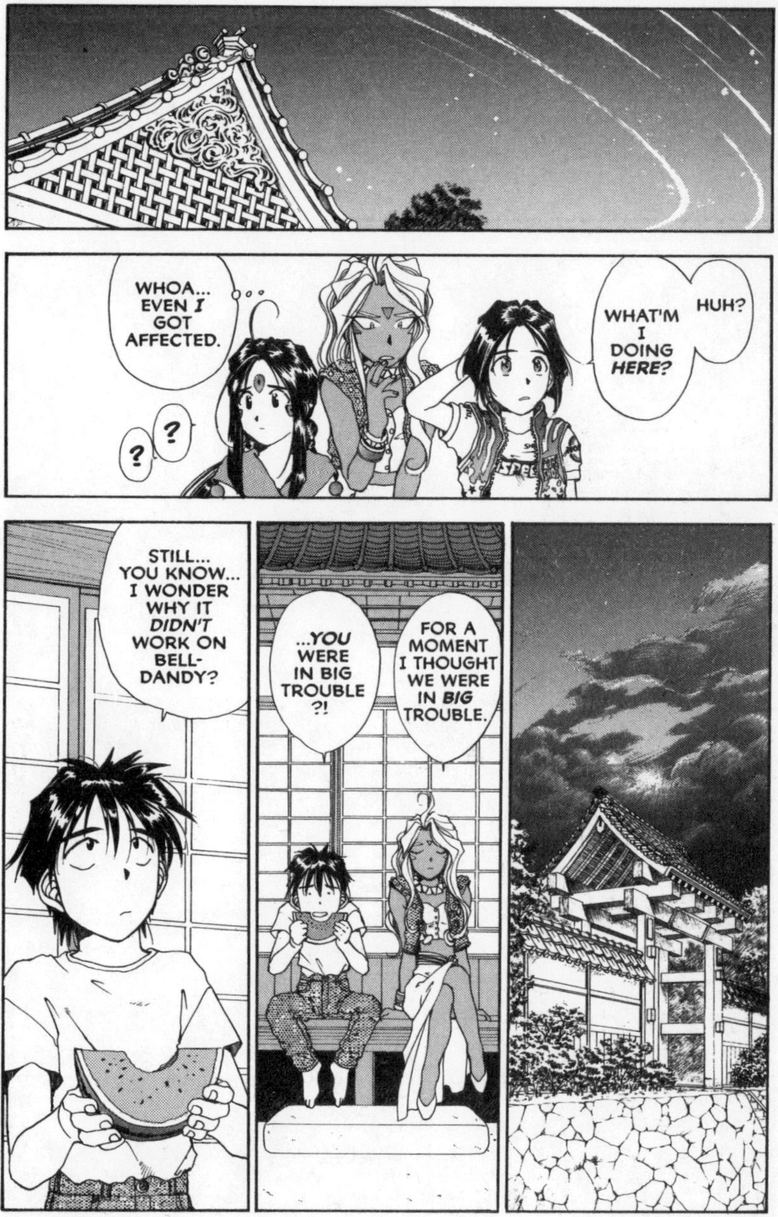

HUH?
WHAT'M I DOING *HERE?*
WHOA... EVEN *I* GOT AFFECTED.
?
?
FOR A MOMENT I THOUGHT WE WERE IN *BIG* TROUBLE.
...*YOU* WERE IN BIG TROUBLE ?!
STILL... YOU KNOW... I WONDER WHY IT *DIDN'T* WORK ON BELL-DANDY?

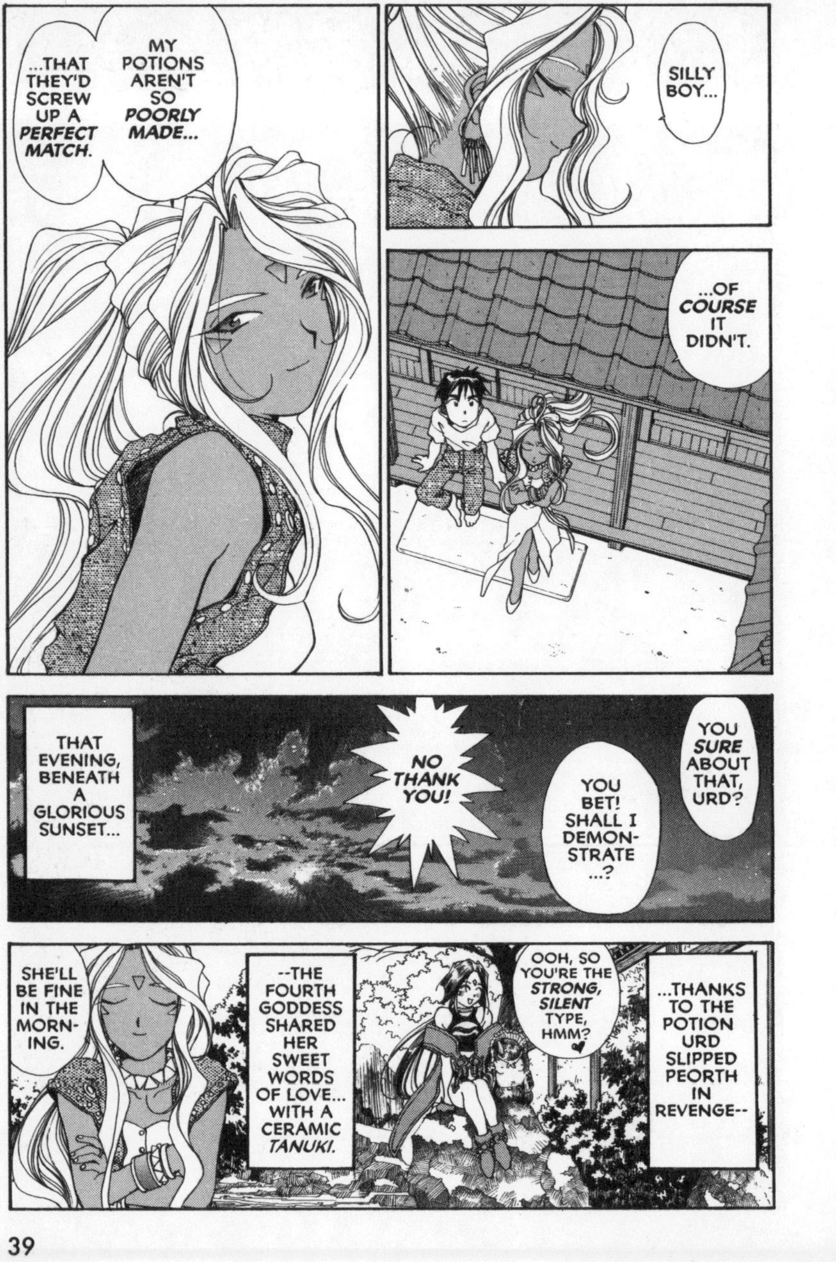
SILLY BOY...
...OF COURSE IT DIDN'T.
MY POTIONS AREN'T SO POORLY MADE...
...THAT THEY'D SCREW UP A PERFECT MATCH.
YOU SURE ABOUT THAT, URD?
YOU BET! SHALL I DEMONSTRATE ...?
NO THANK YOU!
THAT EVENING, BENEATH A GLORIOUS SUNSET...
...THANKS TO THE POTION URD SLIPPED PEORTH IN REVENGE--
OOH, SO YOU'RE THE STRONG, SILENT TYPE, HMM? ♥
--THE FOURTH GODDESS SHARED HER SWEET WORDS OF LOVE... WITH A CERAMIC TANUKI.
SHE'LL BE FINE IN THE MORNING.

THE ADVENTURES OF THE MINI-GODDESSES

◆SO YOU STARTED A BAND--*NOW* WHAT?◆

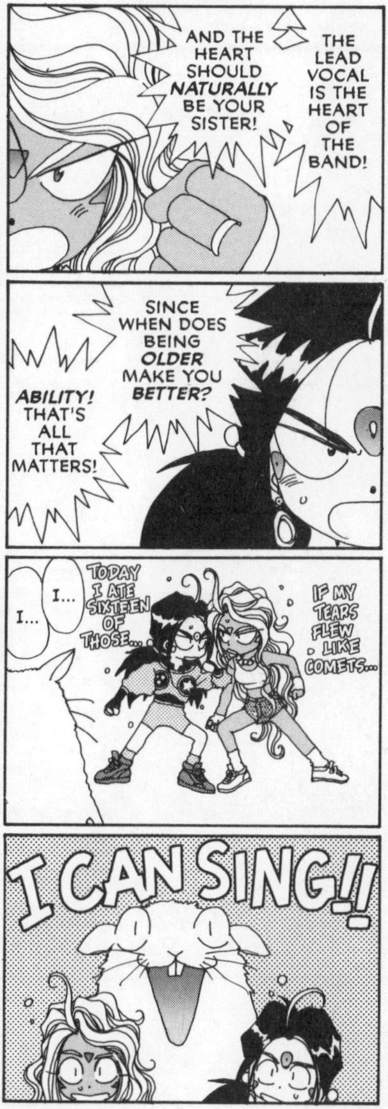
THE LEAD VOCAL IS THE HEART OF THE BAND!
AND THE HEART SHOULD *NATURALLY* BE YOUR SISTER!
SINCE WHEN DOES BEING *OLDER* MAKE YOU *BETTER?*
ABILITY! THAT'S ALL THAT MATTERS!
IF MY TEARS FLEW LIKE COMETS...
TODAY I ATE SIXTEEN OF THOSE...
I...
I...
I CAN SING!!

◆THE SECRET OF SONG◆

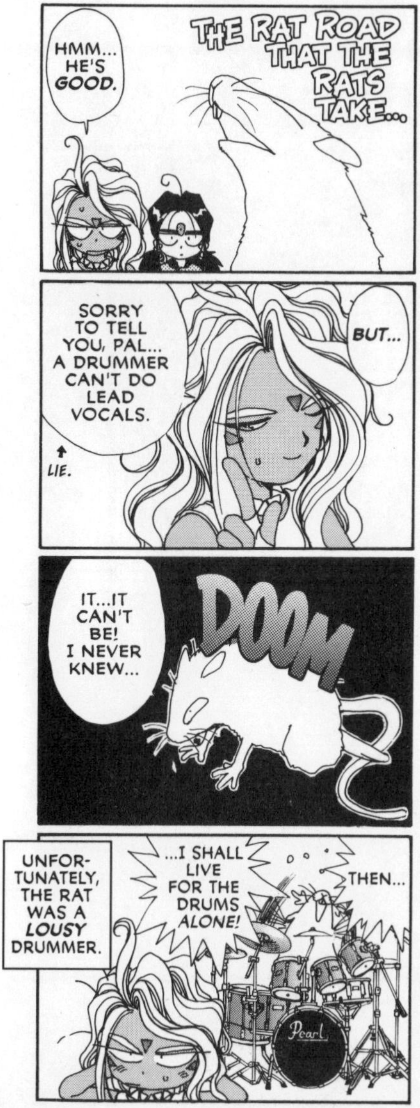
THE RAT ROAD THAT THE RATS TAKE...
HMM... HE'S *GOOD.*
BUT...
SORRY TO TELL YOU, PAL... A DRUMMER CAN'T DO LEAD VOCALS.
LIE.
DOOM
IT...IT CAN'T BE! I NEVER KNEW...
THEN...
...I SHALL LIVE FOR THE DRUMS *ALONE!*
Pearl
UNFORTUNATELY, THE RAT WAS A *LOUSY* DRUMMER.

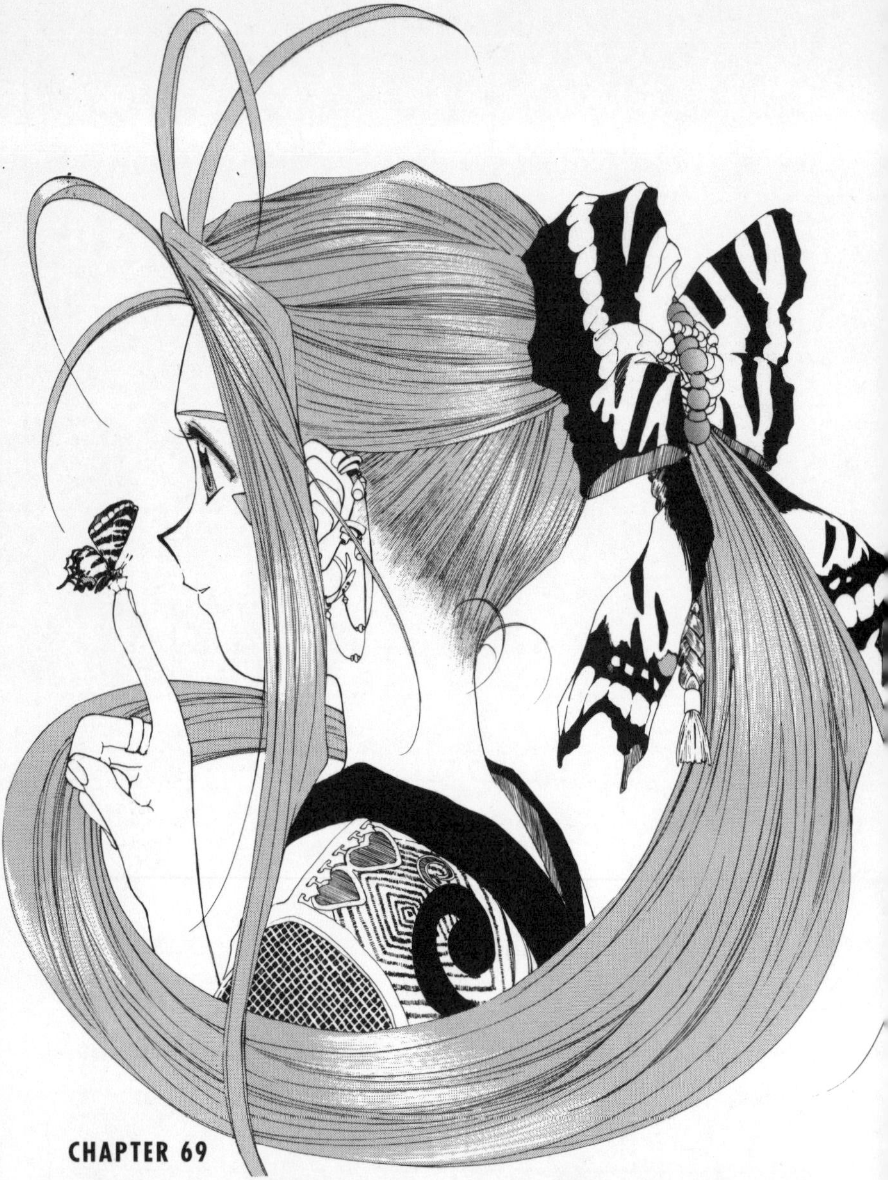

CHAPTER 69

Okay, This Is the Real Date

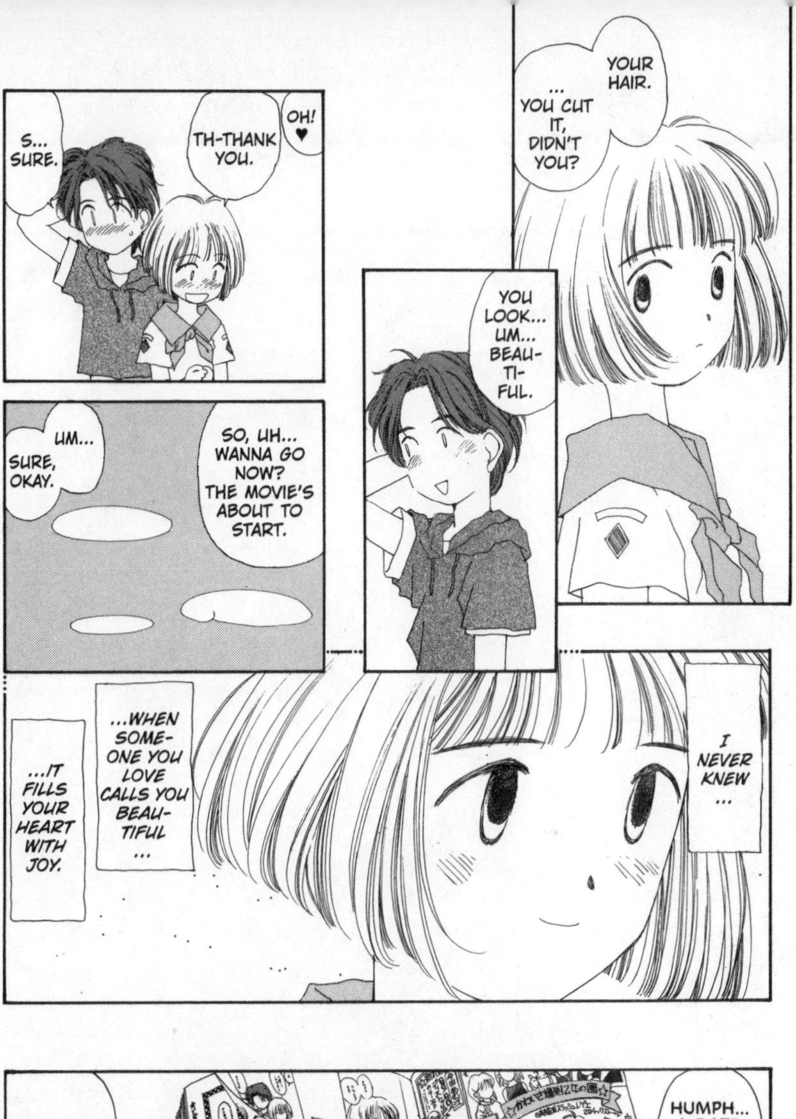
YOUR HAIR.
... YOU CUT IT, DIDN'T YOU?
YOU LOOK... UM... BEAU-TI-FUL.
OH! ♥
TH-THANK YOU.
S... SURE.
SO, UH... WANNA GO NOW? THE MOVIE'S ABOUT TO START.
UM... SURE, OKAY.
I NEVER KNEW ...
...WHEN SOME-ONE YOU LOVE CALLS YOU BEAU-TIFUL ...
...IT FILLS YOUR HEART WITH JOY.
HUMPH... A DATE. WITH THE DUMB BOY-FRIEND.
FLIP
YEAH, RIGHT.

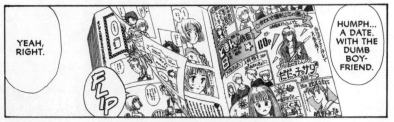

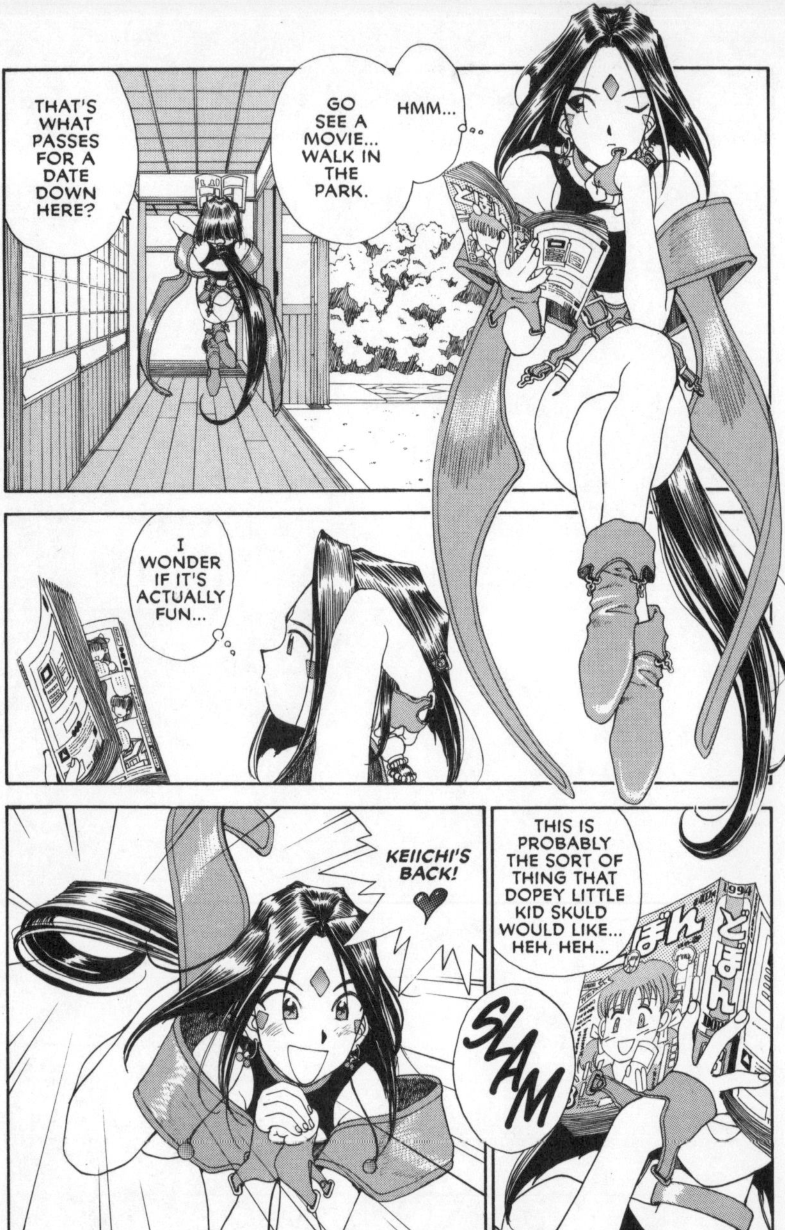
HMM...
GO SEE A MOVIE... WALK IN THE PARK.
THAT'S WHAT PASSES FOR A DATE DOWN HERE?
I WONDER IF IT'S ACTUALLY FUN...
THIS IS PROBABLY THE SORT OF THING THAT DOPEY LITTLE KID SKULD WOULD LIKE... HEH, HEH...
SLAM
KEIICHI'S BACK!

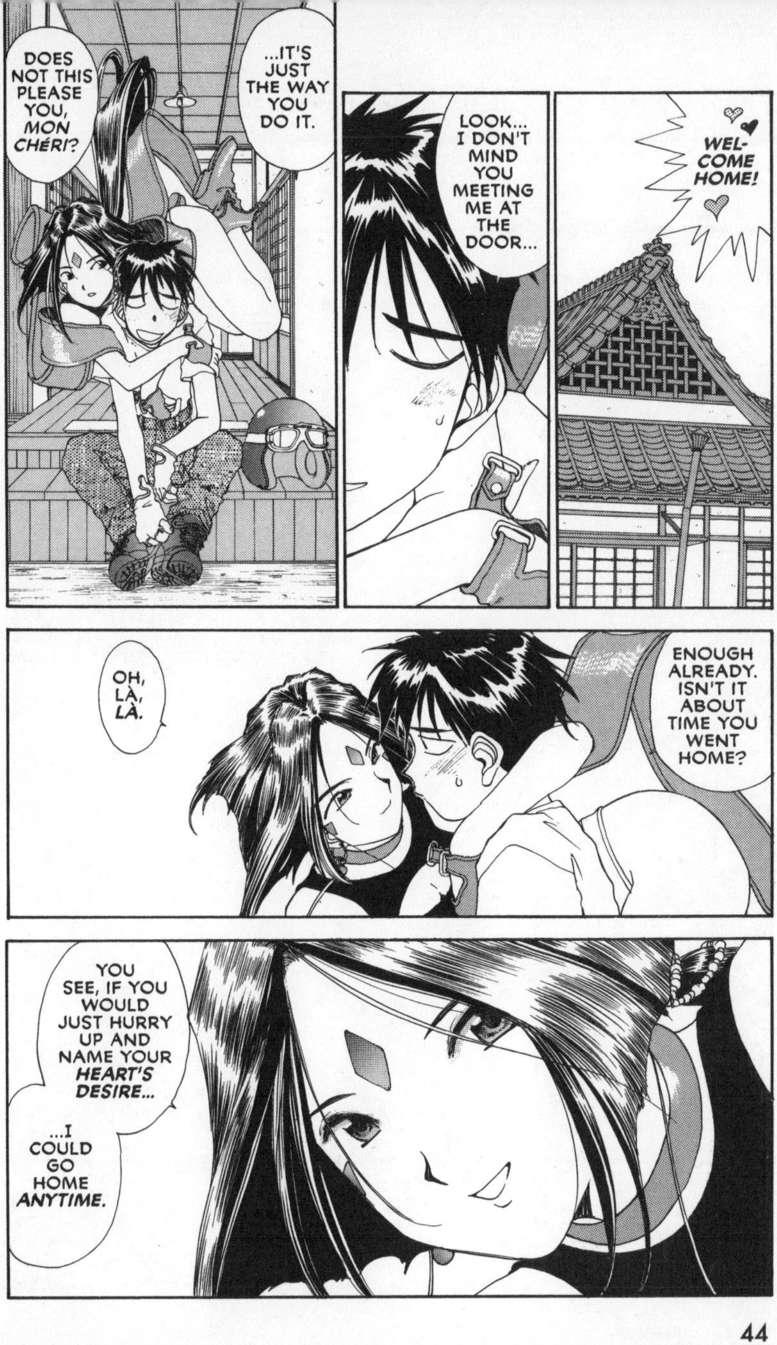
WEL-COME HOME!
LOOK... I DON'T MIND YOU MEETING ME AT THE DOOR...
...IT'S JUST THE WAY YOU DO IT.
DOES NOT THIS PLEASE YOU, *MON CHÉRI*?
ENOUGH ALREADY. ISN'T IT ABOUT TIME YOU WENT HOME?
OH, LÀ, *LÀ*.
YOU SEE, IF YOU WOULD JUST HURRY UP AND NAME YOUR *HEART'S DESIRE*...
...I COULD GO HOME *ANYTIME*.

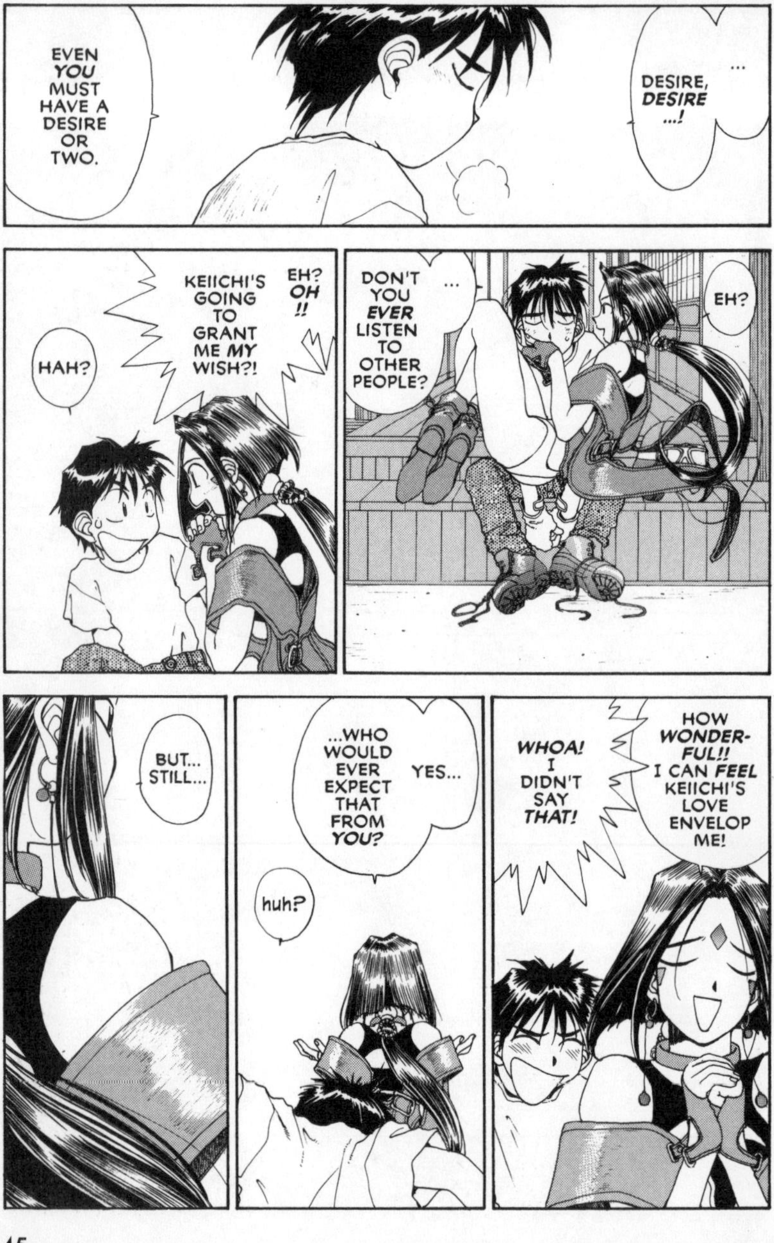
... DESIRE, DESIRE ...!
EVEN YOU MUST HAVE A DESIRE OR TWO.
EH?
...
DON'T YOU EVER LISTEN TO OTHER PEOPLE?
EH? OH !!
KEIICHI'S GOING TO GRANT ME MY WISH?!
HAH?
HOW WONDERFUL!! I CAN FEEL KEIICHI'S LOVE ENVELOP ME!
WHOA! I DIDN'T SAY THAT!
YES...
...WHO WOULD EVER EXPECT THAT FROM YOU?
huh?
BUT... STILL...

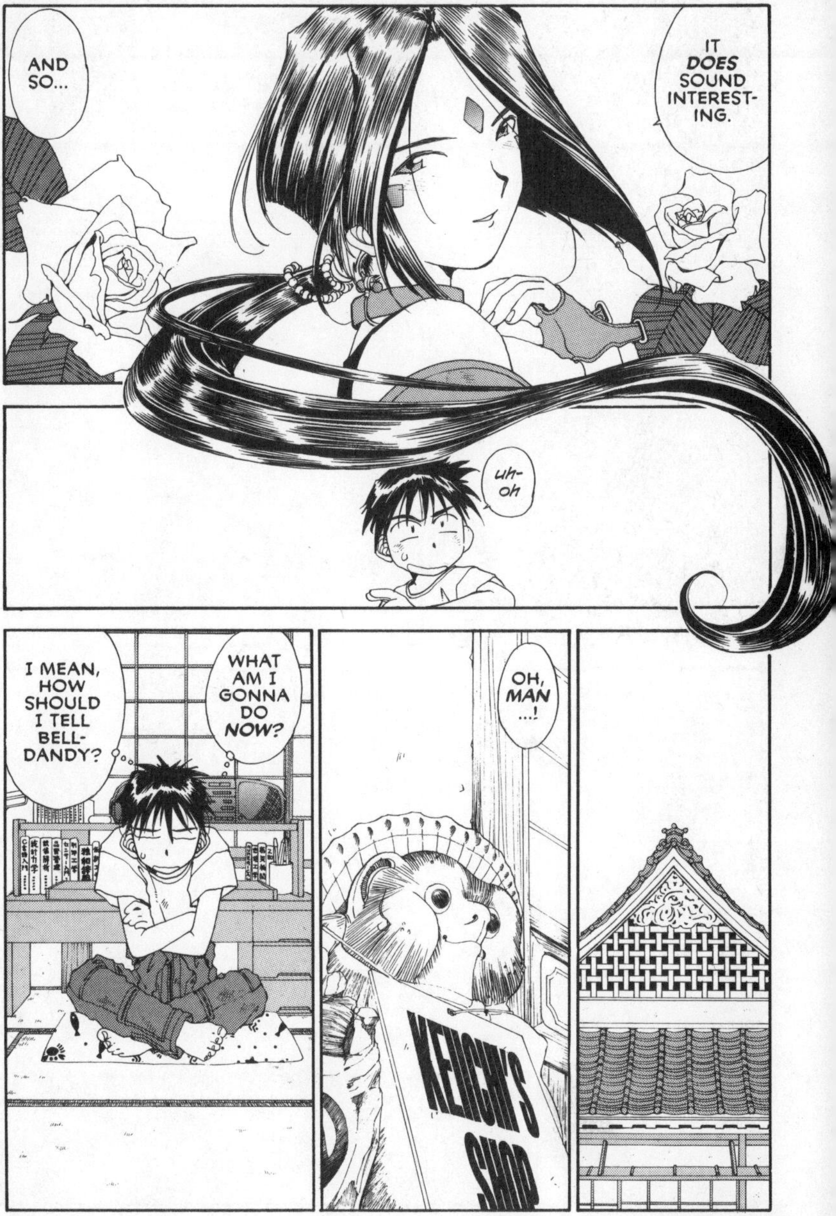
IT DOES SOUND INTERESTING.
AND SO...
uh-oh
OH, MAN ...!
KEIICHI'S SHOP
WHAT AM I GONNA DO NOW?
I MEAN, HOW SHOULD I TELL BELL-DANDY?

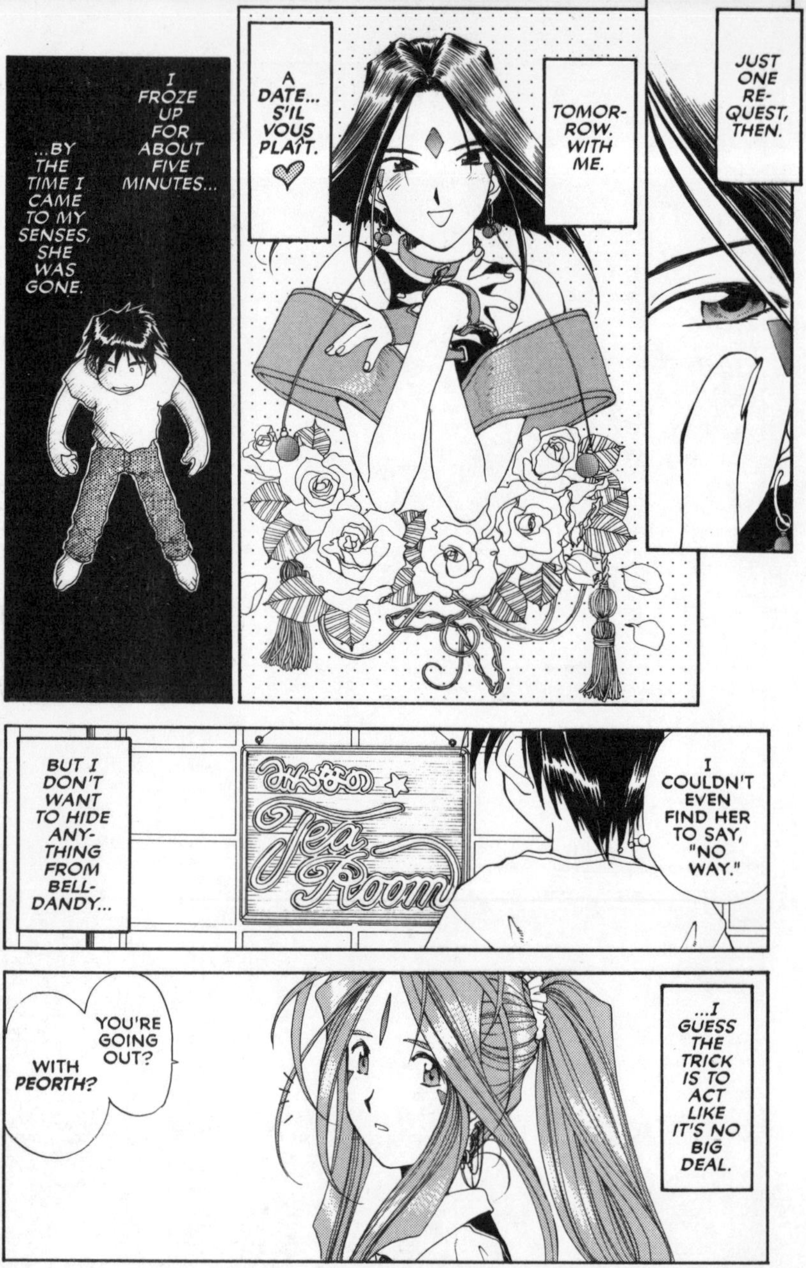
JUST ONE REQUEST, THEN.
TOMORROW. WITH ME.
A DATE... S'IL VOUS PLAÎT. ♥
I FROZE UP FOR ABOUT FIVE MINUTES...
...BY THE TIME I CAME TO MY SENSES, SHE WAS GONE.
I COULDN'T EVEN FIND HER TO SAY, "NO WAY."
みんなの ☆ Tea Room
BUT I DON'T WANT TO HIDE ANYTHING FROM BELLDANDY...
...I GUESS THE TRICK IS TO ACT LIKE IT'S NO BIG DEAL.
YOU'RE GOING OUT? WITH PEORTH?

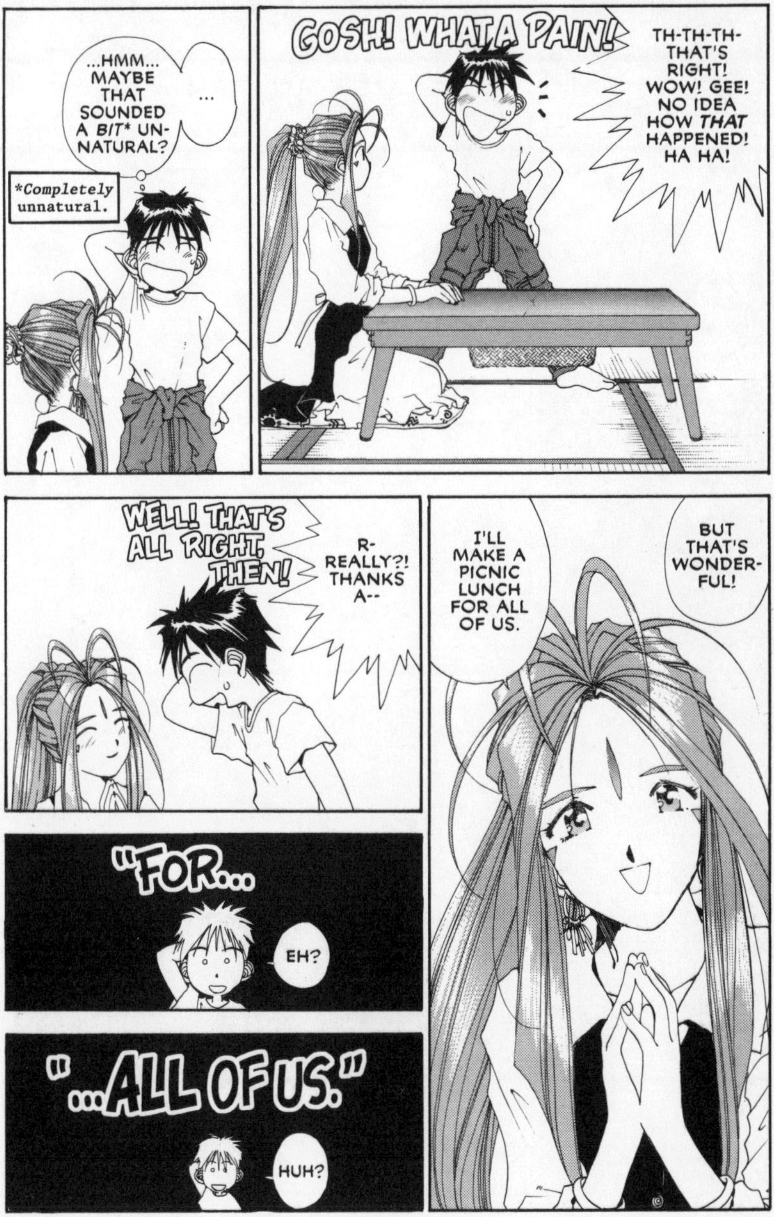
TH-TH-TH-THAT'S RIGHT! WOW! GEE! NO IDEA HOW *THAT* HAPPENED! HA HA!
GOSH! WHAT A PAIN!
...
...HMM... MAYBE THAT SOUNDED A *BIT** UN-NATURAL?
*Completely unnatural.
BUT THAT'S WONDERFUL!
I'LL MAKE A PICNIC LUNCH FOR ALL OF US.
R-REALLY?! THANKS A--
WELL! THAT'S ALL RIGHT, THEN!
"FOR...
EH?
"...ALL OF US."
HUH?

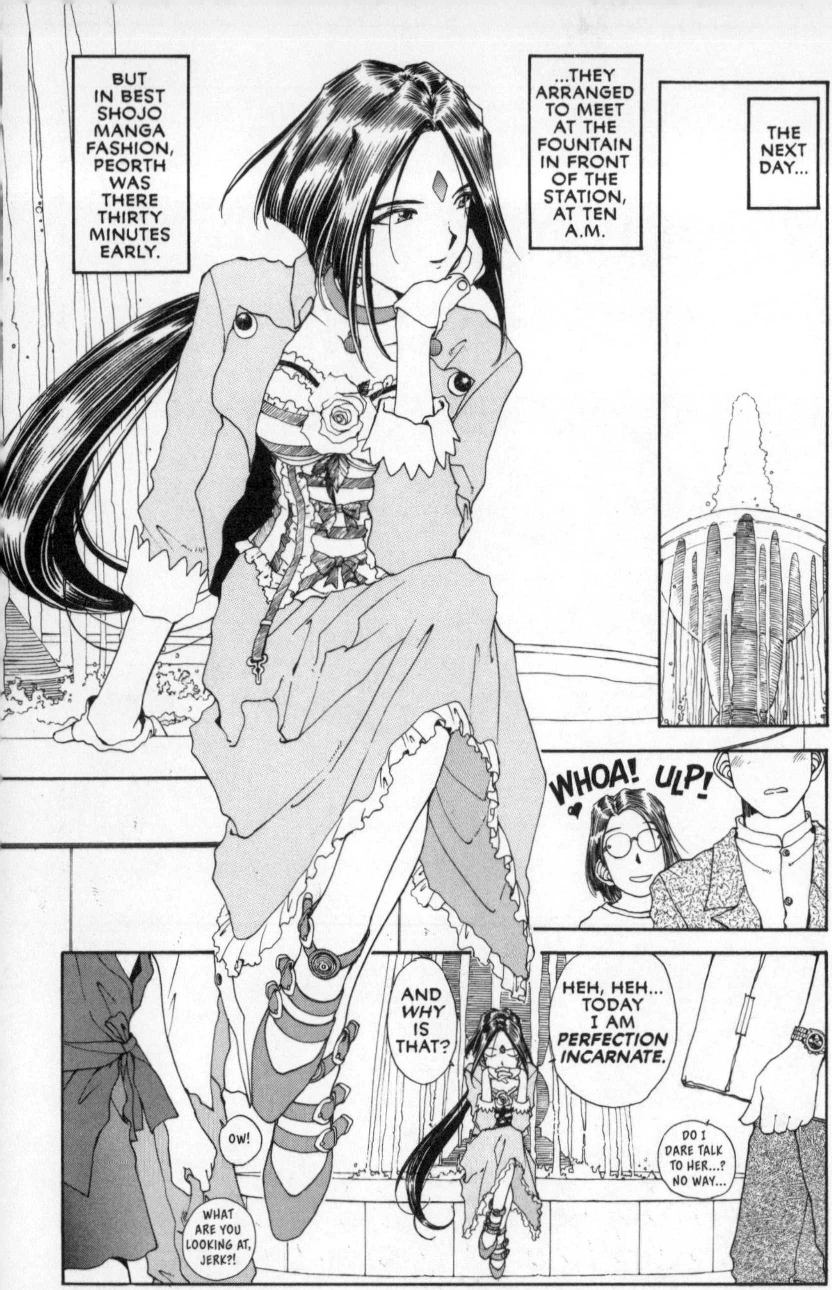
THE NEXT DAY...
...THEY ARRANGED TO MEET AT THE FOUNTAIN IN FRONT OF THE STATION, AT TEN A.M.
BUT IN BEST SHOJO MANGA FASHION, PEORTH WAS THERE THIRTY MINUTES EARLY.
WHOA!
ULP!
DO I DARE TALK TO HER...? NO WAY...
HEH, HEH... TODAY I AM *PERFECTION INCARNATE.*
AND *WHY* IS THAT?
OW!
WHAT ARE YOU LOOKING AT, JERK?!

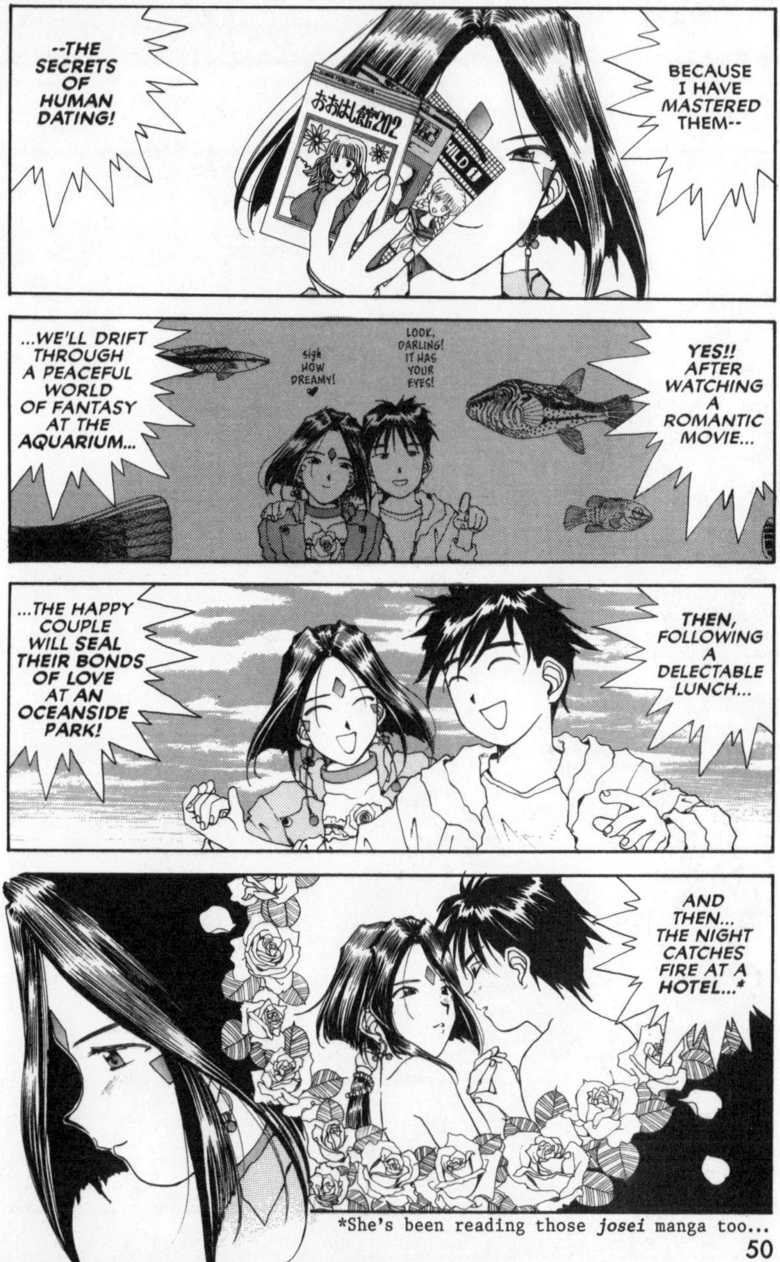
BECAUSE I HAVE MASTERED THEM--
おおはし館202
--THE SECRETS OF HUMAN DATING!
YES!! AFTER WATCHING A ROMANTIC MOVIE...
LOOK, DARLING! IT HAS YOUR EYES!
sigh HOW DREAMY! ♥
...WE'LL DRIFT THROUGH A PEACEFUL WORLD OF FANTASY AT THE AQUARIUM...
THEN, FOLLOWING A DELECTABLE LUNCH...
...THE HAPPY COUPLE WILL SEAL THEIR BONDS OF LOVE AT AN OCEANSIDE PARK!
AND THEN... THE NIGHT CATCHES FIRE AT A HOTEL...*

*She's been reading those *josei* manga too...

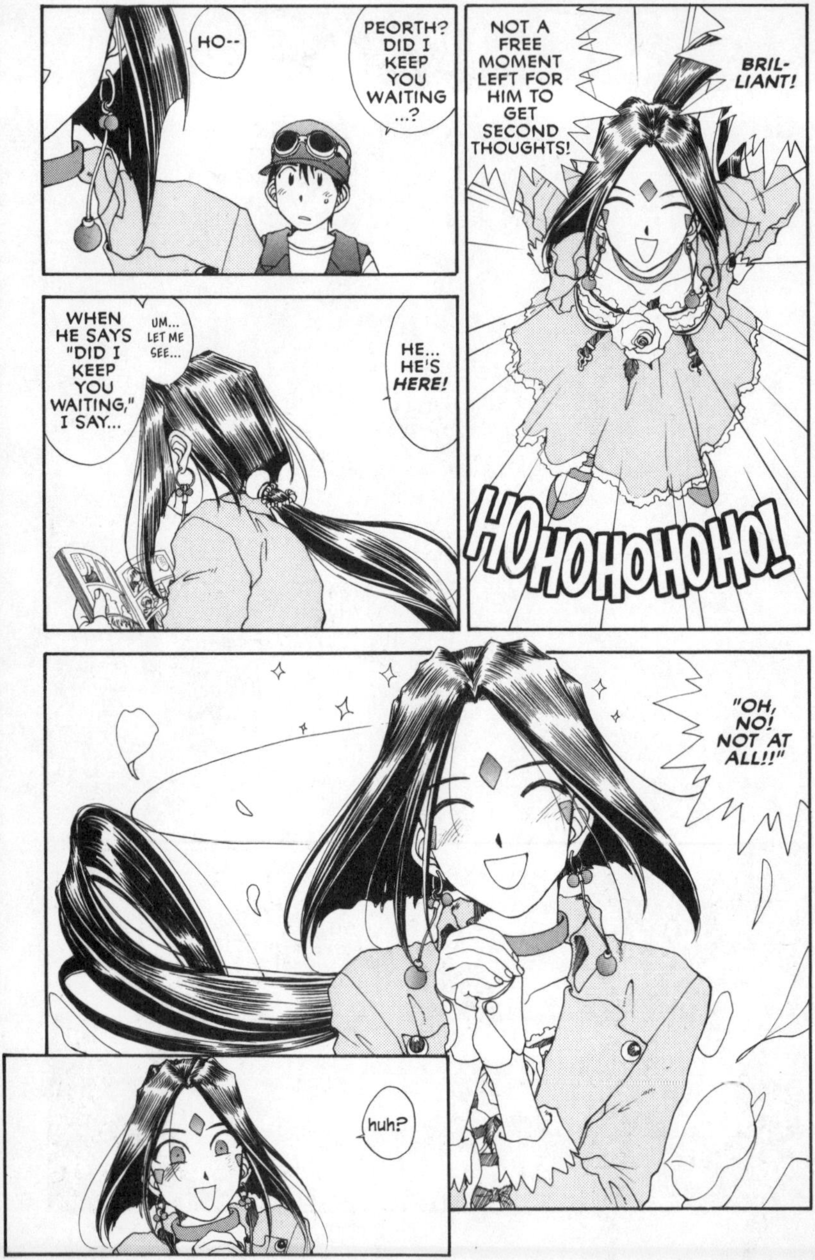
BRIL-LIANT!
NOT A FREE MOMENT LEFT FOR HIM TO GET SECOND THOUGHTS!
HOHOHOHOHOHO!
PEORTH? DID I KEEP YOU WAITING ...?
HO--
HE... HE'S *HERE!*
UM... LET ME SEE...
WHEN HE SAYS "DID I KEEP YOU WAITING," I SAY...
"OH, NO! NOT AT ALL!!"
huh?

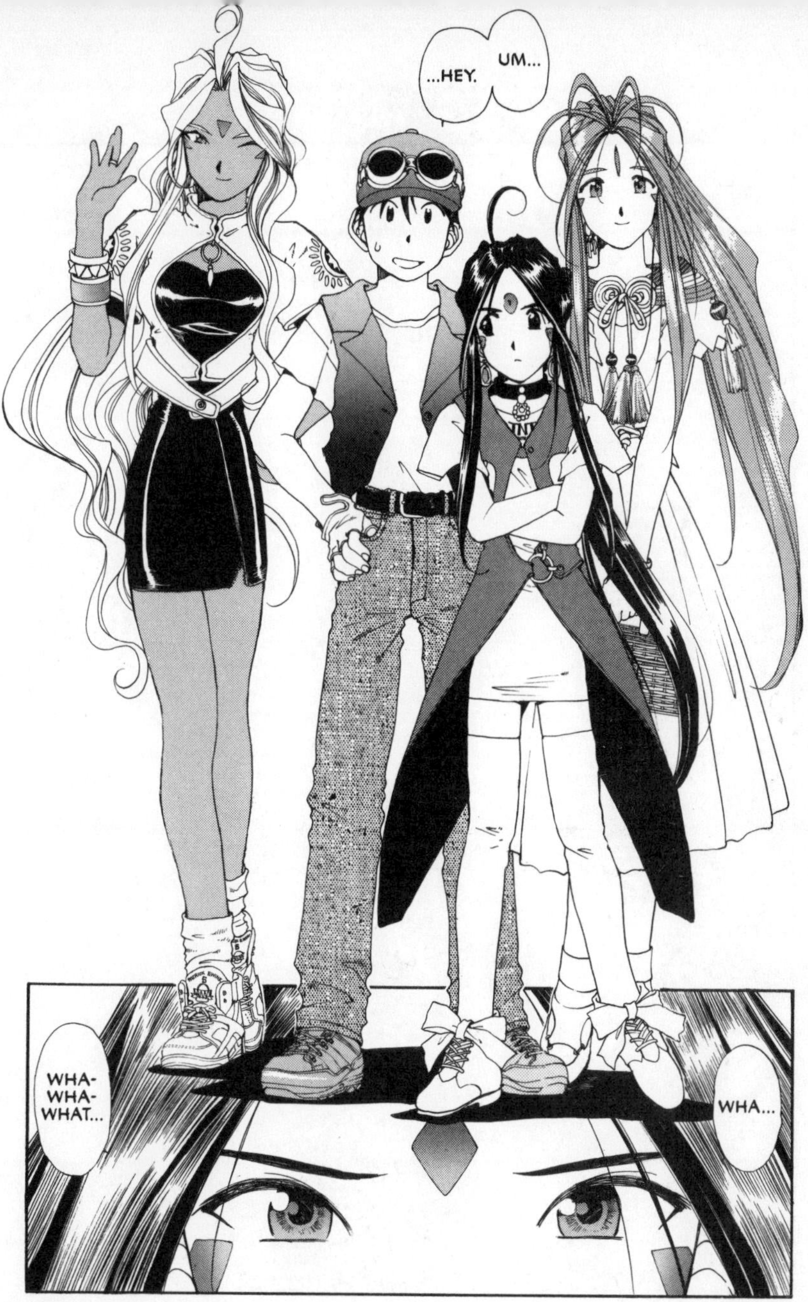
UM...
...HEY.
WHA...
WHA-
WHA-
WHAT...

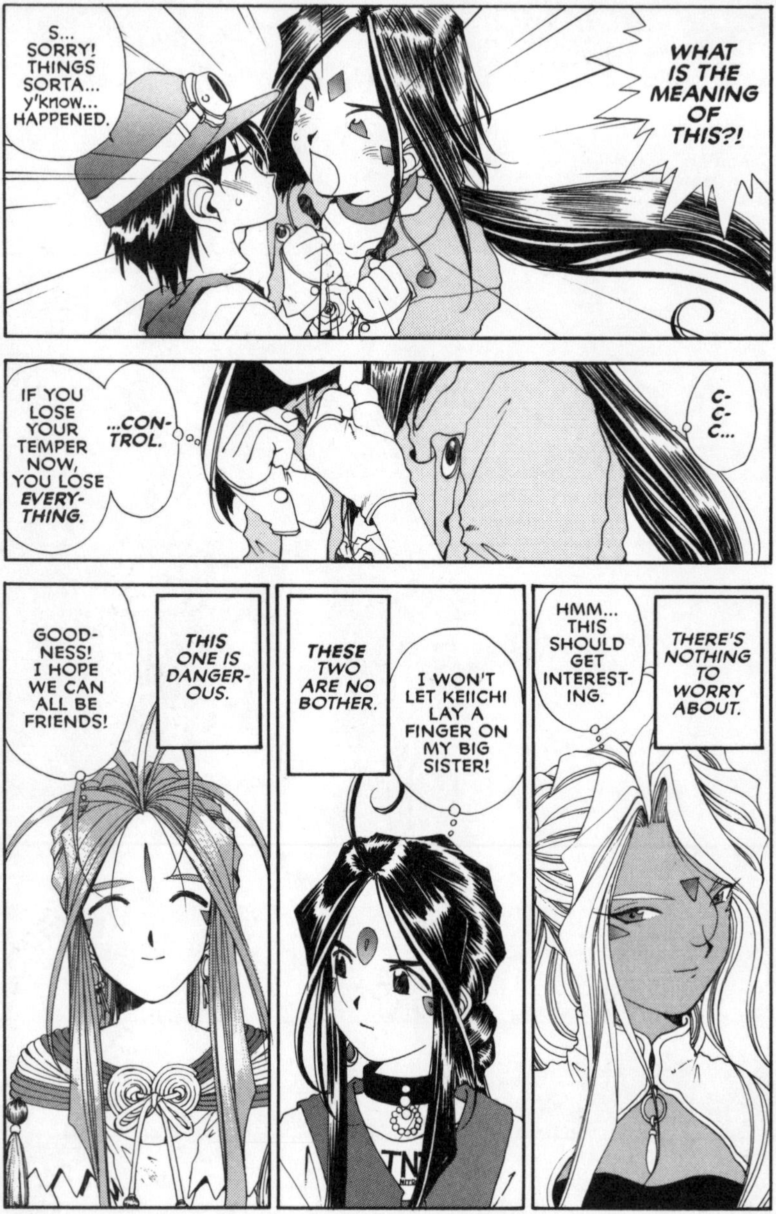
WHAT IS THE MEANING OF THIS?!
S... SORRY! THINGS SORTA... y'know... HAPPENED.
C-C-C...
...CON-TROL.
IF YOU LOSE YOUR TEMPER NOW, YOU LOSE EVERY-THING.
THERE'S NOTHING TO WORRY ABOUT.
HMM... THIS SHOULD GET INTEREST-ING.
I WON'T LET KEIICHI LAY A FINGER ON MY BIG SISTER!
THESE TWO ARE NO BOTHER.
THIS ONE IS DANGER-OUS.
GOOD-NESS! I HOPE WE CAN ALL BE FRIENDS!

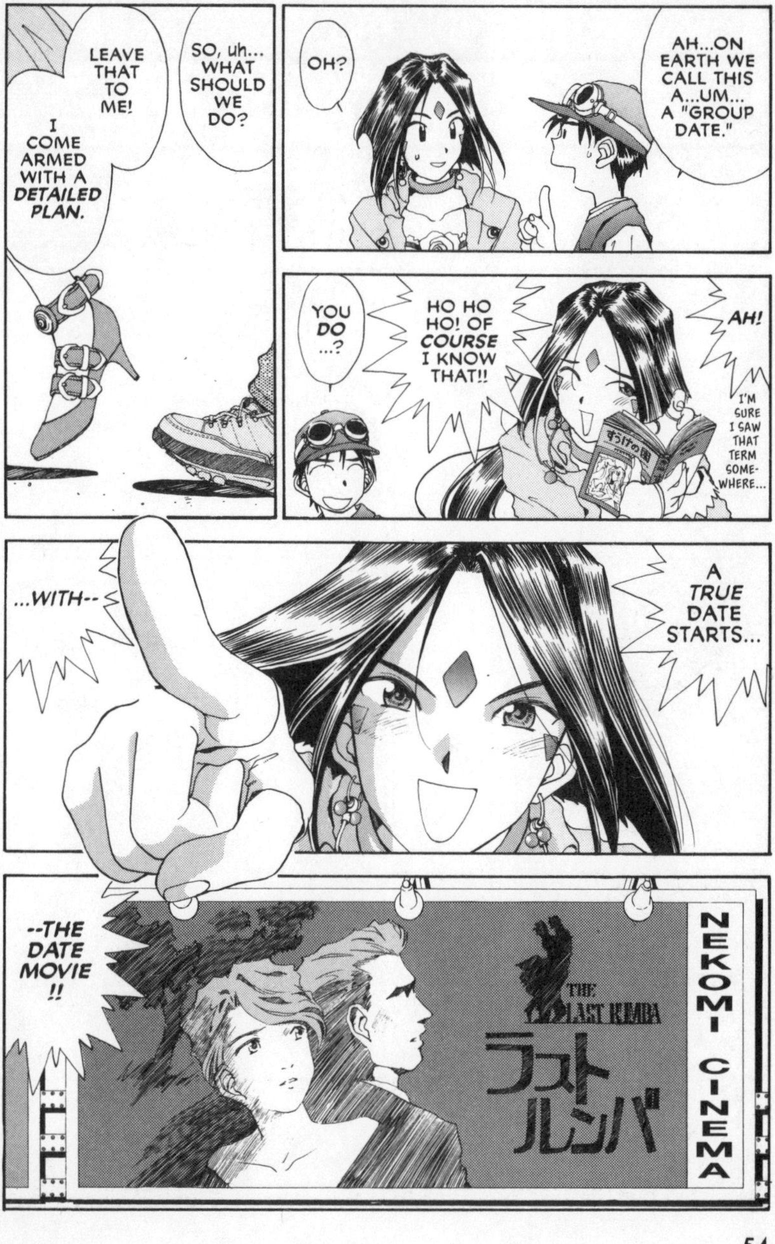
AH...ON EARTH WE CALL THIS A...UM... A "GROUP DATE."
OH?
AH!
I'M SURE I SAW THAT TERM SOME-WHERE...
HO HO HO! OF *COURSE* I KNOW THAT!!
YOU *DO* ...?
SO, uh... WHAT SHOULD WE DO?
LEAVE THAT TO ME!
I COME ARMED WITH A *DETAILED PLAN.*
A *TRUE* DATE STARTS...
...WITH--
--THE DATE MOVIE!!
NEKOMI CINEMA
THE LAST RUMBA
ラスト ルンバ

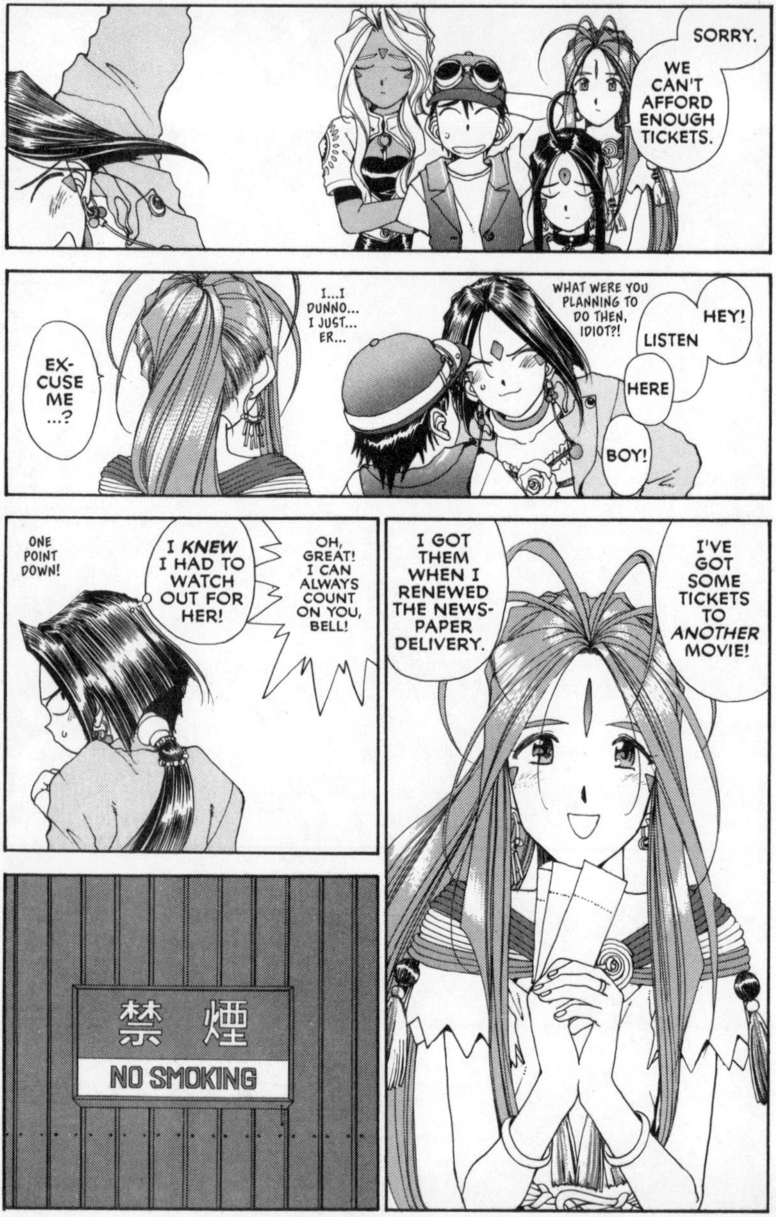
SORRY.
WE CAN'T AFFORD ENOUGH TICKETS.
HEY!
LISTEN
HERE
BOY!
WHAT WERE YOU PLANNING TO DO THEN, IDIOT?!
I...I DUNNO... I JUST... ER...
EX-CUSE ME ...?
I'VE GOT SOME TICKETS TO *ANOTHER* MOVIE!
I GOT THEM WHEN I RENEWED THE NEWS-PAPER DELIVERY.
OH, GREAT! I CAN ALWAYS COUNT ON YOU, BELL!
I ***KNEW*** I HAD TO WATCH OUT FOR HER!
ONE POINT DOWN!
禁煙
NO SMOKING

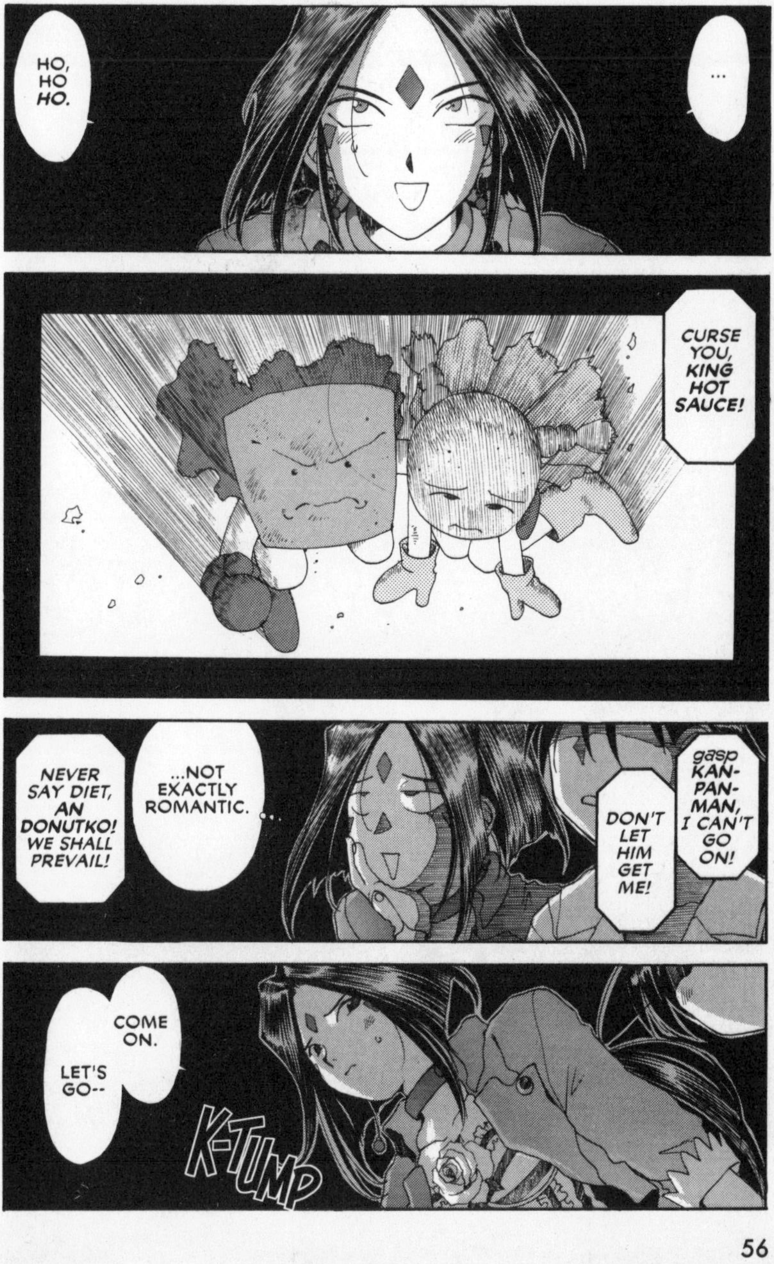
...
HO, HO HO.
CURSE YOU, KING HOT SAUCE!
gasp KAN-PAN-MAN, I CAN'T GO ON!
DON'T LET HIM GET ME!
...NOT EXACTLY ROMANTIC.
NEVER SAY DIET, AN DONUTKO! WE SHALL PREVAIL!
COME ON.
LET'S GO--
K-TUMP

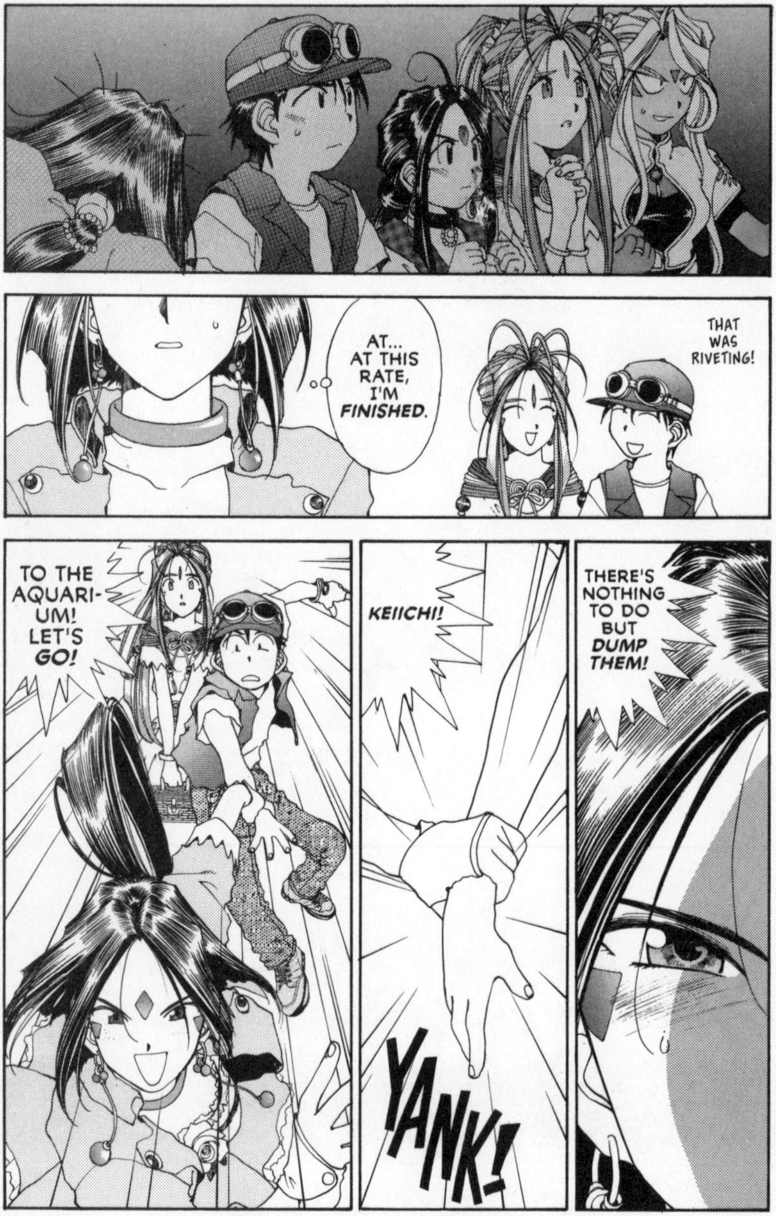
THAT WAS RIVETING!
AT... AT THIS RATE, I'M *FINISHED*.
THERE'S NOTHING TO DO BUT *DUMP THEM!*
KEIICHI!
YANK!
TO THE AQUARI-UM! LET'S *GO!*

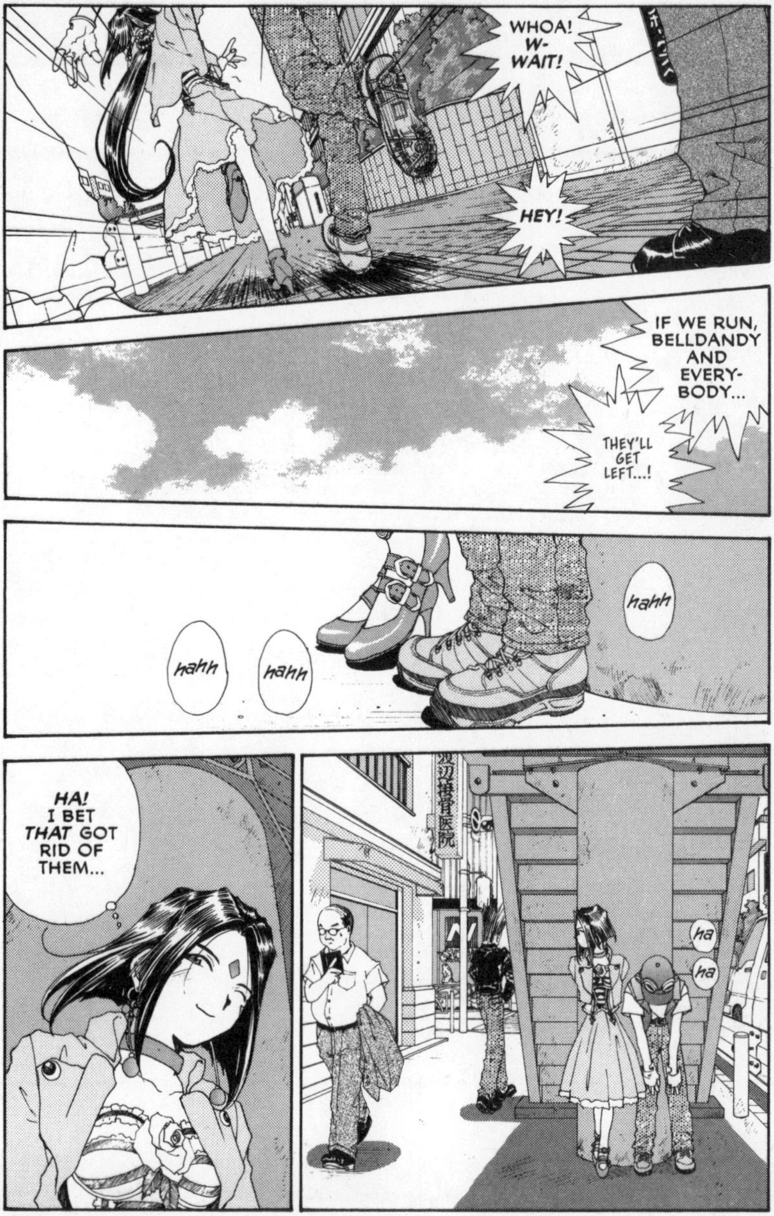
WHOA! W-WAIT!
HEY!
IF WE RUN, BELLDANDY AND EVERY-BODY...
THEY'LL GET LEFT...!
hahh
hahh
hahh
ha
ha
HA! I BET *THAT* GOT RID OF THEM...

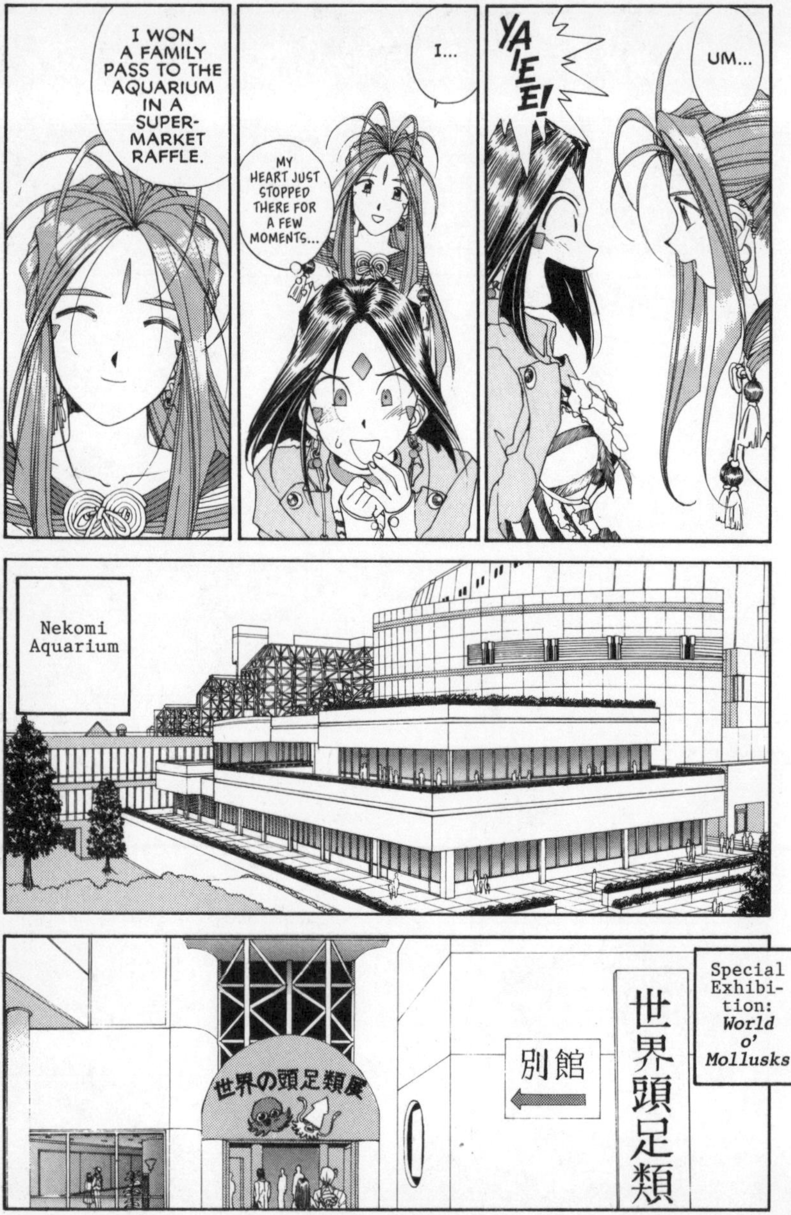
UM...
YAIEE!
I...
MY HEART JUST STOPPED THERE FOR A FEW MOMENTS...
I WON A FAMILY PASS TO THE AQUARIUM IN A SUPER-MARKET RAFFLE.
Nekomi Aquarium
Special Exhibition: *World o' Mollusks*
世界頭足類
別館
世界の頭足類展

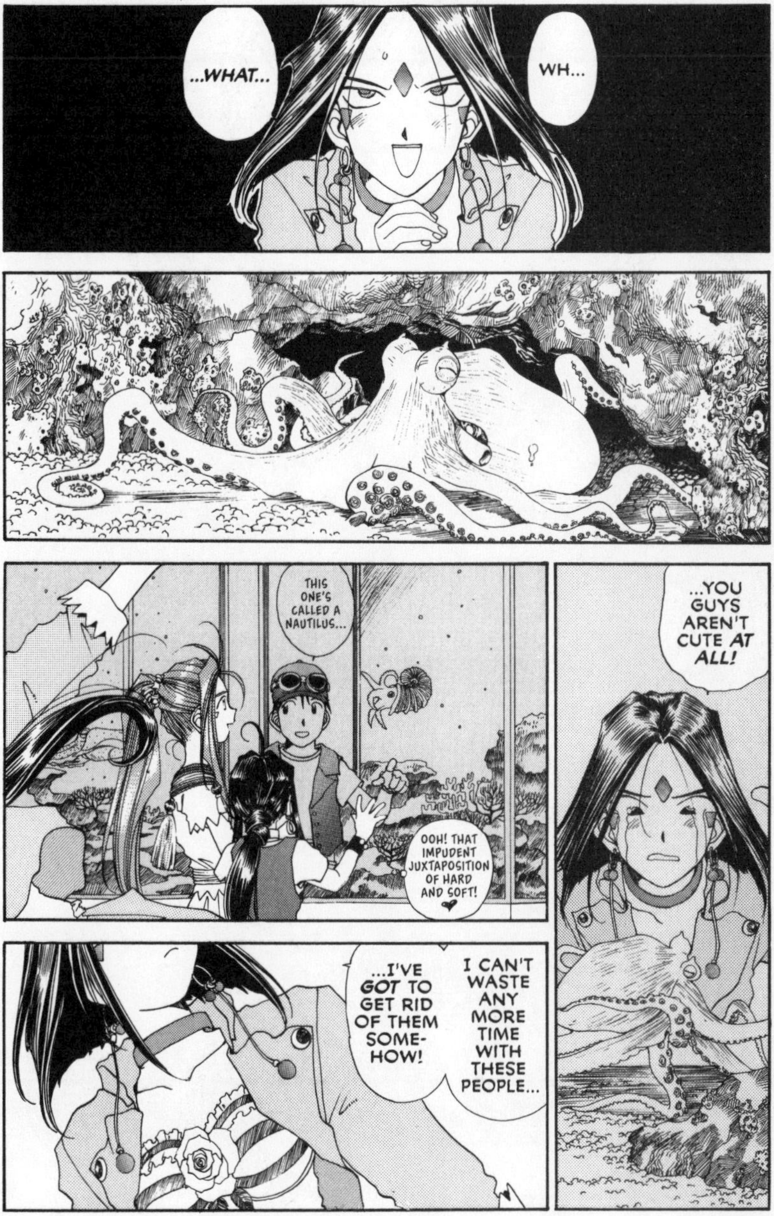
WH...
...WHAT...
...YOU GUYS AREN'T CUTE AT ALL!
THIS ONE'S CALLED A NAUTILUS...
OOH! THAT IMPUDENT JUXTAPOSITION OF HARD AND SOFT!
I CAN'T WASTE ANY MORE TIME WITH THESE PEOPLE...
...I'VE GOT TO GET RID OF THEM SOME-HOW!

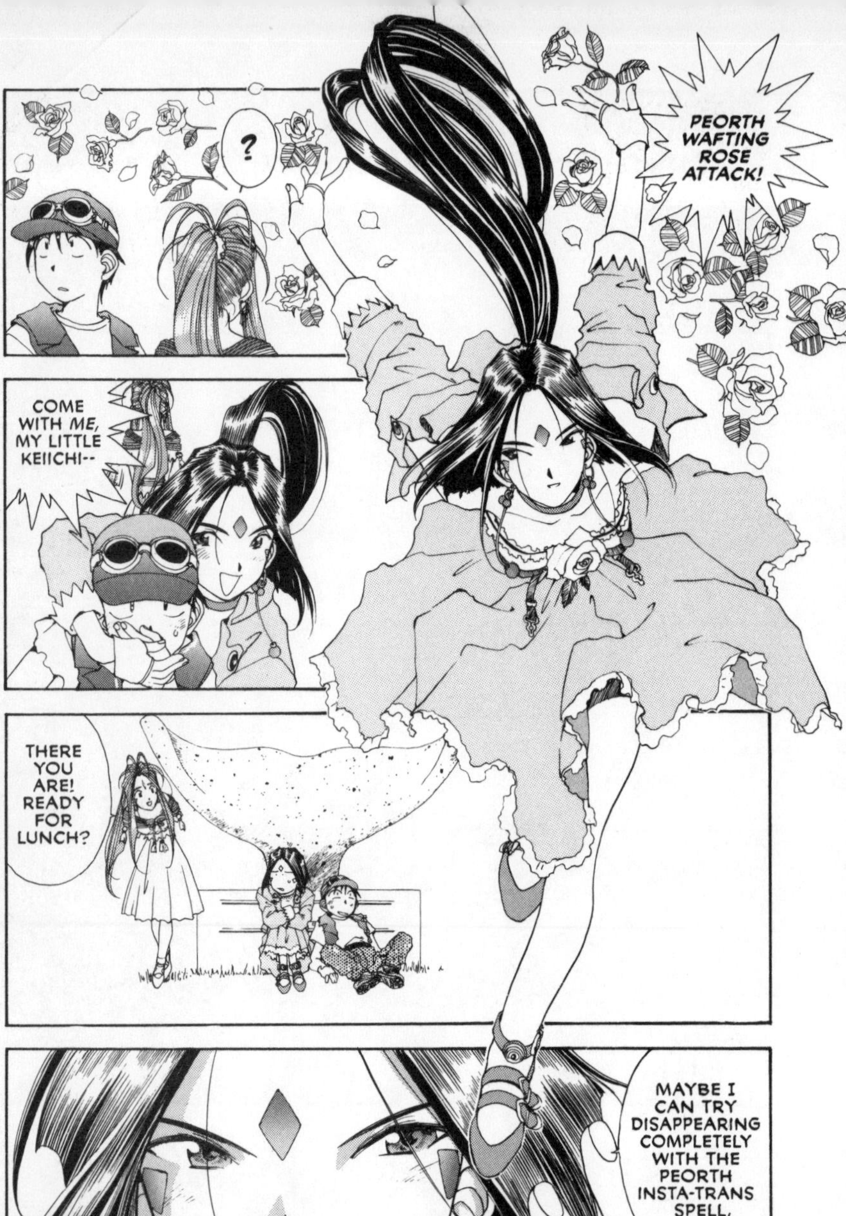
PEORTH WAFTING ROSE ATTACK!
?
COME WITH *ME*, MY LITTLE KEIICHI--
THERE YOU ARE! READY FOR LUNCH?
MAYBE I CAN TRY DISAPPEARING COMPLETELY WITH THE PEORTH INSTA-TRANS SPELL, AND--

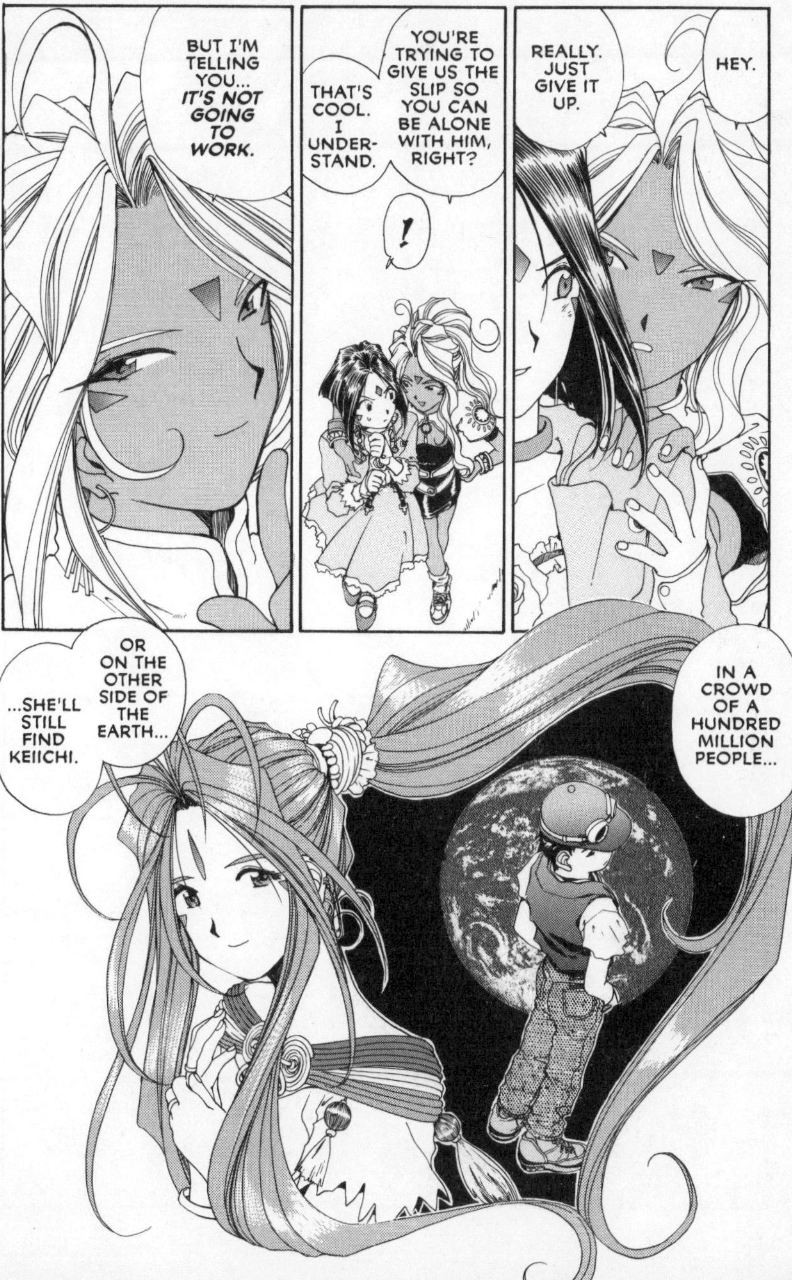
HEY.
REALLY. JUST GIVE IT UP.
YOU'RE TRYING TO GIVE US THE SLIP SO YOU CAN BE ALONE WITH HIM, RIGHT?
THAT'S COOL. I UNDER-STAND.
!
BUT I'M TELLING YOU... *IT'S NOT GOING TO WORK.*
IN A CROWD OF A HUNDRED MILLION PEOPLE...
OR ON THE OTHER SIDE OF THE EARTH...
...SHE'LL STILL FIND KEIICHI.

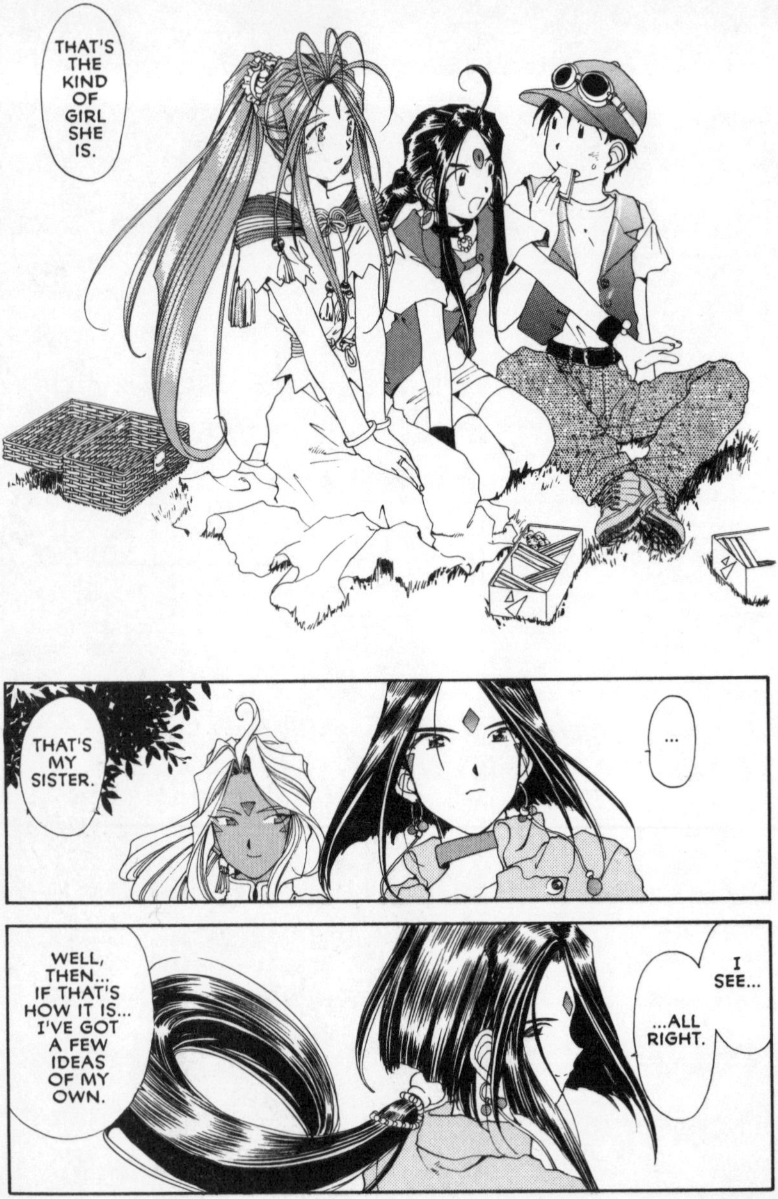
THAT'S THE KIND OF GIRL SHE IS.
...
THAT'S MY SISTER.
I SEE...
...ALL RIGHT.
WELL, THEN... IF THAT'S HOW IT IS... I'VE GOT A FEW IDEAS OF MY OWN.

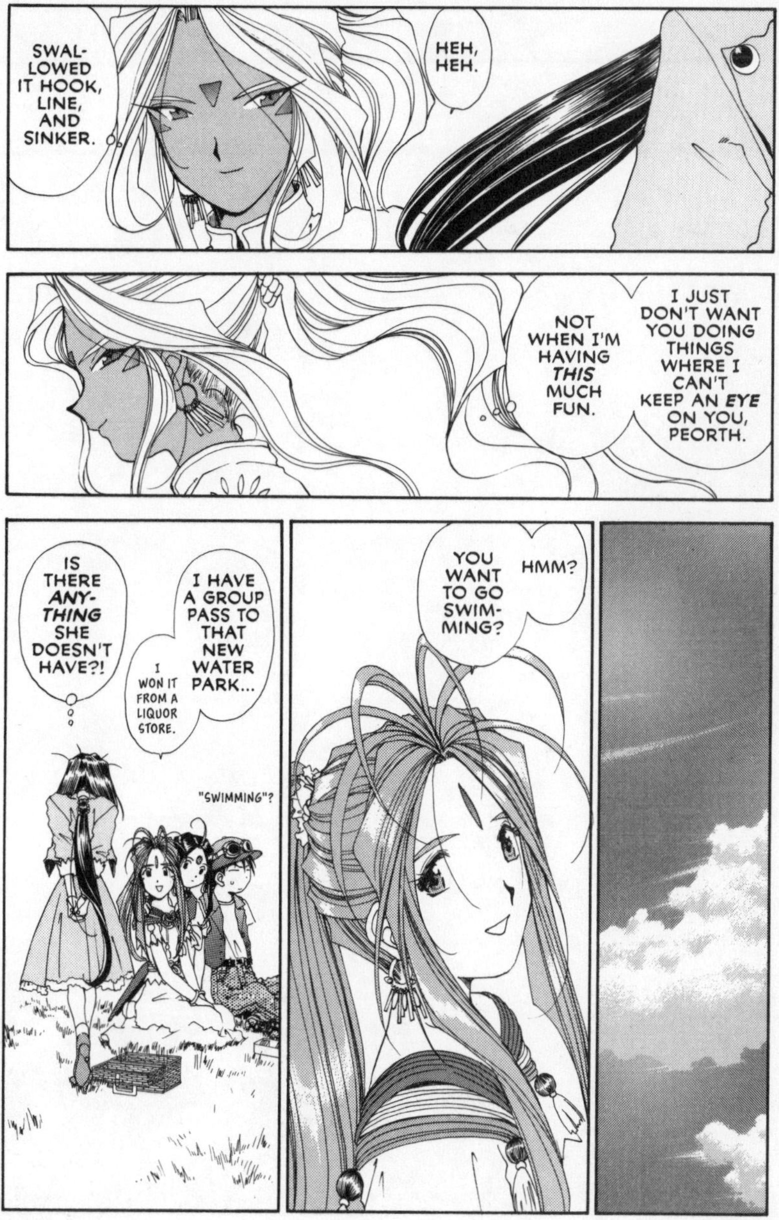
HEH, HEH.
SWAL-LOWED IT HOOK, LINE, AND SINKER.
I JUST DON'T WANT YOU DOING THINGS WHERE I CAN'T KEEP AN *EYE* ON YOU, PEORTH.
NOT WHEN I'M HAVING *THIS* MUCH FUN.
HMM?
YOU WANT TO GO SWIMMING?
I HAVE A GROUP PASS TO THAT NEW WATER PARK...
I WON IT FROM A LIQUOR STORE.
IS THERE *ANYTHING* SHE DOESN'T HAVE?!
"SWIMMING"?

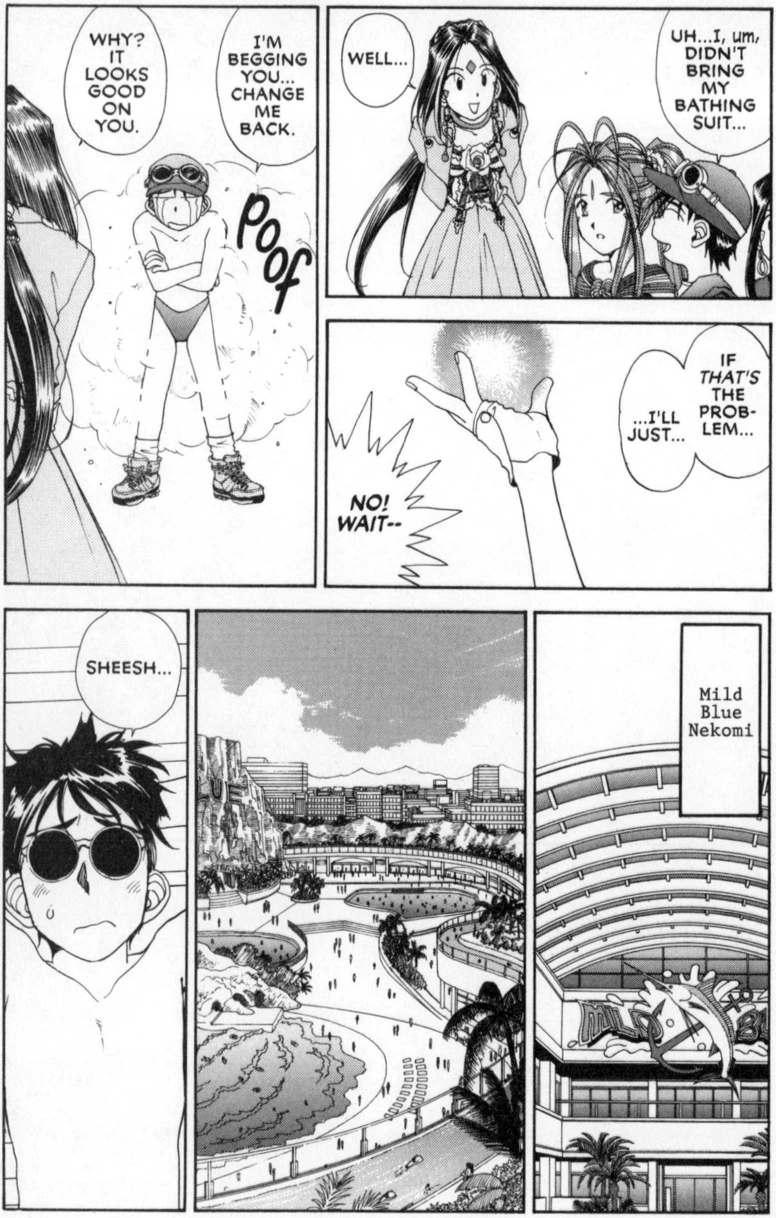
UH...I, um, DIDN'T BRING MY BATHING SUIT...
WELL...
IF THAT'S THE PROBLEM...
...I'LL JUST...
NO! WAIT--
I'M BEGGING YOU... CHANGE ME BACK.
WHY? IT LOOKS GOOD ON YOU.
POOF
Mild Blue Nekomi
SHEESH...

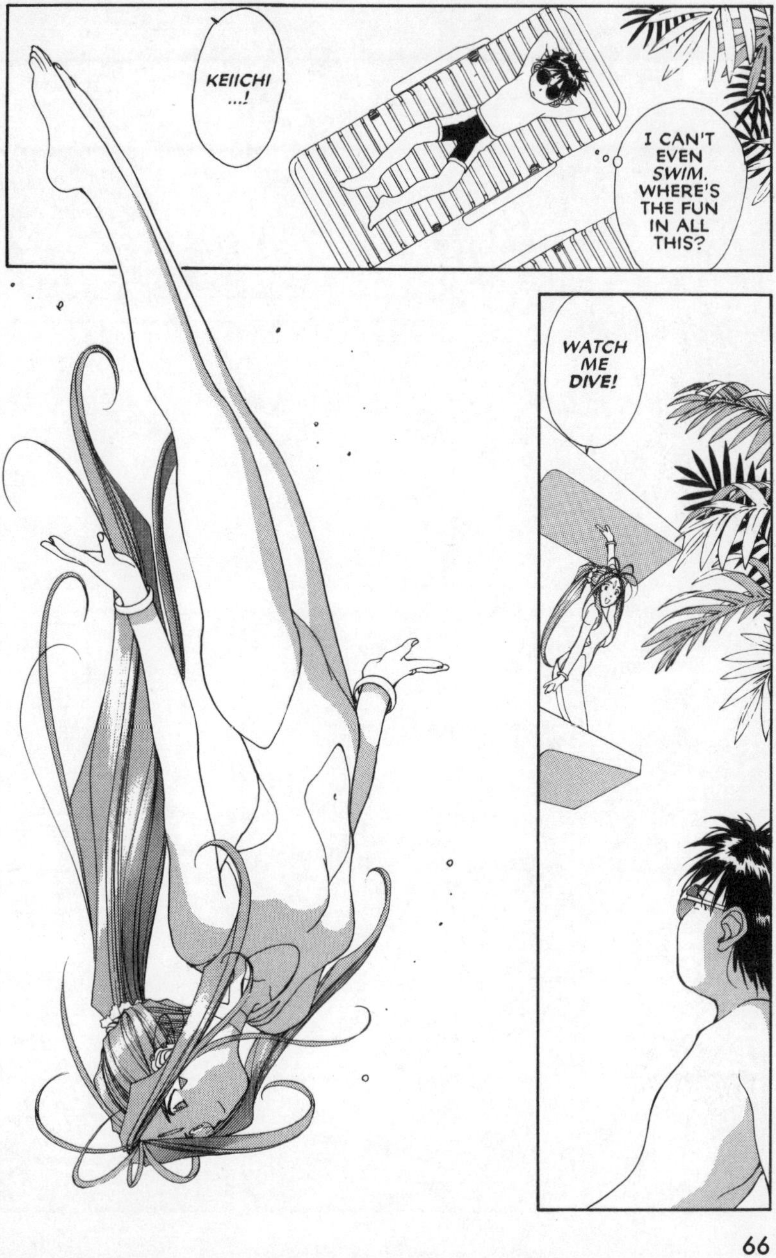
I CAN'T EVEN *SWIM*. WHERE'S THE FUN IN ALL THIS?
KEIICHI ...!
WATCH ME DIVE!

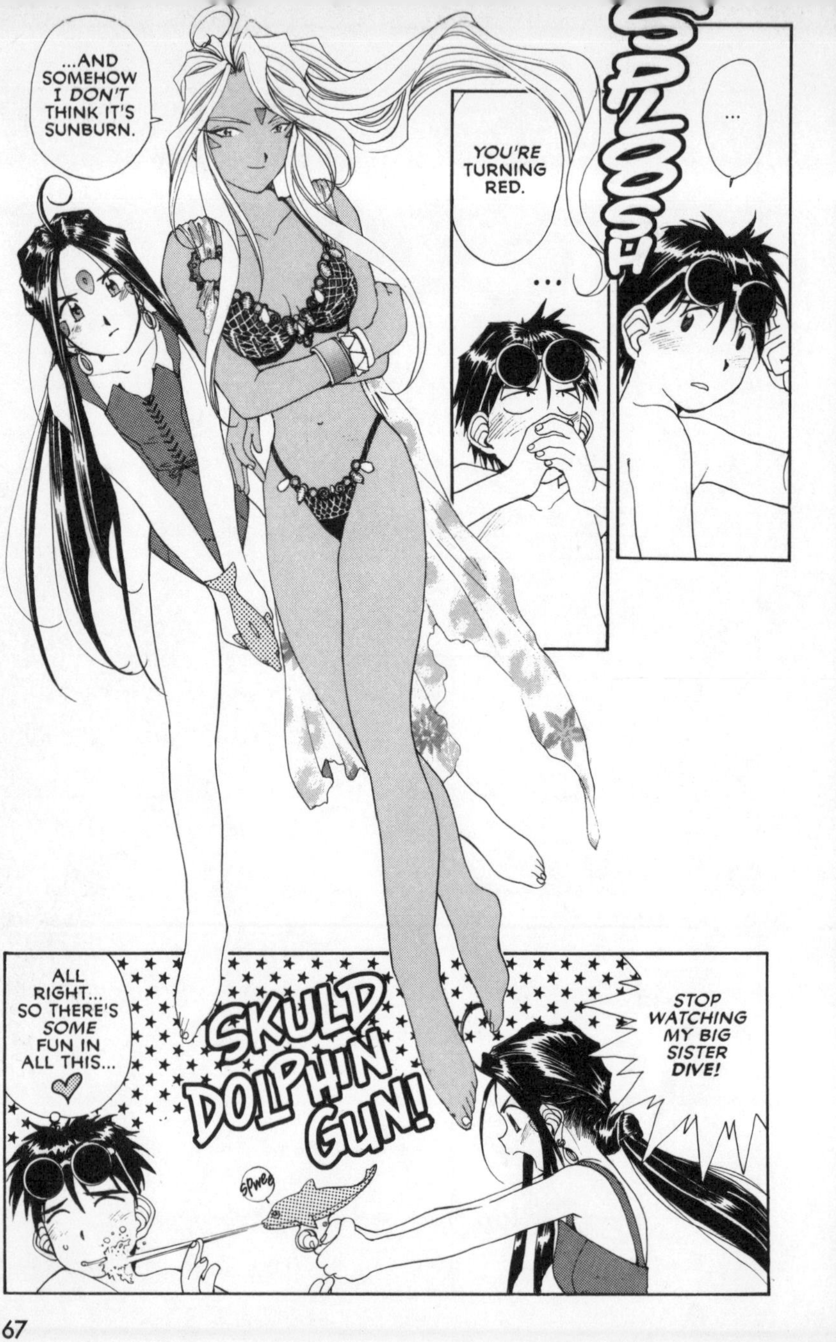
SPLOOSH
...
YOU'RE TURNING RED.
...
...AND SOMEHOW I *DON'T* THINK IT'S SUNBURN.
STOP WATCHING MY BIG SISTER DIVE!
SKULD DOLPHIN GUN!
SPWEE
ALL RIGHT... SO THERE'S *SOME* FUN IN ALL THIS... ♥

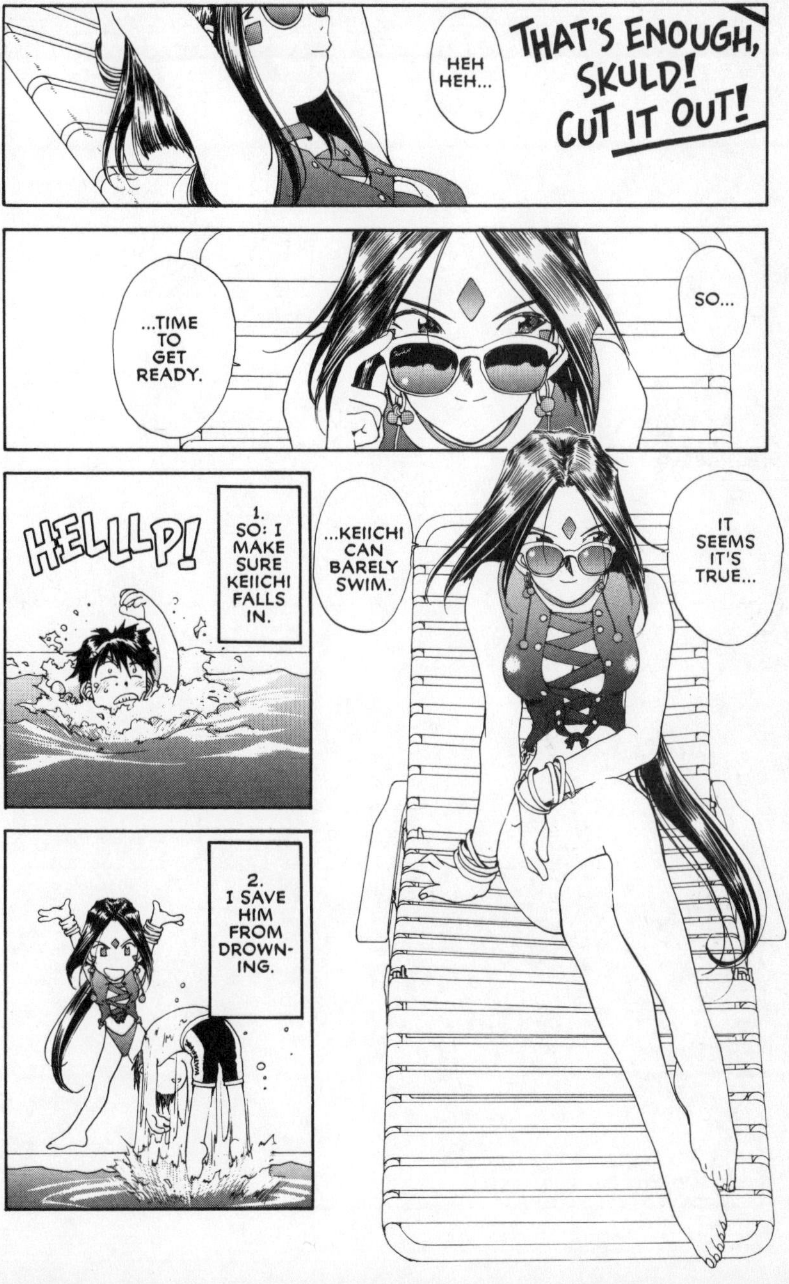
THAT'S ENOUGH, SKULD! CUT IT OUT!
HEH HEH...
SO...
...TIME TO GET READY.
IT SEEMS IT'S TRUE...
...KEIICHI CAN BARELY SWIM.
1. SO: I MAKE SURE KEIICHI FALLS IN.
HELLLP!
2. I SAVE HIM FROM DROWNING.

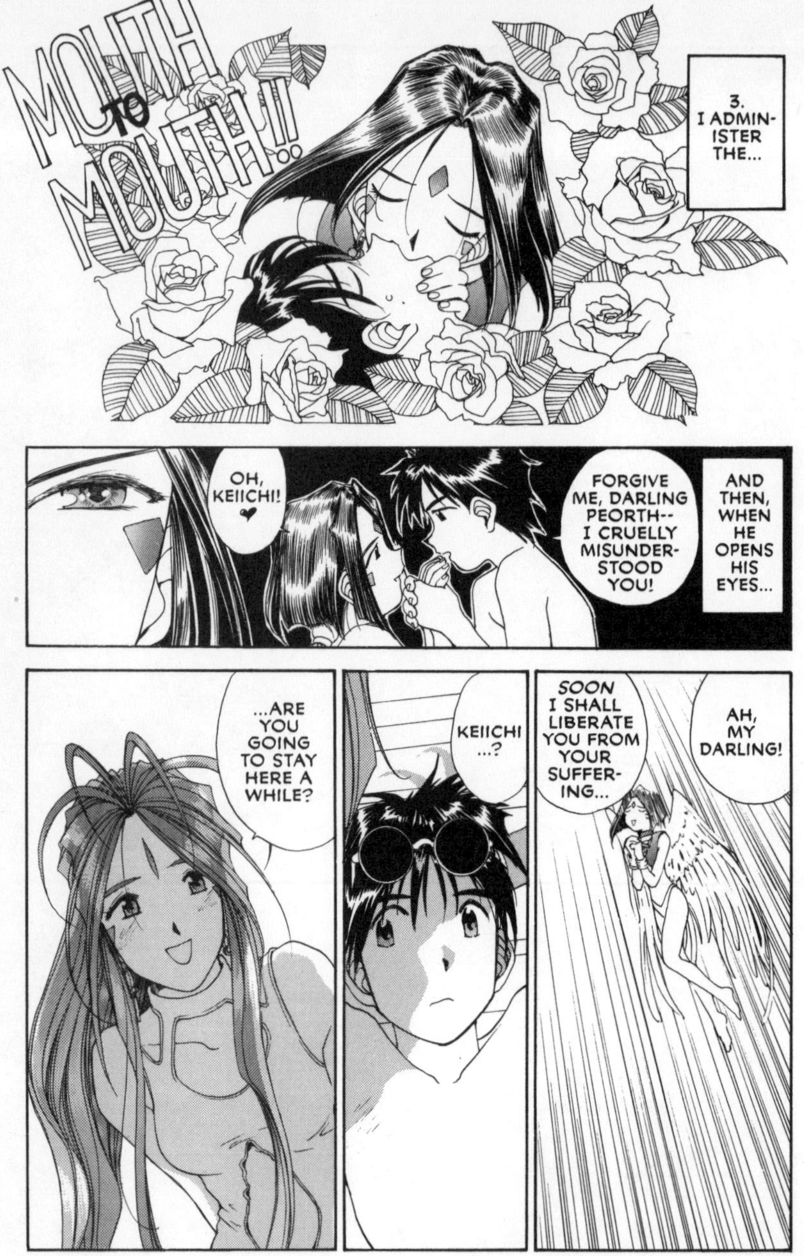
3. I ADMINISTER THE...
MOUTH TO MOUTH!!
AND THEN, WHEN HE OPENS HIS EYES...
FORGIVE ME, DARLING PEORTH-- I CRUELLY MISUNDERSTOOD YOU!
OH, KEIICHI! ♥
AH, MY DARLING!
SOON I SHALL LIBERATE YOU FROM YOUR SUFFERING...
KEIICHI ...?
...ARE YOU GOING TO STAY HERE A WHILE?

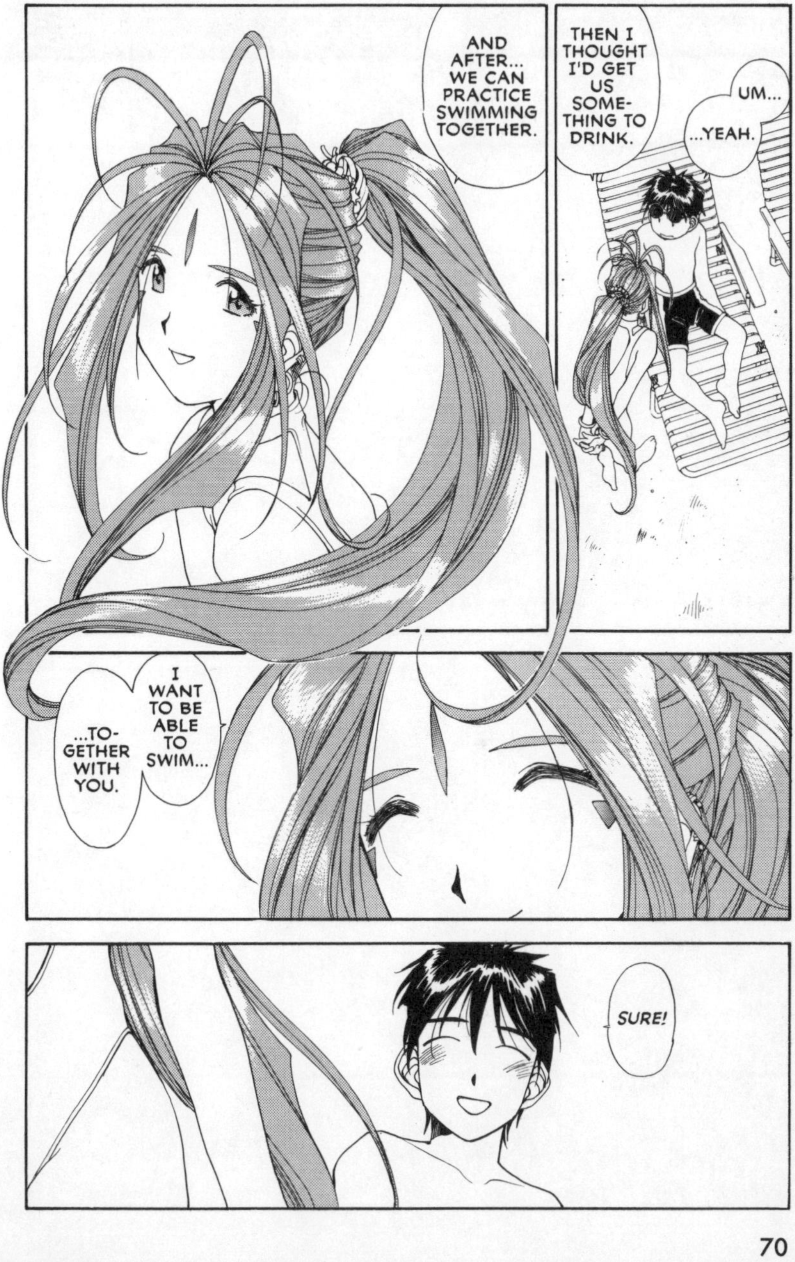
THEN I THOUGHT I'D GET US SOME-THING TO DRINK.
UM...
...YEAH.
AND AFTER... WE CAN PRACTICE SWIMMING TOGETHER.
I WANT TO BE ABLE TO SWIM...
...TO-GETHER WITH YOU.
SURE!

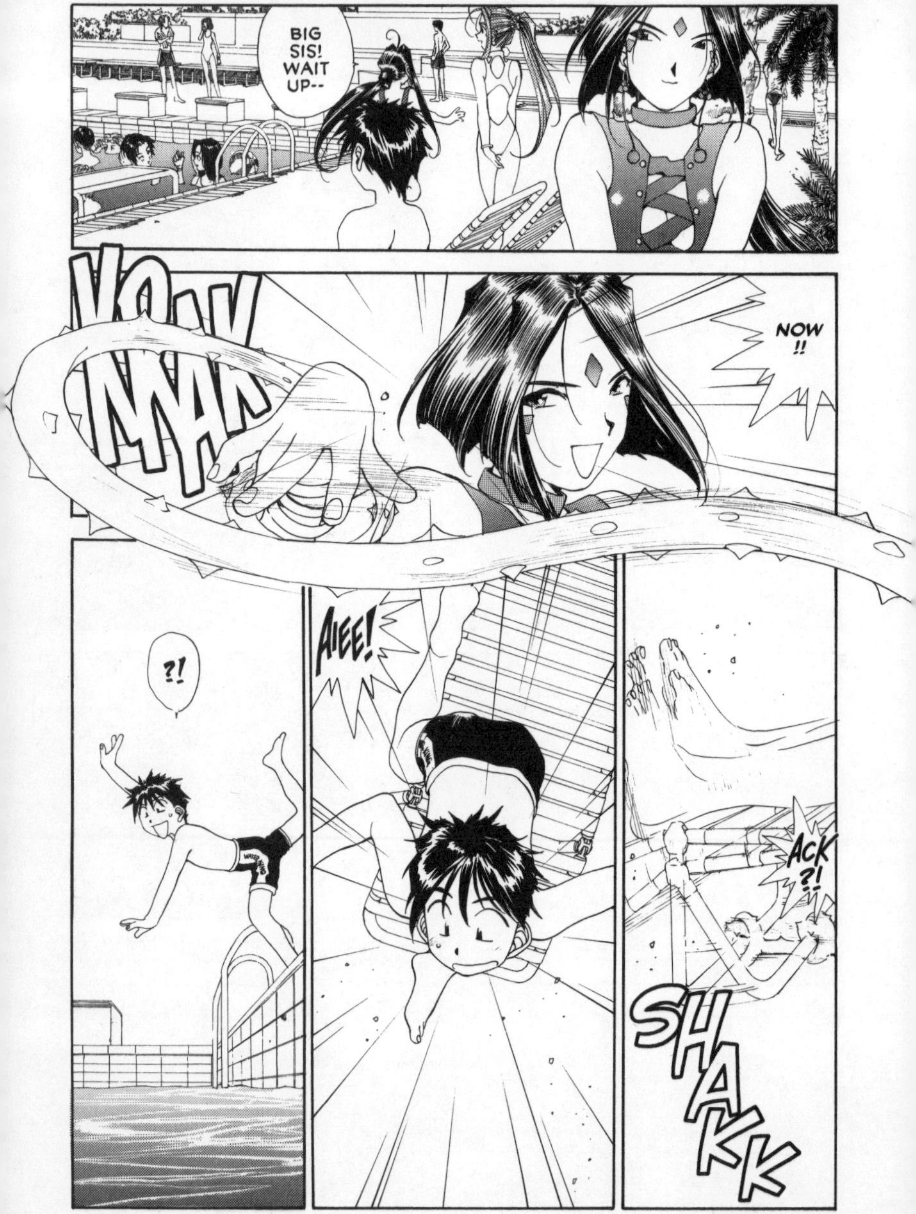
BIG SIS! WAIT UP--
NOW !!
WHAK
ACK ?!
SHAKK
AIEE!
?!

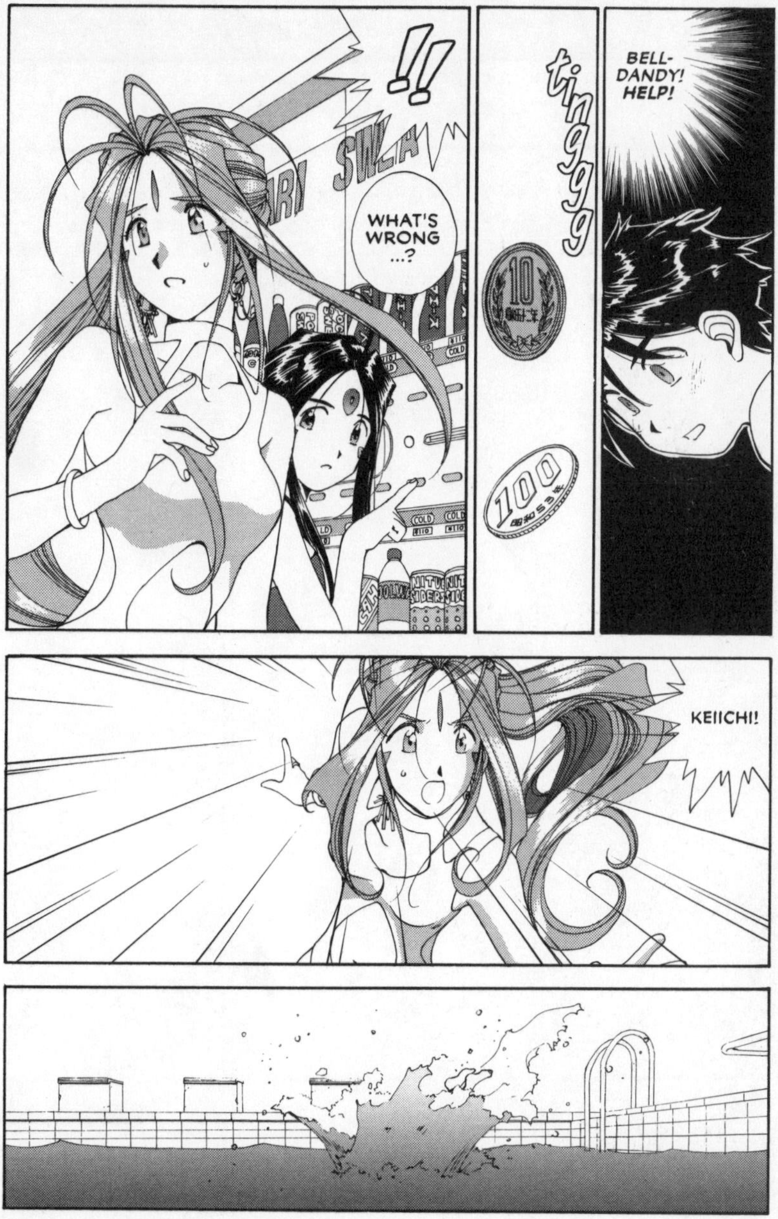
BELL-
DANDY!
HELP!
tinggg
!!
WHAT'S
WRONG
...?
KEIICHI!

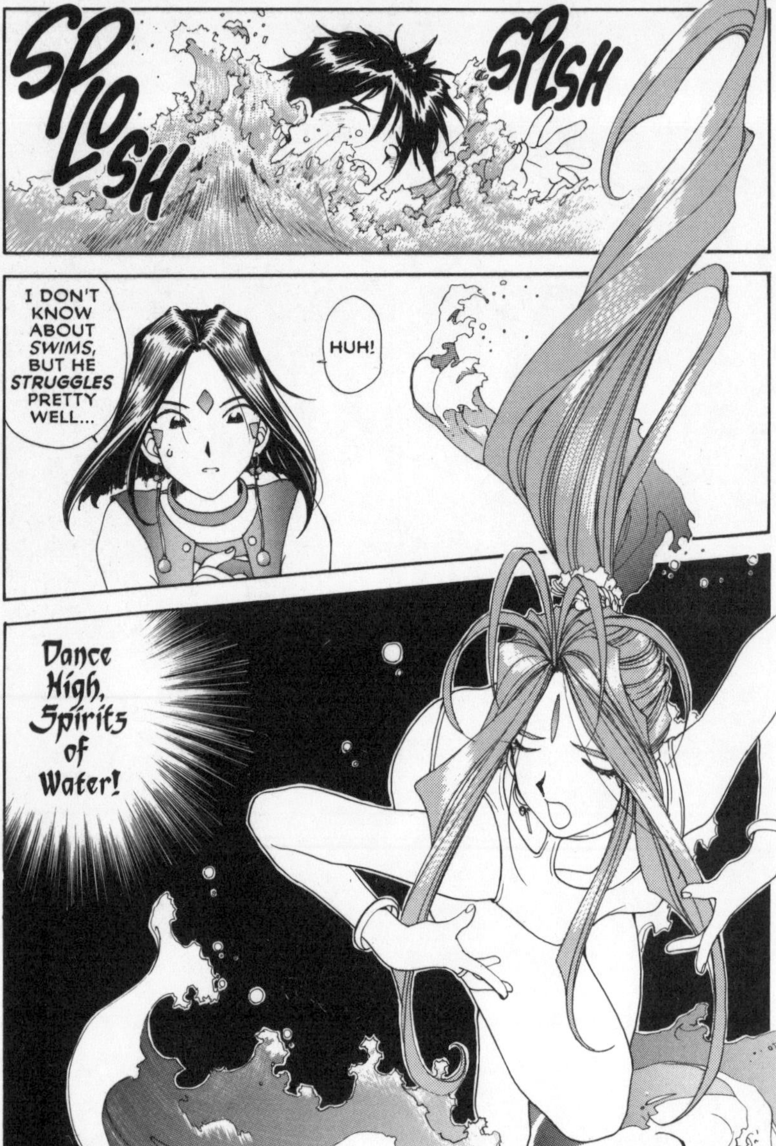
SPLISH
SPLOSH
HUH!
I DON'T KNOW ABOUT *SWIMS*, BUT HE *STRUGGLES* PRETTY WELL...
Dance High, Spirits of Water!

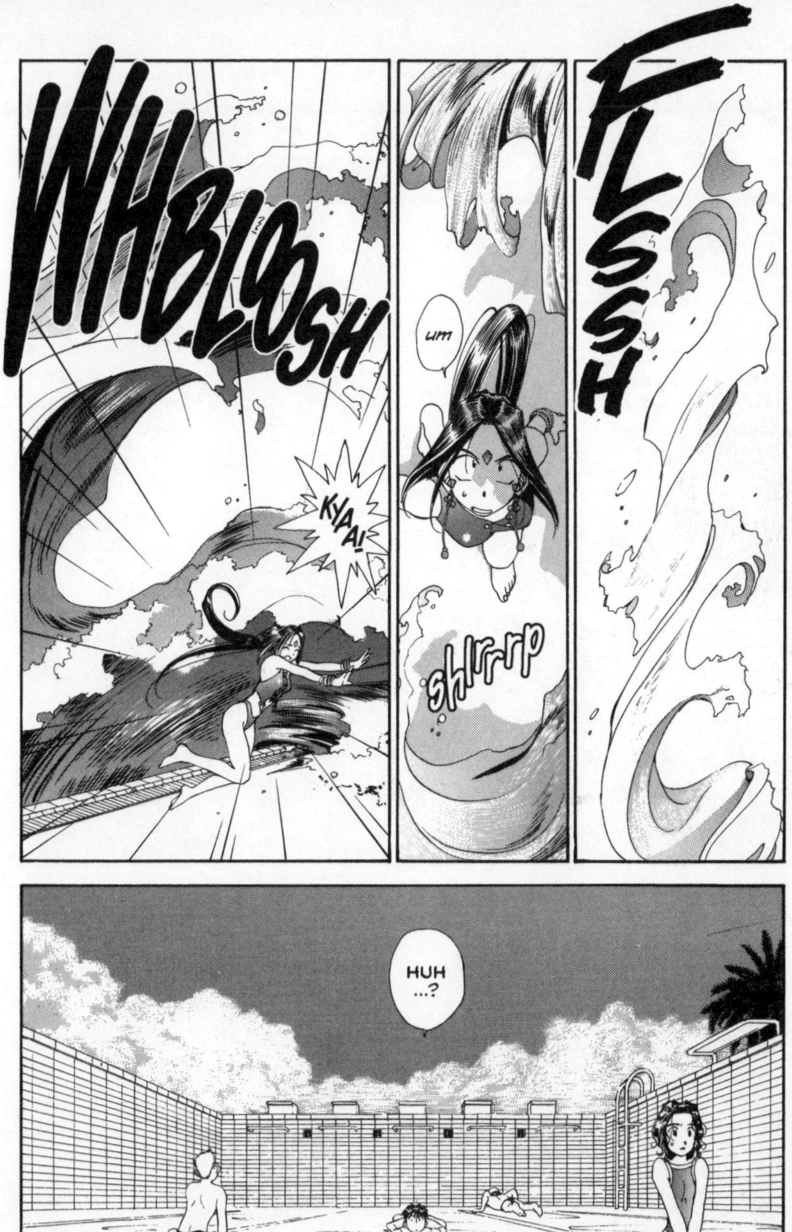
FLSSH
um
shlrrrp
WHABLOOSH
KYAA!
HUH ...?

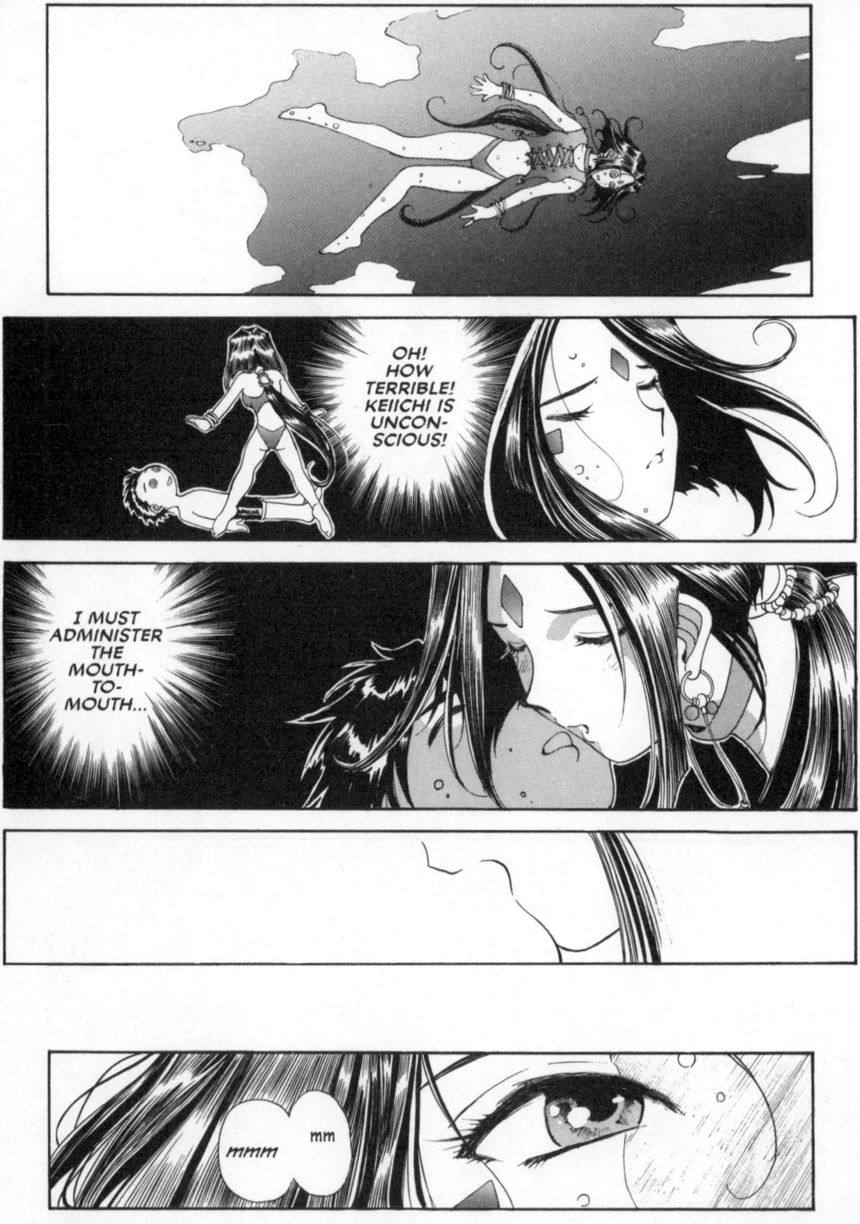
OH! HOW TERRIBLE! KEIICHI IS UNCONSCIOUS!
I MUST ADMINISTER THE MOUTH-TO-MOUTH...
mm
mmm

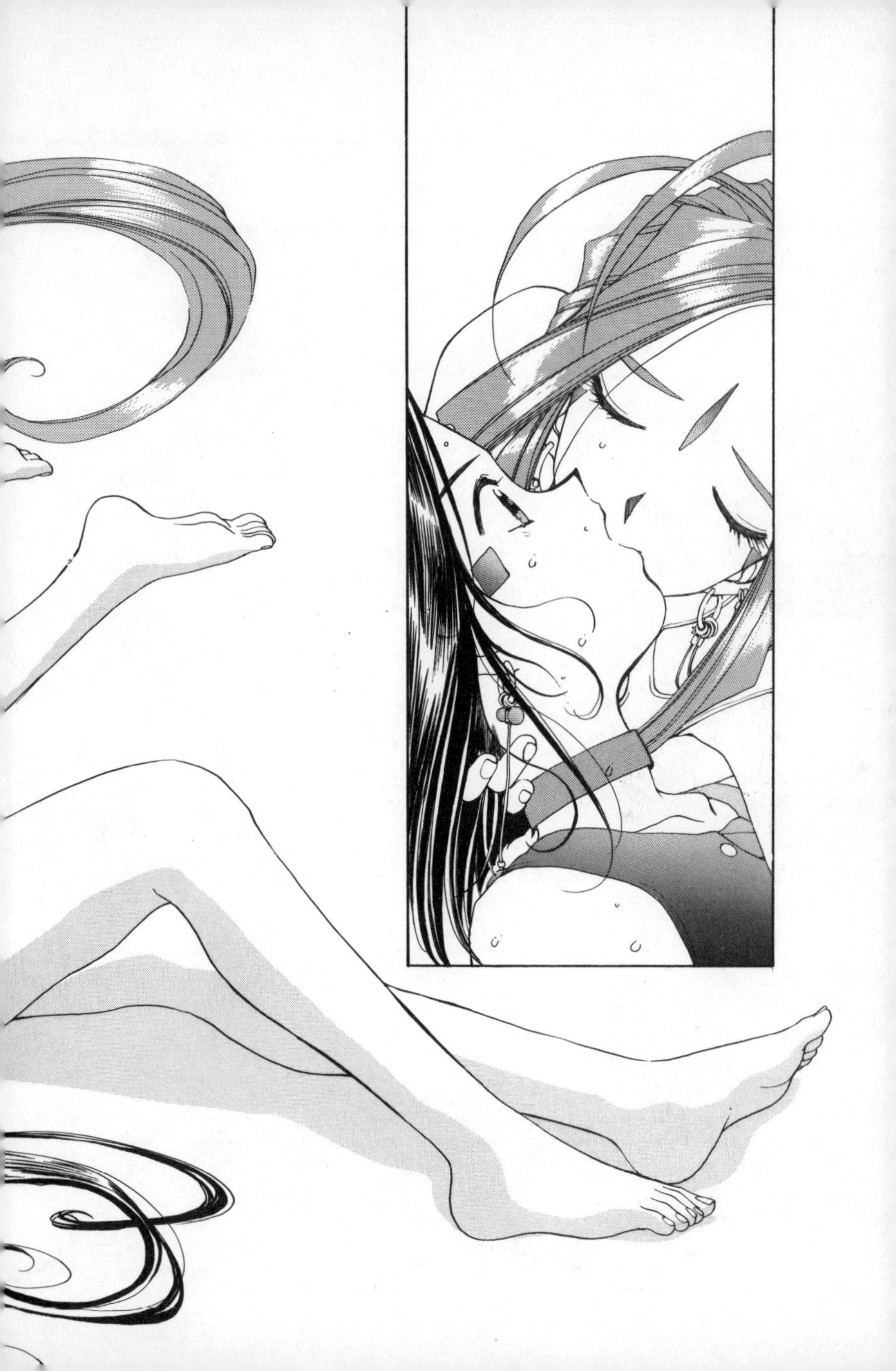

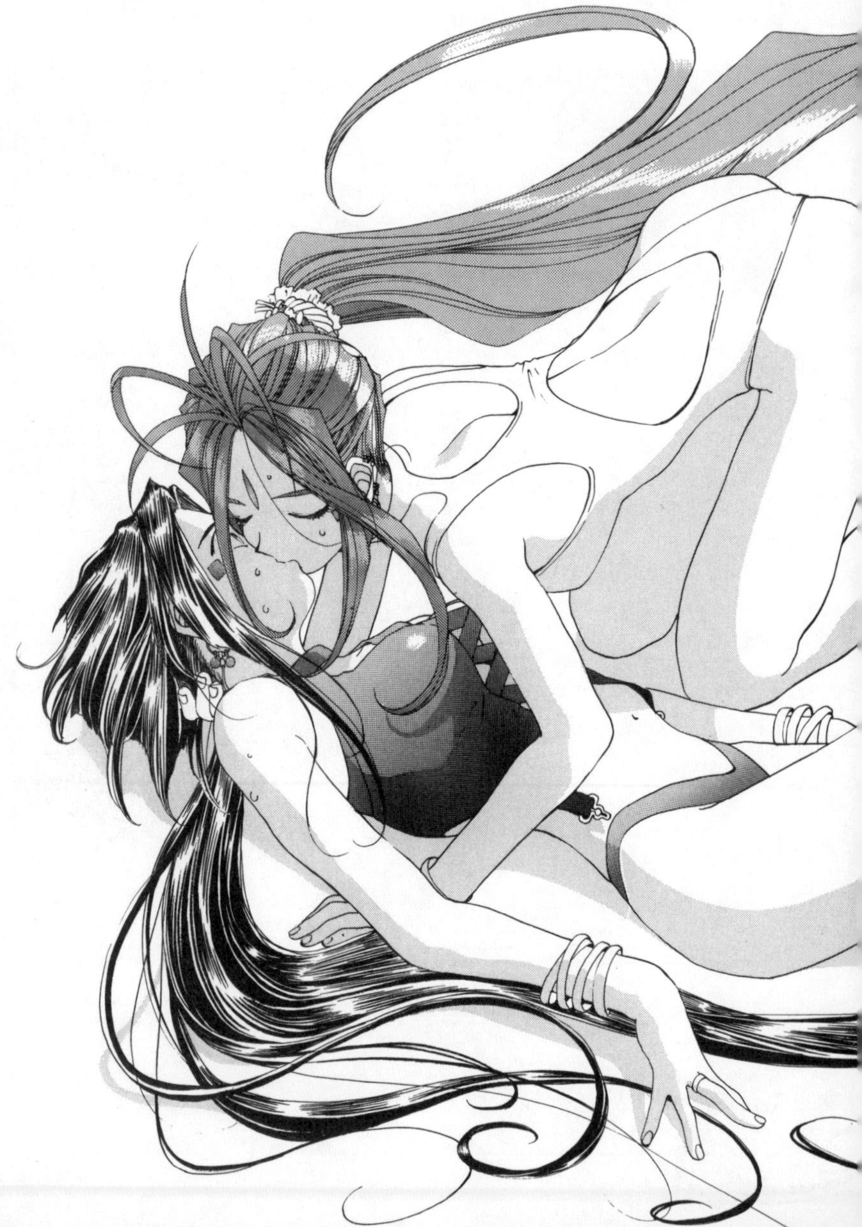

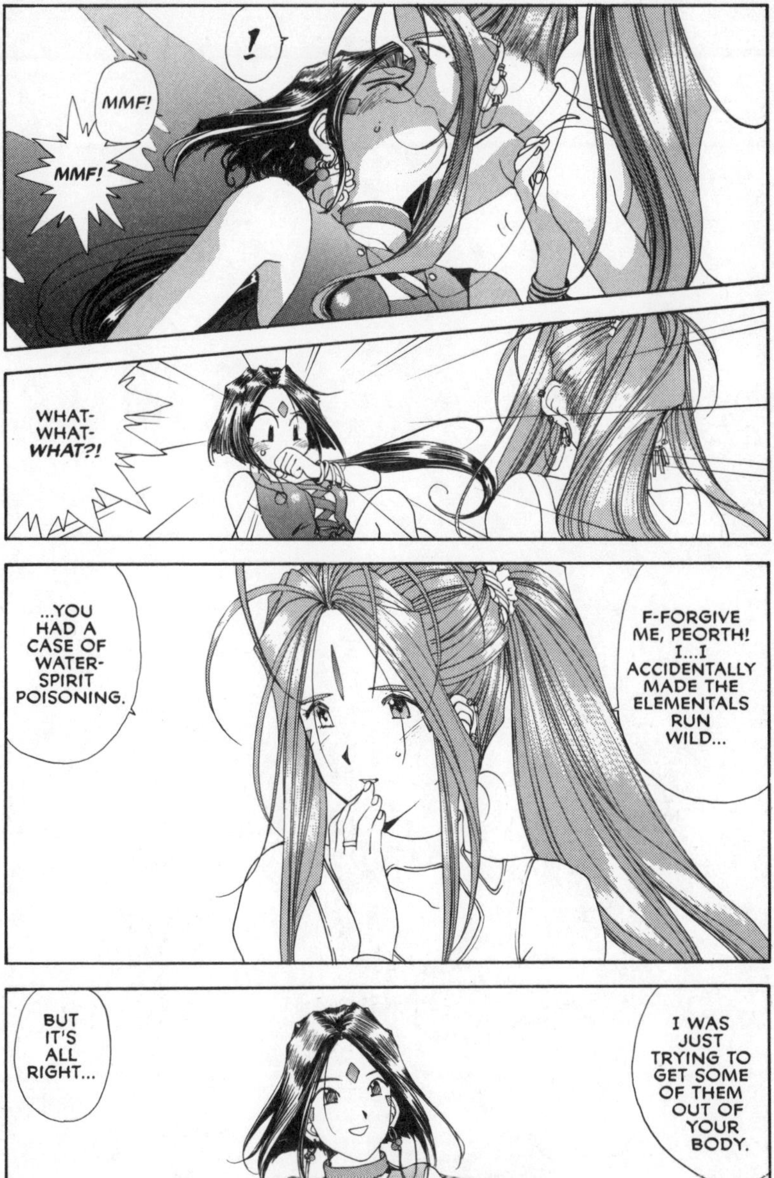
!
MMF!
MMF!
WHAT- WHAT- WHAT?!
F-FORGIVE ME, PEORTH! I...I ACCIDENTALLY MADE THE ELEMENTALS RUN WILD...
...YOU HAD A CASE OF WATER-SPIRIT POISONING.
I WAS JUST TRYING TO GET SOME OF THEM OUT OF YOUR BODY.
BUT IT'S ALL RIGHT...

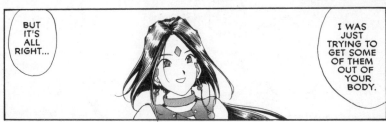

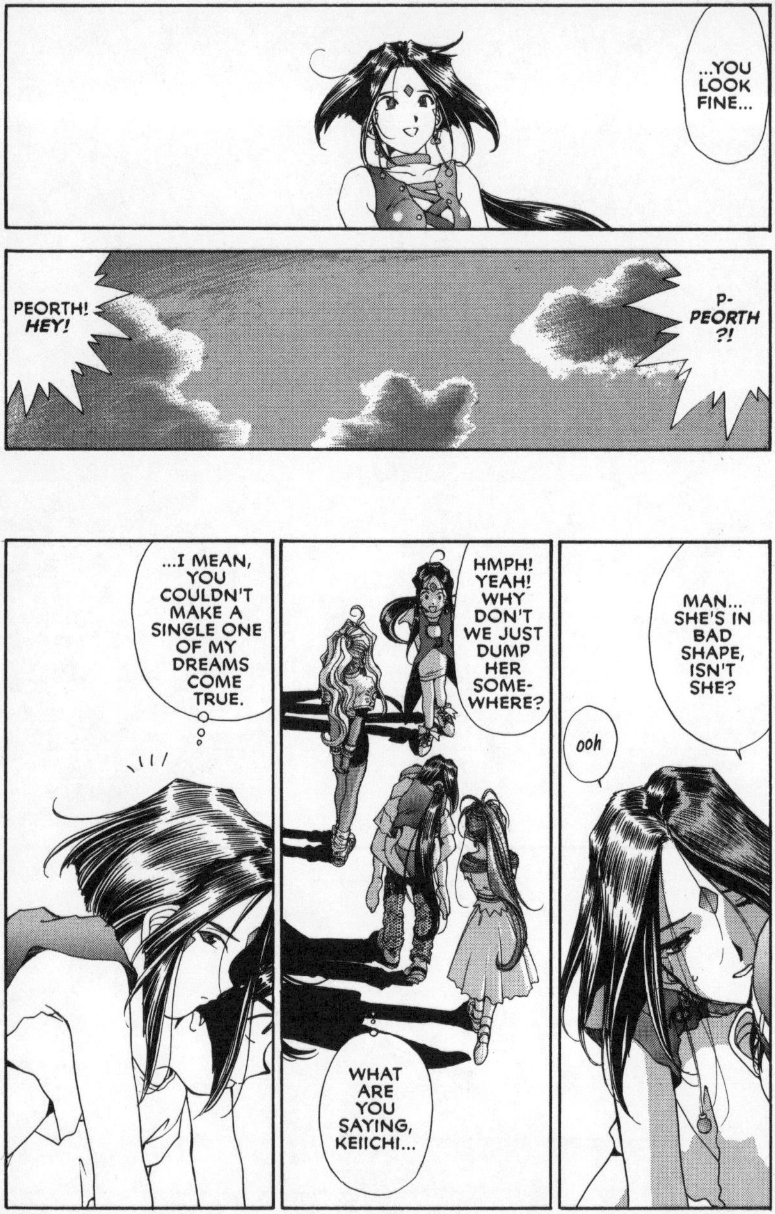
...YOU LOOK FINE...
P- PEORTH?!
PEORTH! HEY!
MAN... SHE'S IN BAD SHAPE, ISN'T SHE?
ooh
HMPH! YEAH! WHY DON'T WE JUST DUMP HER SOME-WHERE?
WHAT ARE YOU SAYING, KEIICHI...
...I MEAN, YOU COULDN'T MAKE A SINGLE ONE OF MY DREAMS COME TRUE.

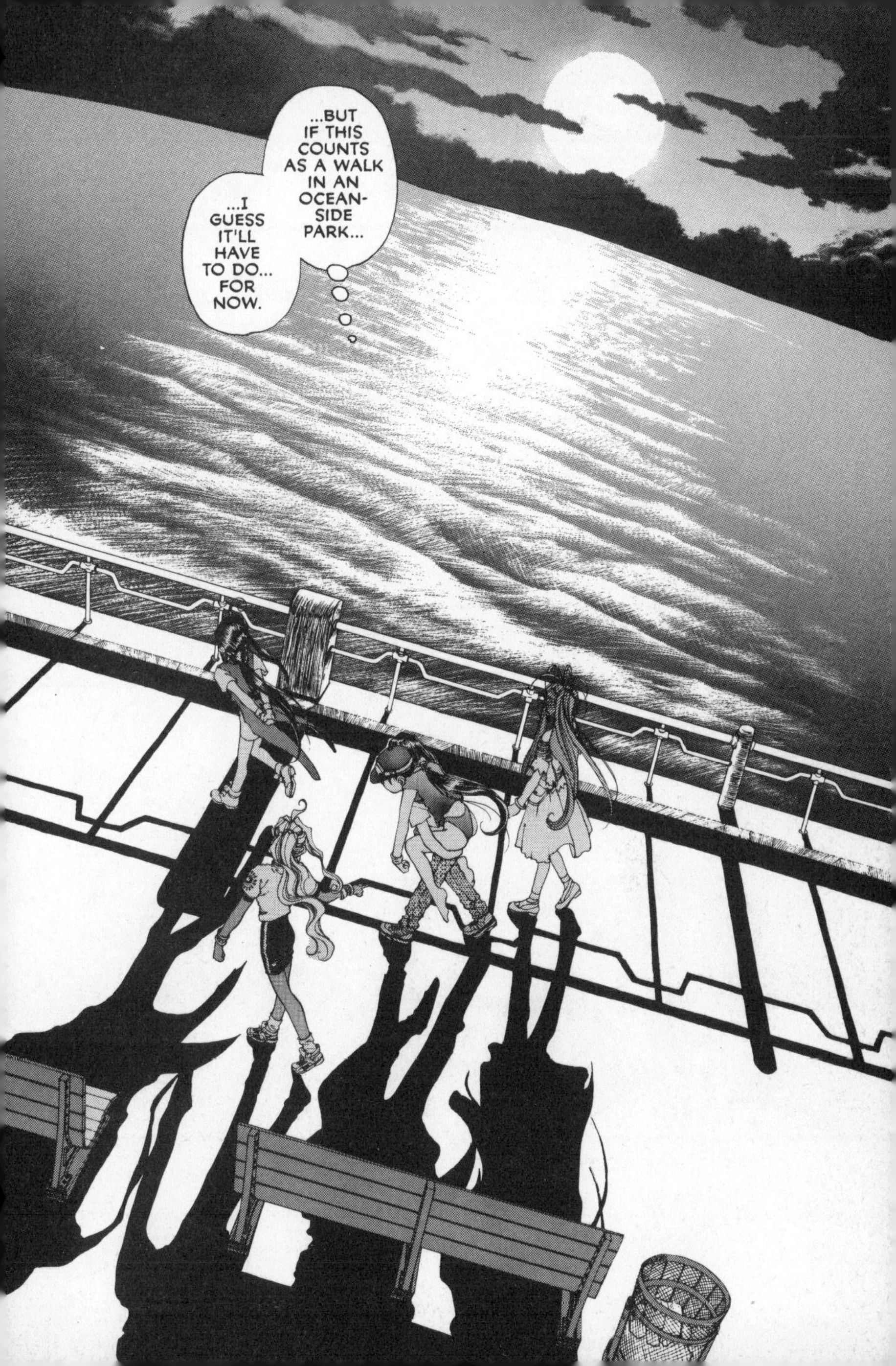
...BUT IF THIS COUNTS AS A WALK IN AN OCEAN-SIDE PARK...
...I GUESS IT'LL HAVE TO DO... FOR NOW.

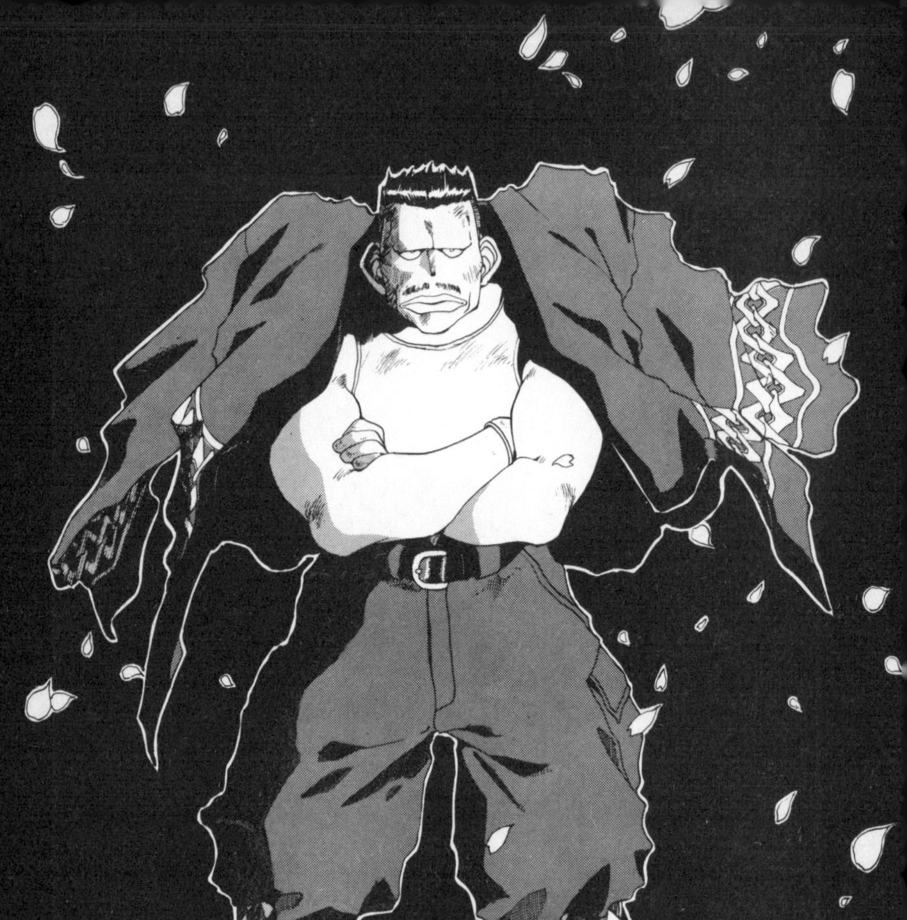

CHAPTER 70

When a Man Loves a Woman

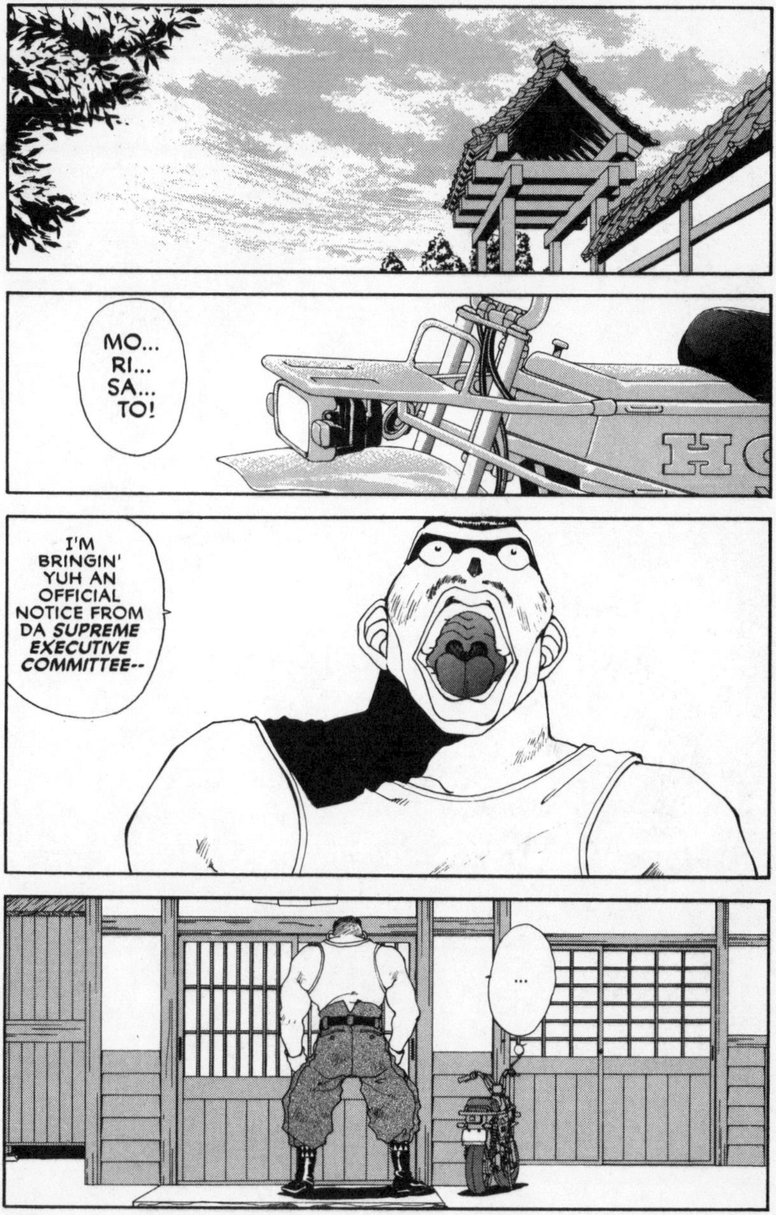
MO... RI... SA... TO!
I'M BRINGIN' YUH AN OFFICIAL NOTICE FROM DA *SUPREME EXECUTIVE COMMITTEE--*
...

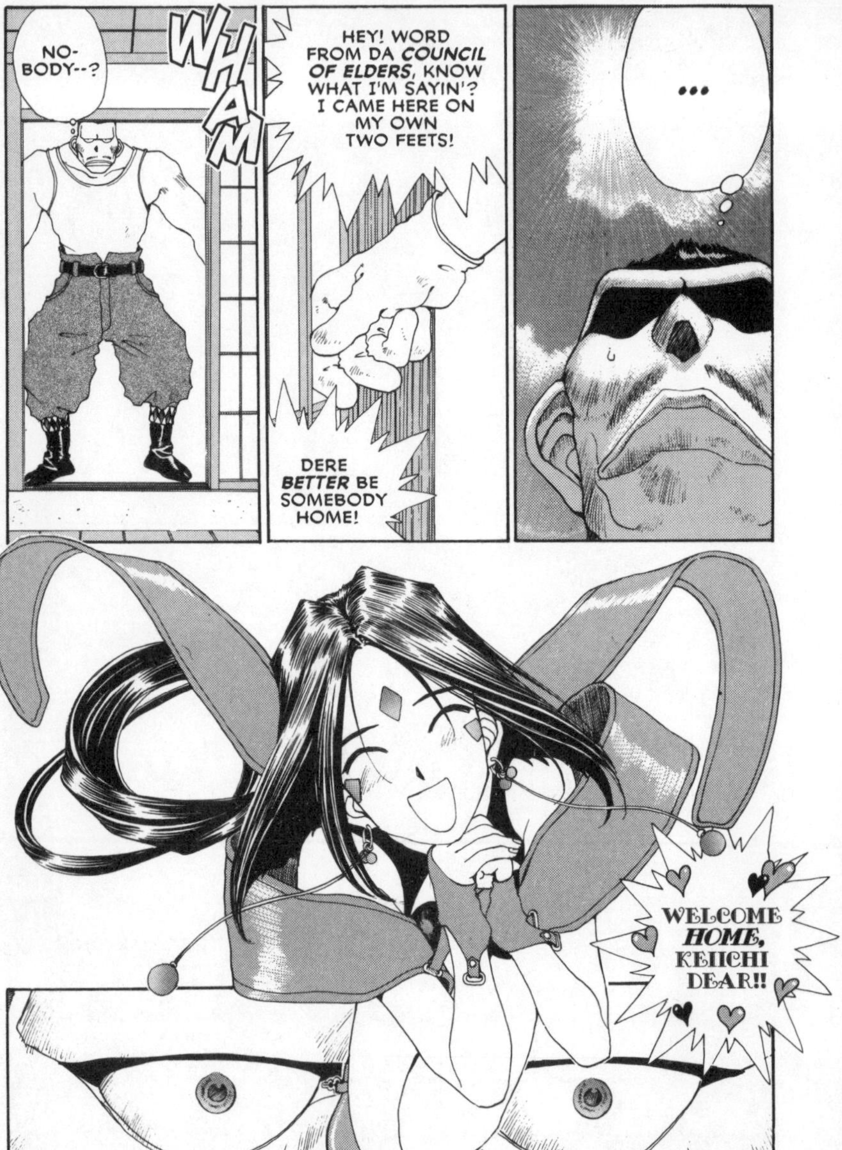
...
HEY! WORD FROM DA COUNCIL OF ELDERS, KNOW WHAT I'M SAYIN'? I CAME HERE ON MY OWN TWO FEETS!
WHAM
DERE BETTER BE SOMEBODY HOME!
NO-BODY--?
WELCOME HOME, KEIICHI DEAR!!

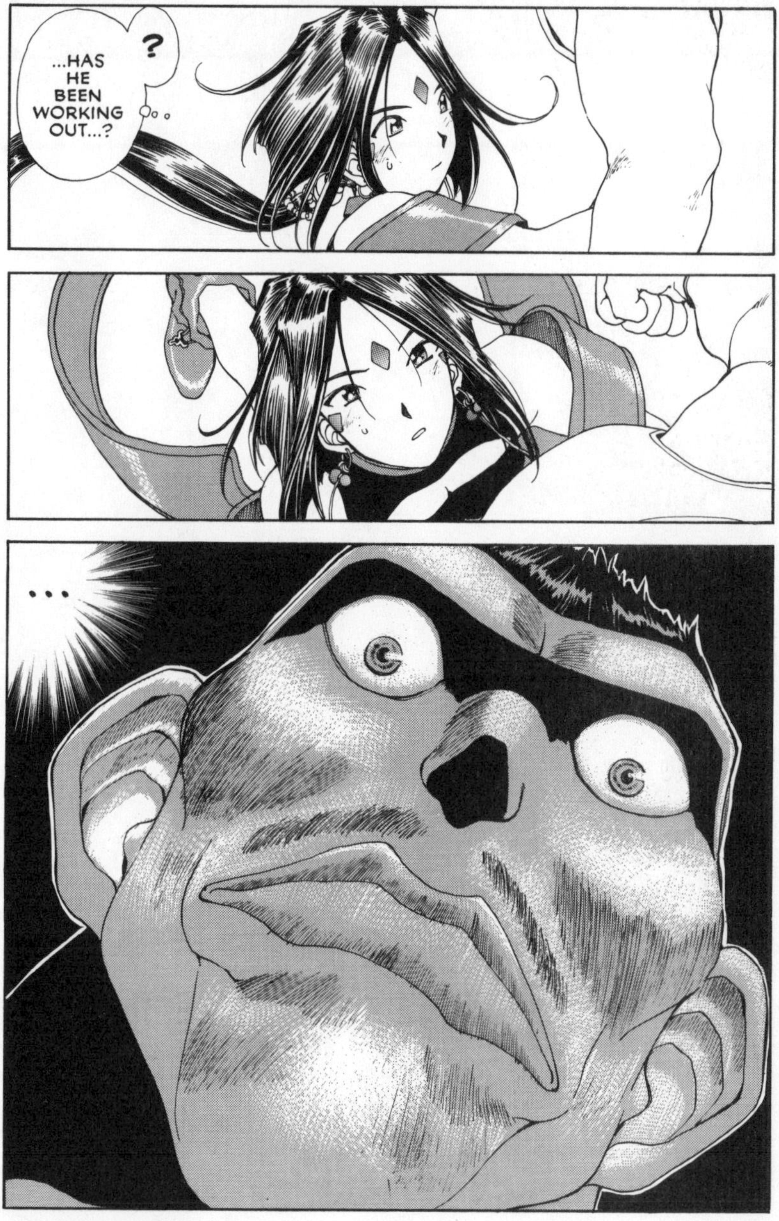
...HAS HE BEEN WORKING OUT...?
?
...

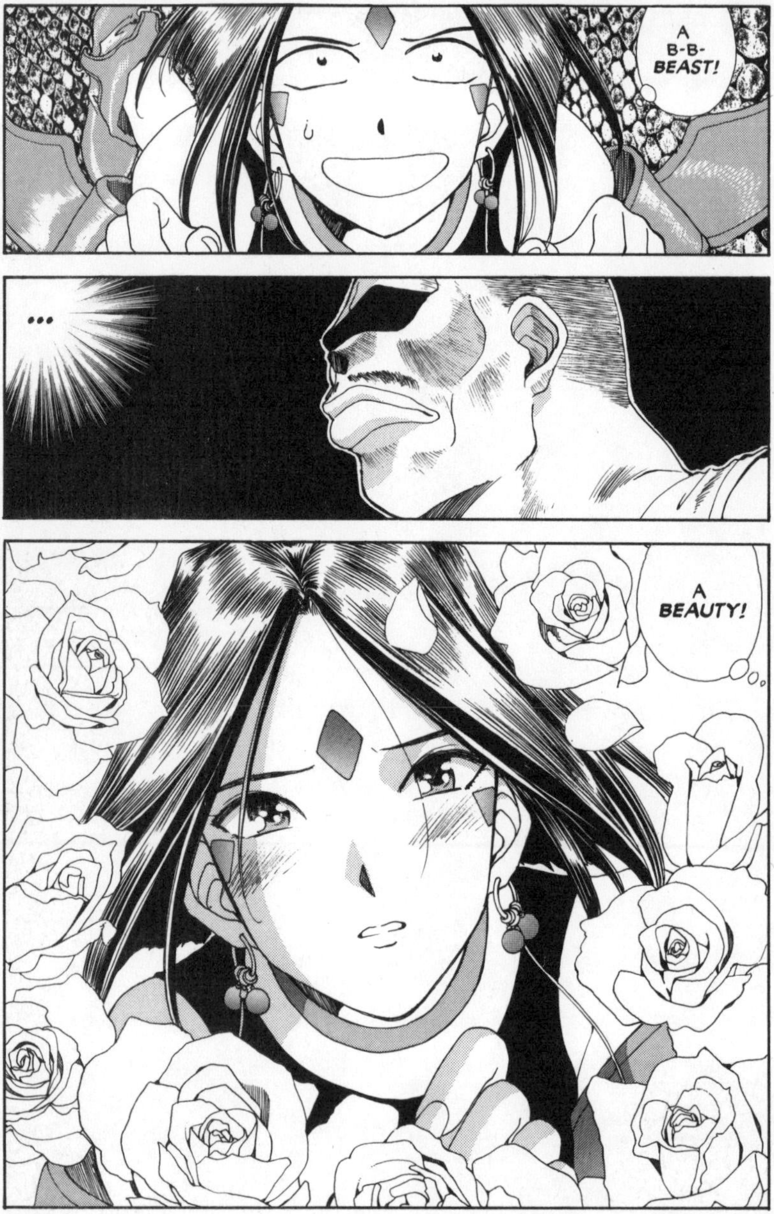
A B-B-BEAST!
...
A BEAUTY!

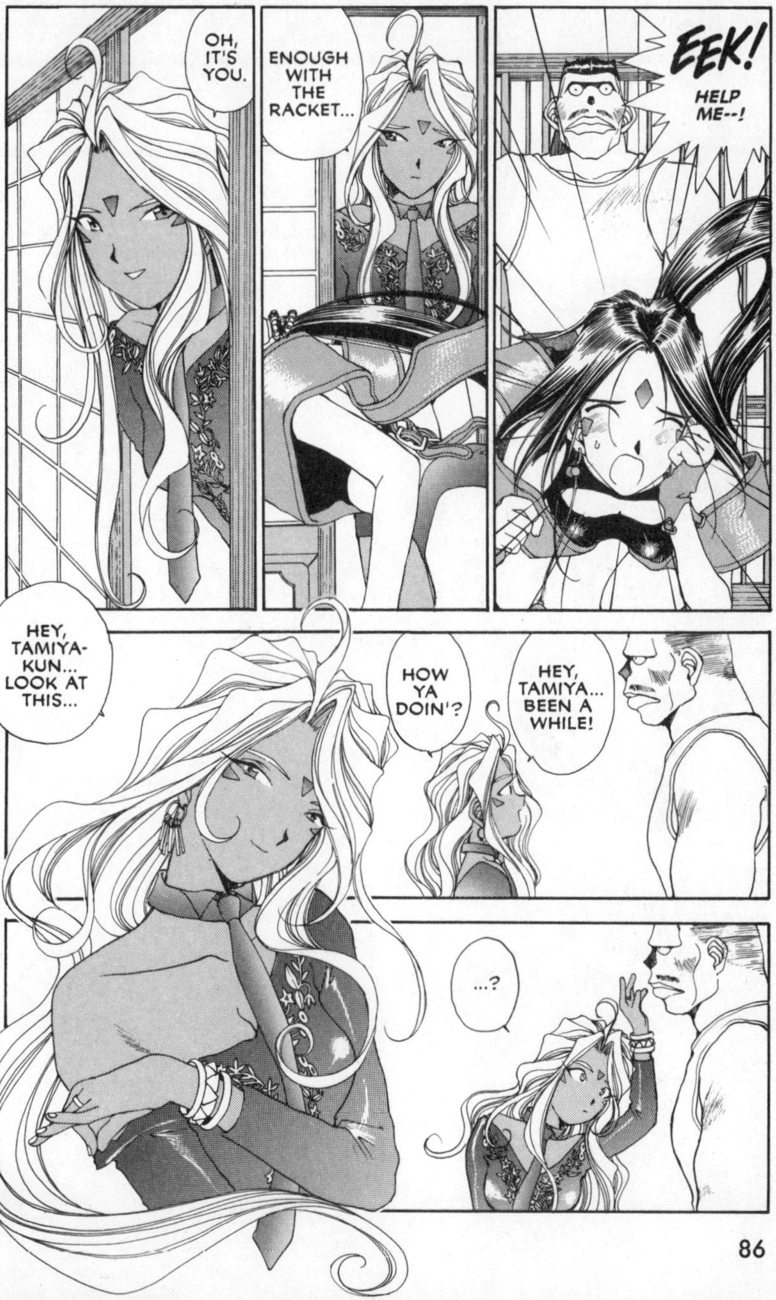
EEK!
HELP ME--!
ENOUGH WITH THE RACKET...
OH, IT'S YOU.
HEY, TAMIYA... BEEN A WHILE!
HOW YA DOIN'?
HEY, TAMIYA-KUN... LOOK AT THIS...
...?

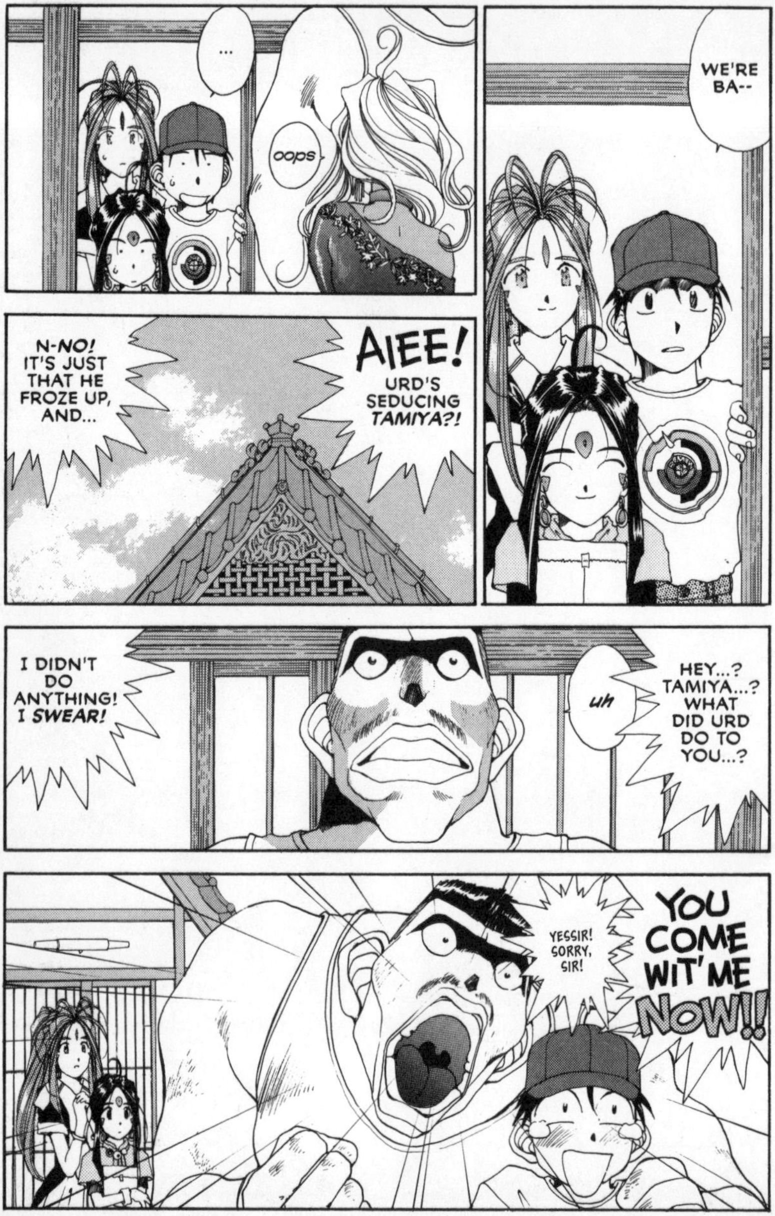

WE'RE BA--
...
oops
AIEE! URD'S SEDUCING *TAMIYA?!*
N-*NO!* IT'S JUST THAT HE FROZE UP, AND...
HEY...? TAMIYA...? WHAT DID URD DO TO YOU...?
uh
I DIDN'T DO ANYTHING! I *SWEAR!*
YOU COME WIT'ME NOW!!
YESSIR! SORRY, SIR!

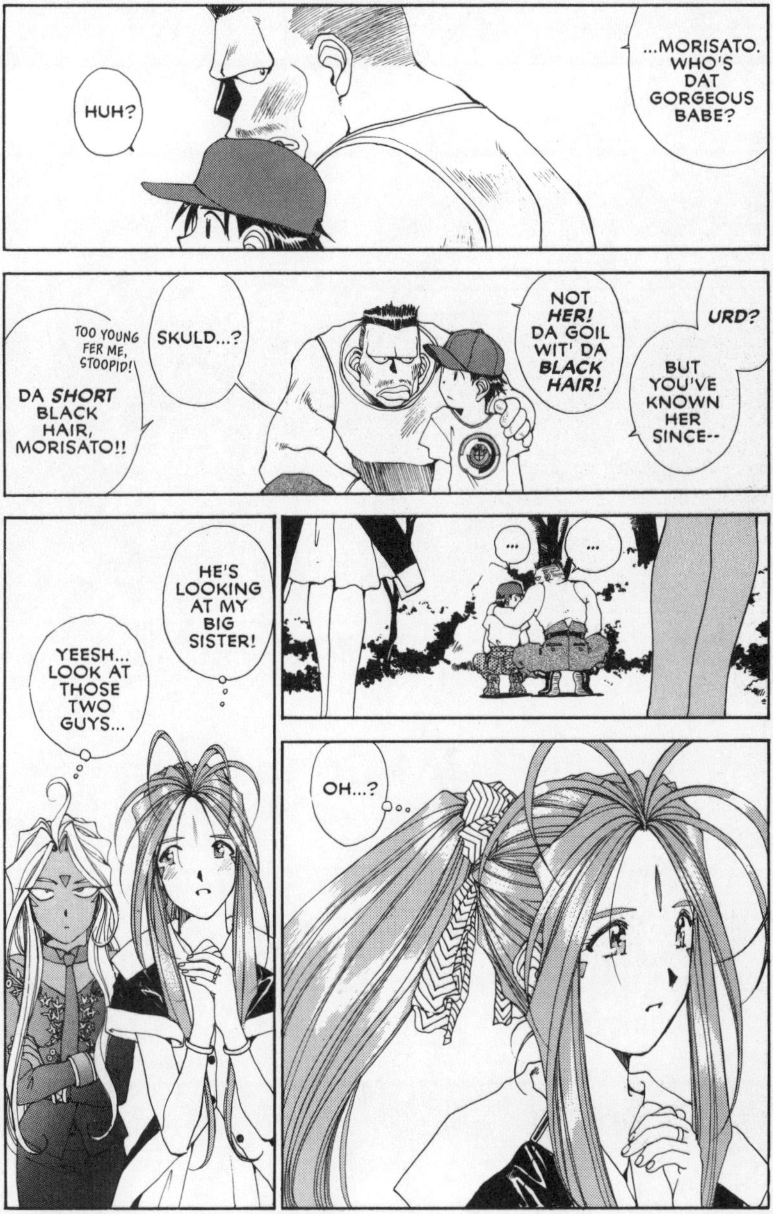
...MORISATO. WHO'S DAT GORGEOUS BABE?
HUH?
URD? BUT YOU'VE KNOWN HER SINCE--
NOT HER! DA GOIL WIT' DA BLACK HAIR!
SKULD...?
TOO YOUNG FER ME, STOOPID!
DA SHORT BLACK HAIR, MORISATO!!
...
...
OH...?
HE'S LOOKING AT MY BIG SISTER!
YEESH... LOOK AT THOSE TWO GUYS...

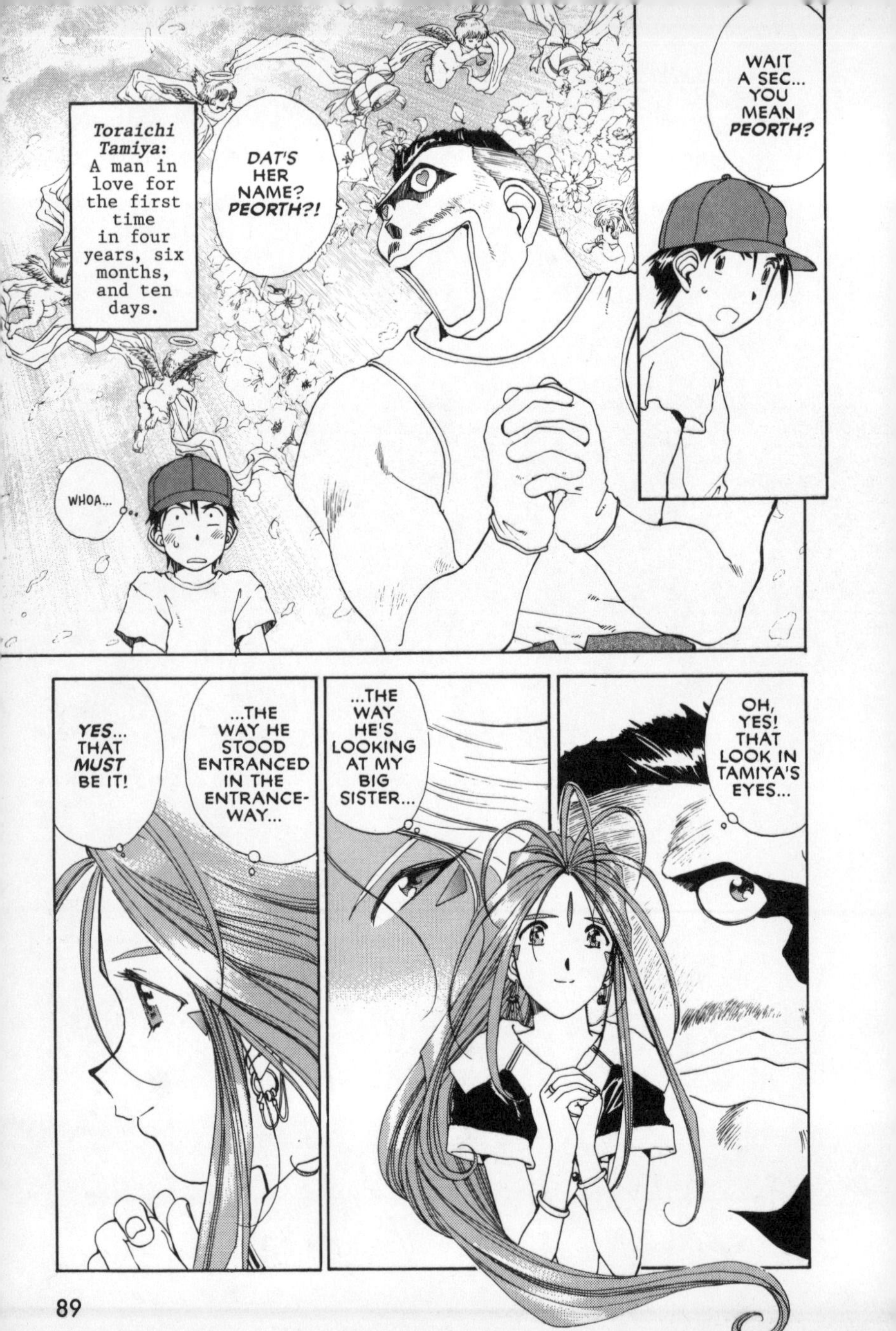
WAIT A SEC... YOU MEAN PEORTH?
DAT'S HER NAME? PEORTH?!
Toraichi Tamiya: A man in love for the first time in four years, six months, and ten days.
WHOA...
OH, YES! THAT LOOK IN TAMIYA'S EYES...
...THE WAY HE'S LOOKING AT MY BIG SISTER...
...THE WAY HE STOOD ENTRANCED IN THE ENTRANCE-WAY...
YES... THAT MUST BE IT!

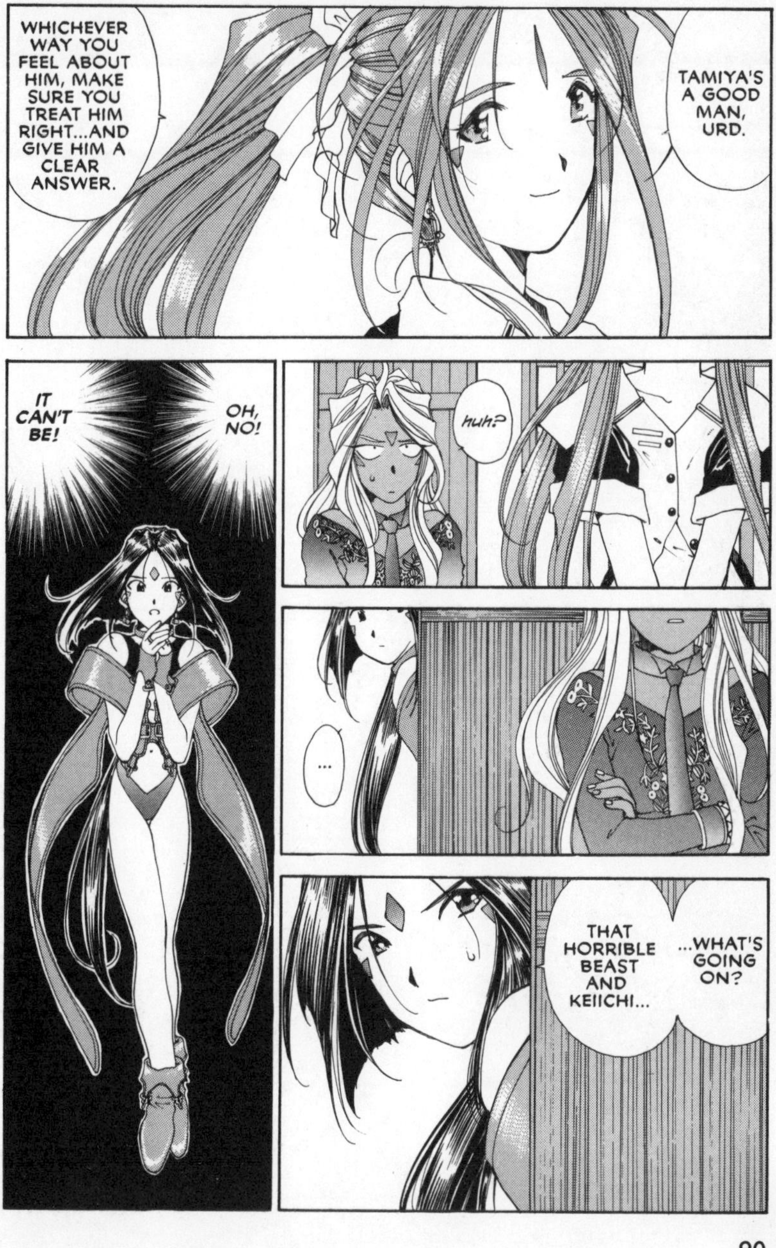
TAMIYA'S A GOOD MAN, URD.
WHICHEVER WAY YOU FEEL ABOUT HIM, MAKE SURE YOU TREAT HIM RIGHT...AND GIVE HIM A CLEAR ANSWER.
huh?
...
...WHAT'S GOING ON?
THAT HORRIBLE BEAST AND KEIICHI...
OH, NO!
IT CAN'T BE!

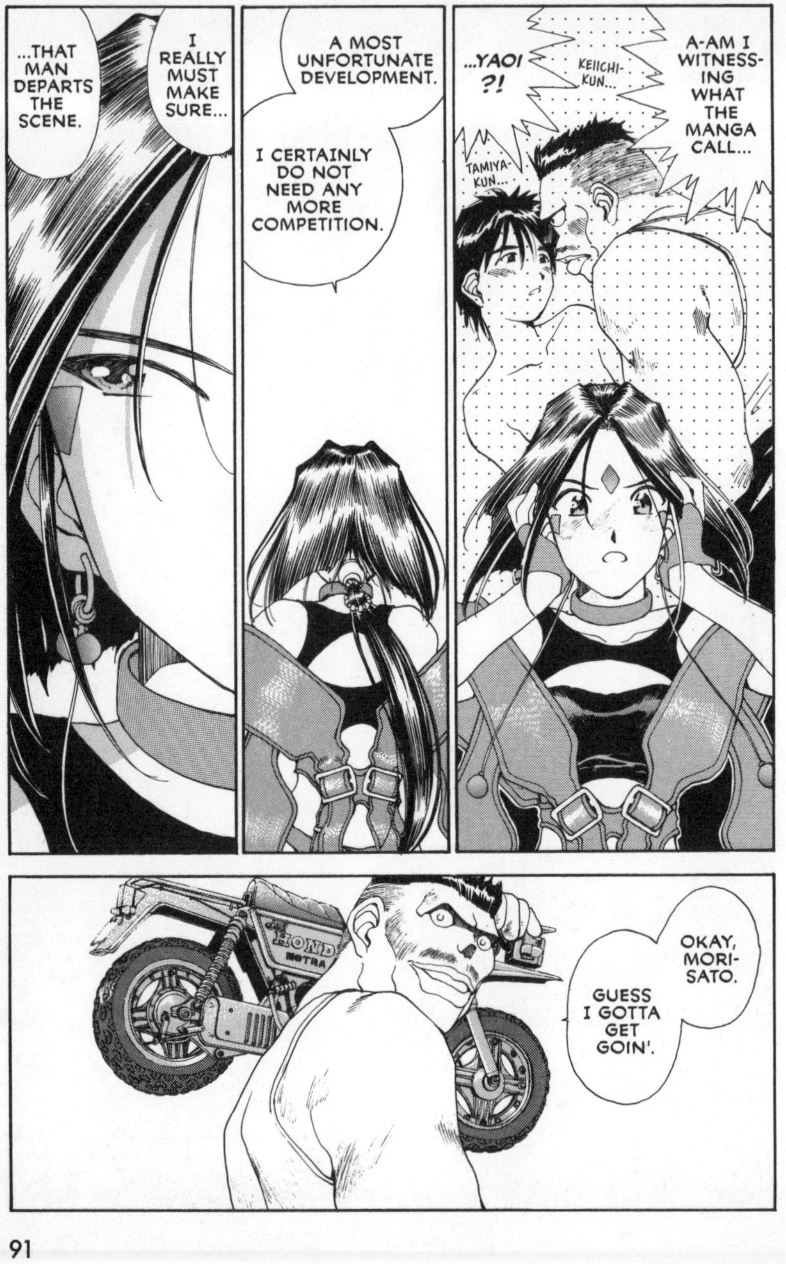
A-AM I WITNESSING WHAT THE MANGA CALL...
KEIICHI-KUN...
...YAOI ?!
TAMIYA-KUN...
A MOST UNFORTUNATE DEVELOPMENT.
I CERTAINLY DO NOT NEED ANY MORE COMPETITION.
I REALLY MUST MAKE SURE...
...THAT MAN DEPARTS THE SCENE.
OKAY, MORI-SATO.
GUESS I GOTTA GET GOIN'.

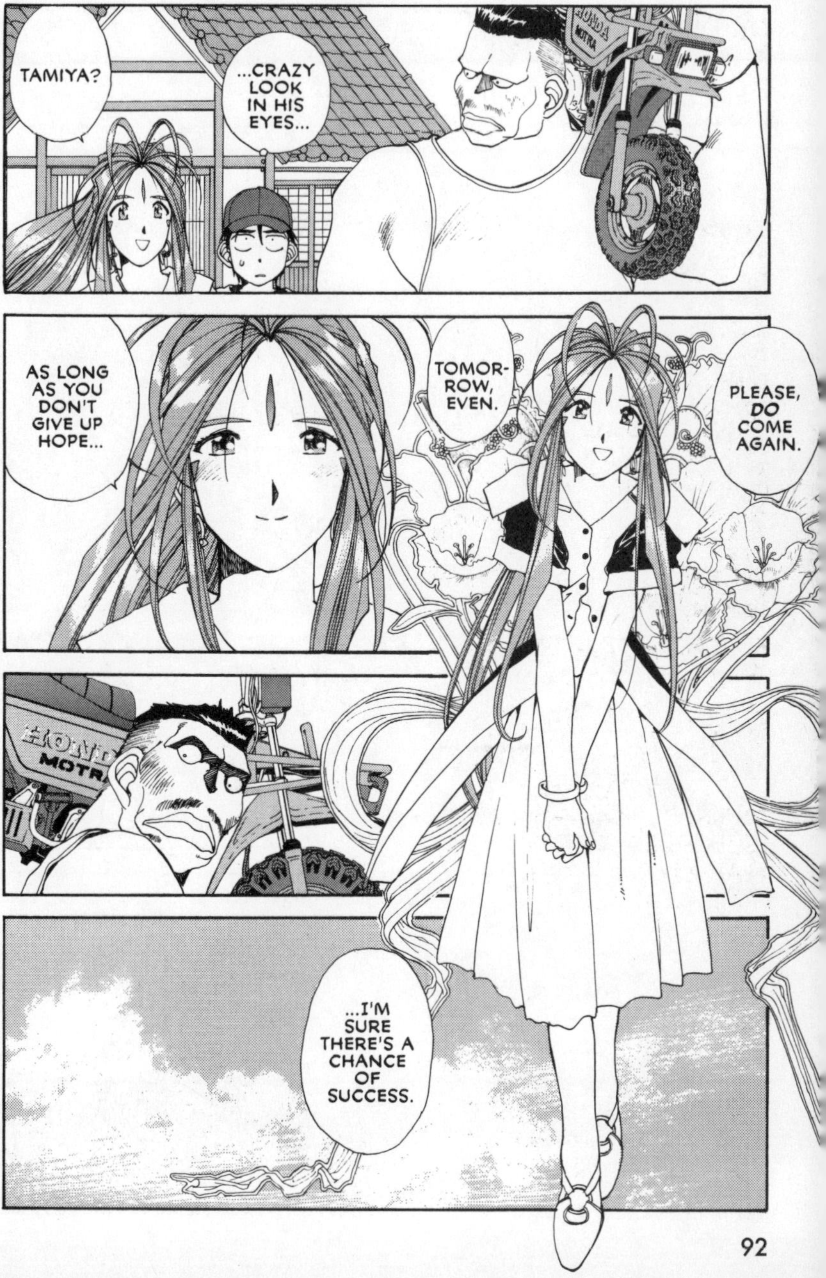
...CRAZY LOOK IN HIS EYES...
TAMIYA?
PLEASE, *DO* COME AGAIN.
TOMOR-ROW, EVEN.
AS LONG AS YOU DON'T GIVE UP HOPE...
...I'M SURE THERE'S A CHANCE OF SUCCESS.

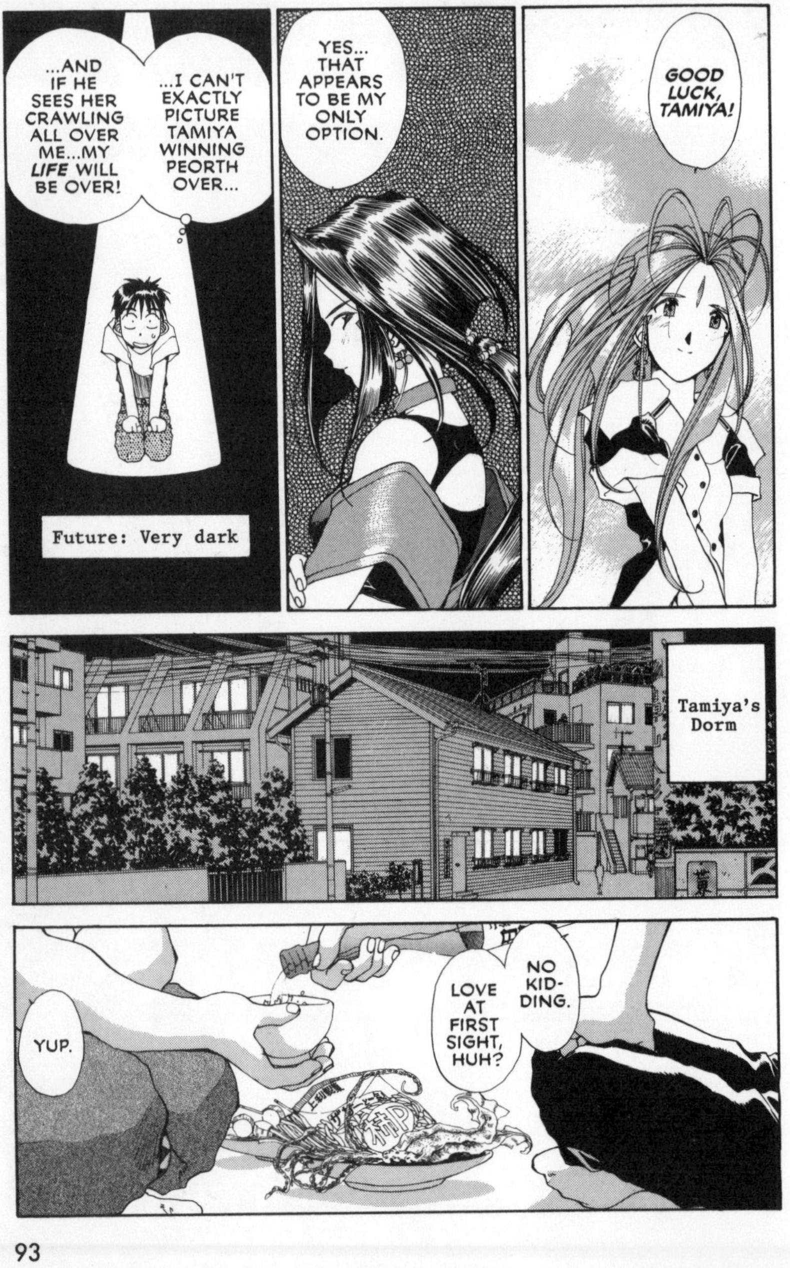
GOOD LUCK, TAMIYA!
YES... THAT APPEARS TO BE MY ONLY OPTION.
...I CAN'T EXACTLY PICTURE TAMIYA WINNING PEORTH OVER...
...AND IF HE SEES HER CRAWLING ALL OVER ME...MY *LIFE* WILL BE OVER!
Future: Very dark
Tamiya's Dorm
NO KIDDING.
LOVE AT FIRST SIGHT, HUH?
YUP.

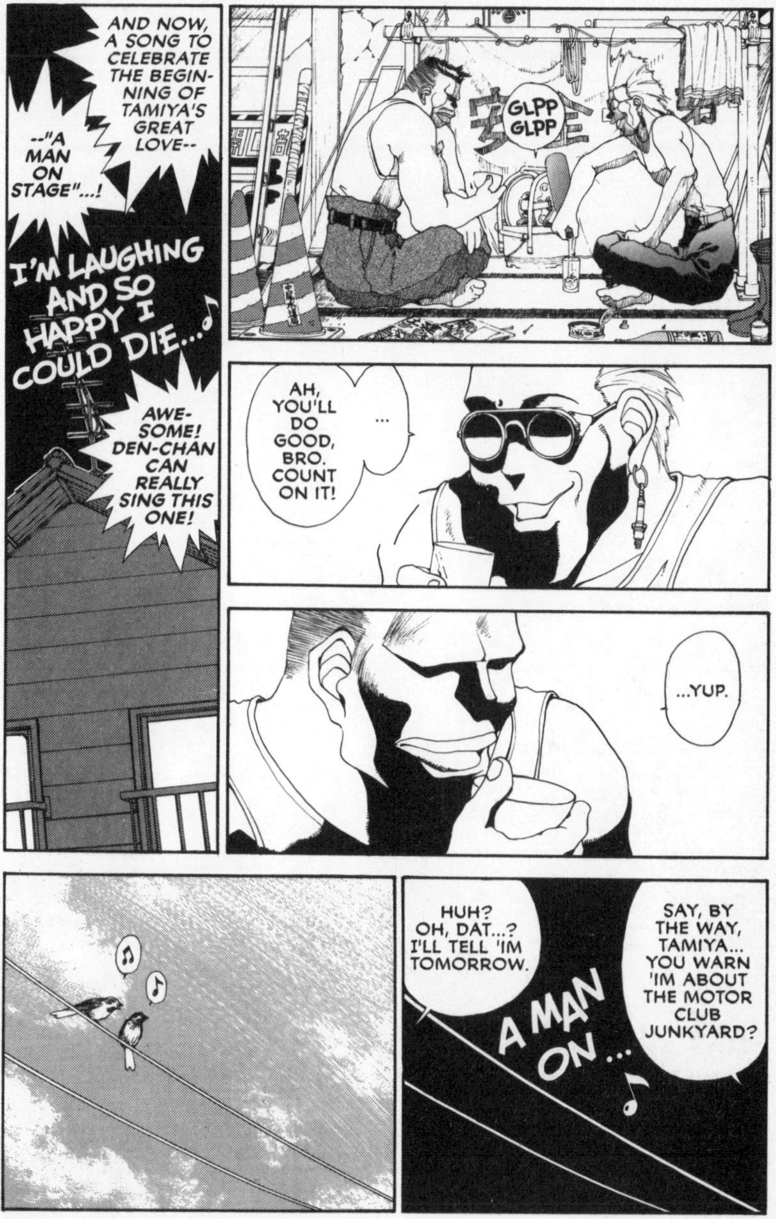
GLPP GLPP
...
AH, YOU'LL DO GOOD, BRO. COUNT ON IT!
...YUP.
AND NOW, A SONG TO CELEBRATE THE BEGIN-NING OF TAMIYA'S GREAT LOVE--
--"A MAN ON STAGE"...!
I'M LAUGHING AND SO HAPPY I COULD DIE...♪
AWE-SOME! DEN-CHAN CAN REALLY SING THIS ONE!
SAY, BY THE WAY, TAMIYA... YOU WARN 'IM ABOUT THE MOTOR CLUB JUNKYARD?
HUH? OH, DAT...? I'LL TELL 'IM TOMORROW.
A MAN ON...♪

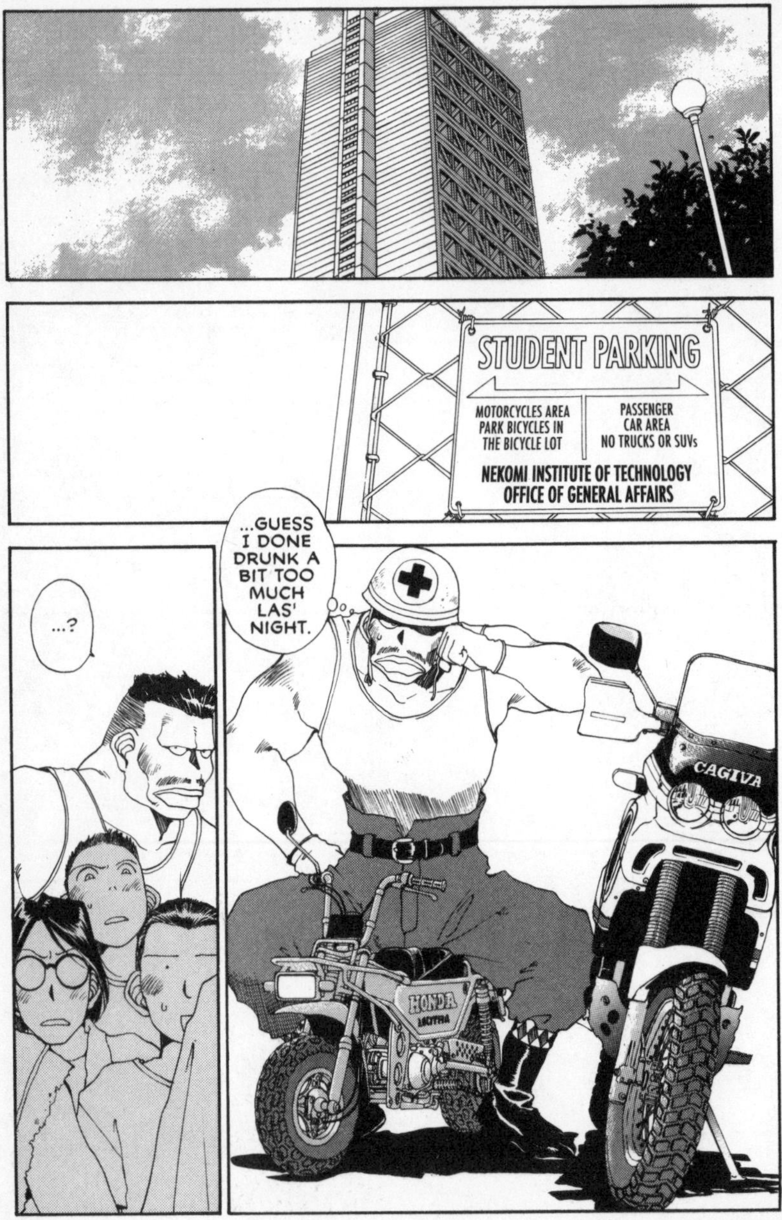
STUDENT PARKING
MOTORCYCLES AREA PARK BICYCLES IN THE BICYCLE LOT
PASSENGER CAR AREA NO TRUCKS OR SUVs
NEKOMI INSTITUTE OF TECHNOLOGY OFFICE OF GENERAL AFFAIRS
...GUESS I DONE DRUNK A BIT TOO MUCH LAS' NIGHT.
CAGIVA
HONDA
...?

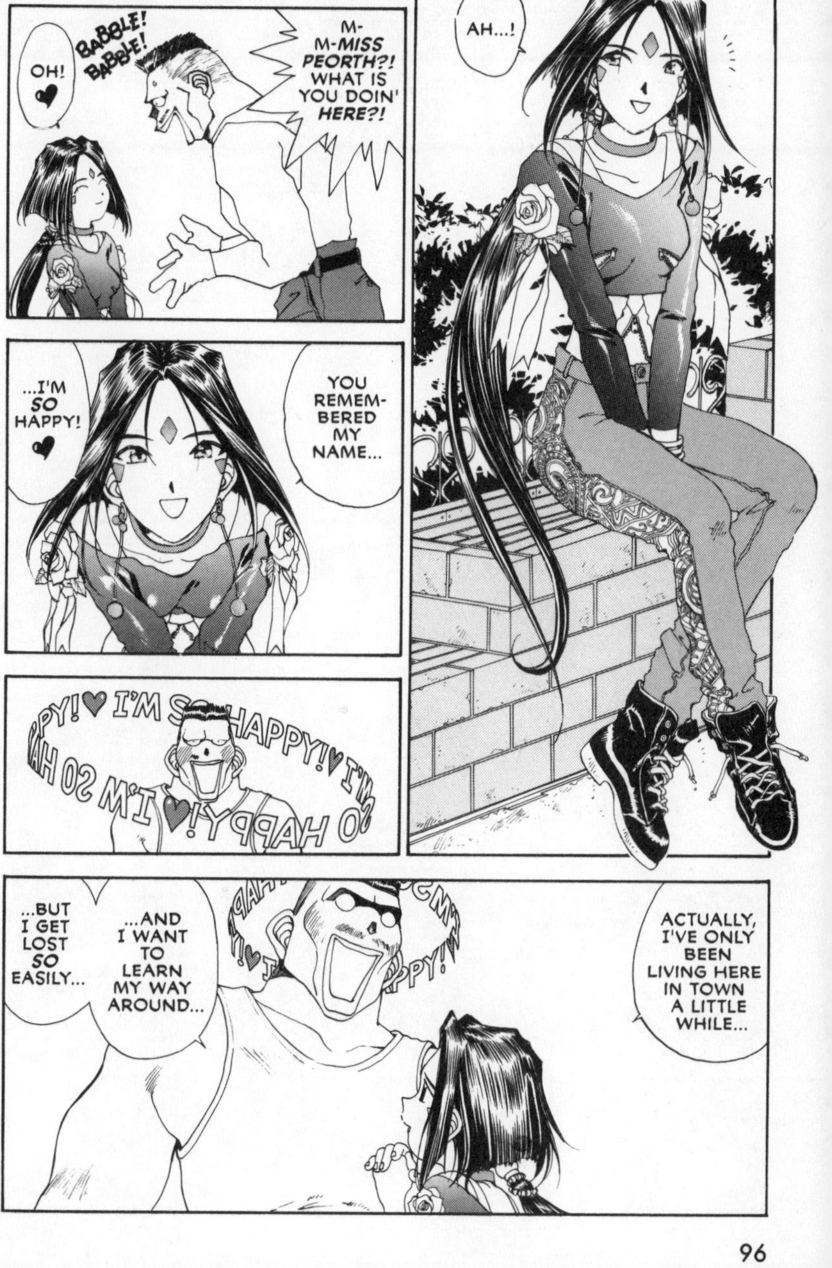
AH...!
M-M-MISS PEORTH?! WHAT IS YOU DOIN' HERE?!
BABBLE! BABBLE!
OH! ♥
YOU REMEMBERED MY NAME...
...I'M SO HAPPY! ♥
I'M SO HAPPY!♥ I'M SO HAPPY!♥ I'M SO HAPPY!♥ I'M SO HAPPY!♥
ACTUALLY, I'VE ONLY BEEN LIVING HERE IN TOWN A LITTLE WHILE...
...AND I WANT TO LEARN MY WAY AROUND...
...BUT I GET LOST SO EASILY...

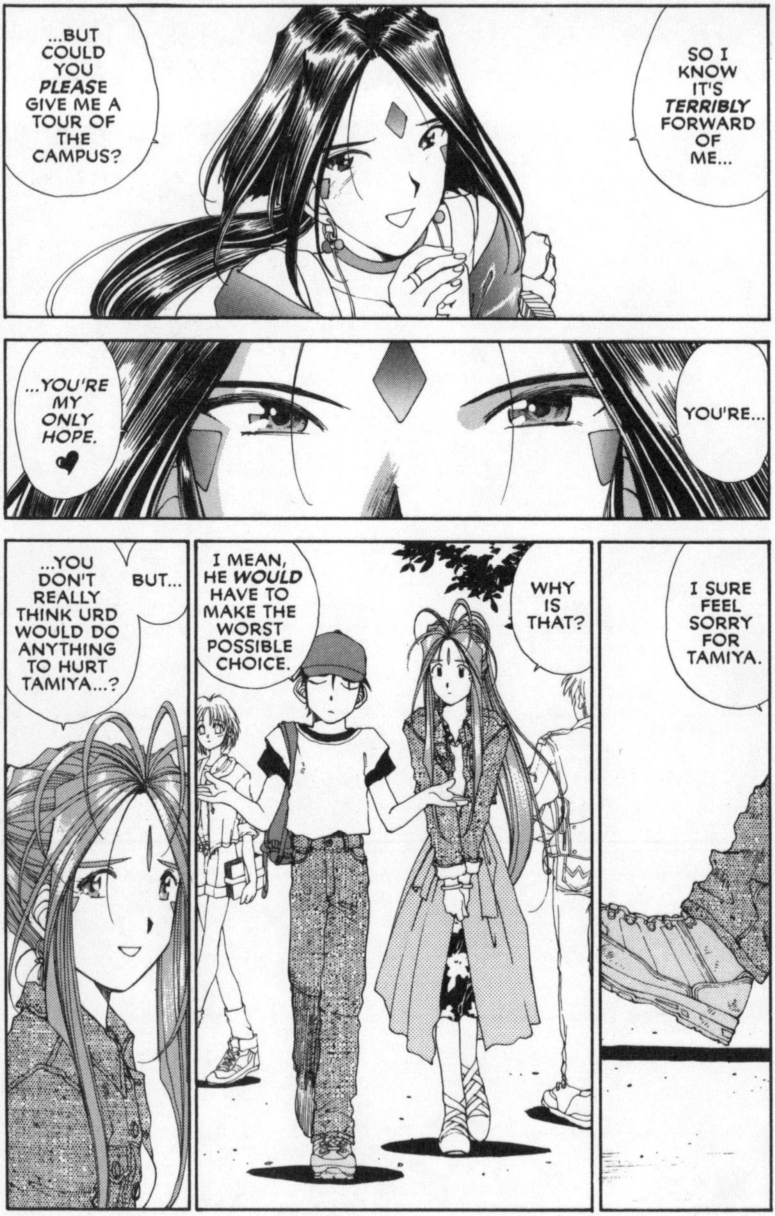
SO I KNOW IT'S *TERRIBLY* FORWARD OF ME...
...BUT COULD YOU *PLEASE* GIVE ME A TOUR OF THE CAMPUS?
YOU'RE...
...*YOU'RE* MY *ONLY* HOPE. ♥
I SURE FEEL SORRY FOR TAMIYA.
WHY IS THAT?
I MEAN, HE ***WOULD*** HAVE TO MAKE THE WORST POSSIBLE CHOICE.
BUT...
...YOU DON'T REALLY THINK URD WOULD DO ANYTHING TO HURT TAMIYA...?

HUH?
TAMIYA'S IN LOVE WITH *PEORTH.*
EH?!
STOMP STOMP
!!
YOU GOTTA SEE THIS!
HE'S OVER *THERE!*
HASE-GAWA?! WHAT'S GOING ON?!
OH, SIR! *LOOK...!*
!!

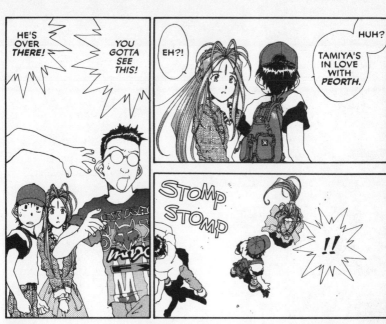

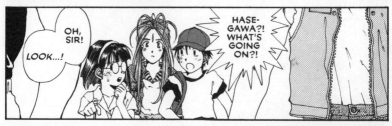

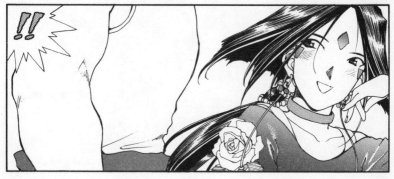

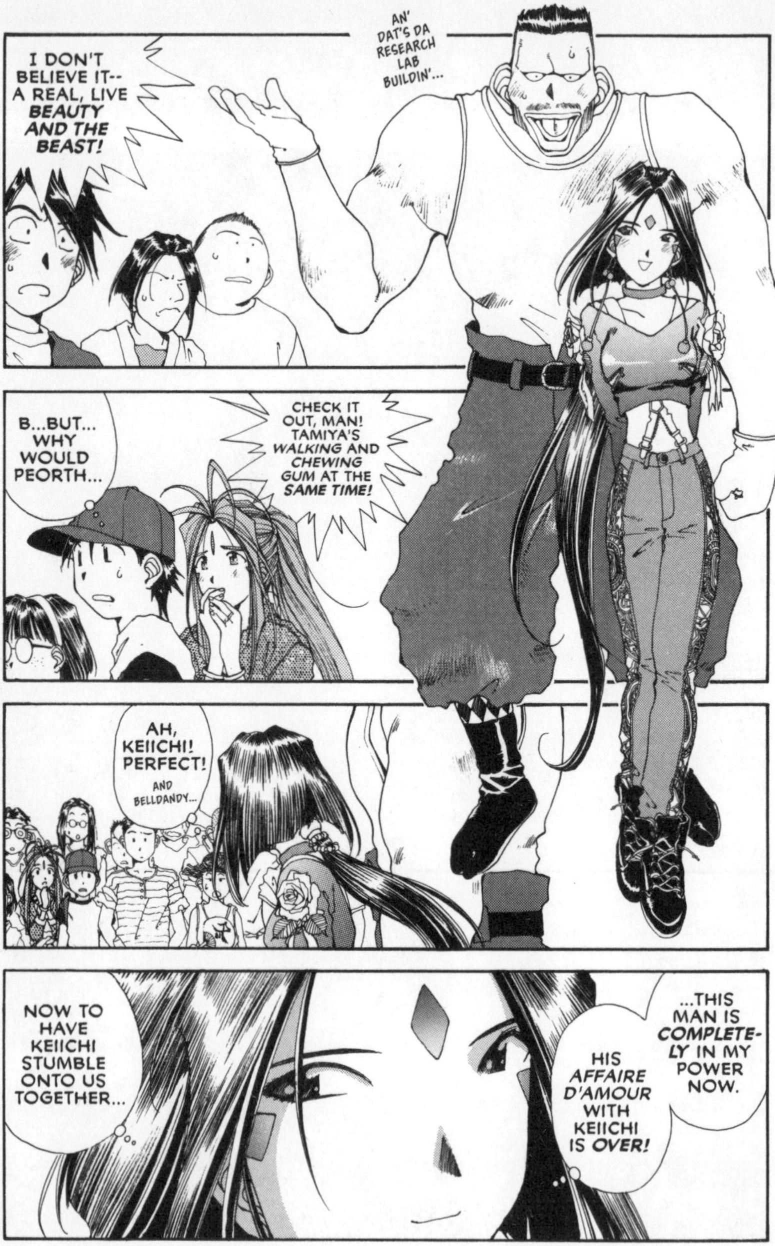
AN' DAT'S DA RESEARCH LAB BUILDIN'...
I DON'T BELIEVE IT-- A REAL, LIVE *BEAUTY AND THE BEAST!*
CHECK IT OUT, MAN! TAMIYA'S *WALKING* AND *CHEWING* GUM AT THE *SAME TIME!*
B...BUT... WHY WOULD PEORTH...
AH, KEIICHI! PERFECT!
AND BELLDANDY...
...THIS MAN IS *COMPLETE-LY* IN MY POWER NOW.
HIS *AFFAIRE D'AMOUR* WITH KEIICHI IS *OVER!*
NOW TO HAVE KEIICHI STUMBLE ONTO US TOGETHER...

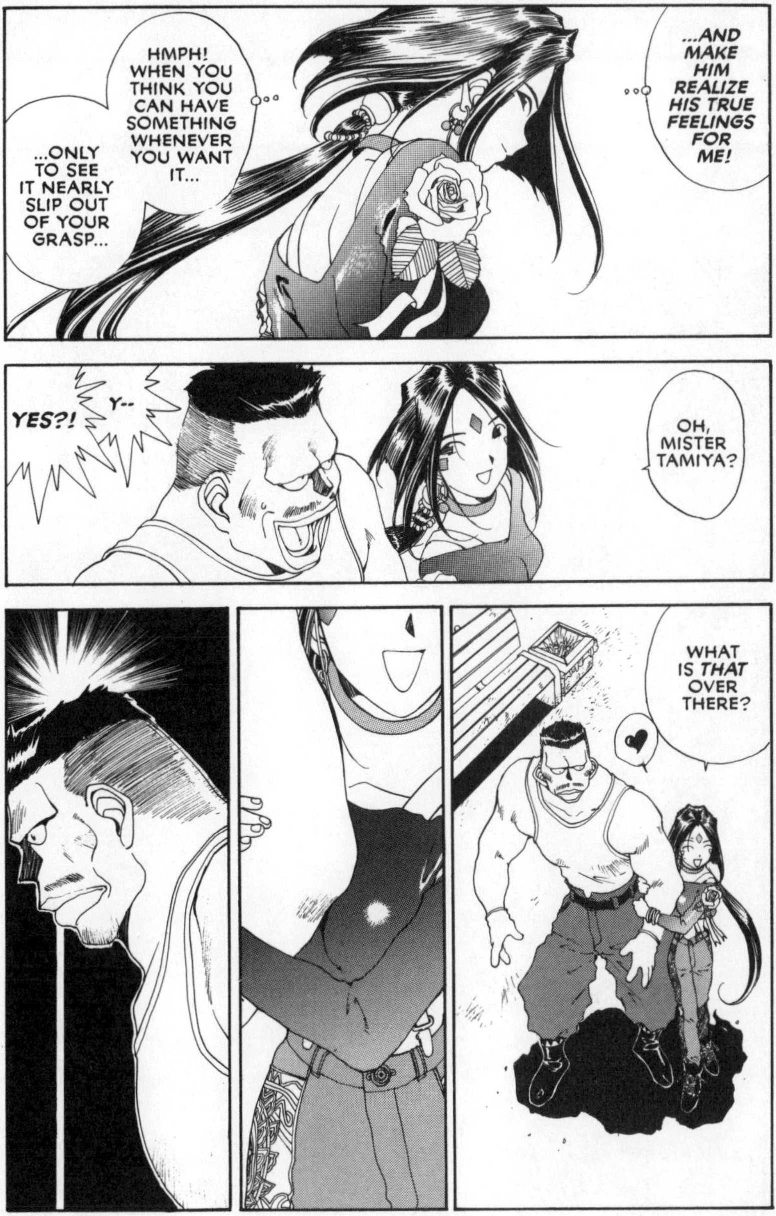
HMPH! WHEN YOU THINK YOU CAN HAVE SOMETHING WHENEVER YOU WANT IT...
...ONLY TO SEE IT NEARLY SLIP OUT OF YOUR GRASP...
...AND MAKE HIM REALIZE HIS TRUE FEELINGS FOR ME!
OH, MISTER TAMIYA?
Y-- YES?!
WHAT IS *THAT* OVER THERE?
♥

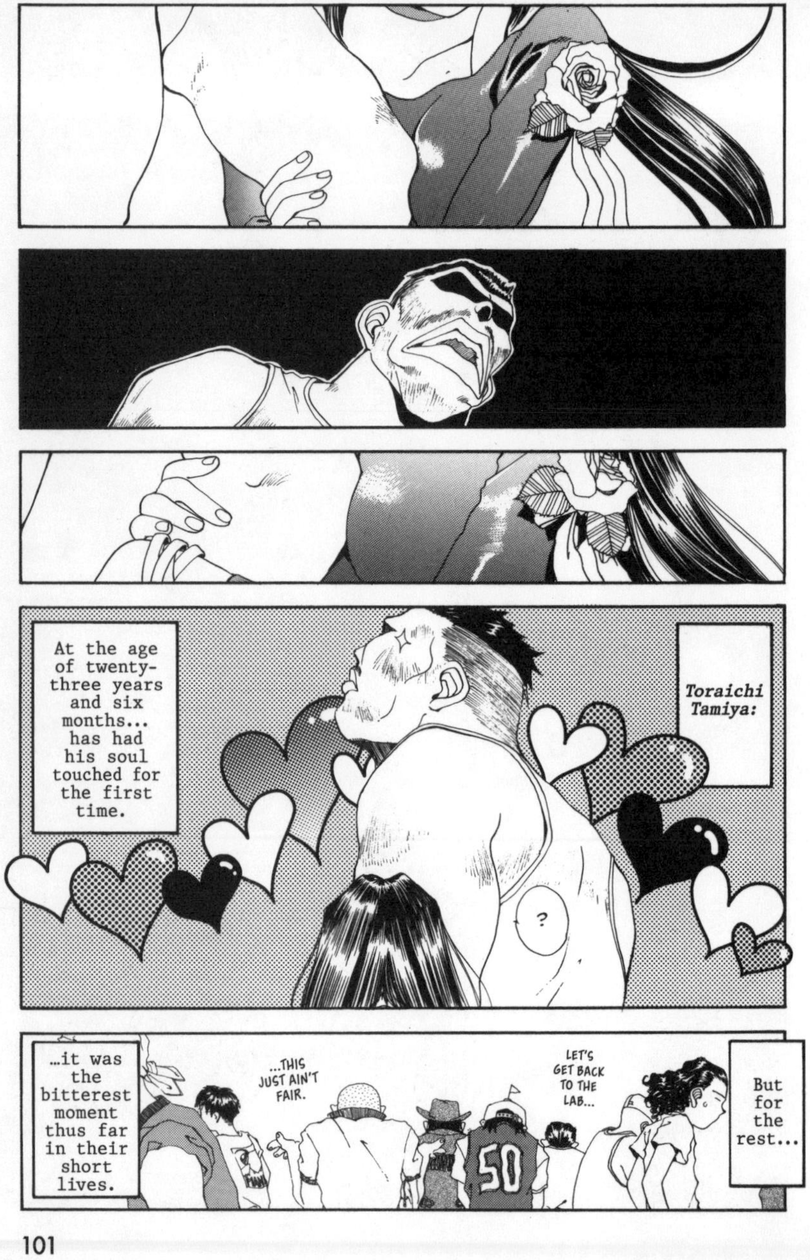
Toraichi Tamiya:
At the age of twenty-three years and six months... has had his soul touched for the first time.
?
But for the rest...
LET'S GET BACK TO THE LAB...
...THIS JUST AIN'T FAIR.
...it was the bitterest moment thus far in their short lives.

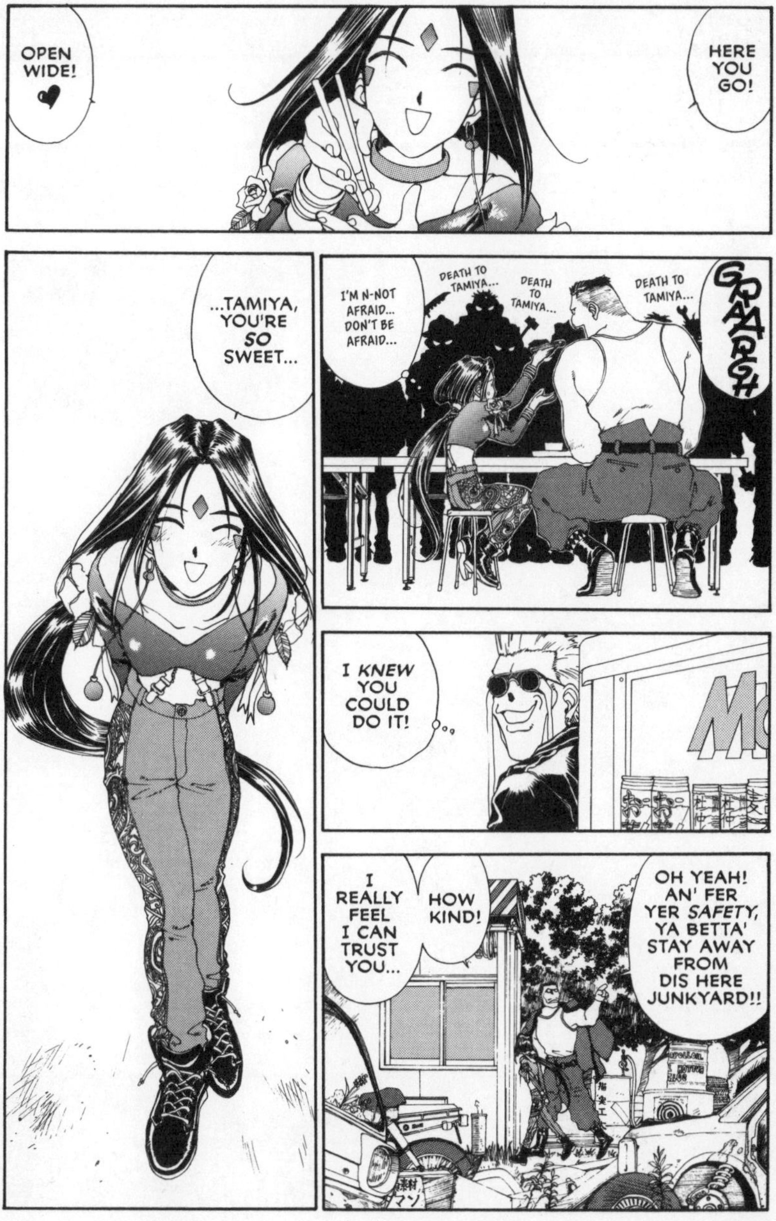
HERE YOU GO!
OPEN WIDE! ♥
GRAAARGH
DEATH TO TAMIYA...
DEATH TO TAMIYA...
DEATH TO TAMIYA...
I'M N-NOT AFRAID... DON'T BE AFRAID...
I *KNEW* YOU COULD DO IT!
OH YEAH! AN' FER YER *SAFETY*, YA BETTA' STAY AWAY FROM DIS HERE JUNKYARD!!
HOW KIND!
I REALLY FEEL I CAN TRUST YOU...
...TAMIYA, YOU'RE *SO* SWEET...

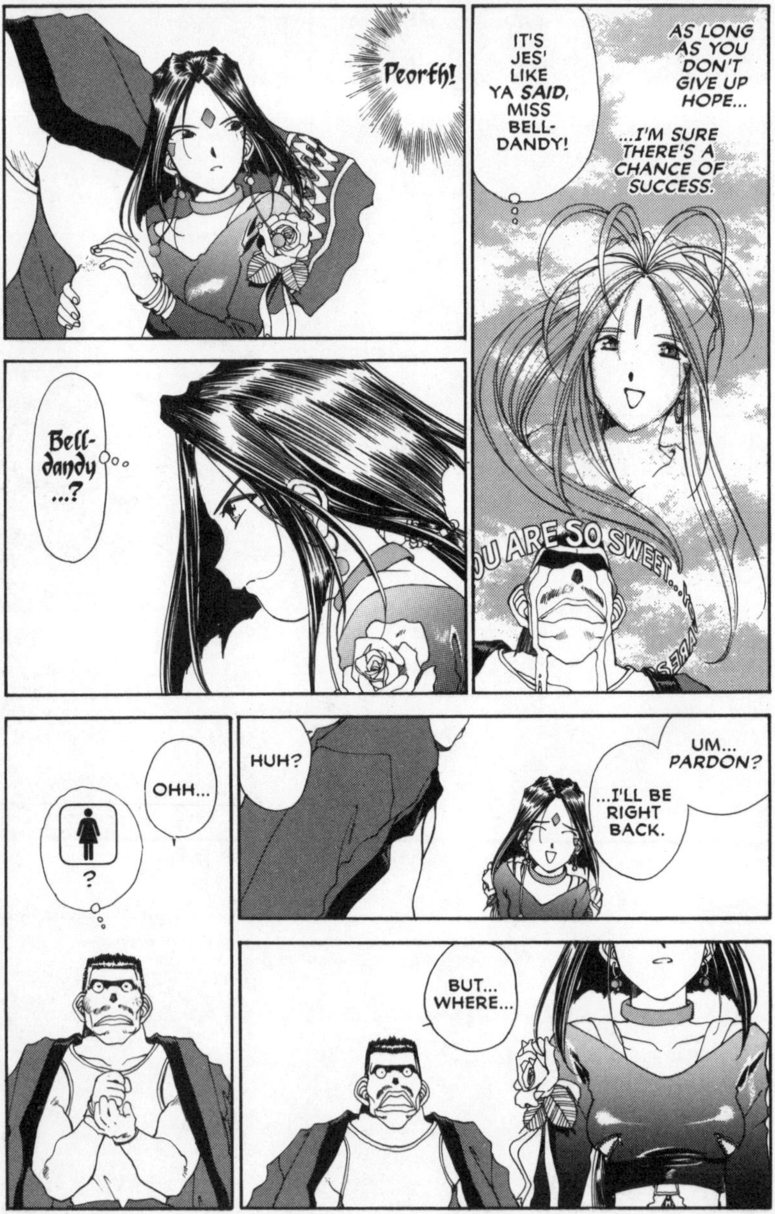
AS LONG AS YOU DON'T GIVE UP HOPE...
...I'M SURE THERE'S A CHANCE OF SUCCESS.
IT'S JES' LIKE YA *SAID*, MISS BELL-DANDY!
OU ARE SO SWEET...
Peorth!
Bell-dandy ...?
UM... PARDON?
...I'LL BE RIGHT BACK.
HUH?
BUT... WHERE...
OHH...
?

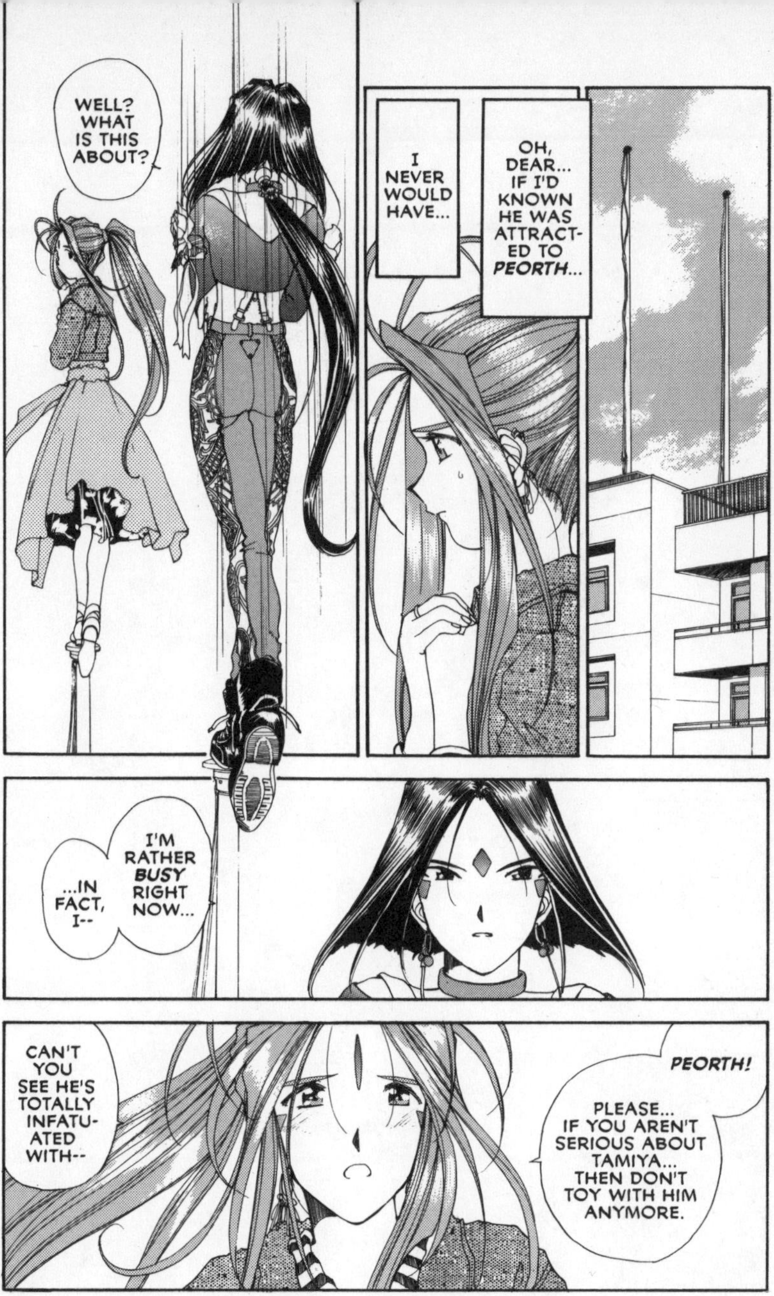
OH, DEAR... IF I'D KNOWN HE WAS ATTRACTED TO *PEORTH*...
I NEVER WOULD HAVE...
WELL? WHAT IS THIS ABOUT?
I'M RATHER *BUSY* RIGHT NOW...
...IN FACT, I--
PEORTH!
PLEASE... IF YOU AREN'T SERIOUS ABOUT TAMIYA... THEN DON'T TOY WITH HIM ANYMORE.
CAN'T YOU SEE HE'S TOTALLY INFATUATED WITH--

IF TAMIYA IS THAT SERIOUS ABOUT HIS FEELINGS FOR KEIICHI, THEN...

WHAT?! I CAN'T BELIEVE YOU'RE SAYING THIS!!

DON'T YOU CARE WHAT HAPPENS TO KEIICHI?!

...HOW CAN YOU JUST SHUT YOUR EYES TO IT?!

YOU KNOW... YOU HAVEN'T CHANGED A BIT.

...I SHALL PROTECT KEIICHI MYSELF.

ENOUGH OF THIS...

WH... WHAT...?

105

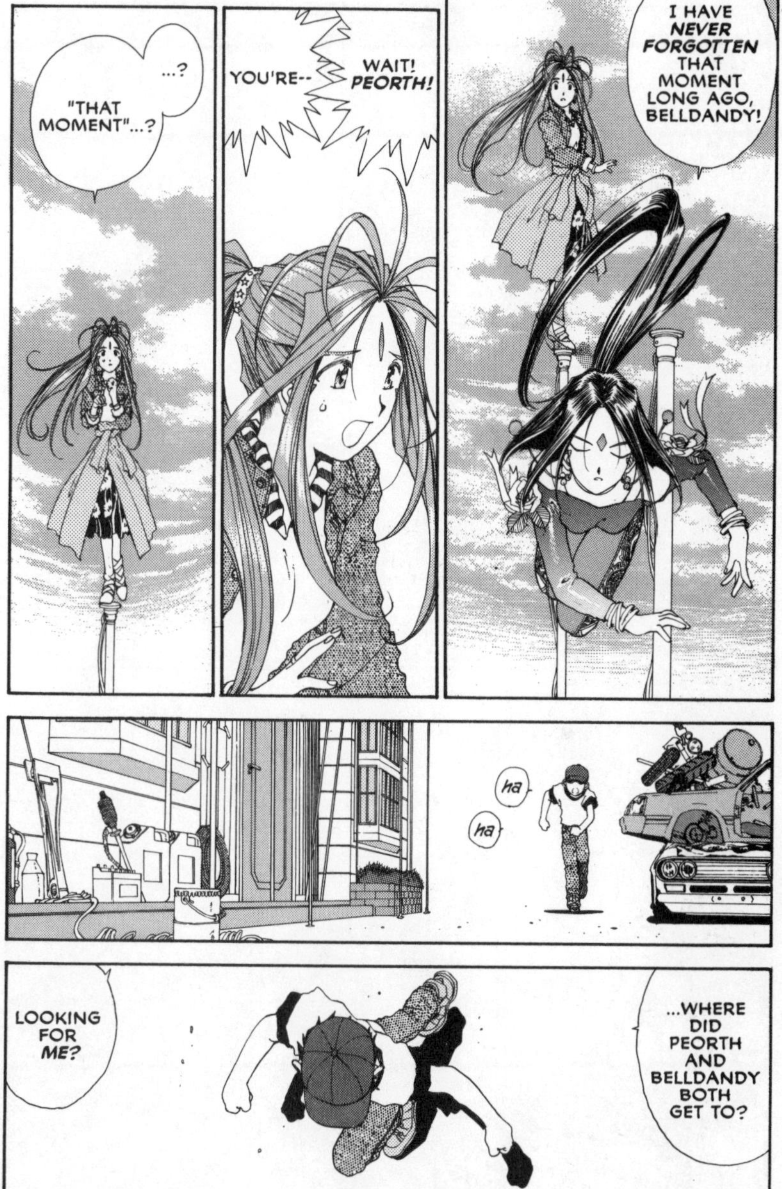
I HAVE NEVER FORGOTTEN THAT MOMENT LONG AGO, BELLDANDY!
WAIT! PEORTH!
YOU'RE--
...?
"THAT MOMENT"...?
ha
ha
...WHERE DID PEORTH AND BELLDANDY BOTH GET TO?
LOOKING FOR ME?

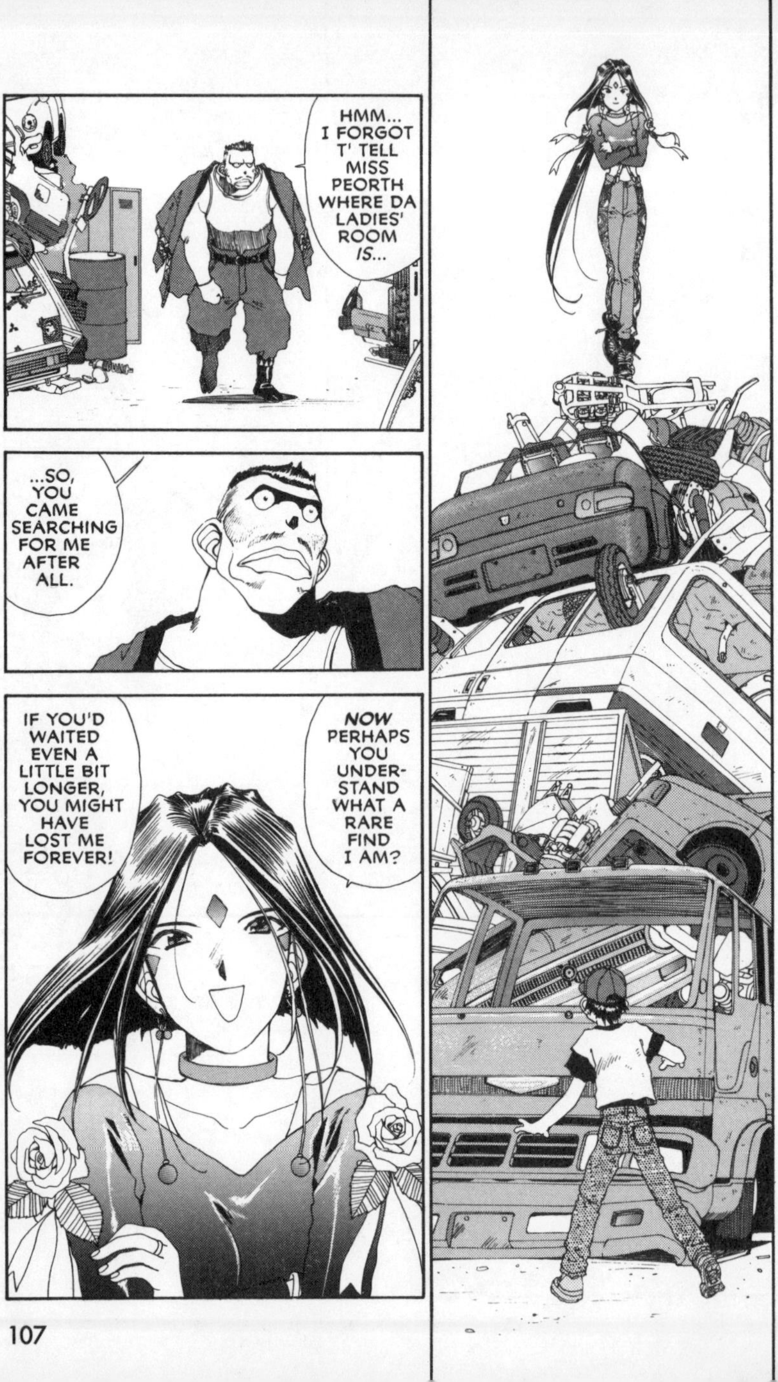
HMM... I FORGOT T' TELL MISS PEORTH WHERE DA LADIES' ROOM IS...
...SO, YOU CAME SEARCHING FOR ME AFTER ALL.
NOW PERHAPS YOU UNDER-STAND WHAT A RARE FIND I AM?
IF YOU'D WAITED EVEN A LITTLE BIT LONGER, YOU MIGHT HAVE LOST ME FOREVER!

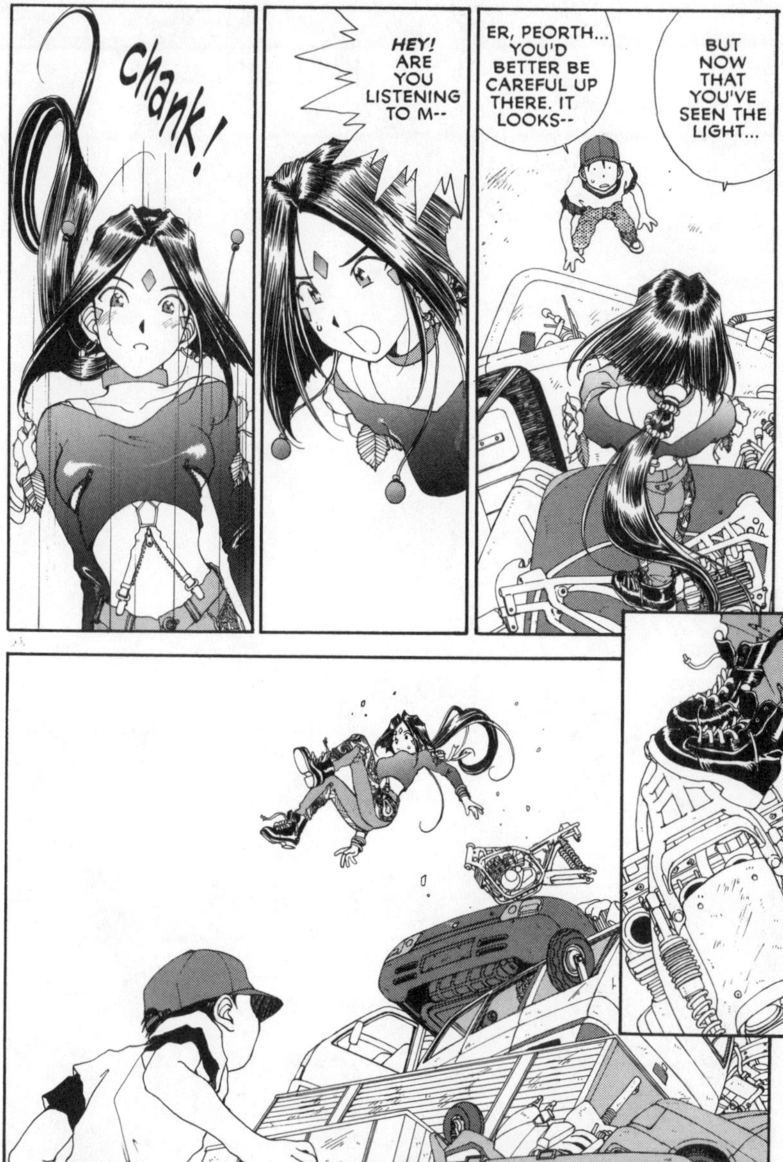
BUT NOW THAT YOU'VE SEEN THE LIGHT...
ER, PEORTH... YOU'D BETTER BE CAREFUL UP THERE. IT LOOKS--
HEY! ARE YOU LISTENING TO M--
Chank!

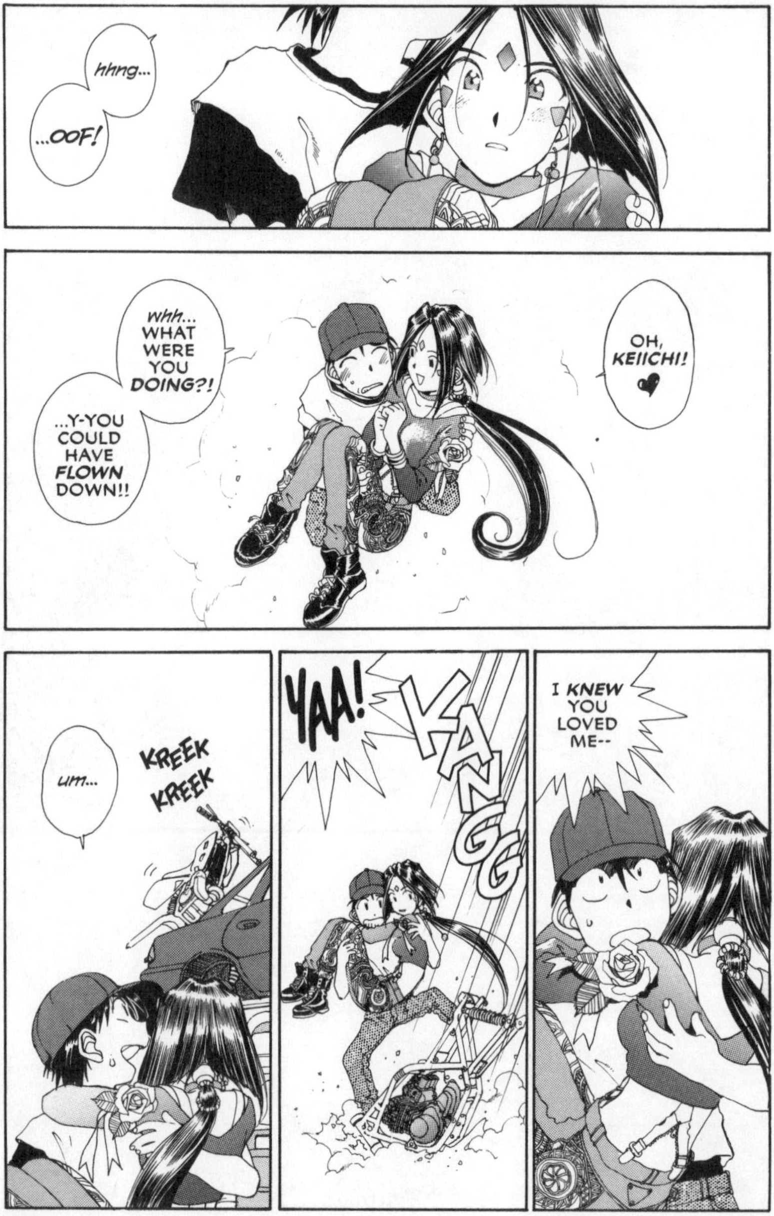
hhng...
...OOF!
OH, KEIICHI! ♥
whh... WHAT WERE YOU DOING?!
...Y-YOU COULD HAVE FLOWN DOWN!!
I KNEW YOU LOVED ME--
YAA!
KANGG
KREEK KREEK
um...

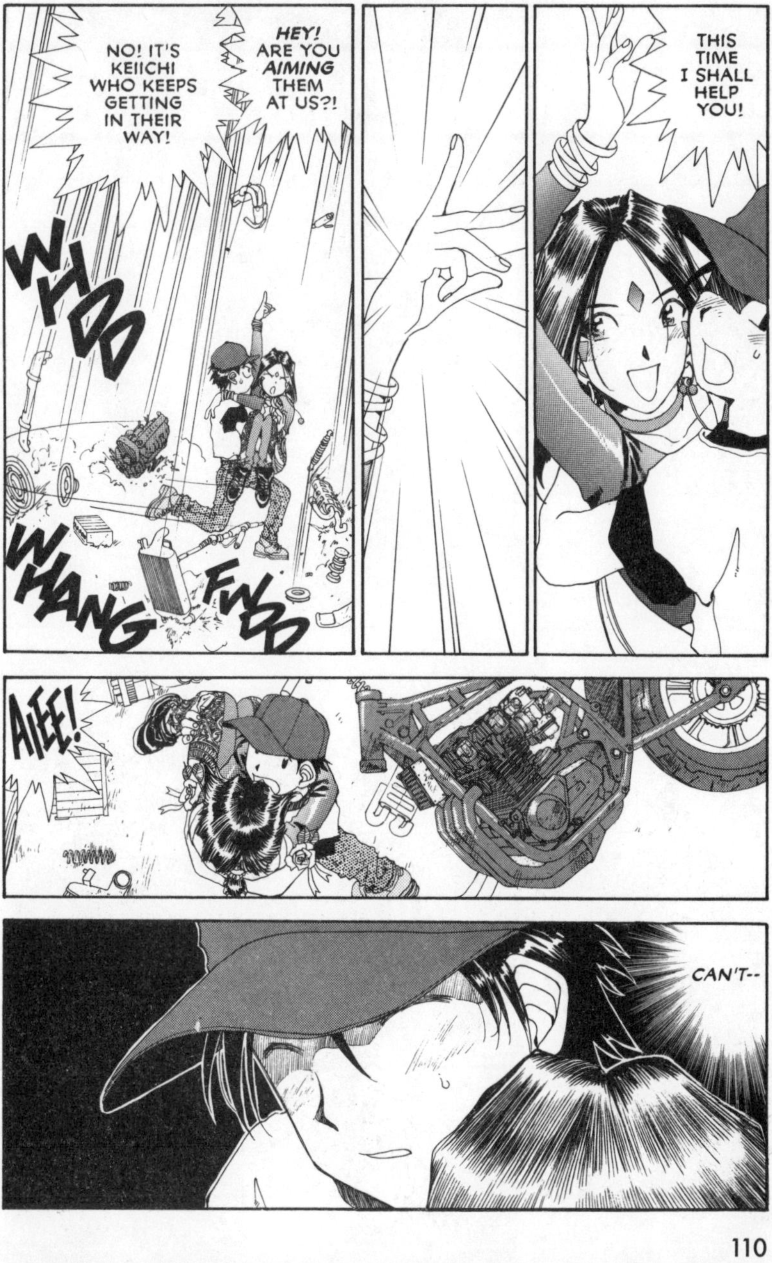
THIS TIME I SHALL HELP YOU!
HEY! ARE YOU AIMING THEM AT US?!
NO! IT'S KEIICHI WHO KEEPS GETTING IN THEIR WAY!
WHANG
AIEE!
CAN'T--

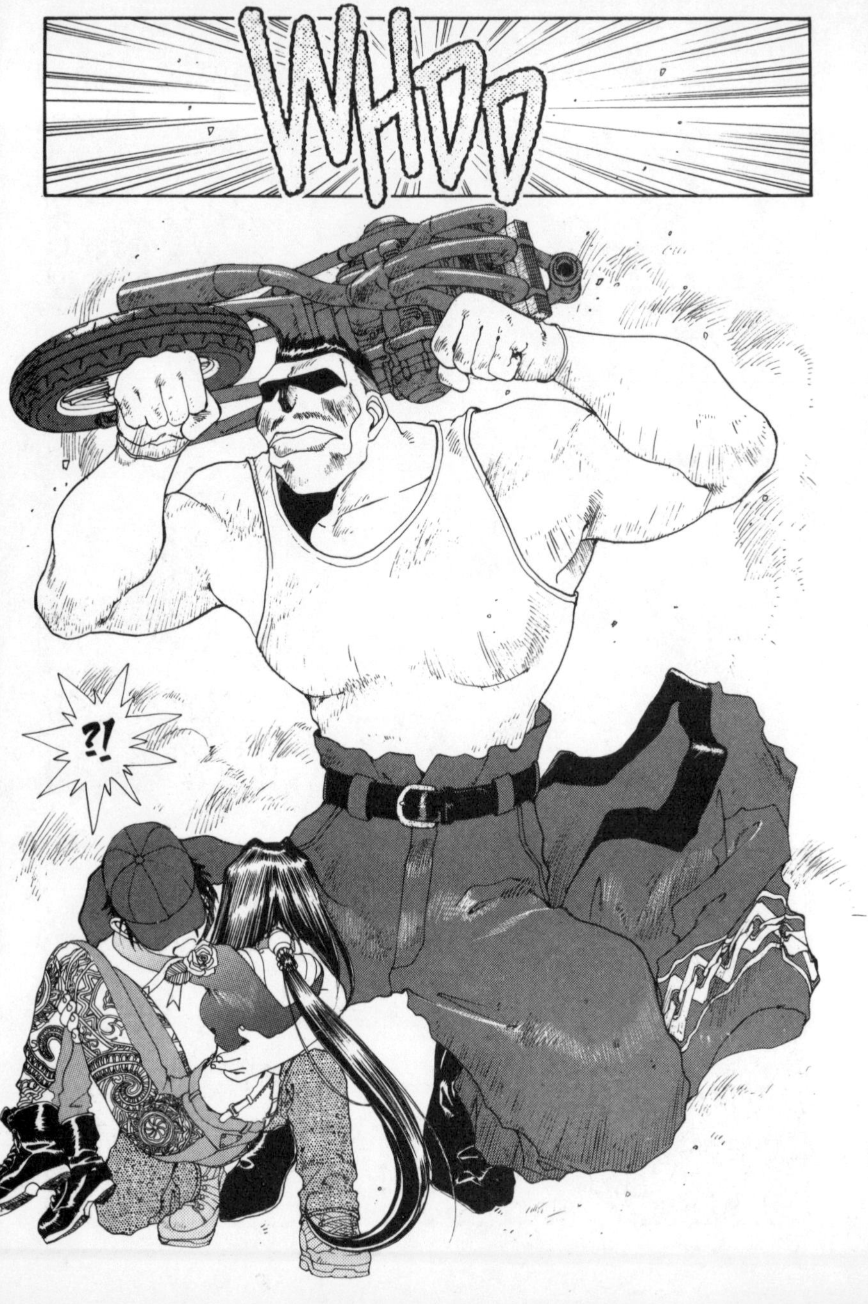
WHOO
?!

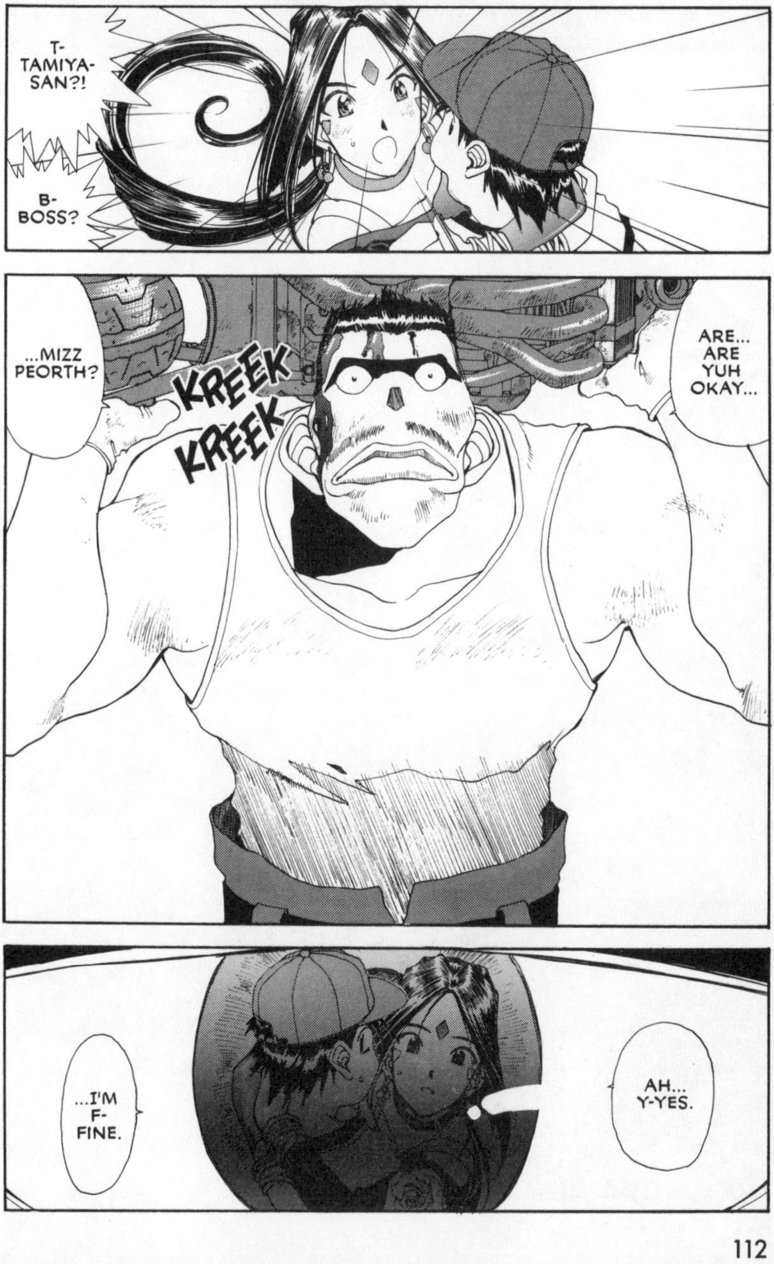
T-TAMIYA-SAN?!
B-BOSS?
ARE... ARE YUH OKAY...
KREEK KREEK
...MIZZ PEORTH?
AH... Y-YES.
...I'M F-FINE.

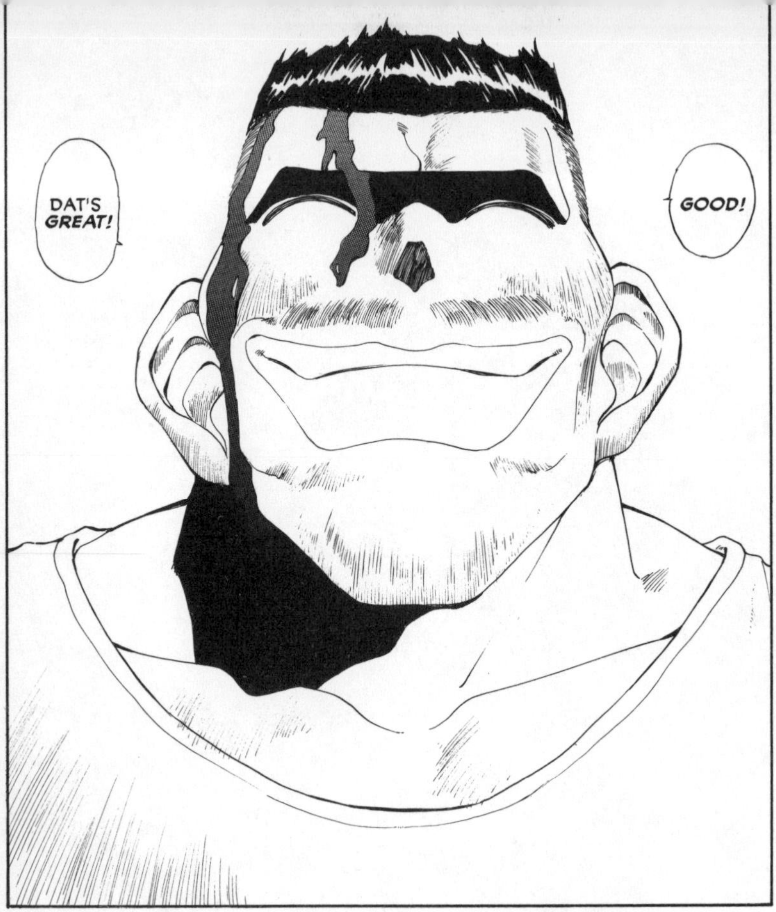
GOOD!
DAT'S GREAT!

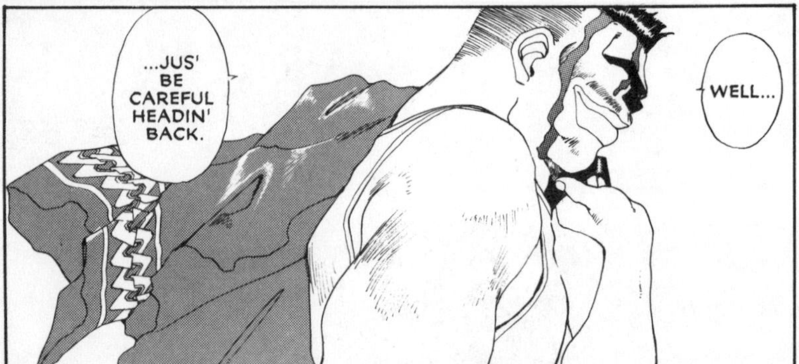
WELL...
...JUS' BE CAREFUL HEADIN' BACK.

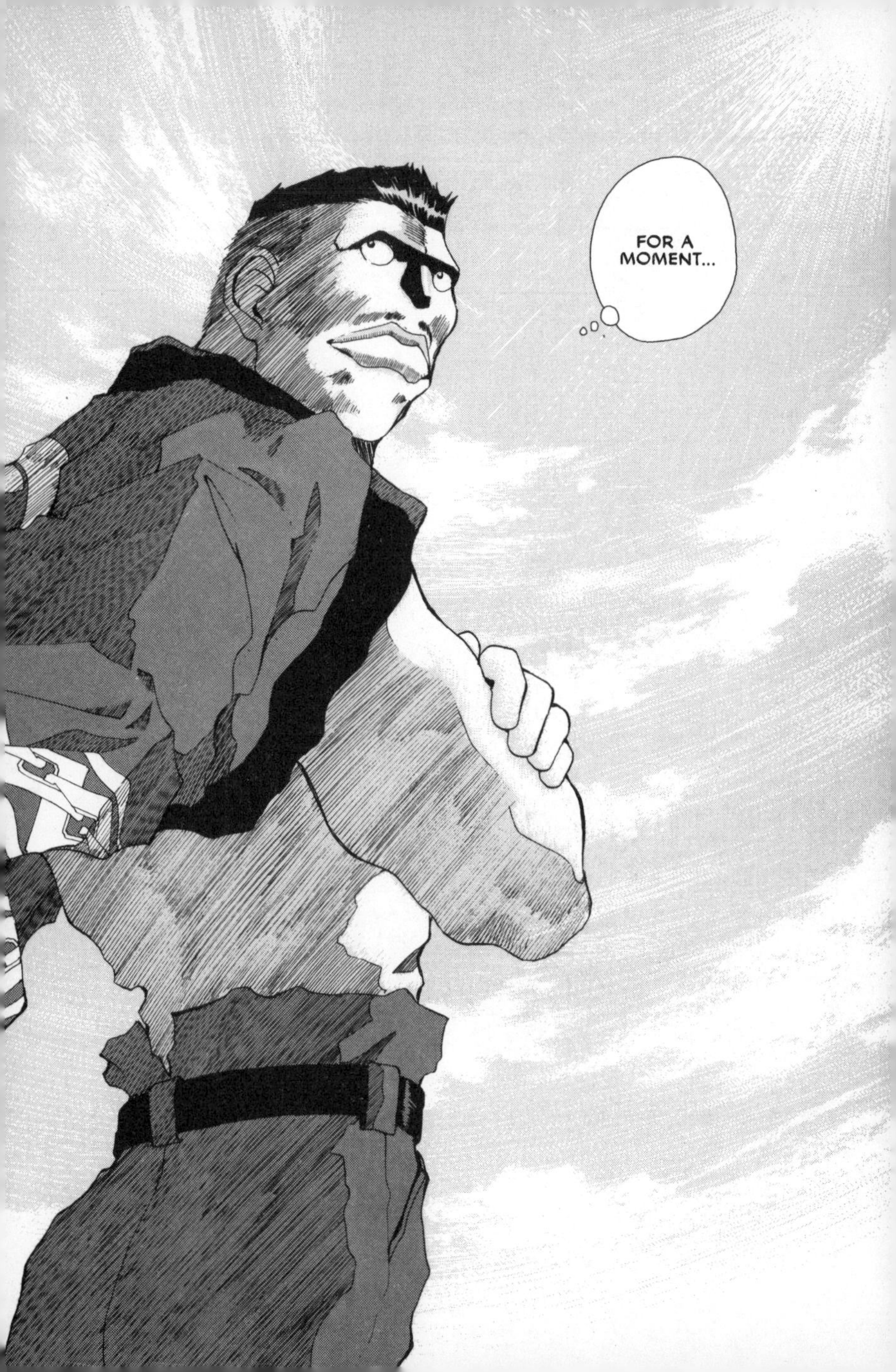
FOR A MOMENT...

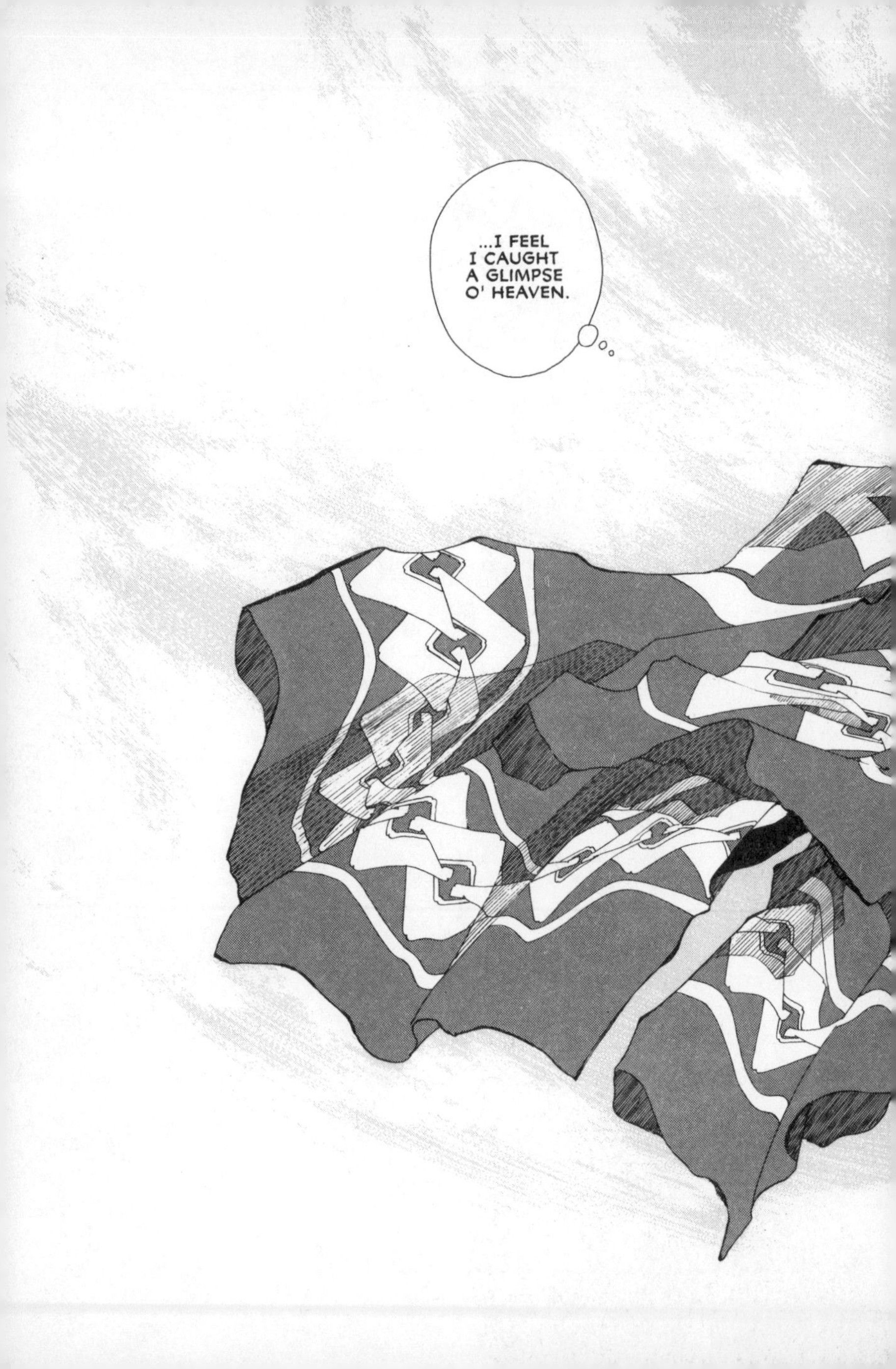
...I FEEL I CAUGHT A GLIMPSE O' HEAVEN.

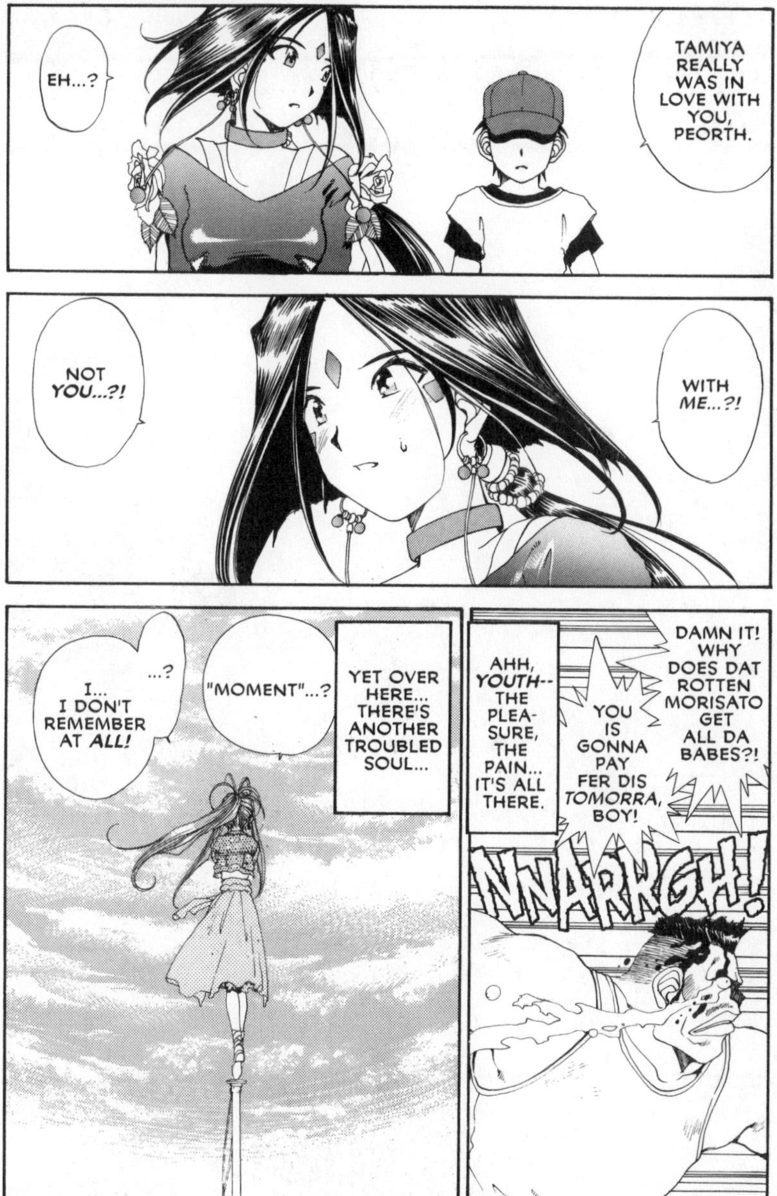
TAMIYA REALLY WAS IN LOVE WITH YOU, PEORTH.
EH...?
WITH *ME...?!*
NOT *YOU...?!*
DAMN IT! WHY DOES DAT ROTTEN MORISATO GET ALL DA BABES?!
YOU IS GONNA PAY FER DIS *TOMORRA,* BOY!
AHH, *YOUTH*-- THE PLEA-SURE, THE PAIN... IT'S ALL THERE.
NNARRGH!
YET OVER HERE... THERE'S ANOTHER TROUBLED SOUL...
"MOMENT"...?
...? I... I DON'T REMEMBER AT *ALL!*

CHAPTER 71

Meeting a Goddess's Troubles Halfway

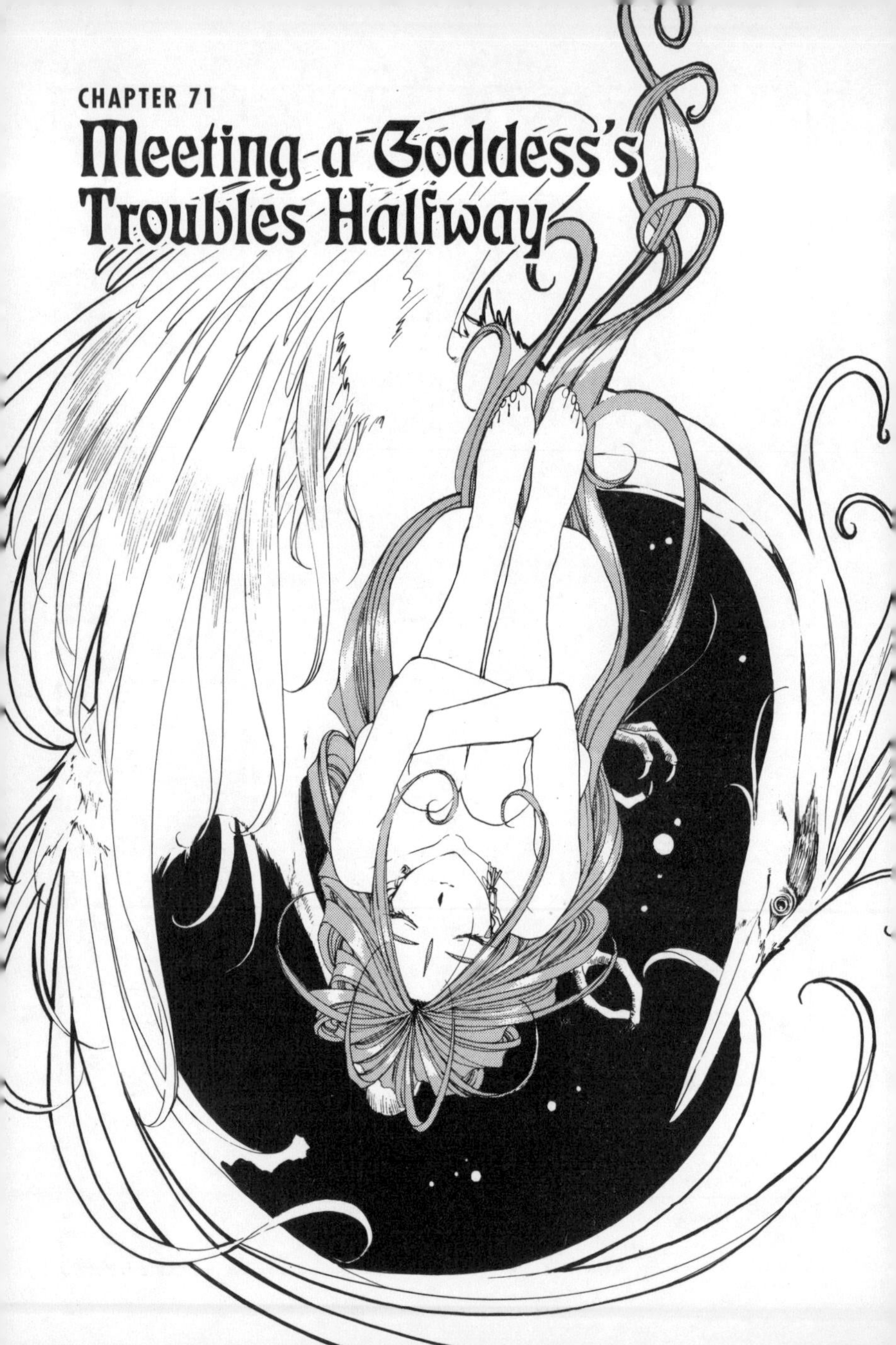

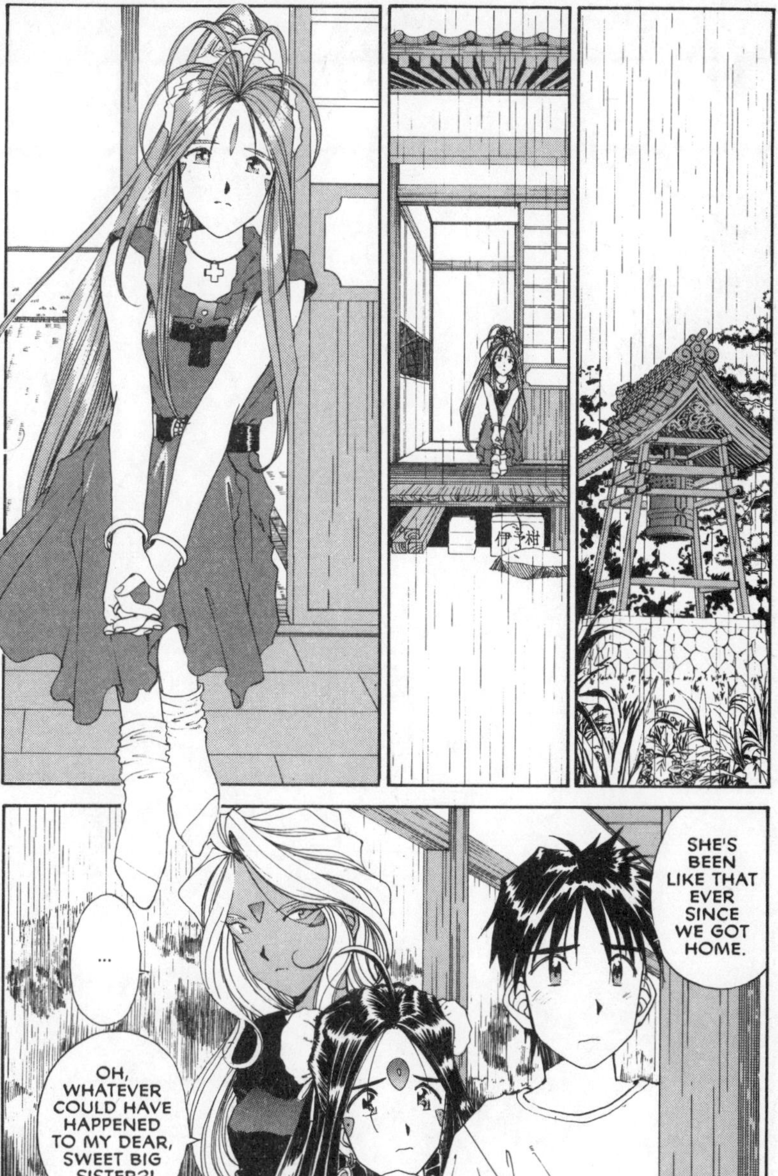
伊予柑
SHE'S BEEN LIKE THAT EVER SINCE WE GOT HOME.
...
OH, WHATEVER COULD HAVE HAPPENED TO MY DEAR, SWEET BIG SISTER?!

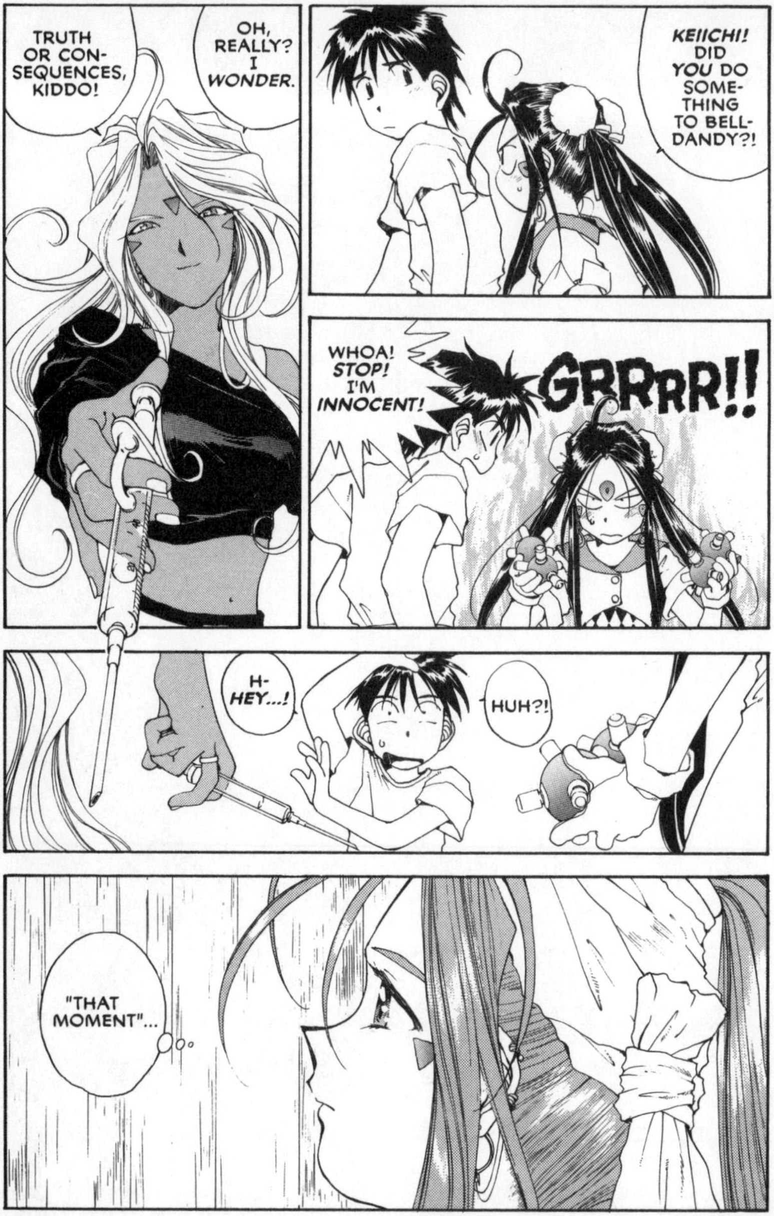
KEIICHI! DID YOU DO SOME-THING TO BELL-DANDY?!
GRRRR!!
WHOA! STOP! I'M INNOCENT!
OH, REALLY? I WONDER.
TRUTH OR CON-SEQUENCES, KIDDO!
HUH?!
H-HEY...!
"THAT MOMENT"...

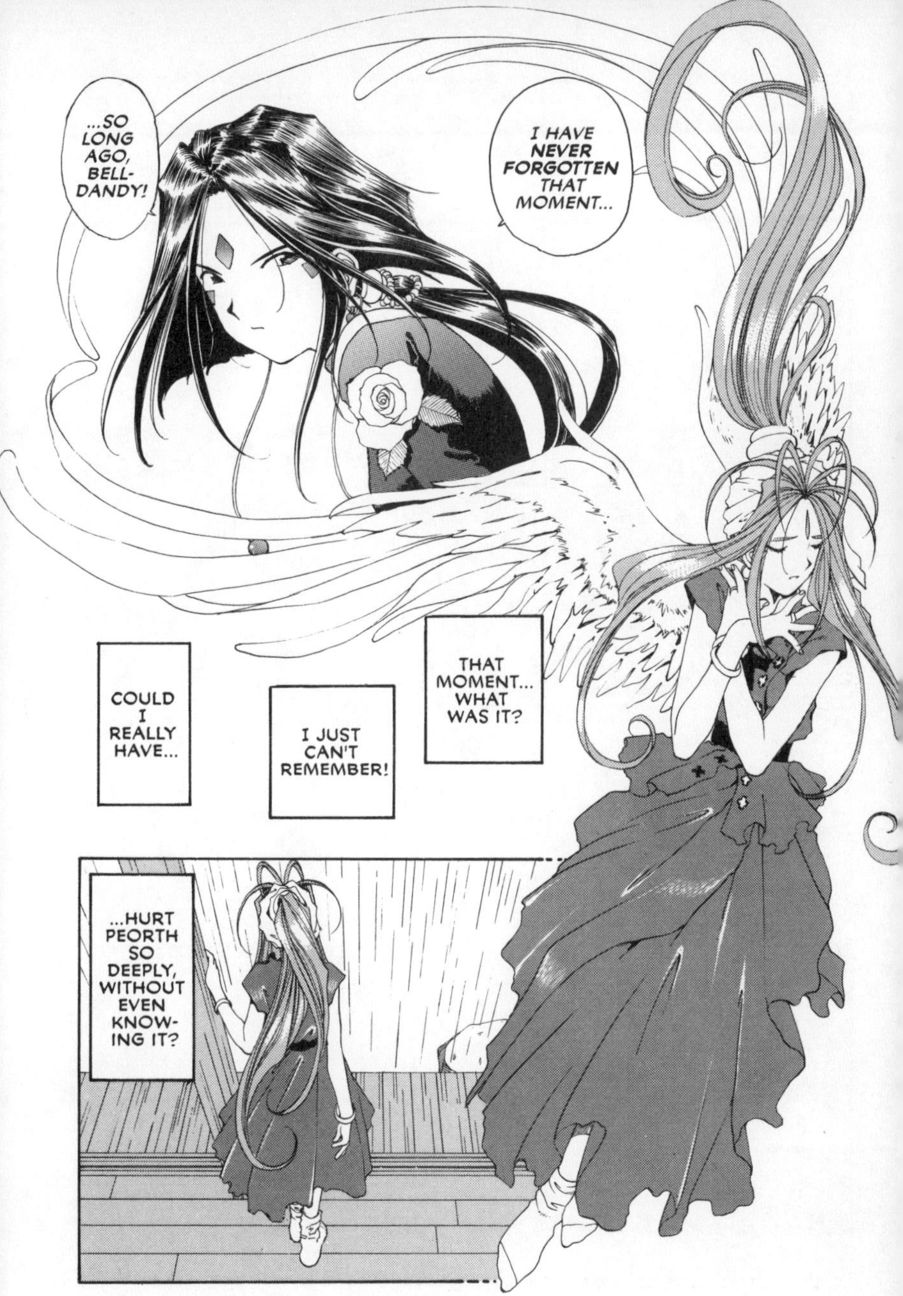
I HAVE NEVER FORGOTTEN THAT MOMENT...
...SO LONG AGO, BELL-DANDY!
THAT MOMENT... WHAT WAS IT?
I JUST CAN'T REMEMBER!
COULD I REALLY HAVE...
...HURT PEORTH SO DEEPLY, WITHOUT EVEN KNOW-ING IT?

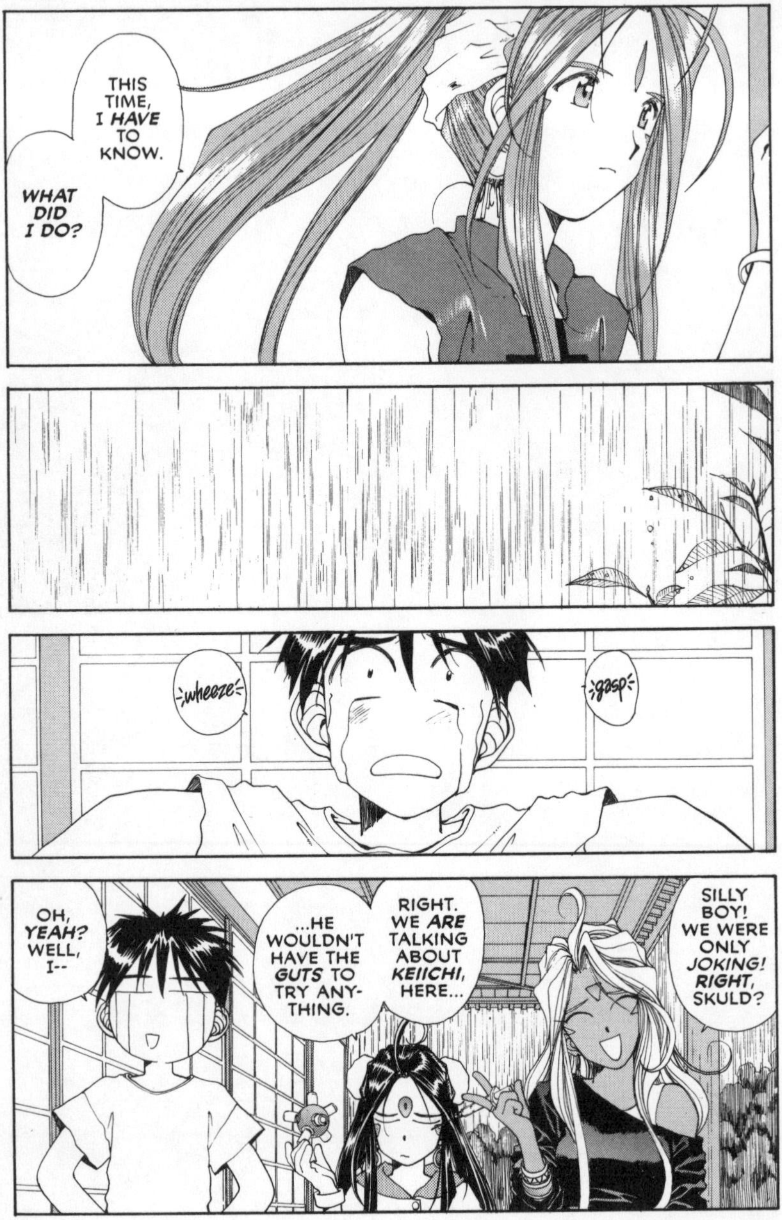
THIS TIME, I HAVE TO KNOW.
WHAT DID I DO?
gasp
wheeze
SILLY BOY! WE WERE ONLY JOKING! RIGHT, SKULD?
RIGHT. WE ARE TALKING ABOUT KEIICHI, HERE...
...HE WOULDN'T HAVE THE GUTS TO TRY ANY-THING.
OH, YEAH? WELL, I--

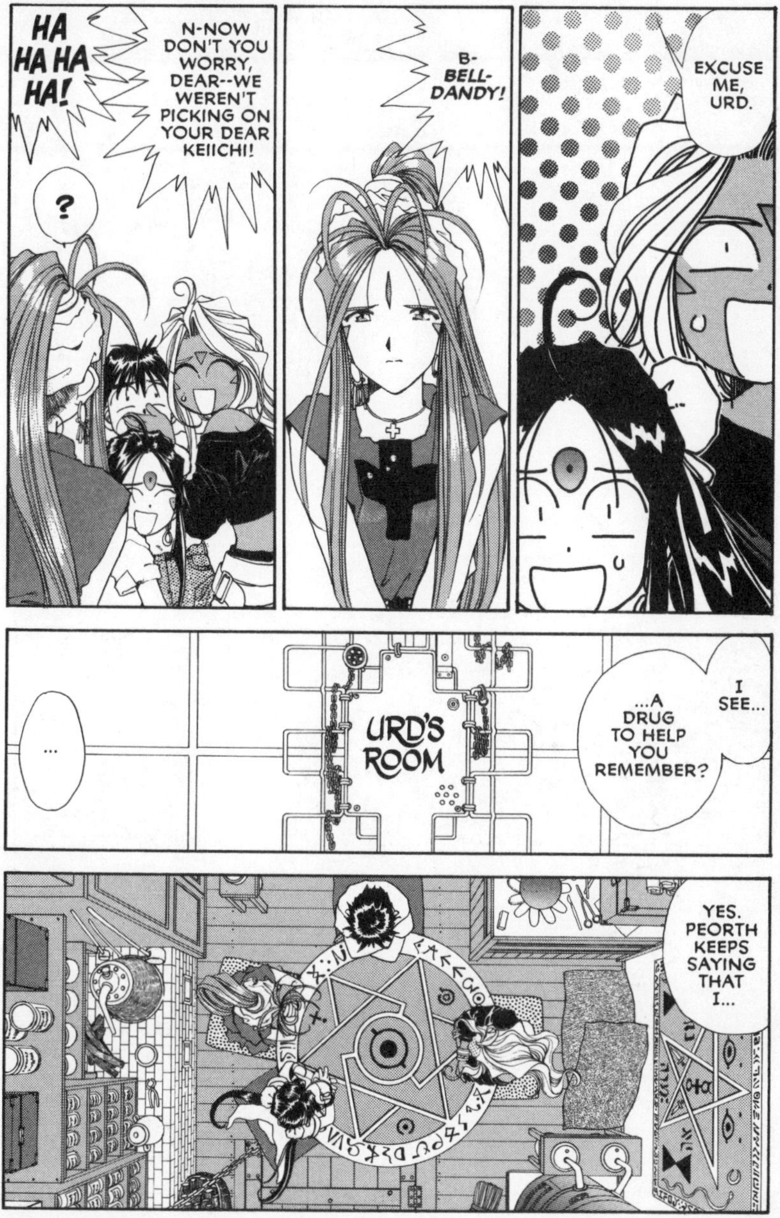
EXCUSE ME, URD.
B-BELL-DANDY!
N-NOW DON'T YOU WORRY, DEAR--WE WEREN'T PICKING ON YOUR DEAR KEIICHI!
HA HA HA HA!
?
I SEE...
...A DRUG TO HELP YOU REMEMBER?
URD'S ROOM
...
YES. PEORTH KEEPS SAYING THAT I...

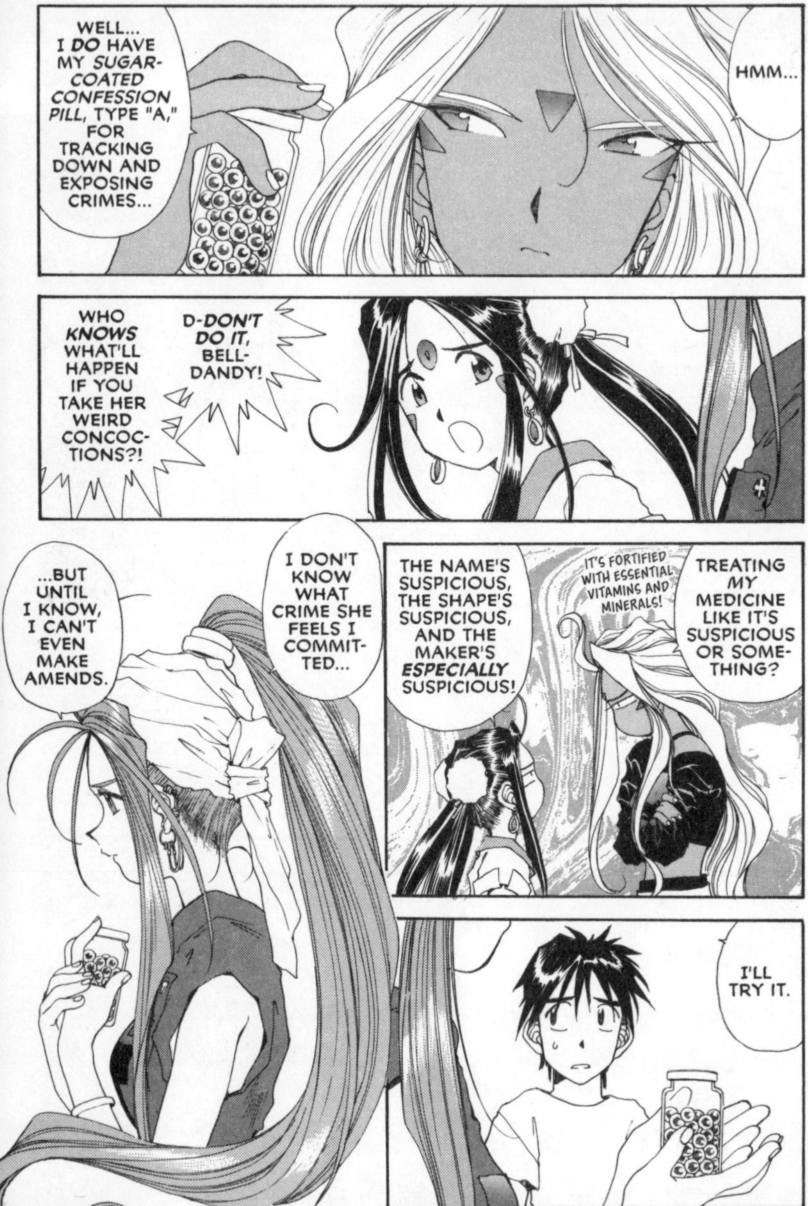
HMM...
WELL... I DO HAVE MY SUGAR-COATED CONFESSION PILL, TYPE "A," FOR TRACKING DOWN AND EXPOSING CRIMES...
D-DON'T DO IT, BELL-DANDY!
WHO KNOWS WHAT'LL HAPPEN IF YOU TAKE HER WEIRD CONCOC-TIONS?!
TREATING MY MEDICINE LIKE IT'S SUSPICIOUS OR SOME-THING?
IT'S FORTIFIED WITH ESSENTIAL VITAMINS AND MINERALS!
THE NAME'S SUSPICIOUS, THE SHAPE'S SUSPICIOUS, AND THE MAKER'S ESPECIALLY SUSPICIOUS!
I'LL TRY IT.
I DON'T KNOW WHAT CRIME SHE FEELS I COMMIT-TED...
...BUT UNTIL I KNOW, I CAN'T EVEN MAKE AMENDS.

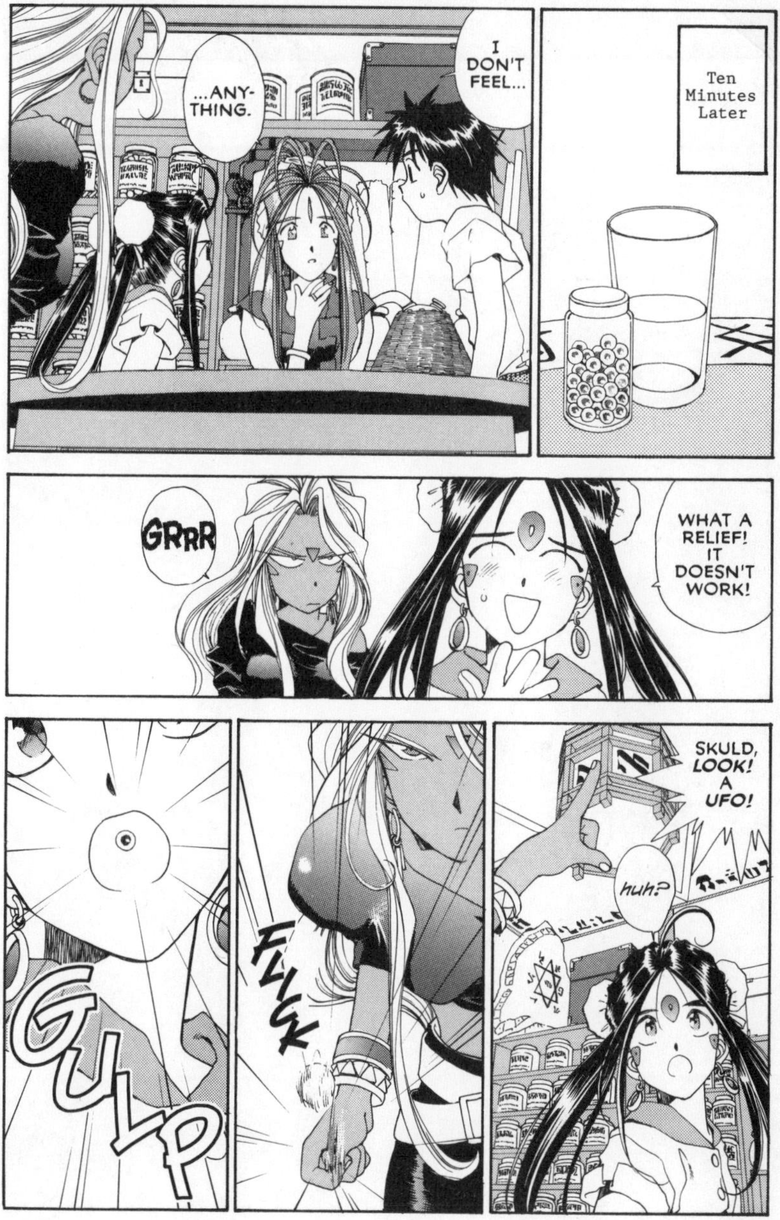
Ten Minutes Later
I DON'T FEEL...
...ANY-THING.
WHAT A RELIEF! IT DOESN'T WORK!
GRRR
SKULD, LOOK! A UFO!
huh?
FLICK
GULP

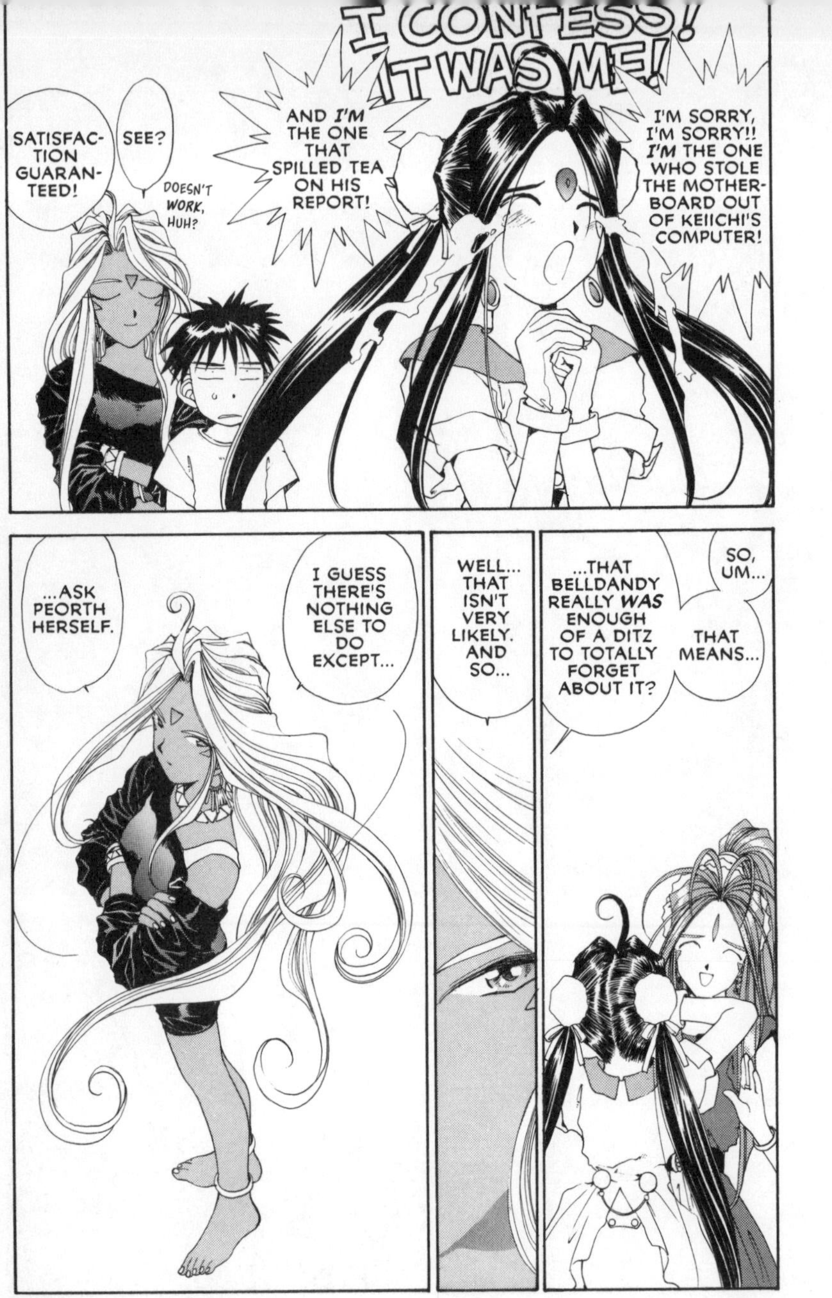
I CONFESS! IT WAS ME!
I'M SORRY, I'M SORRY!! I'M THE ONE WHO STOLE THE MOTHERBOARD OUT OF KEIICHI'S COMPUTER!
AND I'M THE ONE THAT SPILLED TEA ON HIS REPORT!
SEE?
SATISFACTION GUARANTEED!
DOESN'T WORK, HUH?
SO, UM... THAT MEANS...
...THAT BELLDANDY REALLY WAS ENOUGH OF A DITZ TO TOTALLY FORGET ABOUT IT?
WELL... THAT ISN'T VERY LIKELY. AND SO...
I GUESS THERE'S NOTHING ELSE TO DO EXCEPT...
...ASK PEORTH HERSELF.

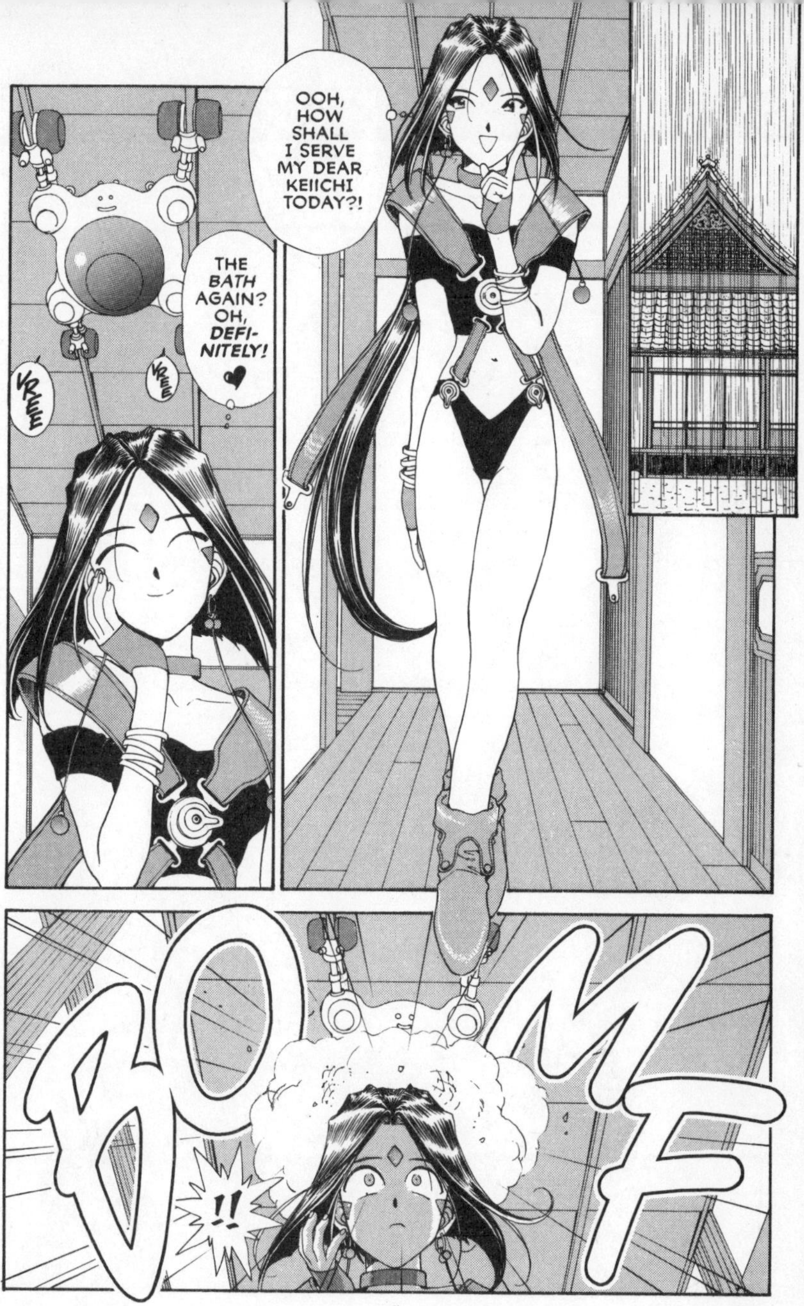
OOH, HOW SHALL I SERVE MY DEAR KEIICHI TODAY?!
THE BATH AGAIN? OH, DEFINITELY! ♥
VREE
VREE
BOMF
!!

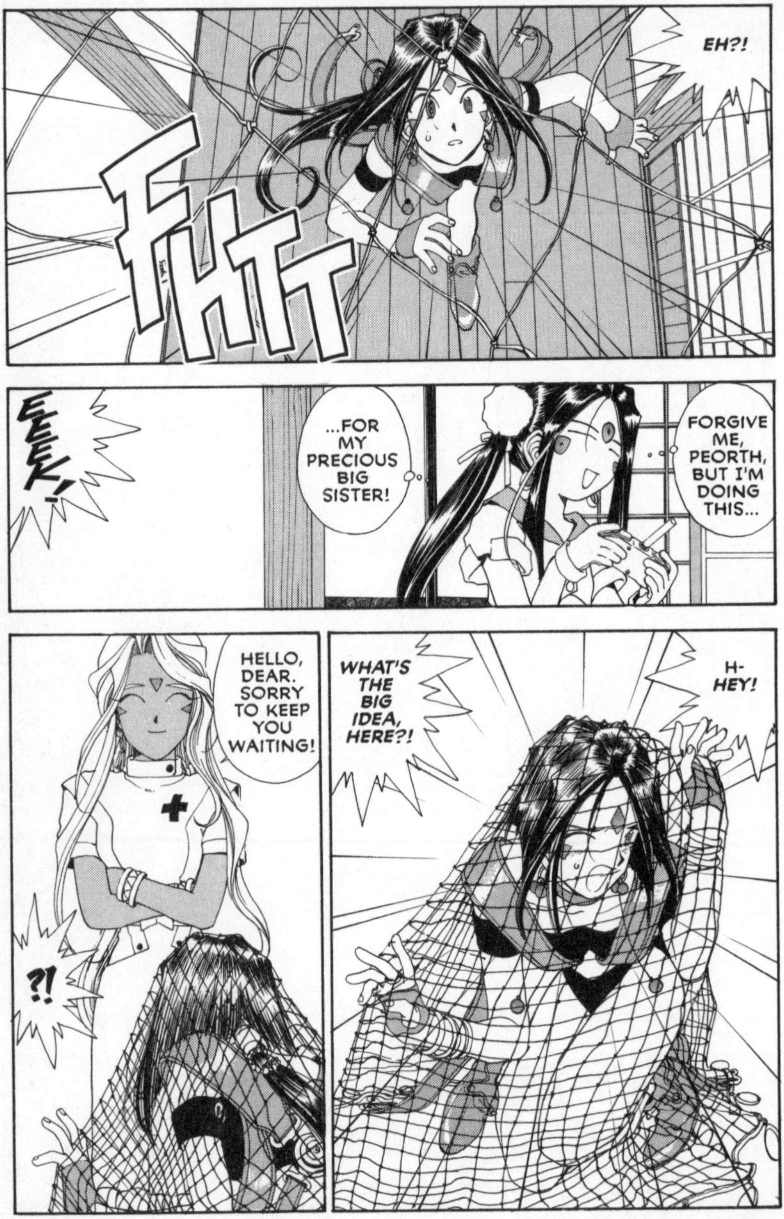
EH?!
FHTT
FORGIVE ME, PEORTH, BUT I'M DOING THIS...
...FOR MY PRECIOUS BIG SISTER!
EEEEK!
H-HEY!
WHAT'S THE BIG IDEA, HERE?!
HELLO, DEAR. SORRY TO KEEP YOU WAITING!
?!

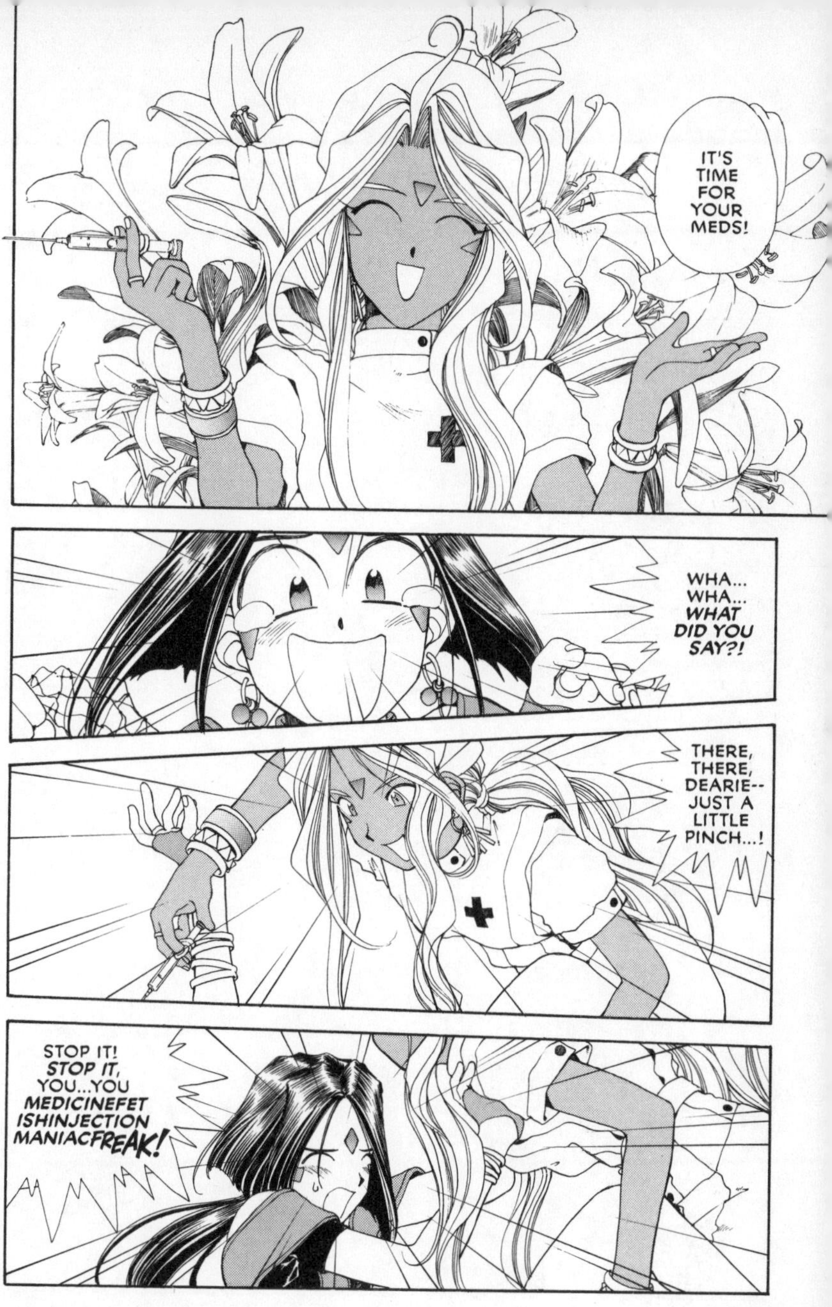
IT'S TIME FOR YOUR MEDS!
WHA... WHA... WHAT DID YOU SAY?!
THERE, THERE, DEARIE-- JUST A LITTLE PINCH...!
STOP IT! STOP IT, YOU...YOU MEDICINEFETISHINJECTIONMANIACFREAK!

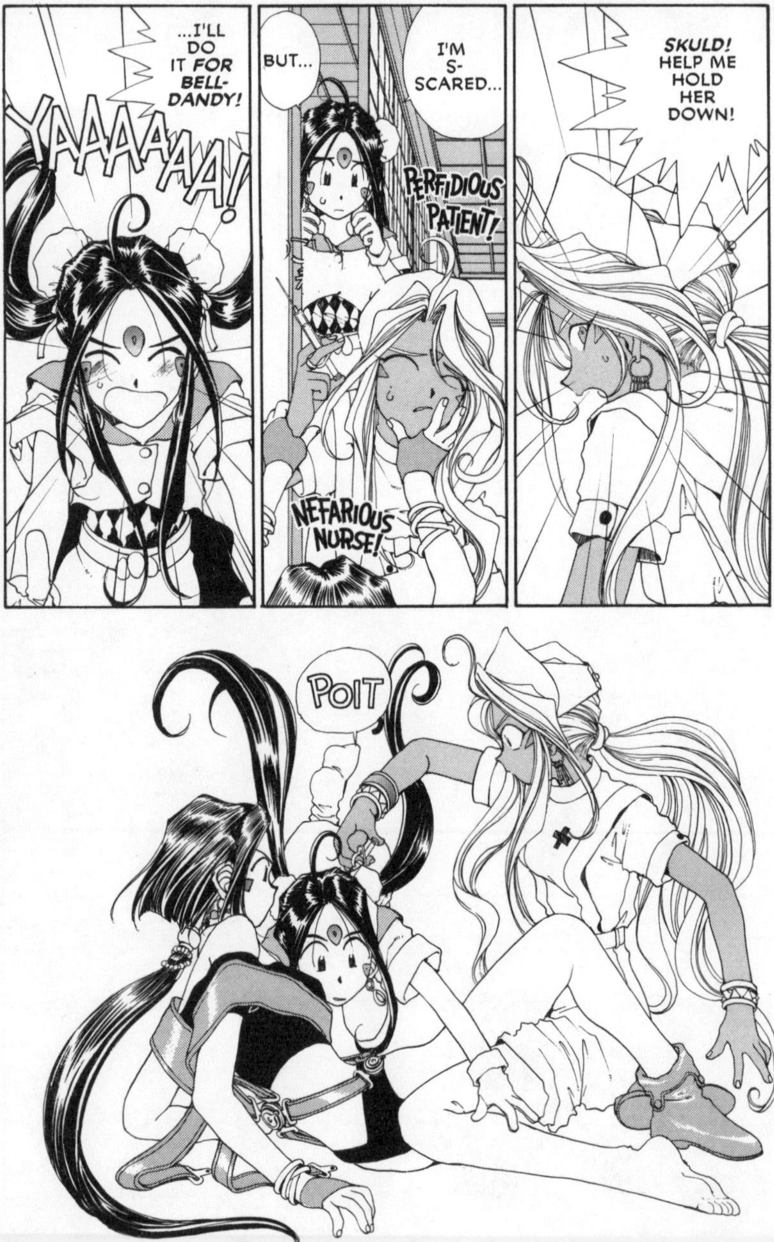
SKULD! HELP ME HOLD HER DOWN!
I'M S-SCARED...
BUT...
PERFIDIOUS PATIENT!
NEFARIOUS NURSE!
...I'LL DO IT FOR BELL-DANDY!
YAAAAAAA!
POIT

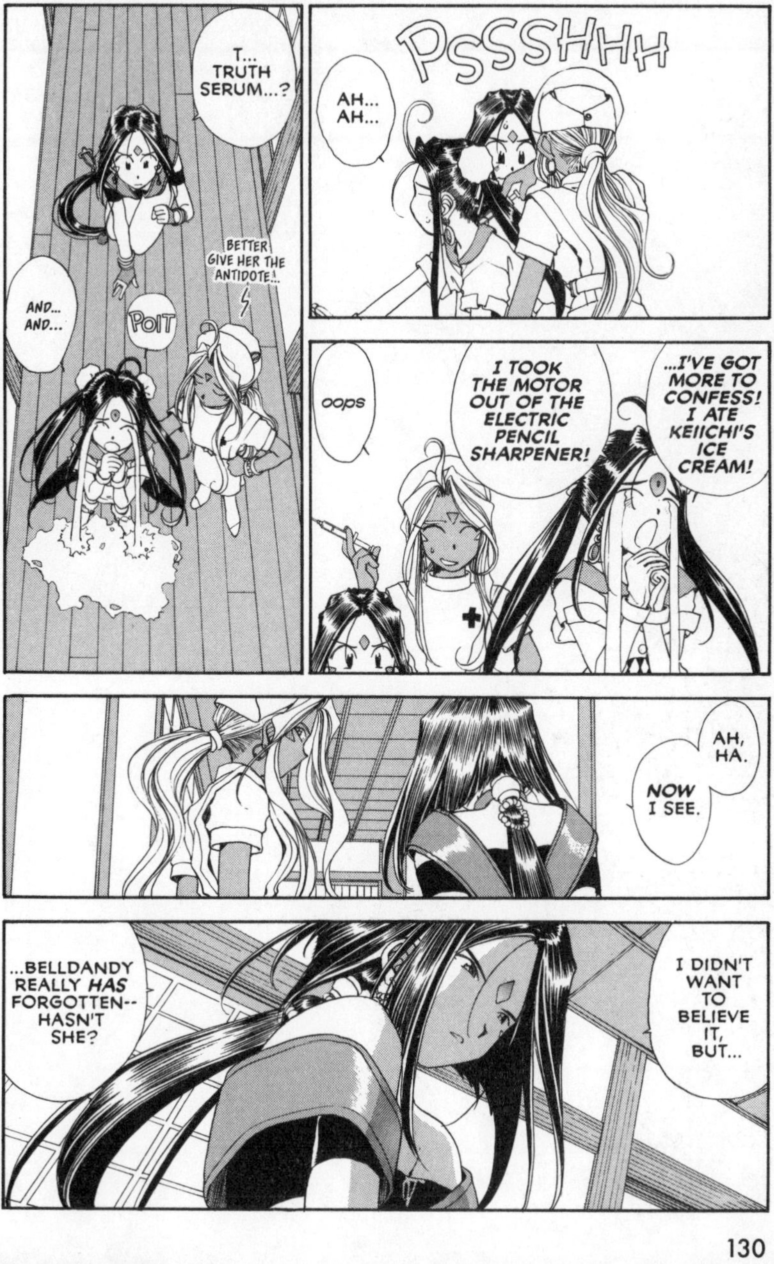
PSSSHHH
AH... AH...
...I'VE GOT MORE TO CONFESS! I ATE KEIICHI'S ICE CREAM!
I TOOK THE MOTOR OUT OF THE ELECTRIC PENCIL SHARPENER!
oops
T... TRUTH SERUM...?
BETTER GIVE HER THE ANTIDOTE...
AND... AND...
POIT
AH, HA. *NOW* I SEE.
I DIDN'T WANT TO BELIEVE IT, BUT...
...BELLDANDY REALLY *HAS* FORGOTTEN-- HASN'T SHE?

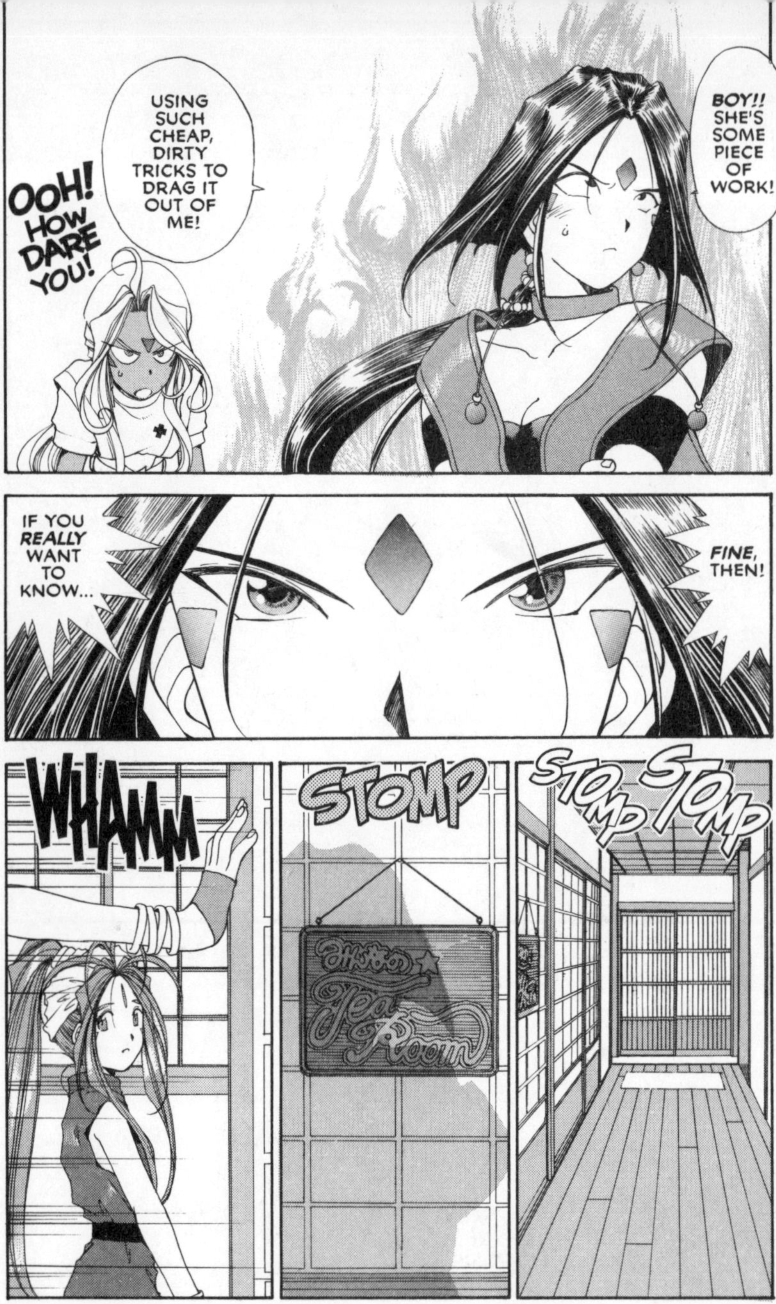
BOY!! SHE'S SOME PIECE OF WORK!
USING SUCH CHEAP, DIRTY TRICKS TO DRAG IT OUT OF ME!
OOH! HOW DARE YOU!
FINE, THEN!
IF YOU *REALLY* WANT TO KNOW...
STOMP STOMP
STOMP
Tea Room
WHAMM

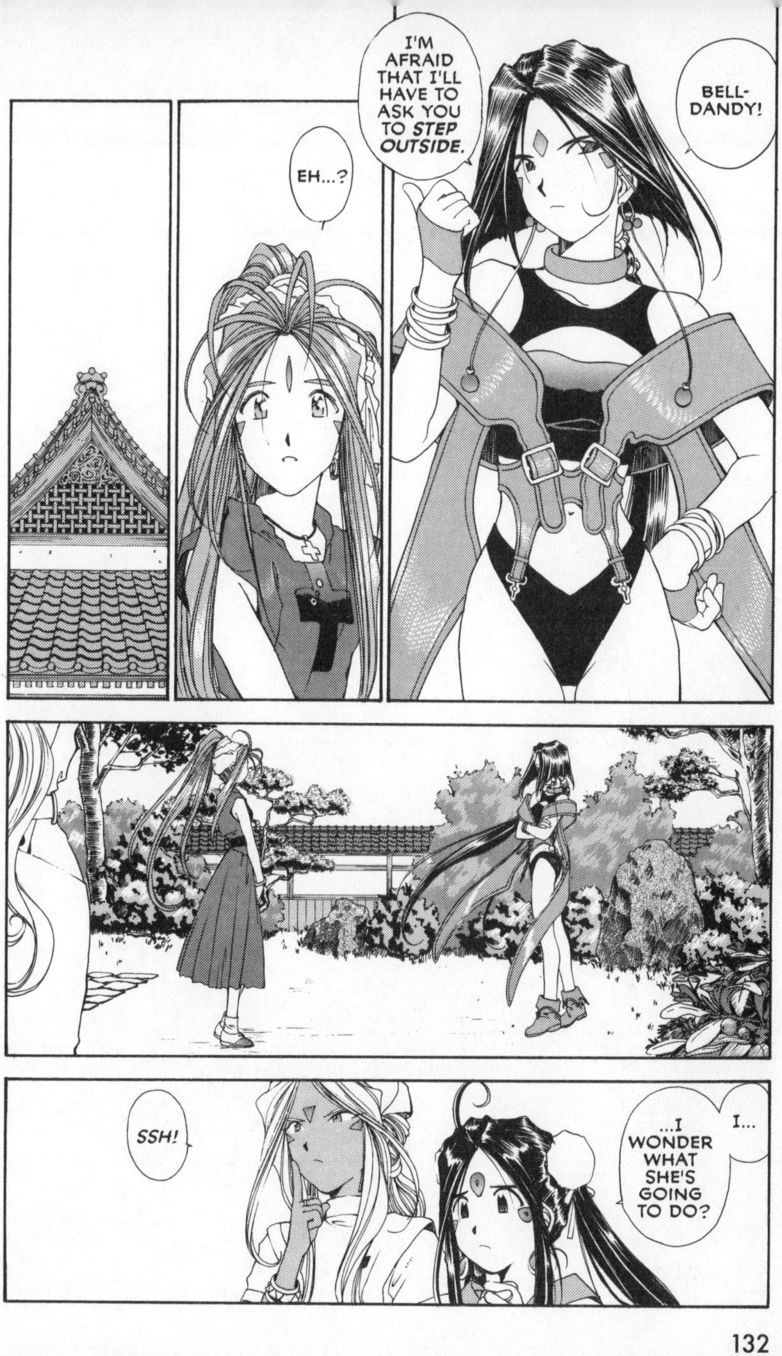
BELL-DANDY!
I'M AFRAID THAT I'LL HAVE TO ASK YOU TO *STEP OUTSIDE.*
EH...?
I...
...I WONDER WHAT SHE'S GOING TO DO?
SSH!

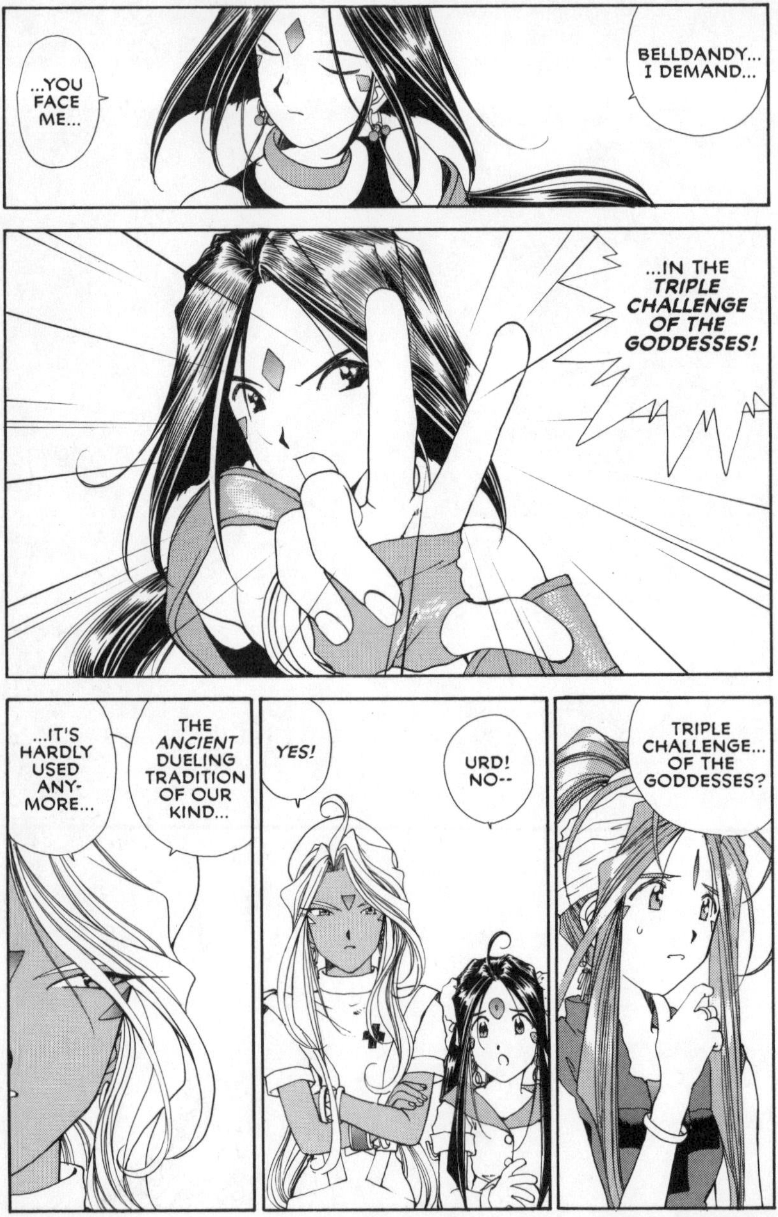
BELLDANDY... I DEMAND...
...YOU FACE ME...
...IN THE *TRIPLE CHALLENGE* OF THE GODDESSES!
TRIPLE CHALLENGE... OF THE GODDESSES?
URD! NO--
YES!
THE *ANCIENT* DUELING TRADITION OF OUR KIND...
...IT'S HARDLY USED ANY-MORE...

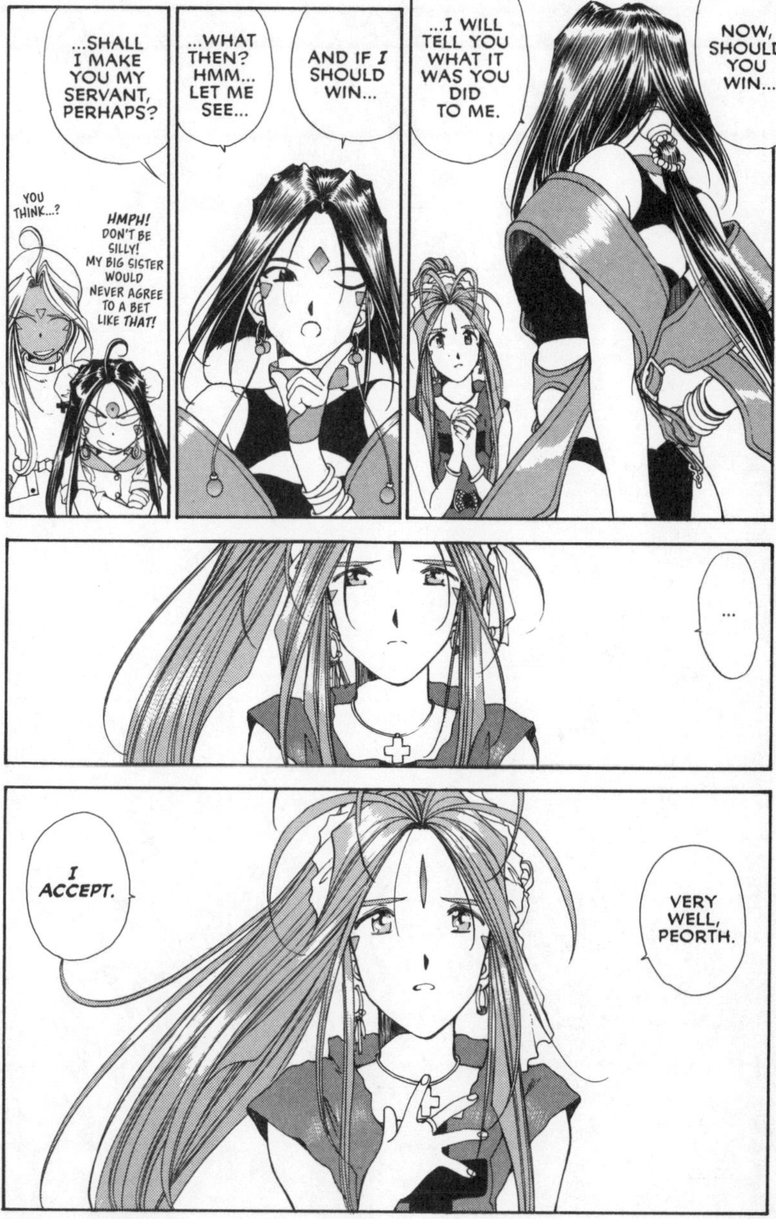
NOW, SHOULD YOU WIN...
...I WILL TELL YOU WHAT IT WAS YOU DID TO ME.
AND IF *I* SHOULD WIN...
...WHAT THEN? HMM... LET ME SEE...
...SHALL I MAKE YOU MY SERVANT, PERHAPS?
HMPH! DON'T BE SILLY! MY BIG SISTER WOULD NEVER AGREE TO A BET LIKE *THAT!*
YOU THINK...?
...
VERY WELL, PEORTH.
I ACCEPT.

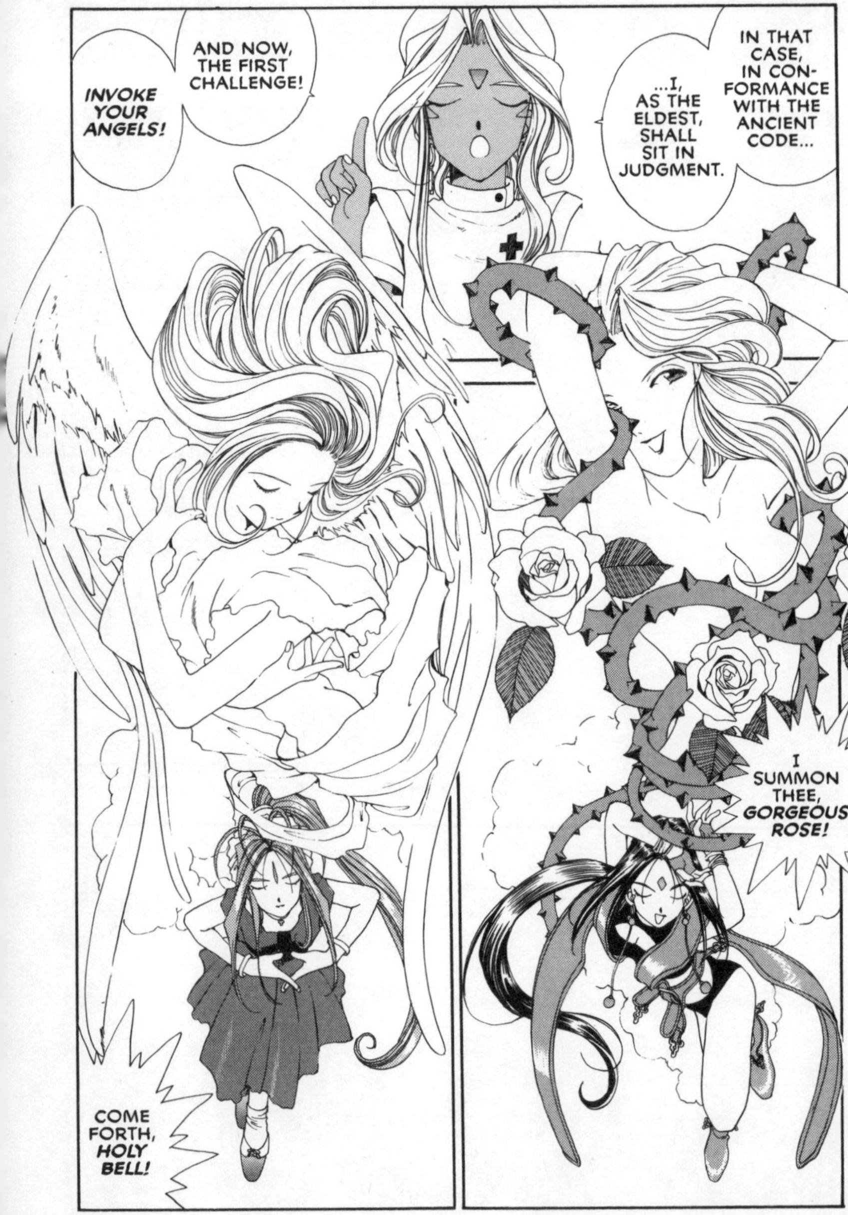
IN THAT CASE, IN CONFORMANCE WITH THE ANCIENT CODE...
...I, AS THE ELDEST, SHALL SIT IN JUDGMENT.
AND NOW, THE FIRST CHALLENGE!
INVOKE YOUR ANGELS!
I SUMMON THEE, *GORGEOUS ROSE!*
COME FORTH, *HOLY BELL!*

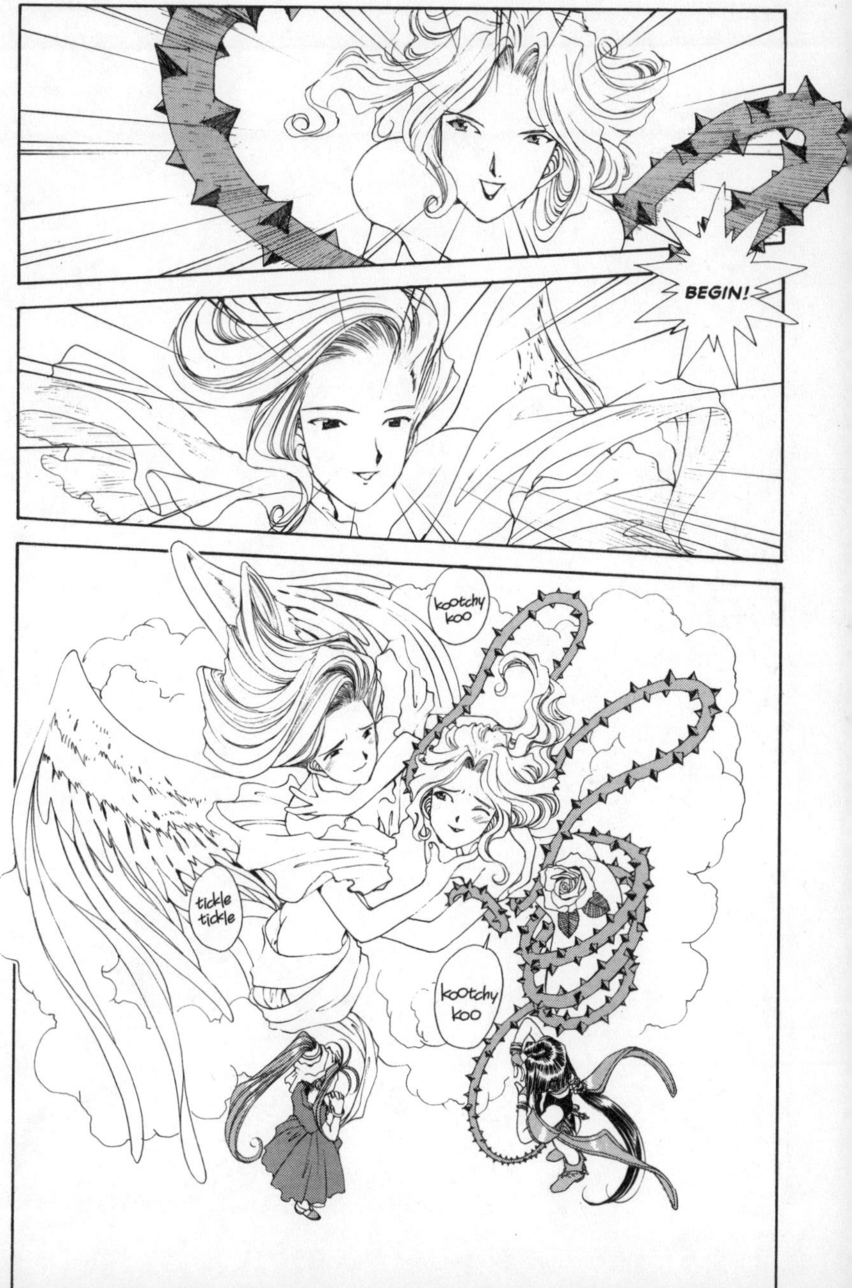
BEGIN!
kootchy koo
tickle tickle
kootchy koo

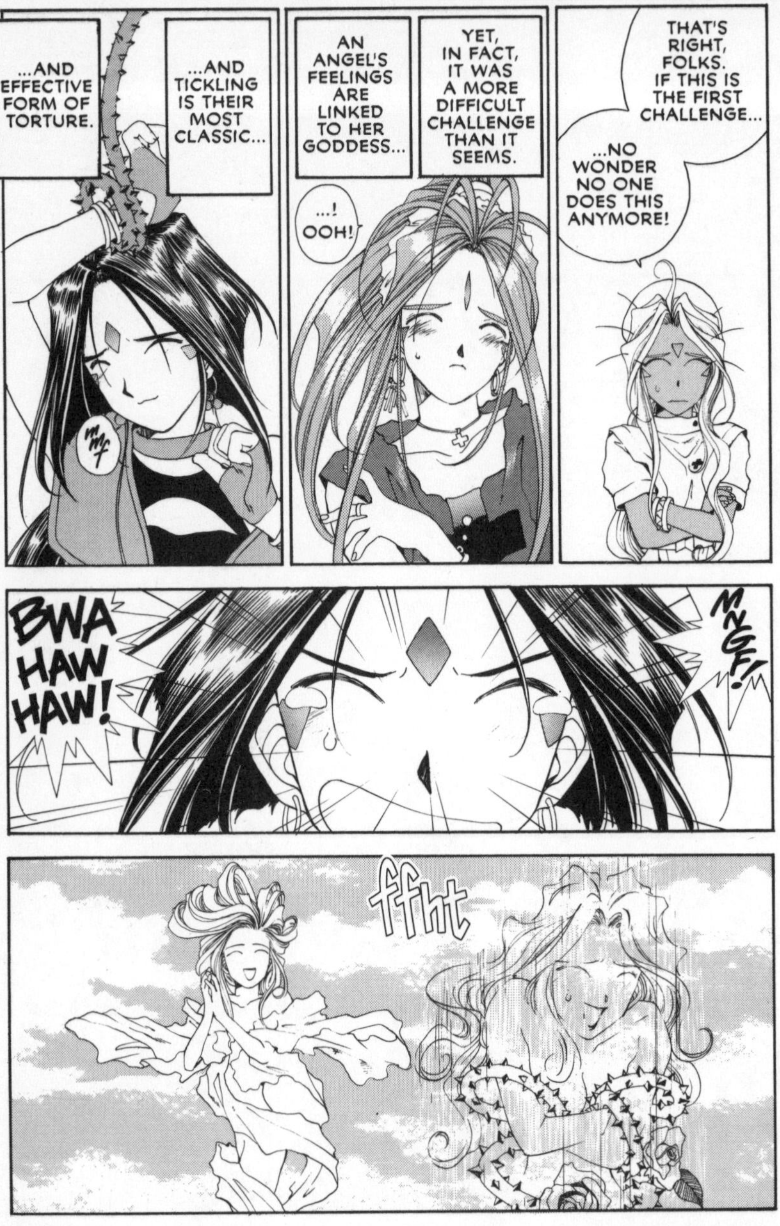
THAT'S RIGHT, FOLKS. IF THIS IS THE FIRST CHALLENGE...
...NO WONDER NO ONE DOES THIS ANYMORE!
YET, IN FACT, IT WAS A MORE DIFFICULT CHALLENGE THAN IT SEEMS.
AN ANGEL'S FEELINGS ARE LINKED TO HER GODDESS...
...! OOH!
...AND TICKLING IS THEIR MOST CLASSIC...
...AND EFFECTIVE FORM OF TORTURE.
mmf
MNGF!
BWA HAW HAW!
ffht

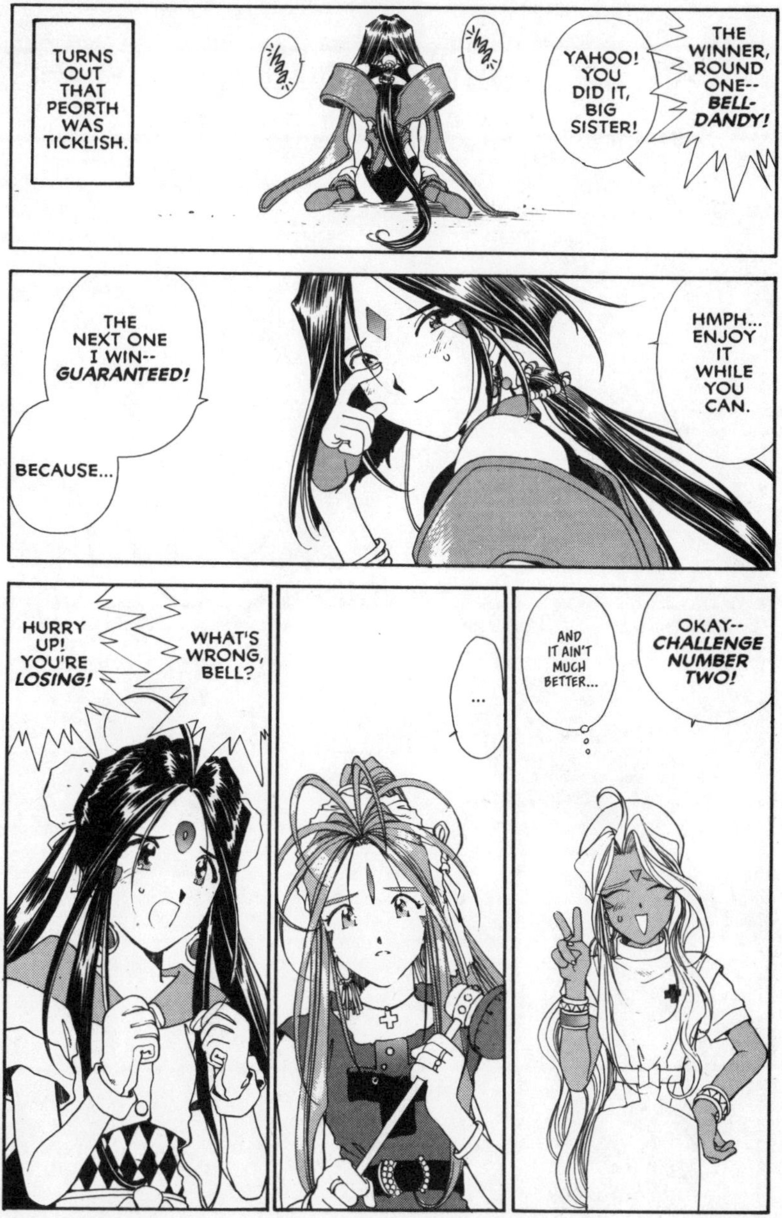
THE WINNER, ROUND ONE-- *BELL-DANDY!*
YAHOO! YOU DID IT, BIG SISTER!
TURNS OUT THAT PEORTH WAS TICKLISH.
HMPH... ENJOY IT WHILE YOU CAN.
THE NEXT ONE I WIN-- *GUARANTEED!*
BECAUSE...
OKAY-- *CHALLENGE NUMBER TWO!*
AND IT AIN'T MUCH BETTER...
...
WHAT'S WRONG, BELL?
HURRY UP! YOU'RE *LOSING!*

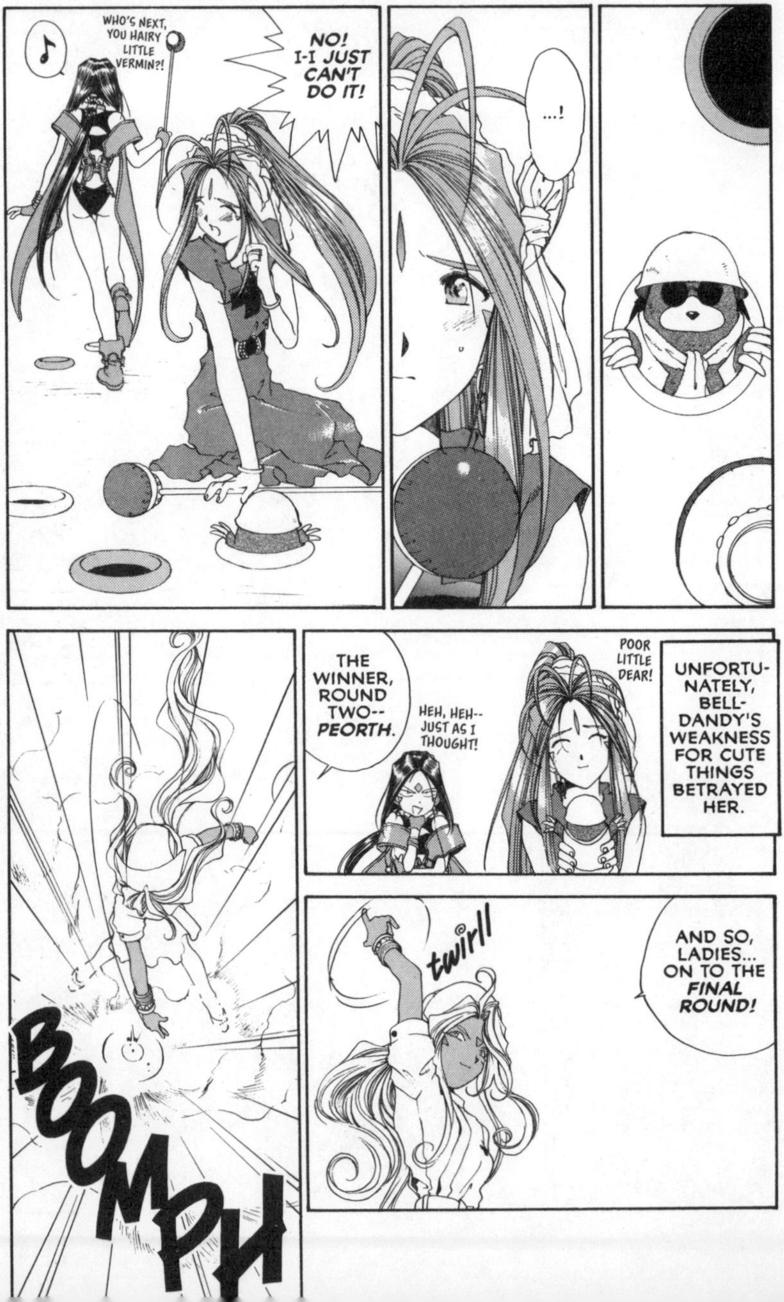
...!
NO! I-I JUST CAN'T DO IT!
WHO'S NEXT, YOU HAIRY LITTLE VERMIN?!
♪
UNFORTU-NATELY, BELL-DANDY'S WEAKNESS FOR CUTE THINGS BETRAYED HER.
POOR LITTLE DEAR!
THE WINNER, ROUND TWO-- PEORTH.
HEH, HEH-- JUST AS I THOUGHT!
AND SO, LADIES... ON TO THE FINAL ROUND!
twirll
BOOMPH

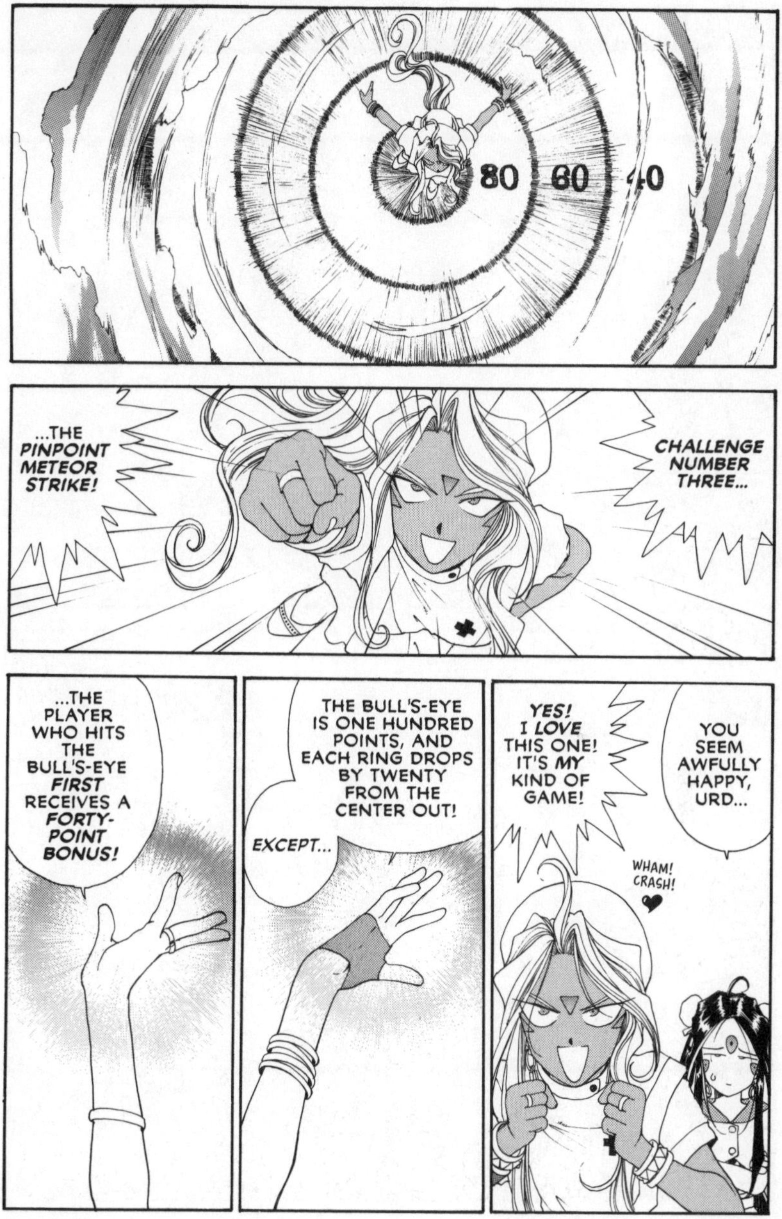
80 60 40
CHALLENGE NUMBER THREE...
...THE PINPOINT METEOR STRIKE!
YOU SEEM AWFULLY HAPPY, URD...
YES! I LOVE THIS ONE! IT'S MY KIND OF GAME!
WHAM! CRASH!
THE BULL'S-EYE IS ONE HUNDRED POINTS, AND EACH RING DROPS BY TWENTY FROM THE CENTER OUT!
EXCEPT...
...THE PLAYER WHO HITS THE BULL'S-EYE FIRST RECEIVES A FORTY-POINT BONUS!

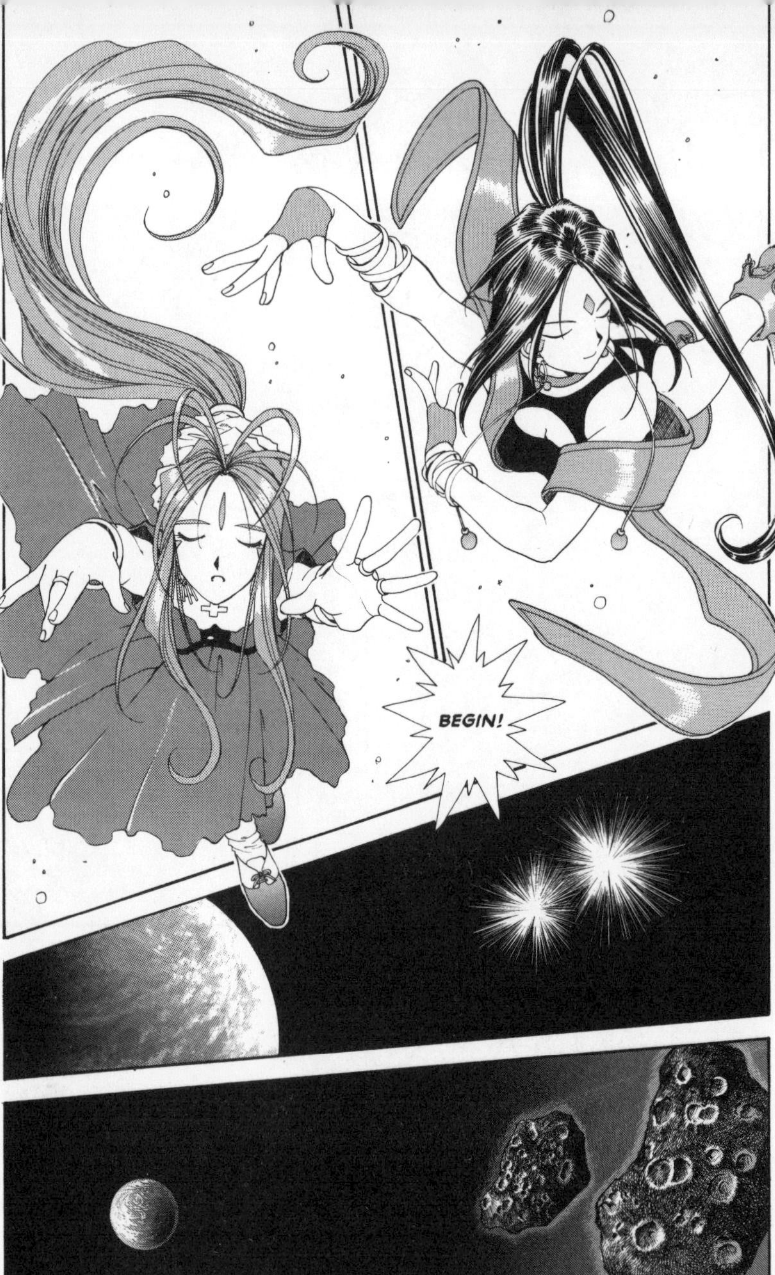
BEGIN!

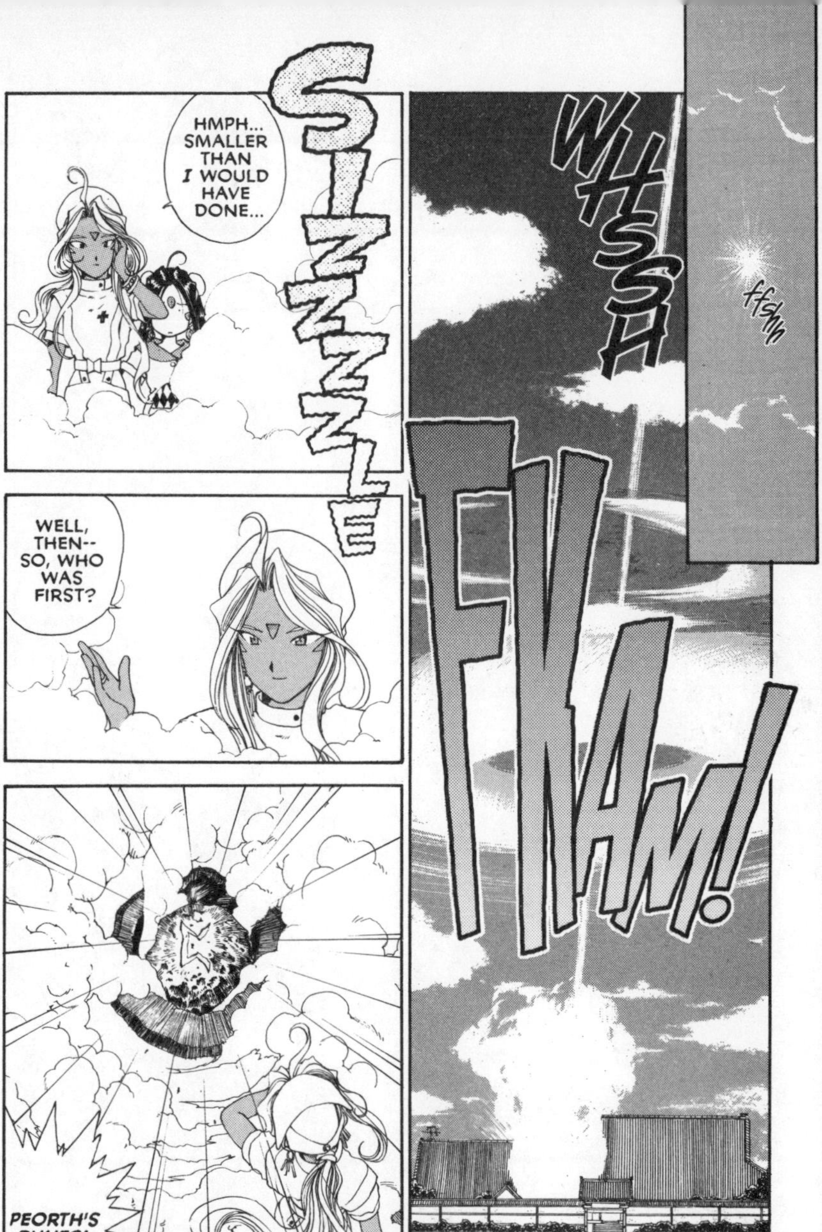
ffshh
WHSSH
FWAM!
SIZZZZZLE
HMPH... SMALLER THAN I WOULD HAVE DONE...
WELL, THEN-- SO, WHO WAS FIRST?
PEORTH'S RUNE?!

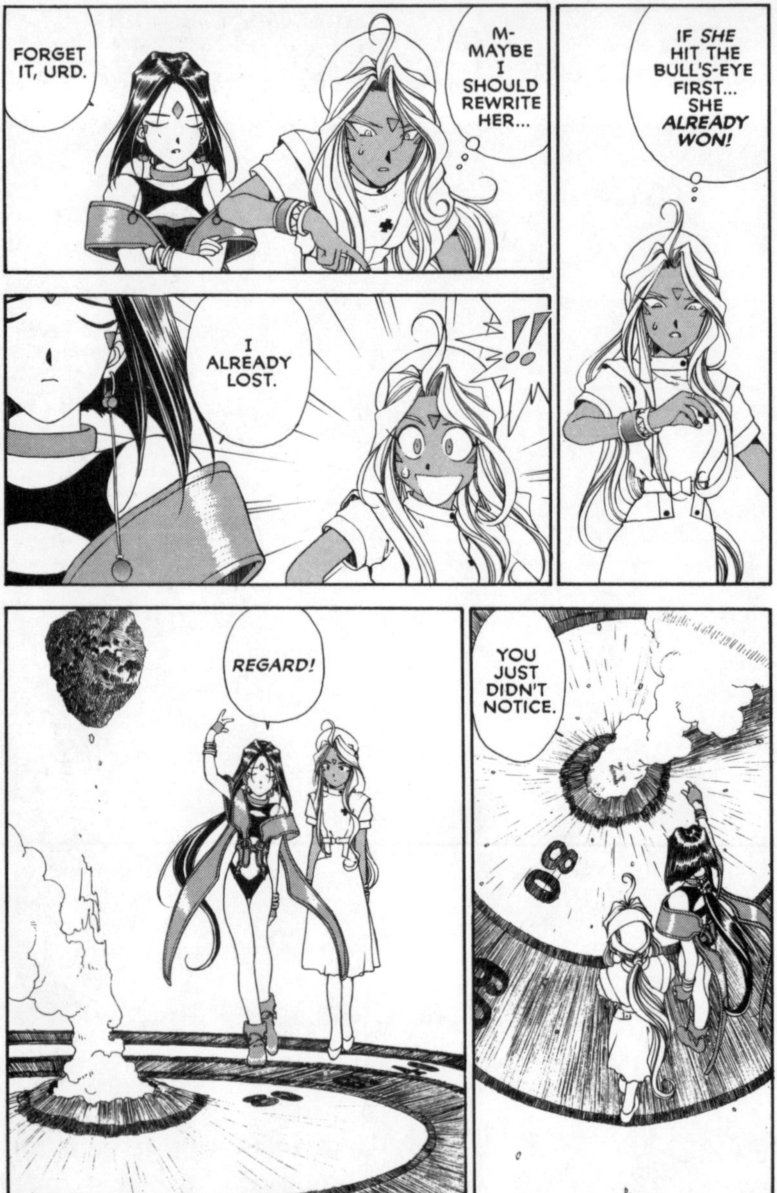
IF *SHE* HIT THE BULL'S-EYE FIRST... SHE ***ALREADY WON!***
M-MAYBE I SHOULD REWRITE HER...
FORGET IT, URD.
!!
I ALREADY LOST.
YOU JUST DIDN'T NOTICE.
REGARD!

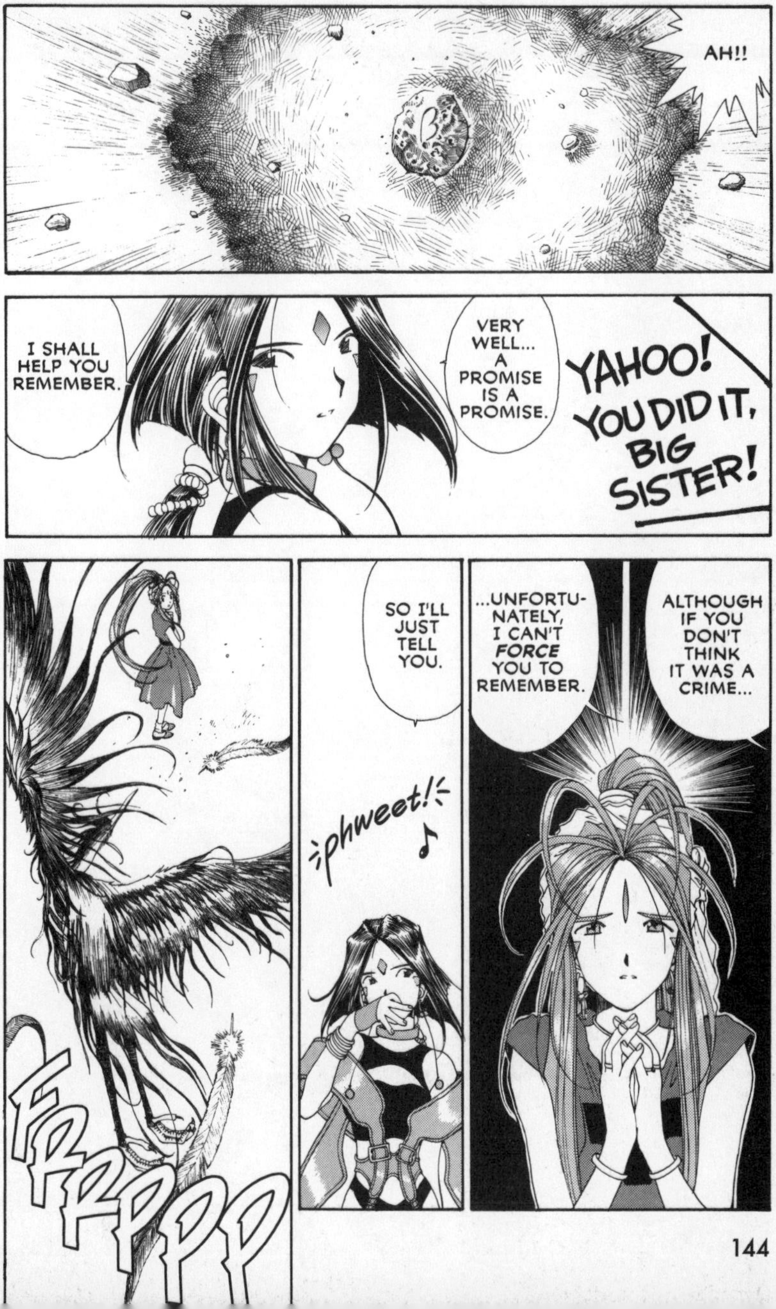
AH!!
YAHOO! YOU DID IT, BIG SISTER!
VERY WELL... A PROMISE IS A PROMISE.
I SHALL HELP YOU REMEMBER.
ALTHOUGH IF YOU DON'T THINK IT WAS A CRIME...
...UNFORTU-NATELY, I CAN'T *FORCE* YOU TO REMEMBER.
SO I'LL JUST TELL YOU.
phweet!
FRRPPP

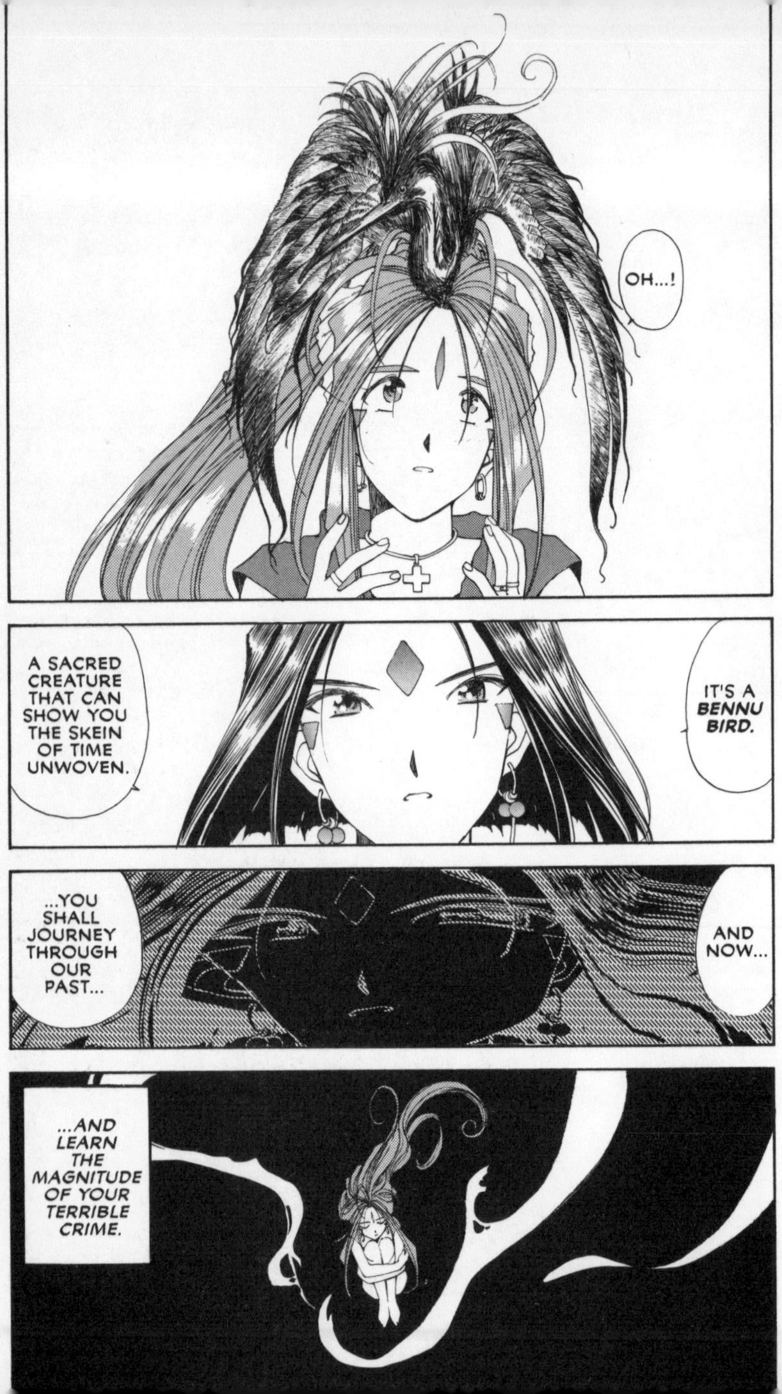
OH...!
IT'S A *BENNU BIRD.*
A SACRED CREATURE THAT CAN SHOW YOU THE SKEIN OF TIME UNWOVEN.
AND NOW...
...YOU SHALL JOURNEY THROUGH OUR PAST...
...AND LEARN THE MAGNITUDE OF YOUR TERRIBLE CRIME.

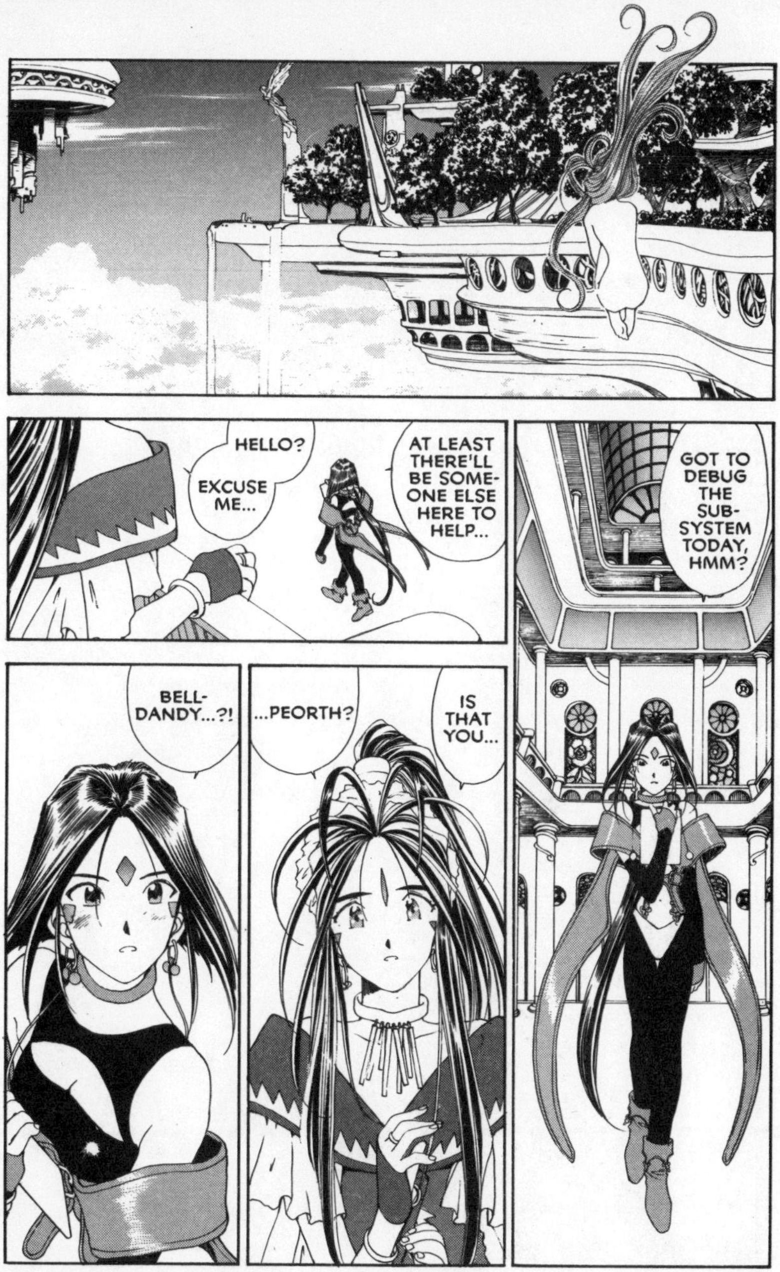
GOT TO DEBUG THE SUB-SYSTEM TODAY, HMM?
AT LEAST THERE'LL BE SOME-ONE ELSE HERE TO HELP...
HELLO?
EXCUSE ME...
IS THAT YOU...
...PEORTH?
BELL-DANDY...?!

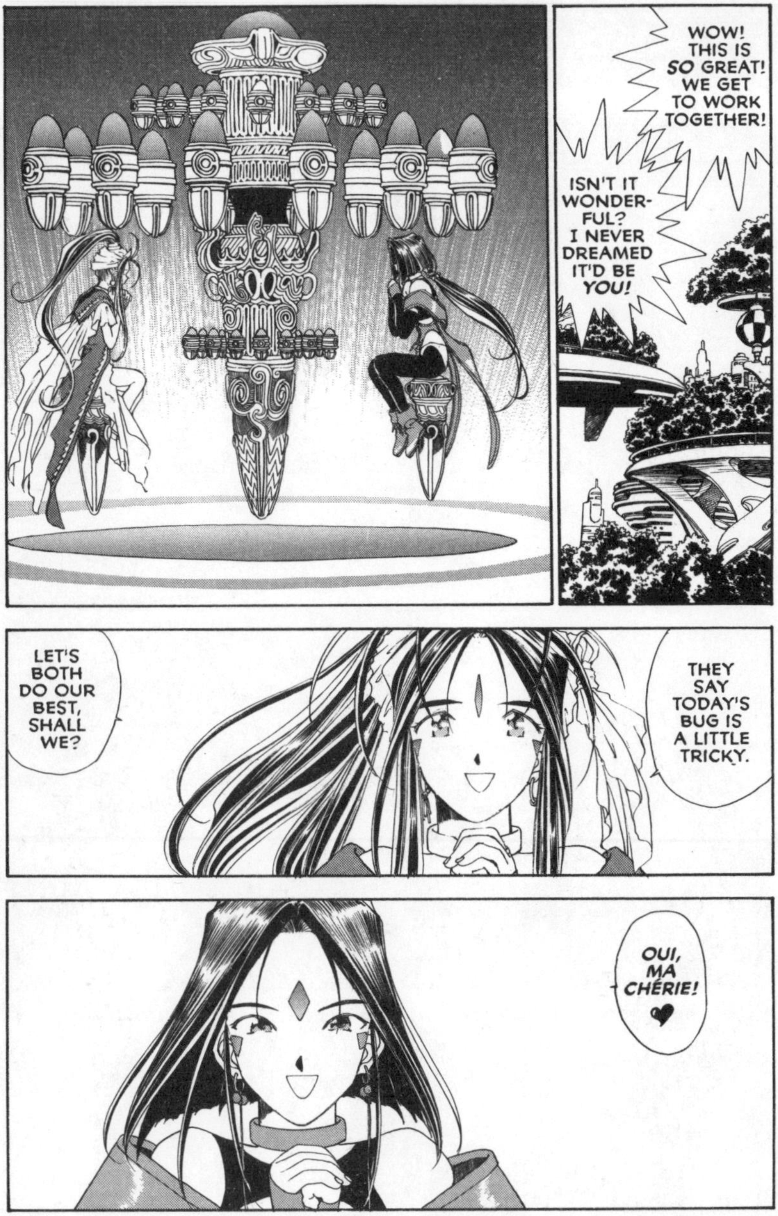
WOW! THIS IS *SO* GREAT! WE GET TO WORK TOGETHER!
ISN'T IT WONDER-FUL? I NEVER DREAMED IT'D BE *YOU!*
THEY SAY TODAY'S BUG IS A LITTLE TRICKY.
LET'S BOTH DO OUR BEST, SHALL WE?
OUI, MA CHÉRIE! ♥

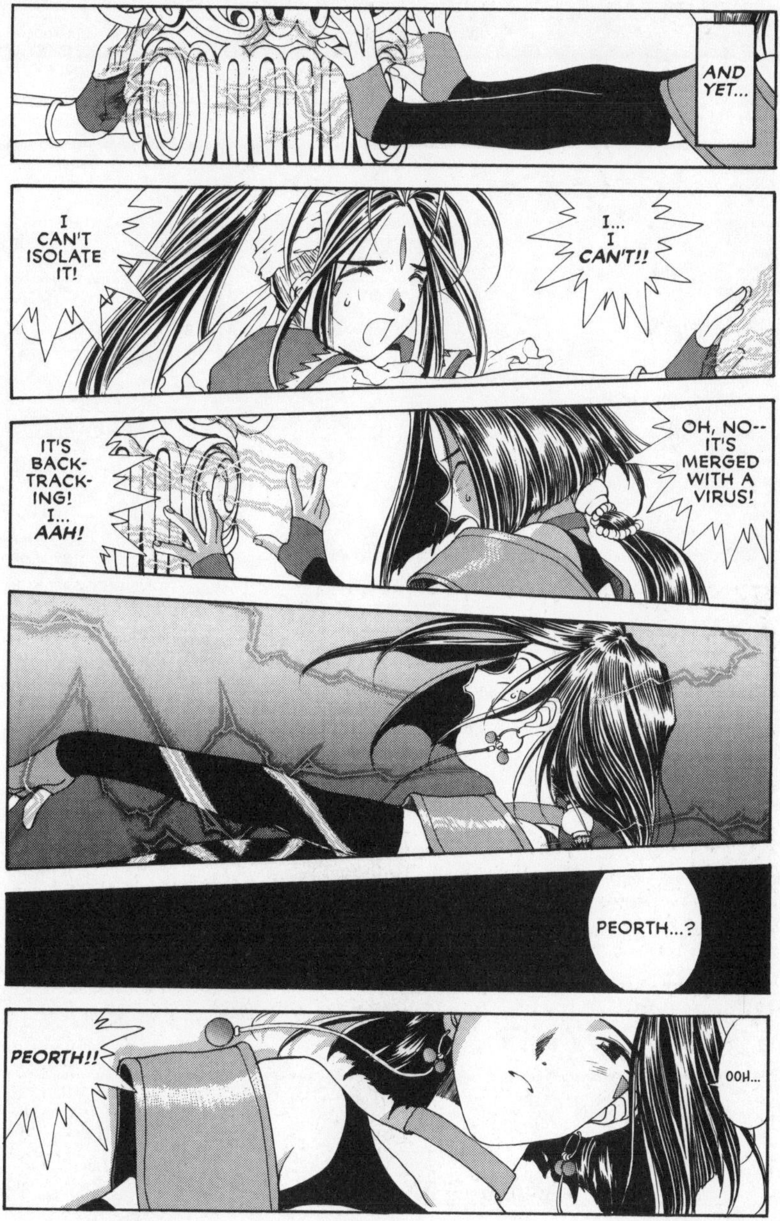
AND YET...
I... I CAN'T!!
I CAN'T ISOLATE IT!
OH, NO-- IT'S MERGED WITH A VIRUS!
IT'S BACK-TRACKING! I... AAH!
PEORTH...?
OOH...
PEORTH!!

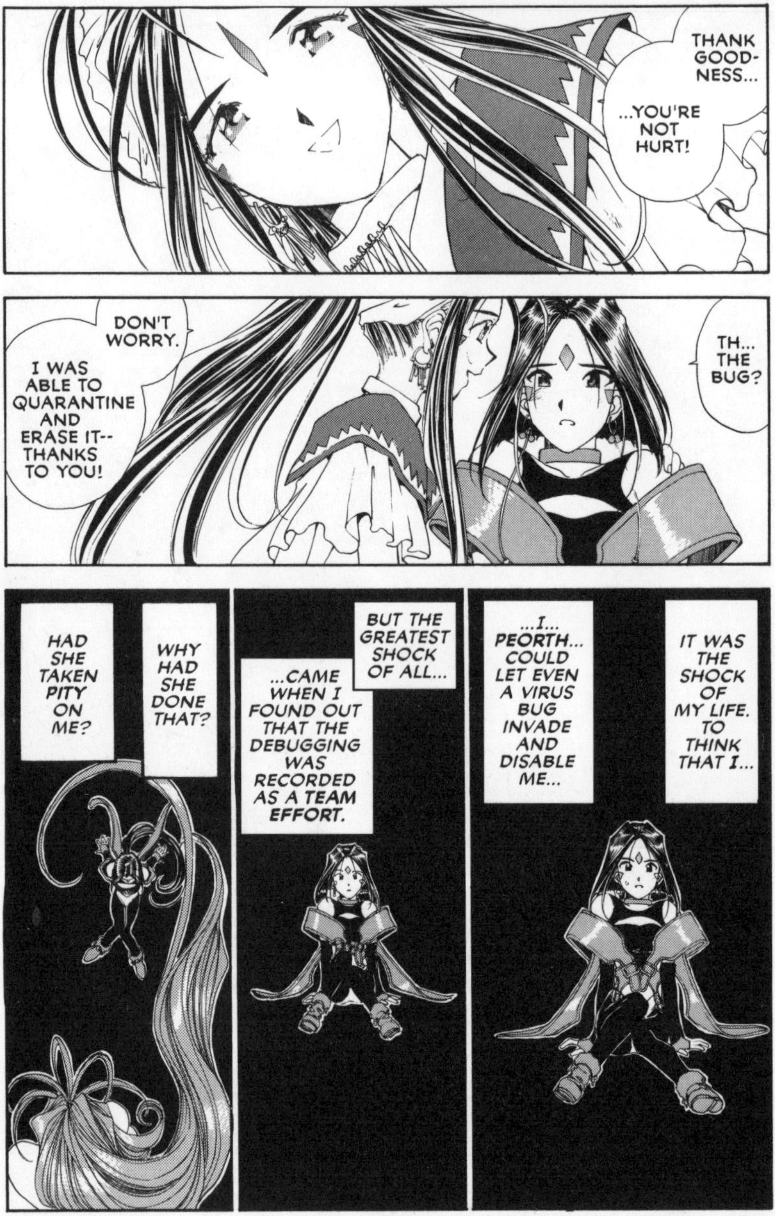
THANK GOODNESS...
...YOU'RE NOT HURT!
TH... THE BUG?
DON'T WORRY.
I WAS ABLE TO QUARANTINE AND ERASE IT--THANKS TO YOU!
IT WAS THE SHOCK OF MY LIFE. TO THINK THAT I...
...I... PEORTH... COULD LET EVEN A VIRUS BUG INVADE AND DISABLE ME...
BUT THE GREATEST SHOCK OF ALL...
...CAME WHEN I FOUND OUT THAT THE DEBUGGING WAS RECORDED AS A TEAM EFFORT.
WHY HAD SHE DONE THAT?
HAD SHE TAKEN PITY ON ME?

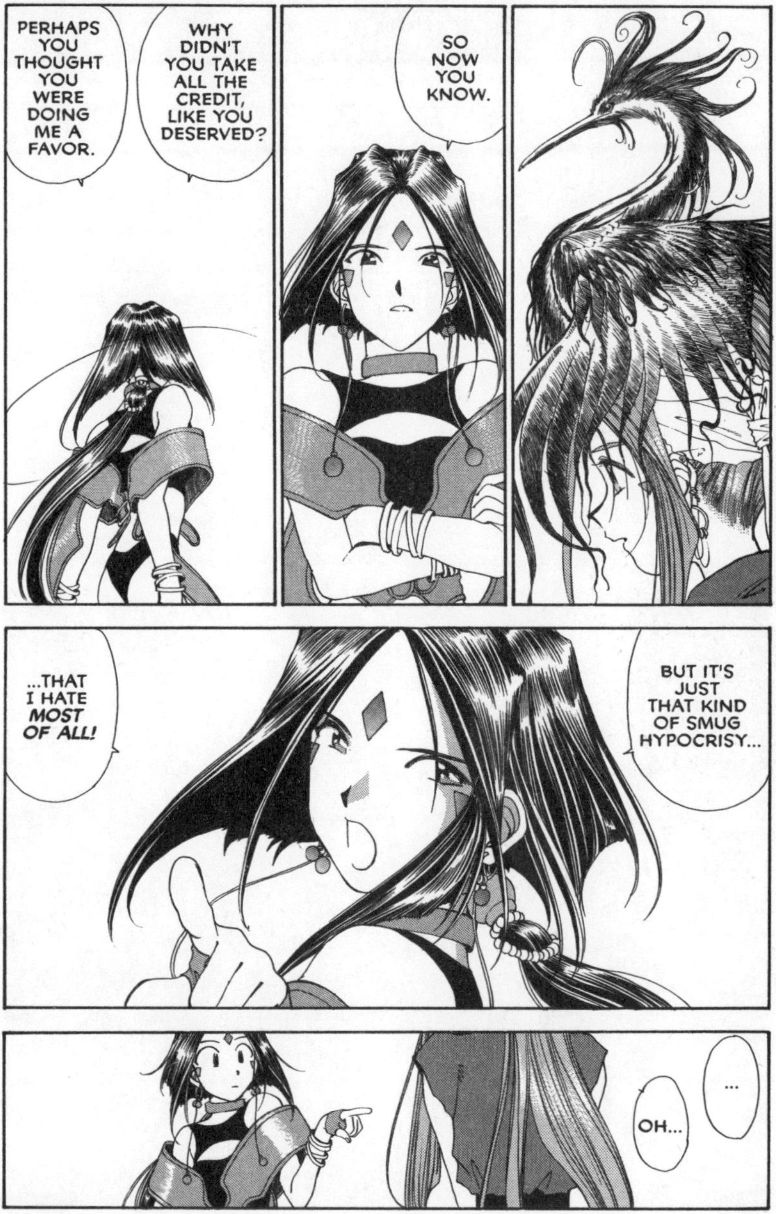
SO NOW YOU KNOW.
WHY DIDN'T YOU TAKE ALL THE CREDIT, LIKE YOU DESERVED?
PERHAPS YOU THOUGHT YOU WERE DOING ME A FAVOR.
BUT IT'S JUST THAT KIND OF SMUG HYPOCRISY...
...THAT I HATE *MOST OF ALL!*
...
OH...

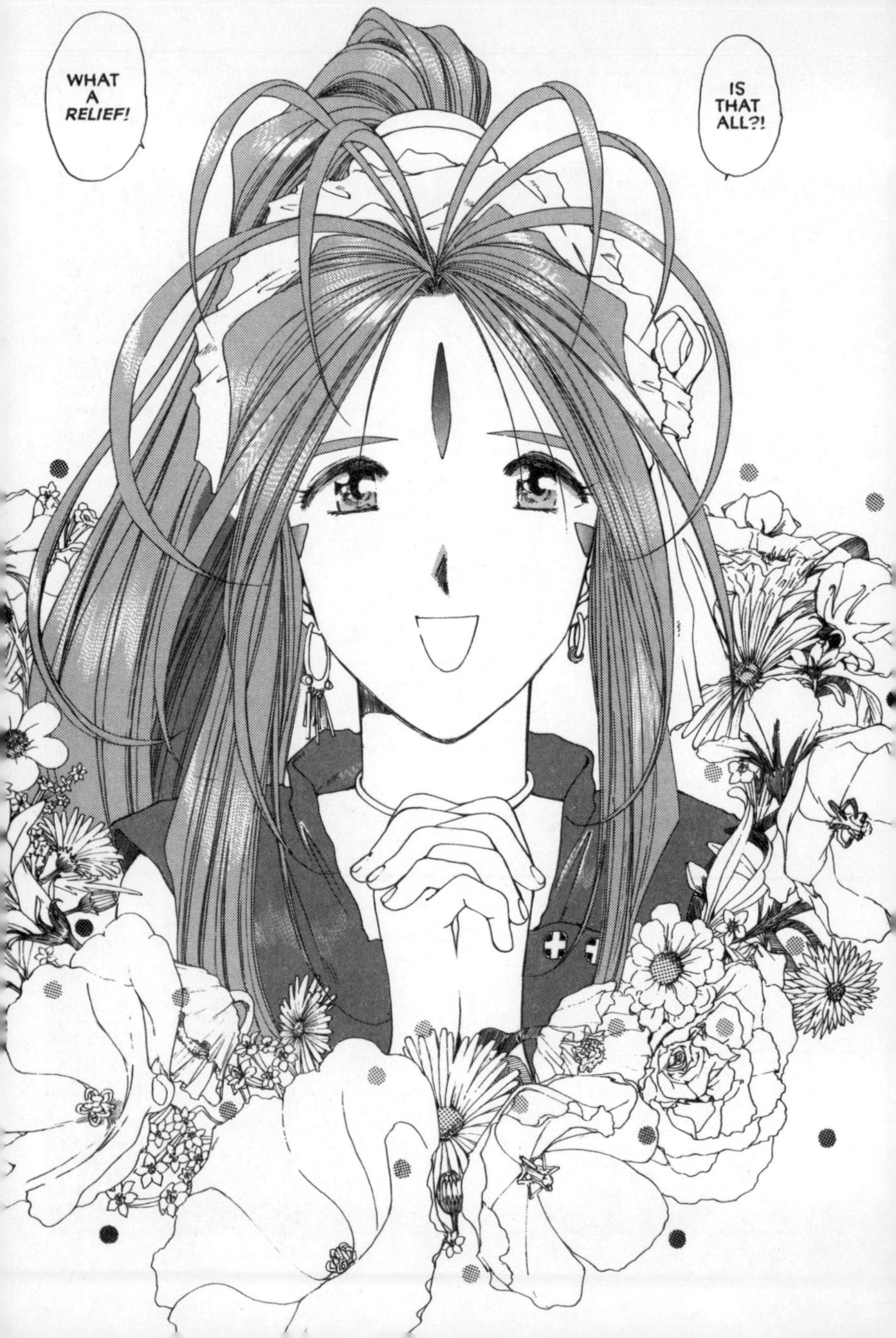
IS THAT ALL?!
WHAT A *RELIEF!*

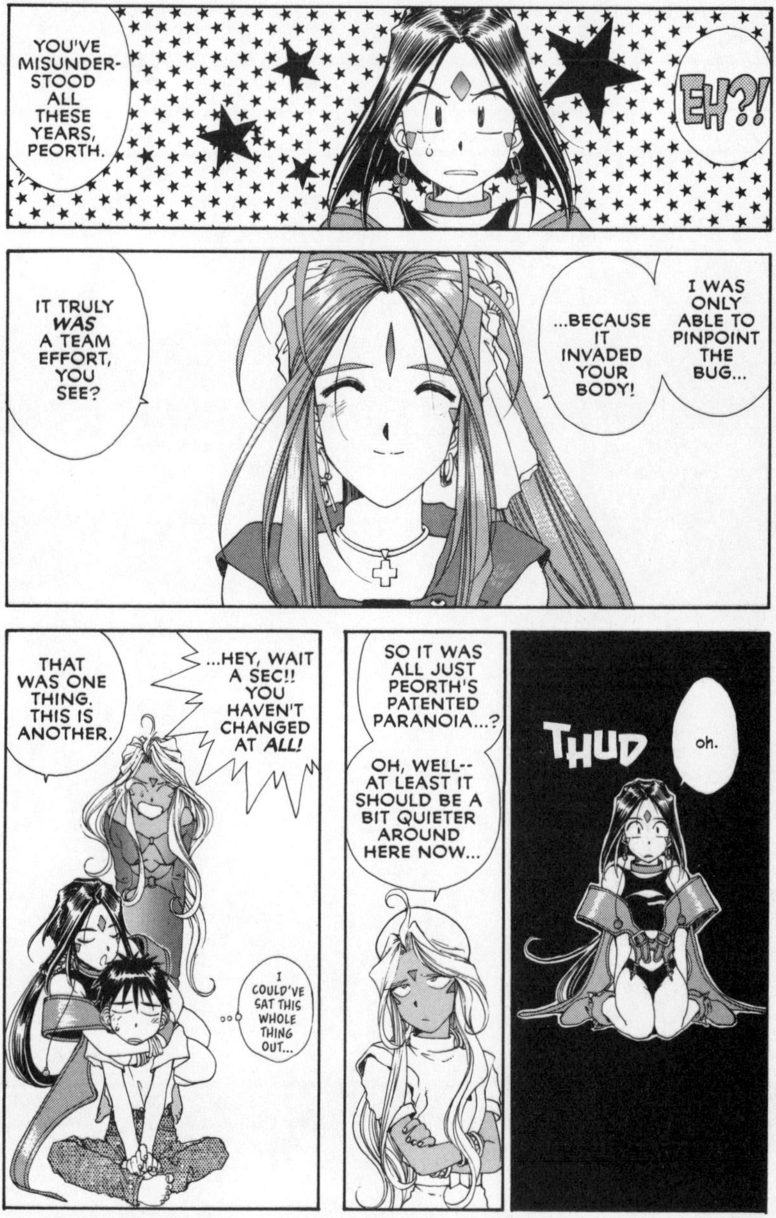
EH?!
YOU'VE MISUNDERSTOOD ALL THESE YEARS, PEORTH.
I WAS ONLY ABLE TO PINPOINT THE BUG...
...BECAUSE IT INVADED YOUR BODY!
IT TRULY WAS A TEAM EFFORT, YOU SEE?
THUD
oh.
SO IT WAS ALL JUST PEORTH'S PATENTED PARANOIA...?
OH, WELL-- AT LEAST IT SHOULD BE A BIT QUIETER AROUND HERE NOW...
...HEY, WAIT A SEC!! YOU HAVEN'T CHANGED AT ALL!
THAT WAS ONE THING. THIS IS ANOTHER.
I COULD'VE SAT THIS WHOLE THING OUT...

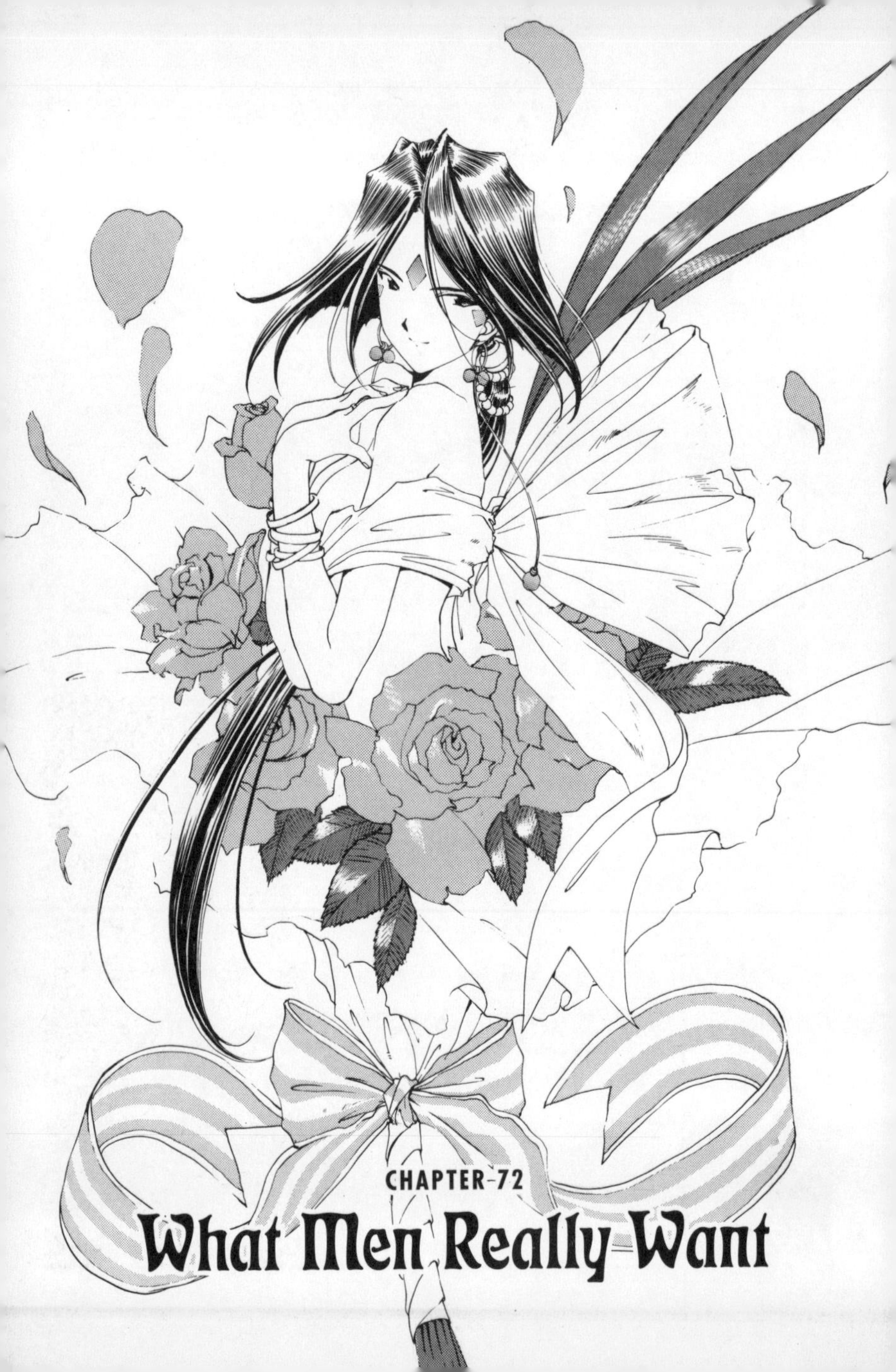

CHAPTER-72

What Men Really Want

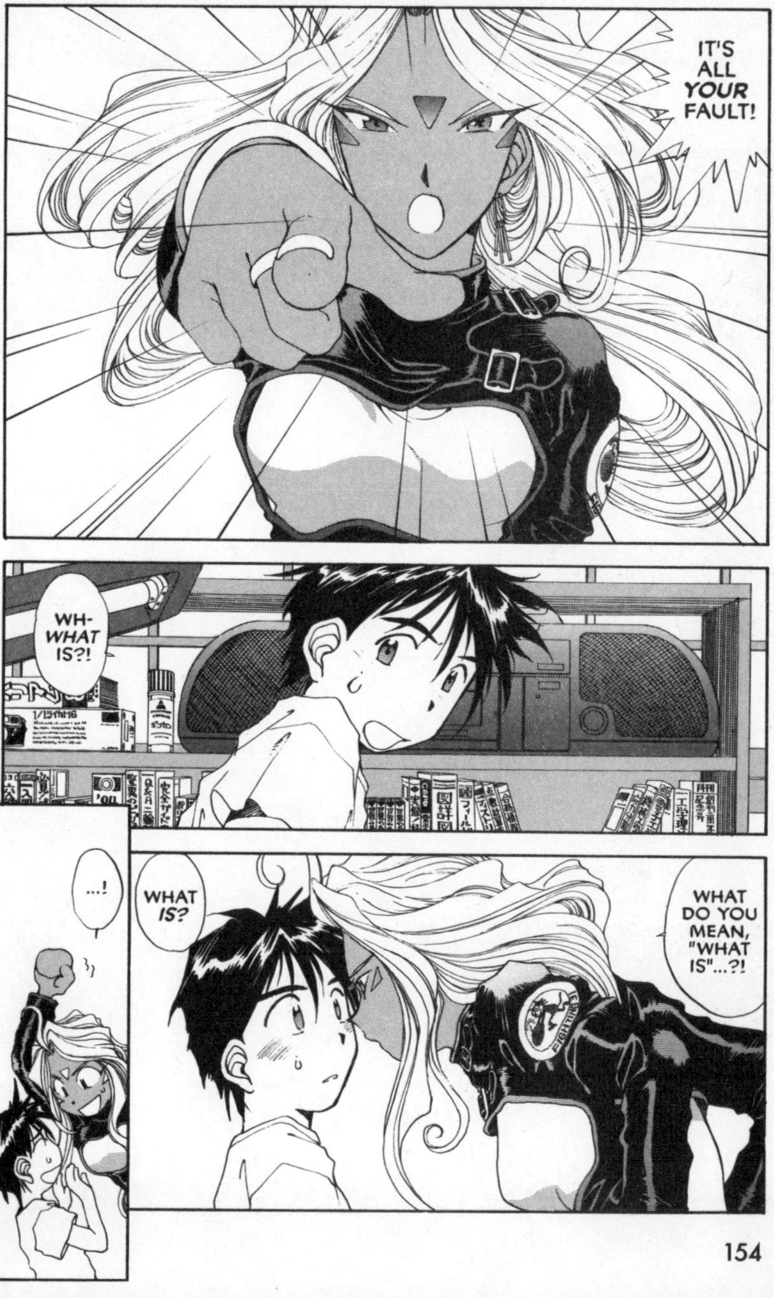
IT'S ALL *YOUR* FAULT!
WH- *WHAT* IS?!
WHAT DO YOU MEAN, "WHAT IS"...?!
WHAT *IS*?
...!

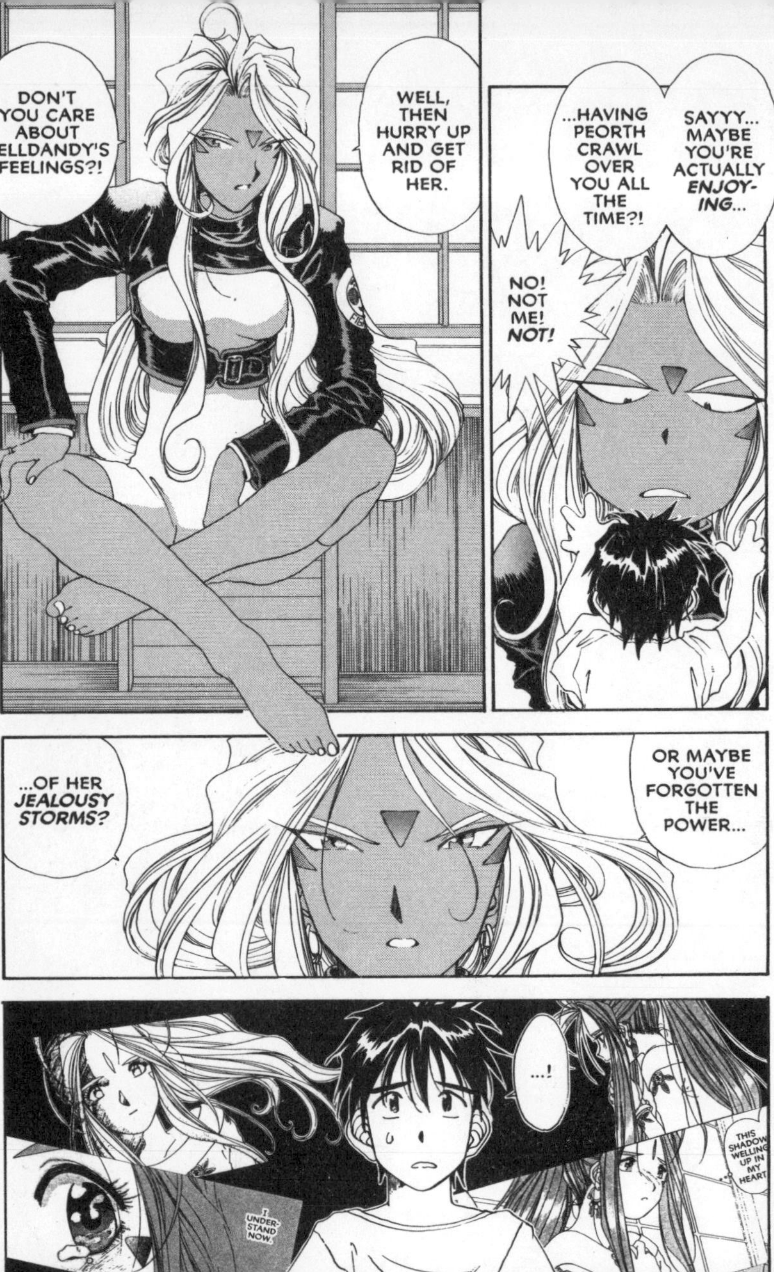
SAYYY... MAYBE YOU'RE ACTUALLY *ENJOYING*...
...HAVING PEORTH CRAWL OVER YOU ALL THE TIME?!
NO! NOT ME! ***NOT!***
WELL, THEN HURRY UP AND GET RID OF HER.
DON'T YOU CARE ABOUT BELLDANDY'S FEELINGS?!
OR MAYBE YOU'VE FORGOTTEN THE POWER...
...OF HER *JEALOUSY STORMS?*
...!
THIS SHADOW WELLING UP IN MY HEART
I UNDERSTAND NOW.

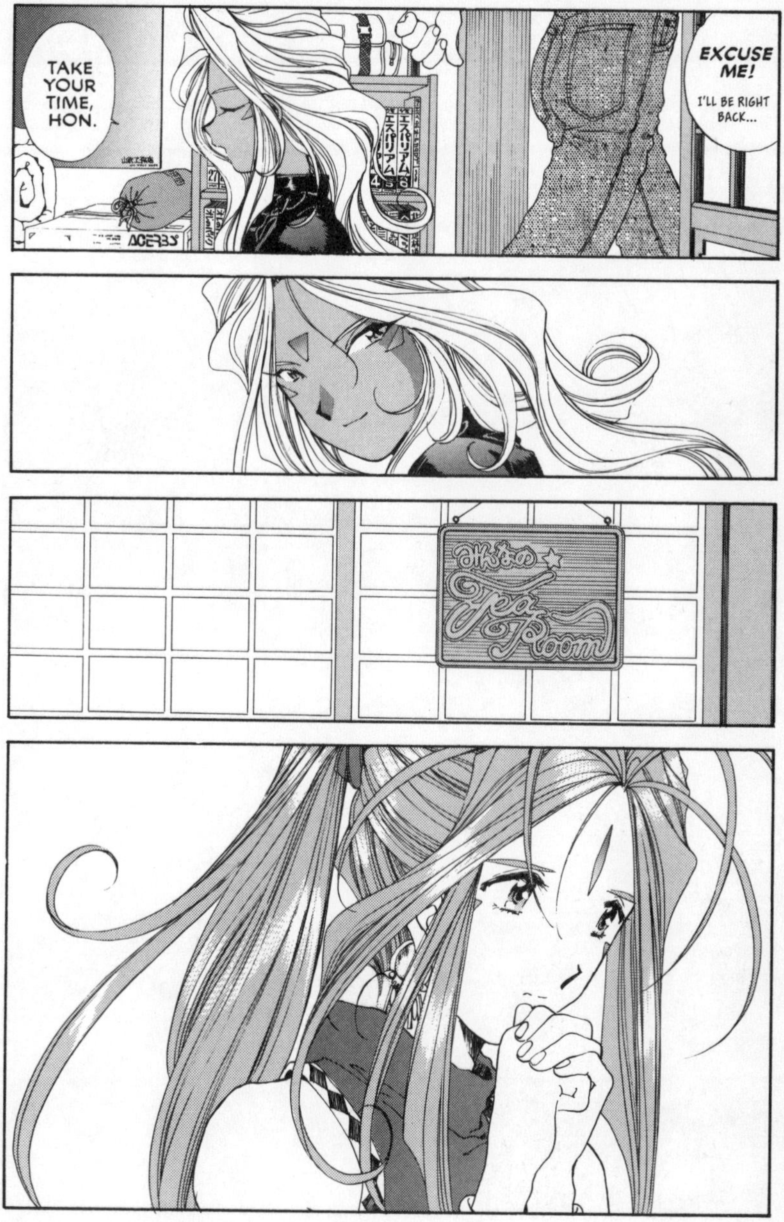
EXCUSE ME! I'LL BE RIGHT BACK...
TAKE YOUR TIME, HON.
Tea Room

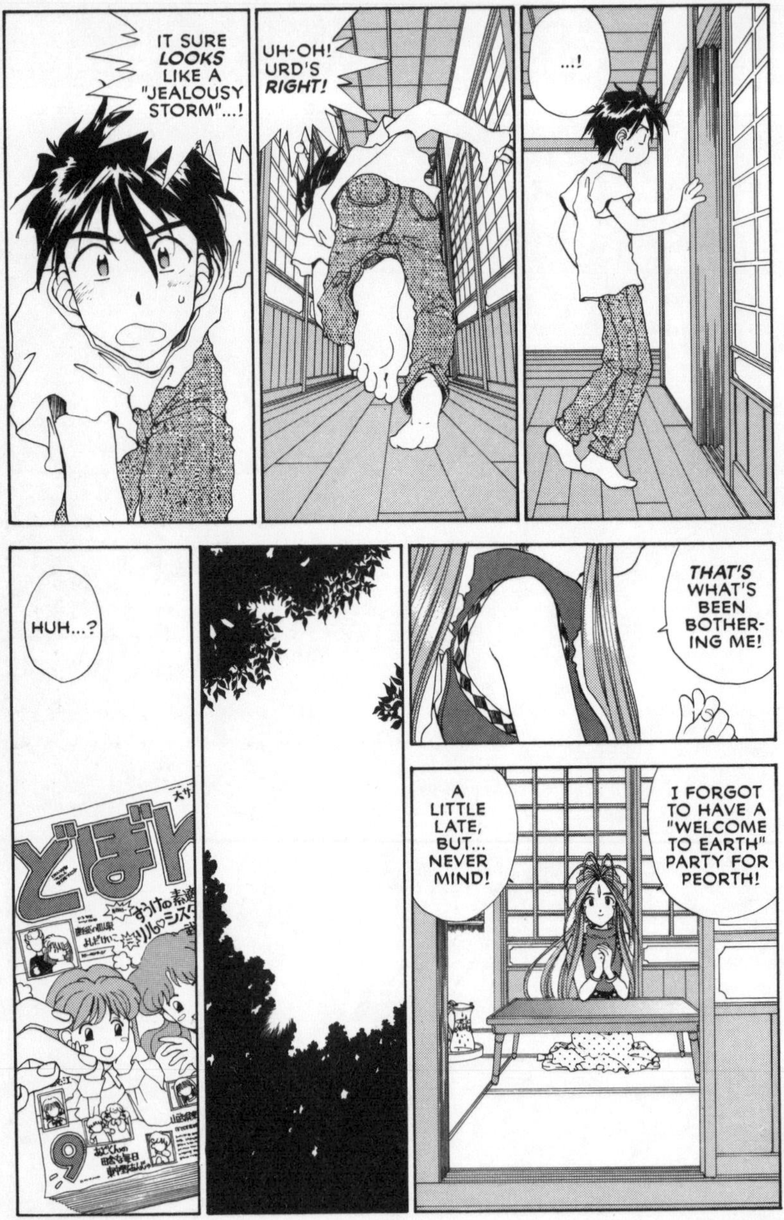
...!
UH-OH! URD'S *RIGHT!*
IT SURE *LOOKS* LIKE A "JEALOUSY STORM"...!
THAT'S WHAT'S BEEN BOTHER-ING ME!
I FORGOT TO HAVE A "WELCOME TO EARTH" PARTY FOR PEORTH!
A LITTLE LATE, BUT... NEVER MIND!
HUH...?

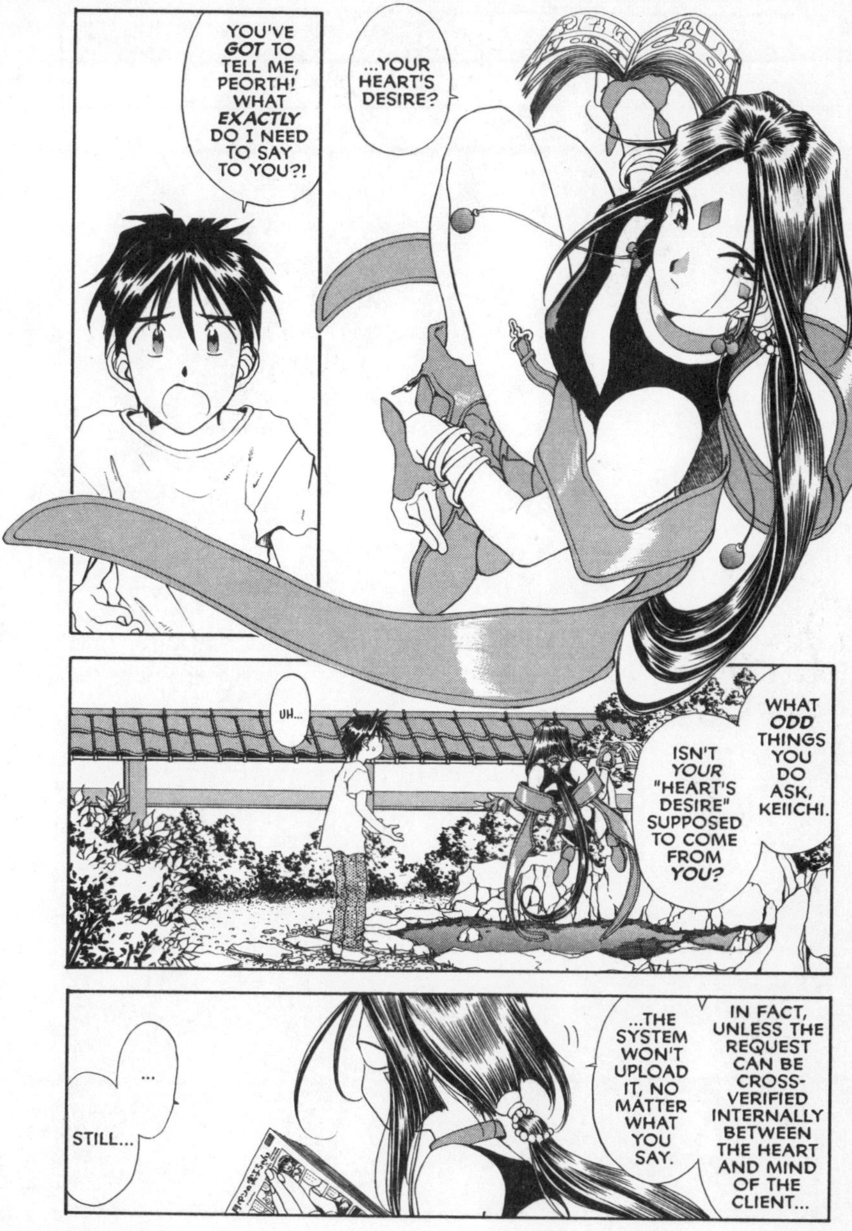
...YOUR HEART'S DESIRE?
YOU'VE GOT TO TELL ME, PEORTH! WHAT EXACTLY DO I NEED TO SAY TO YOU?!
WHAT ODD THINGS YOU DO ASK, KEIICHI.
ISN'T YOUR "HEART'S DESIRE" SUPPOSED TO COME FROM YOU?
UH...
IN FACT, UNLESS THE REQUEST CAN BE CROSS-VERIFIED INTERNALLY BETWEEN THE HEART AND MIND OF THE CLIENT...
...THE SYSTEM WON'T UPLOAD IT, NO MATTER WHAT YOU SAY.
...
STILL...

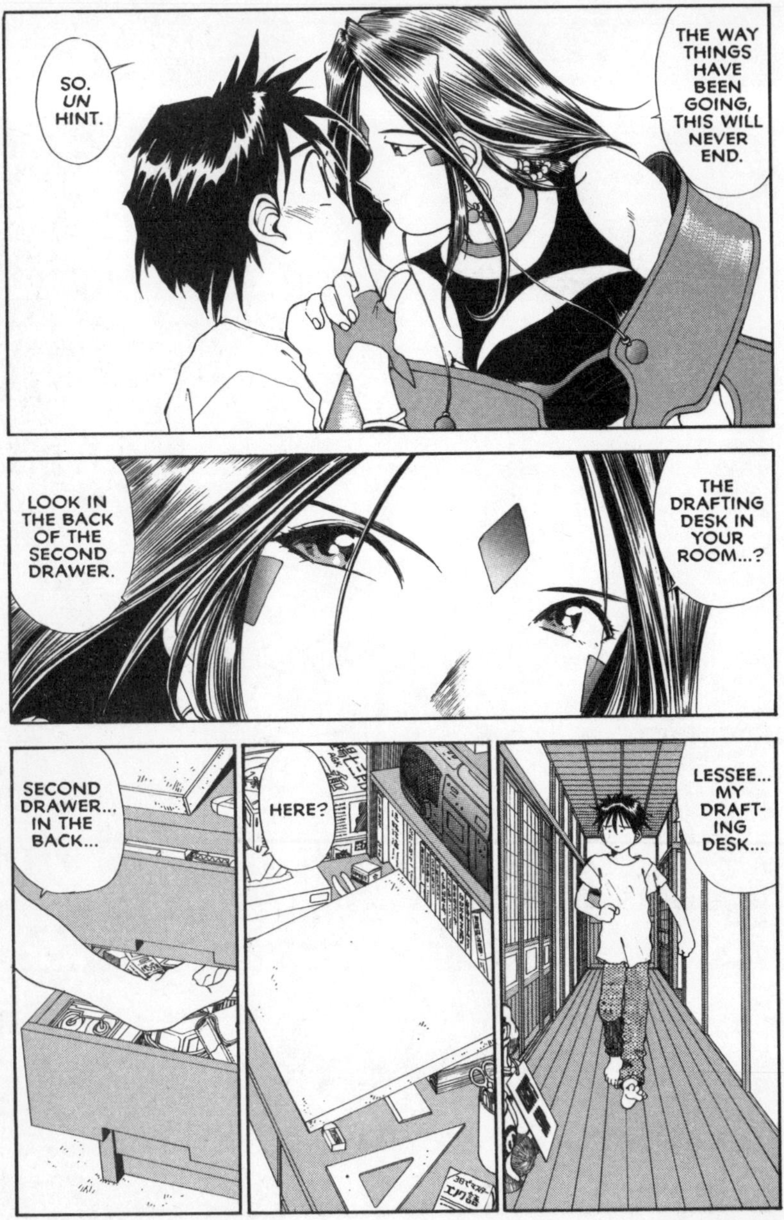
THE WAY THINGS HAVE BEEN GOING, THIS WILL NEVER END.
SO. *UN* HINT.
THE DRAFTING DESK IN YOUR ROOM...?
LOOK IN THE BACK OF THE SECOND DRAWER.
LESSEE... MY DRAFT-ING DESK...
HERE?
SECOND DRAWER... IN THE BACK...

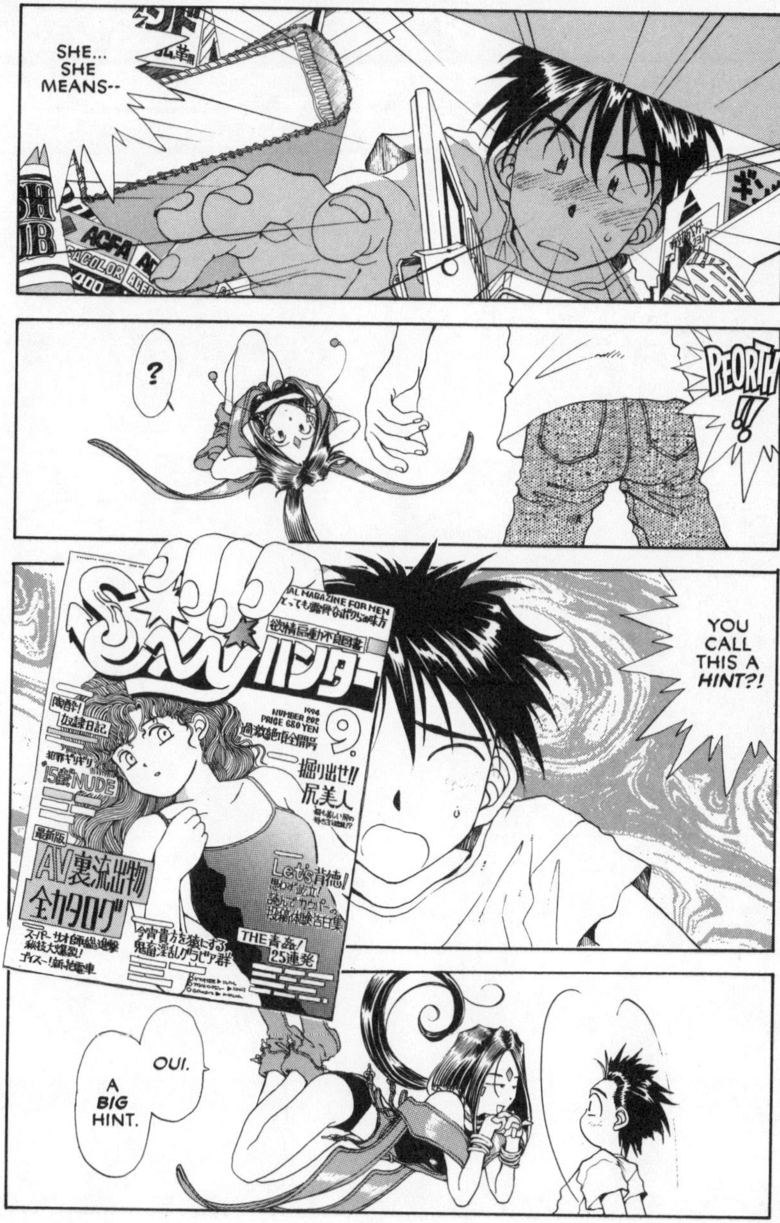

SHE... SHE MEANS--
PEORTH!!
?
YOU CALL THIS A HINT?!
MAGAZINE FOR MEN
ハンター
1994
NUMBER 202
PRICE 680 YEN
9.
掘り出せ!!
尻美人
'15歳'NUDE
最新版
AV裏流出物
全カタログ
Let's背徳!
THE青姦!
25連発
OUI.
A BIG HINT.

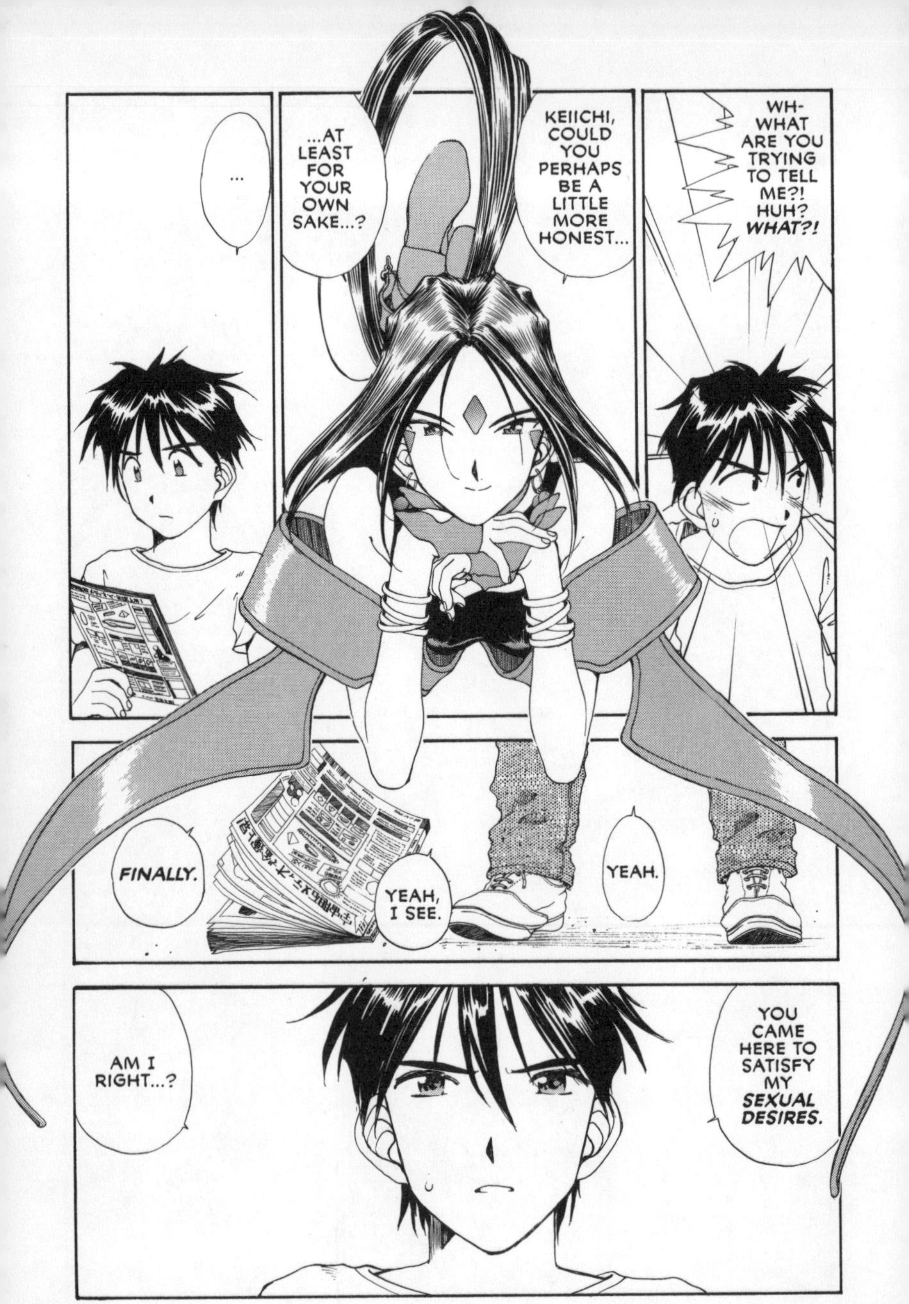
WH- WHAT ARE YOU TRYING TO TELL ME?! HUH? *WHAT?!*
KEIICHI, COULD YOU PERHAPS BE A LITTLE MORE HONEST...
...AT LEAST FOR YOUR OWN SAKE...?
...
YEAH.
YEAH, I SEE.
FINALLY.
YOU CAME HERE TO SATISFY MY *SEXUAL DESIRES.*
AM I RIGHT...?

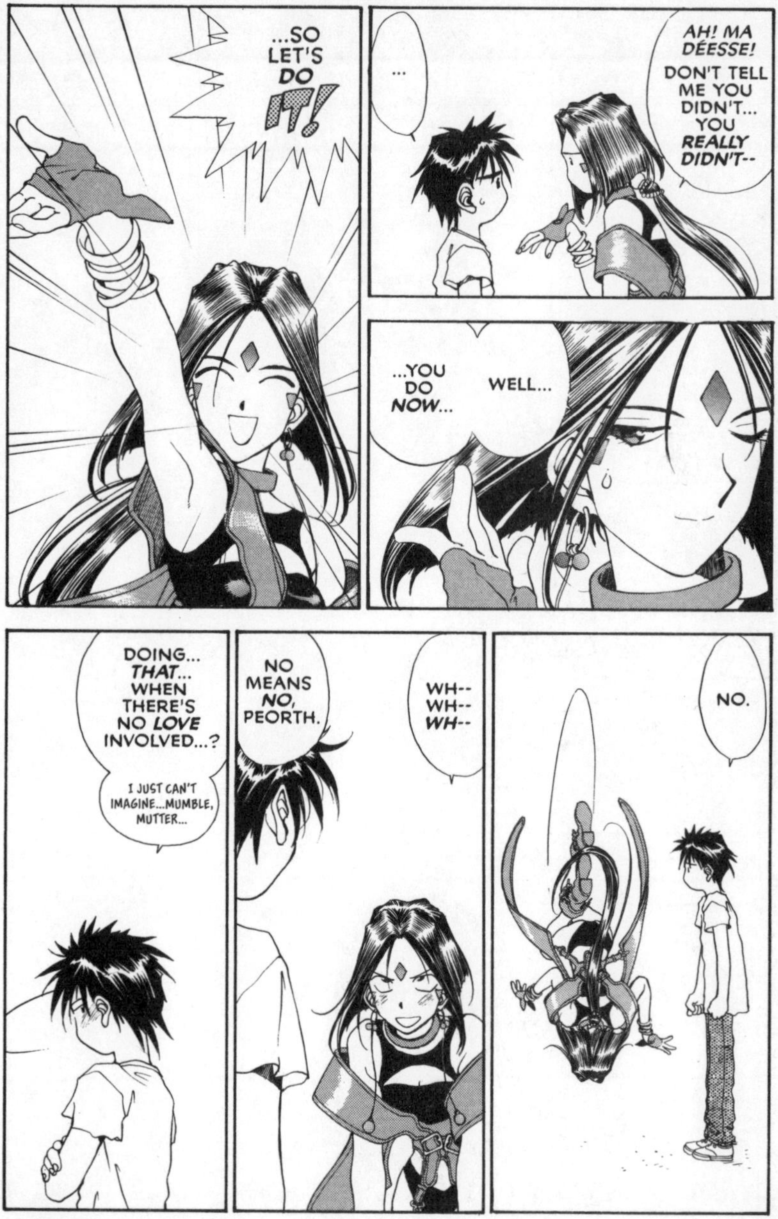
AH! MA DÉESSE! DON'T TELL ME YOU DIDN'T... YOU REALLY DIDN'T--
...
WELL...
...YOU DO NOW...
...SO LET'S DO IT!
NO.
WH-- WH-- WH--
NO MEANS NO, PEORTH.
DOING... THAT... WHEN THERE'S NO LOVE INVOLVED...?
I JUST CAN'T IMAGINE...MUMBLE, MUTTER...

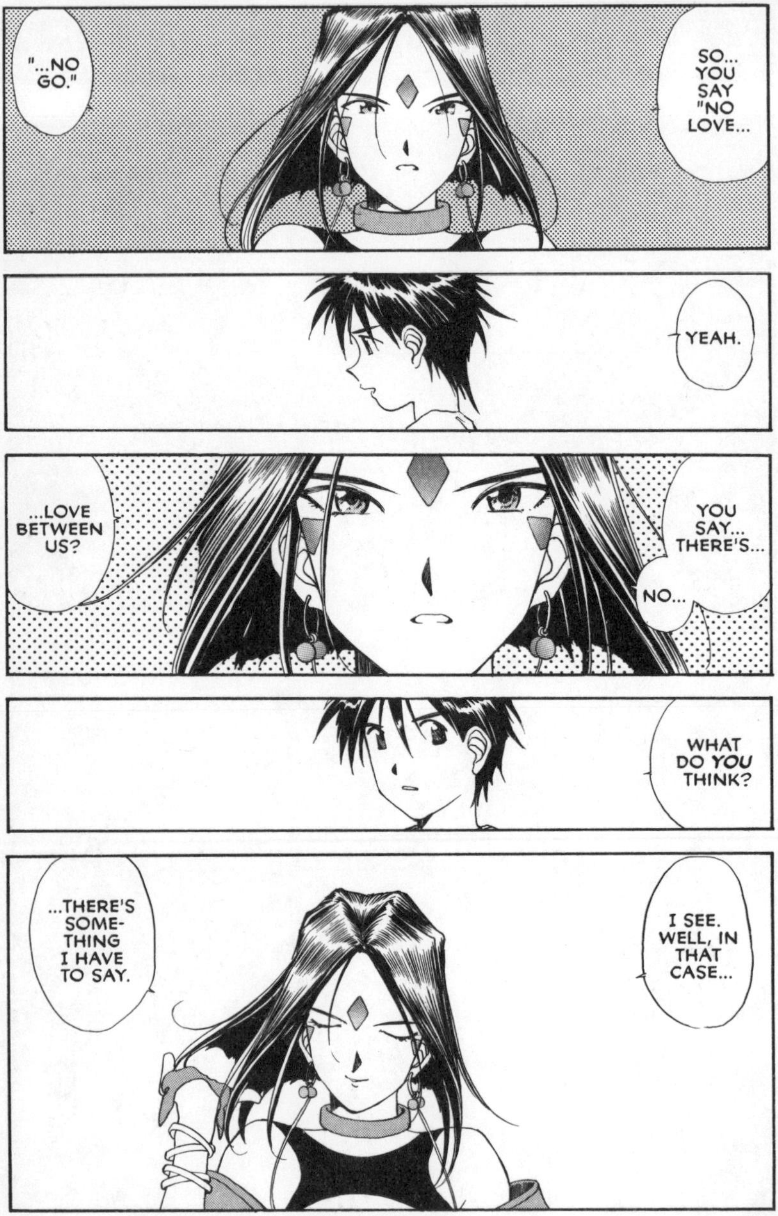
SO... YOU SAY "NO LOVE...
"...NO GO."
YEAH.
YOU SAY... THERE'S...
NO...
...LOVE BETWEEN US?
WHAT DO *YOU* THINK?
I SEE. WELL, IN THAT CASE...
...THERE'S SOME- THING I HAVE TO SAY.

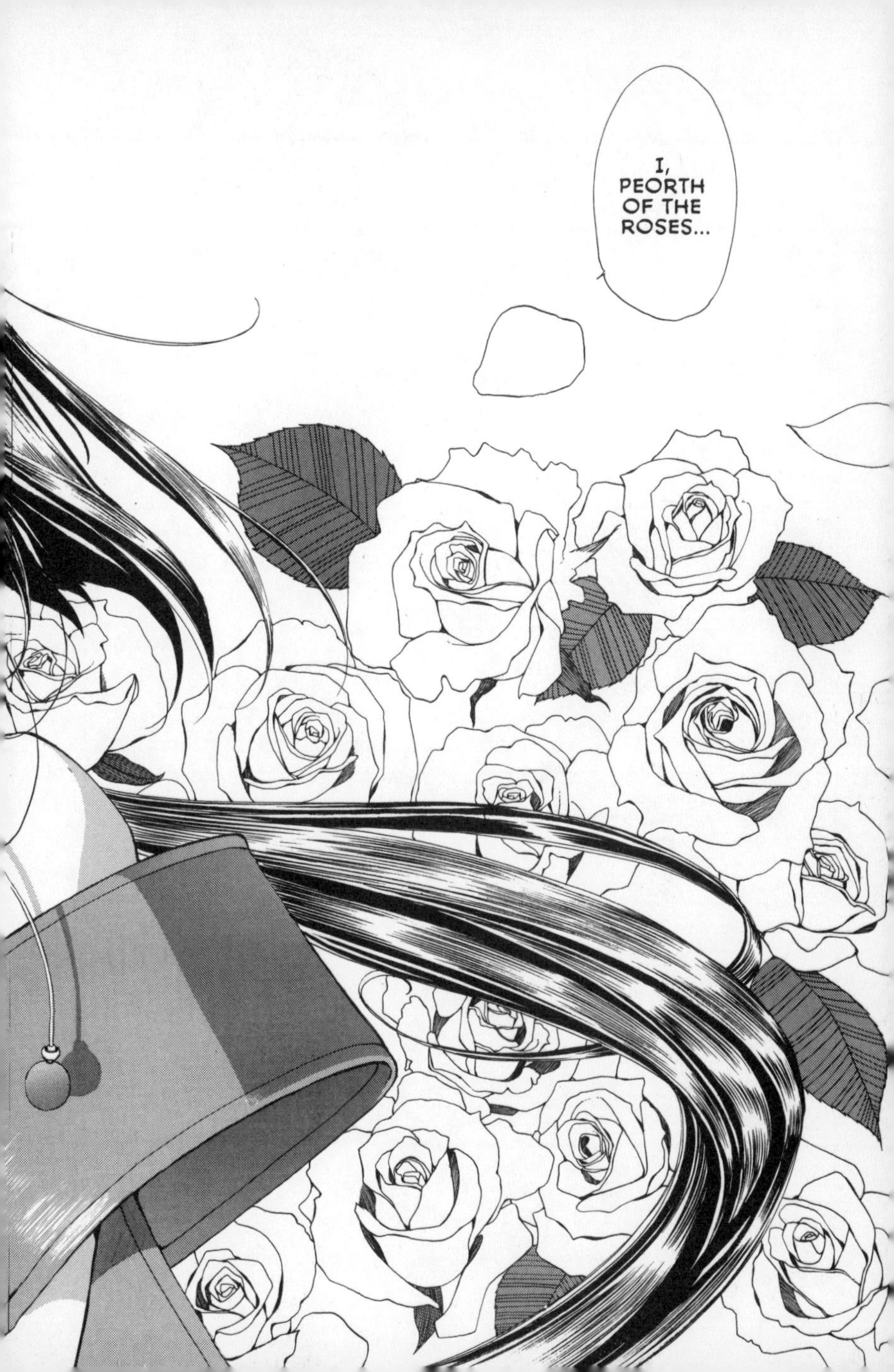
I, PEORTH OF THE ROSES...

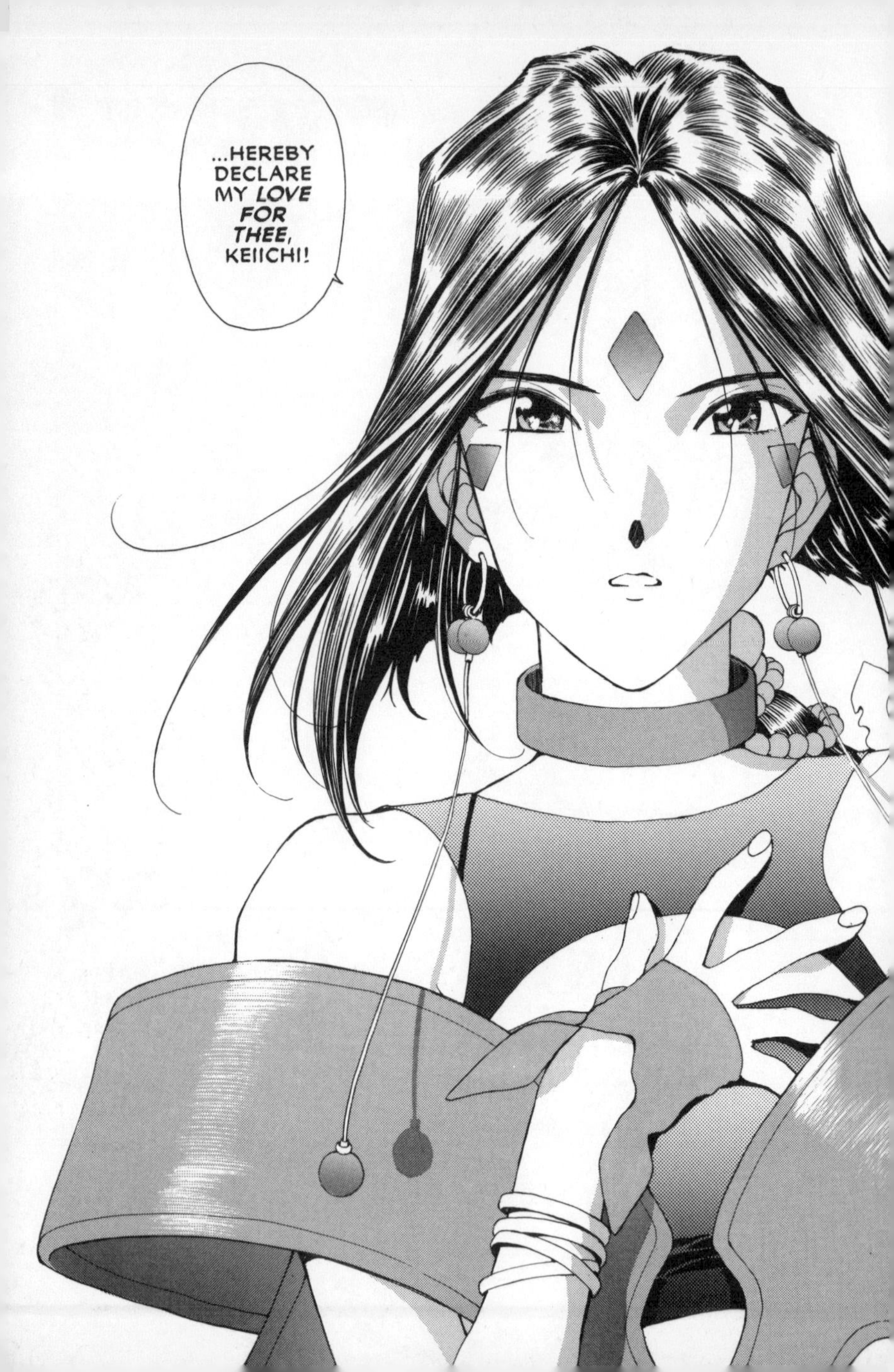
...HEREBY DECLARE MY *LOVE FOR THEE,* KEIICHI!

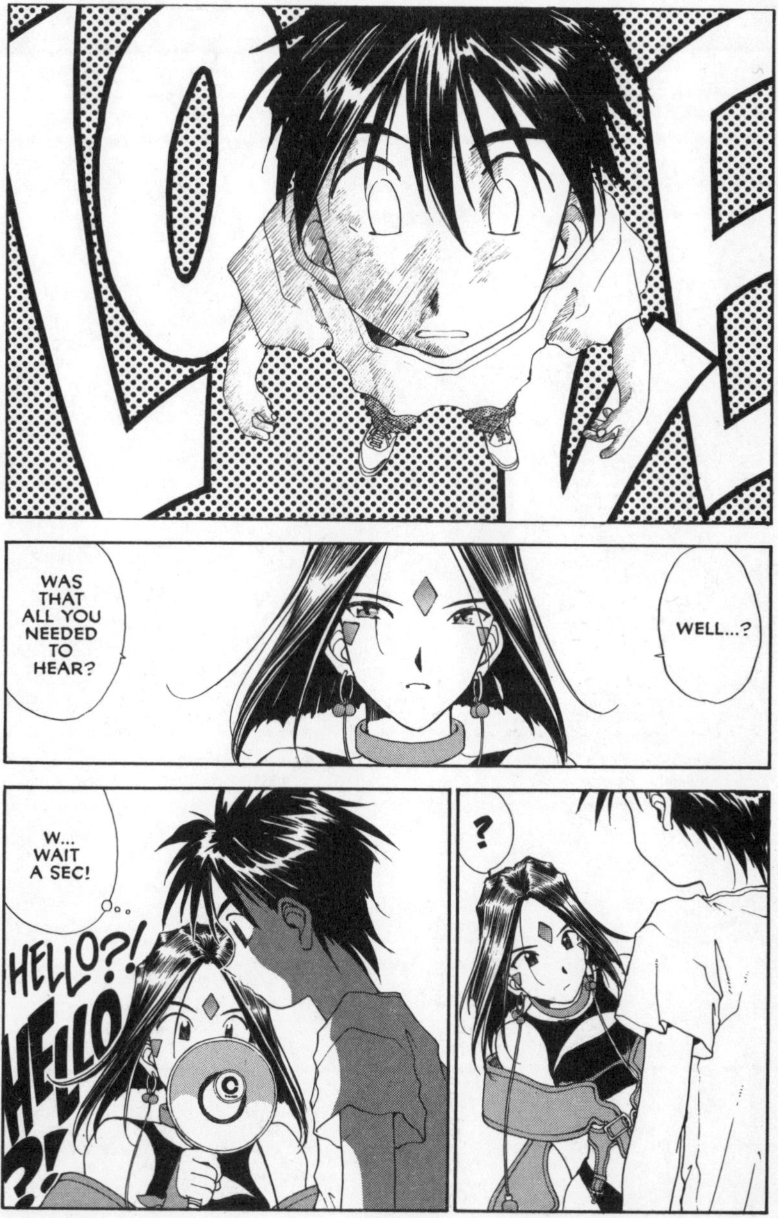
WELL...?
WAS THAT ALL YOU NEEDED TO HEAR?
?
W... WAIT A SEC!
HELLO?!
HELLO?!

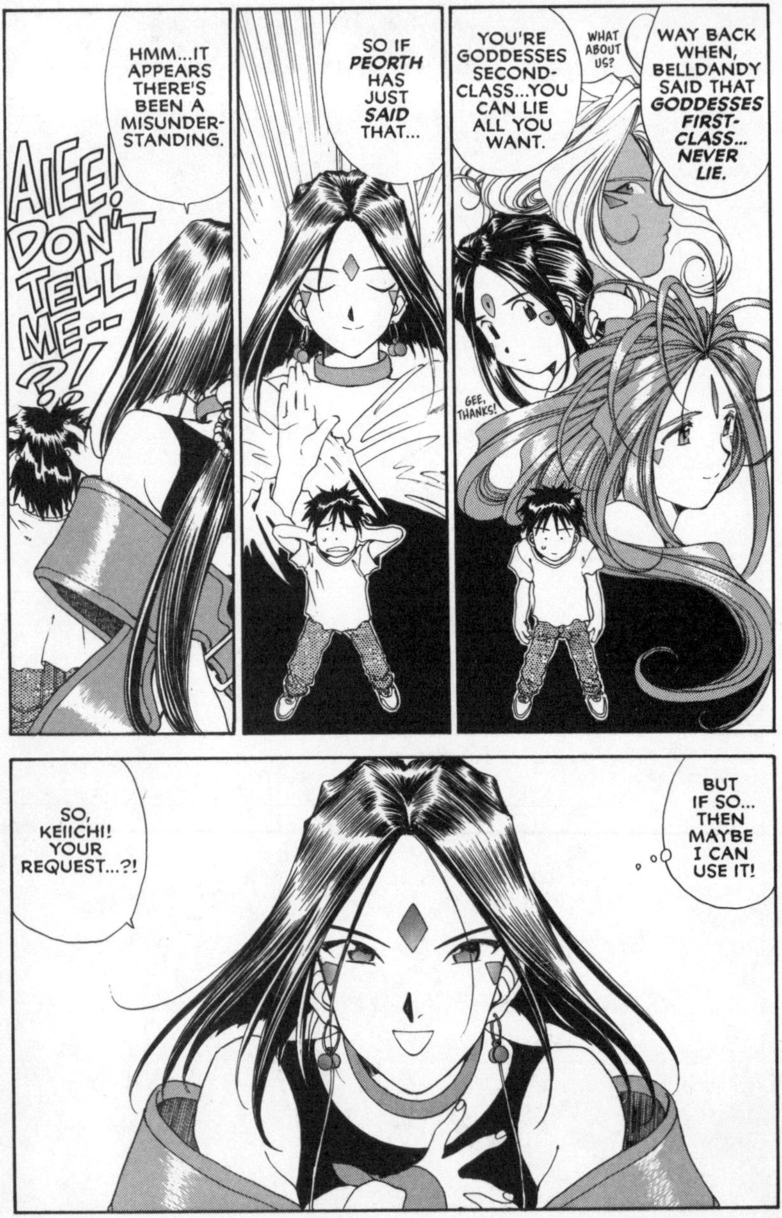
WAY BACK WHEN, BELLDANDY SAID THAT *GODDESSES FIRST-CLASS... NEVER LIE.*
WHAT ABOUT US?
YOU'RE GODDESSES SECOND-CLASS...YOU CAN LIE ALL YOU WANT.
GEE, THANKS!
SO IF *PEORTH* HAS JUST *SAID* THAT...
HMM...IT APPEARS THERE'S BEEN A MISUNDERSTANDING.
AIEEE! DON'T TELL ME..?!
BUT IF SO... THEN MAYBE I CAN USE IT!
SO, KEIICHI! YOUR REQUEST...?!

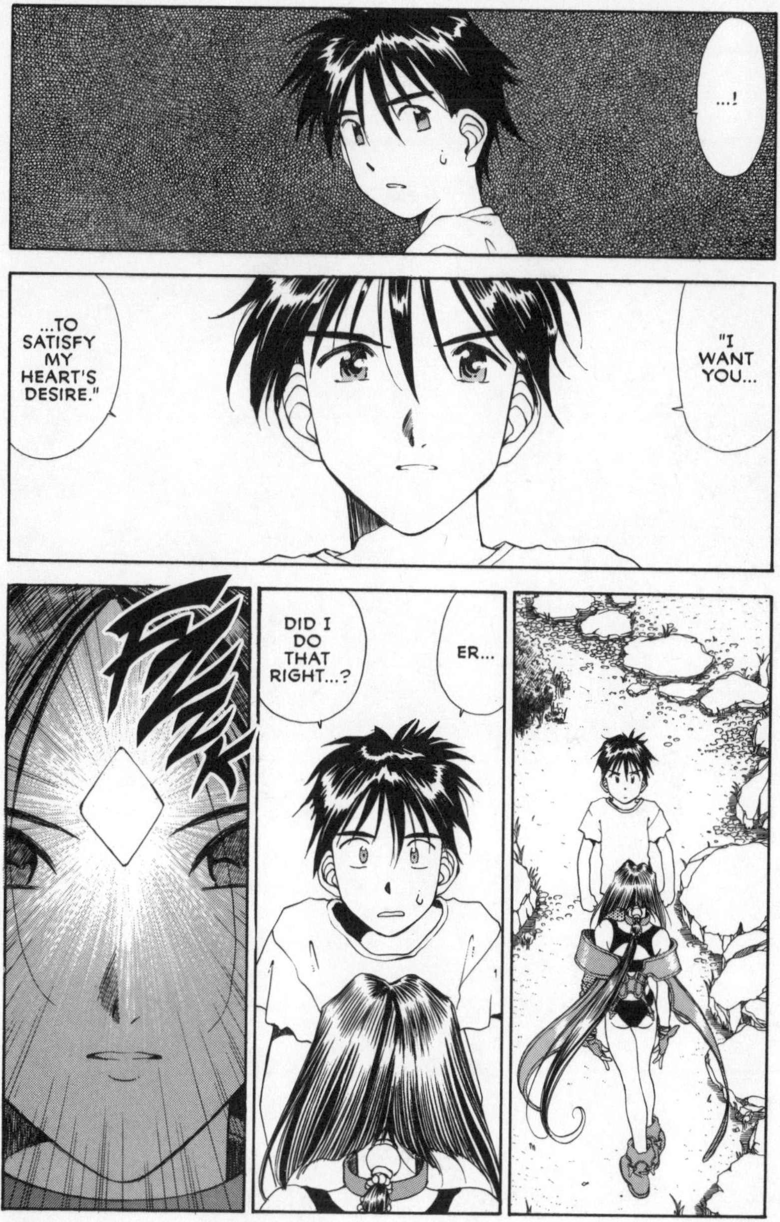
...!
"I WANT YOU...
...TO SATISFY MY HEART'S DESIRE."
ER...
DID I DO THAT RIGHT...?

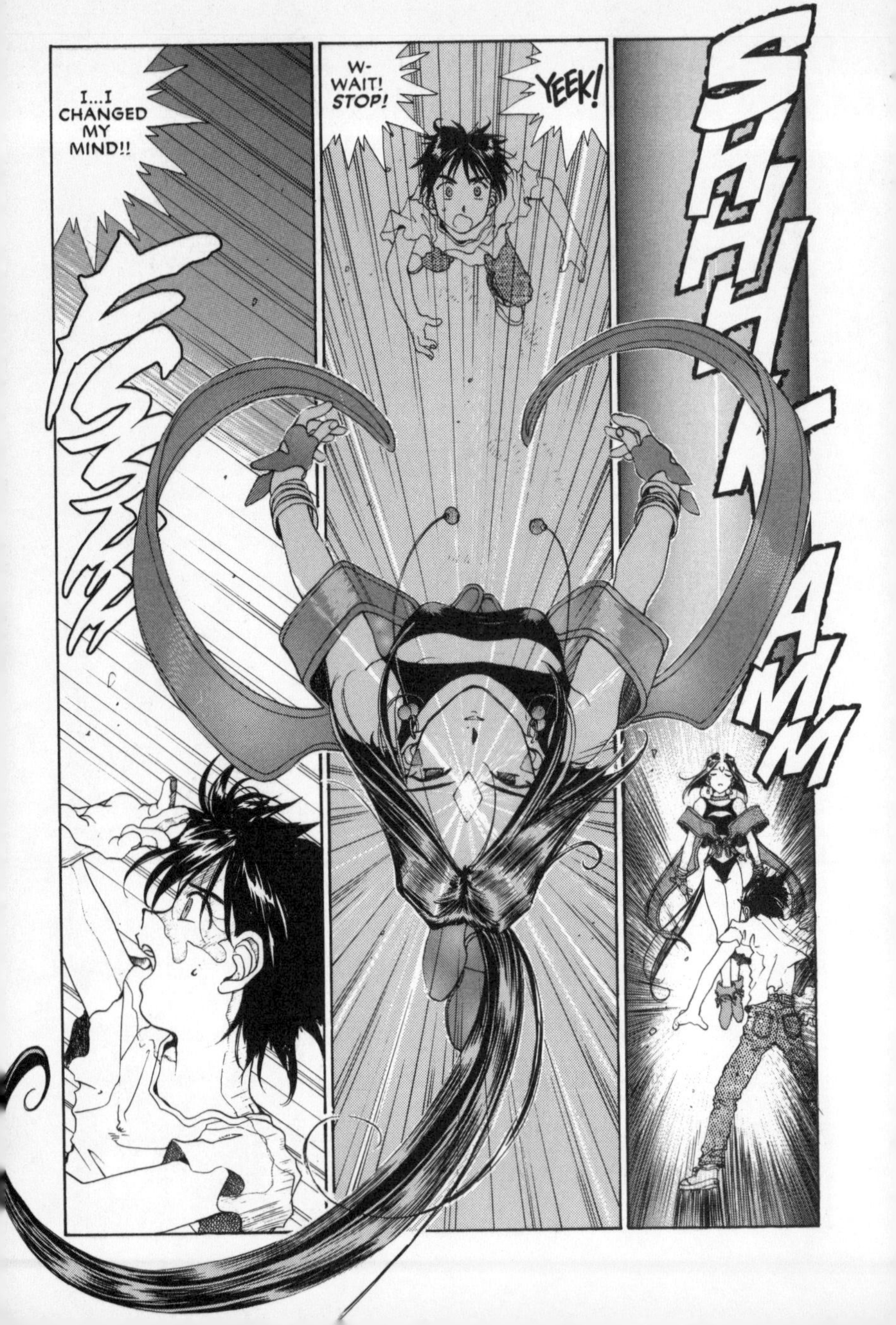

SHHHAMM
YEEK!
W-WAIT! STOP!
I...I CHANGED MY MIND!!

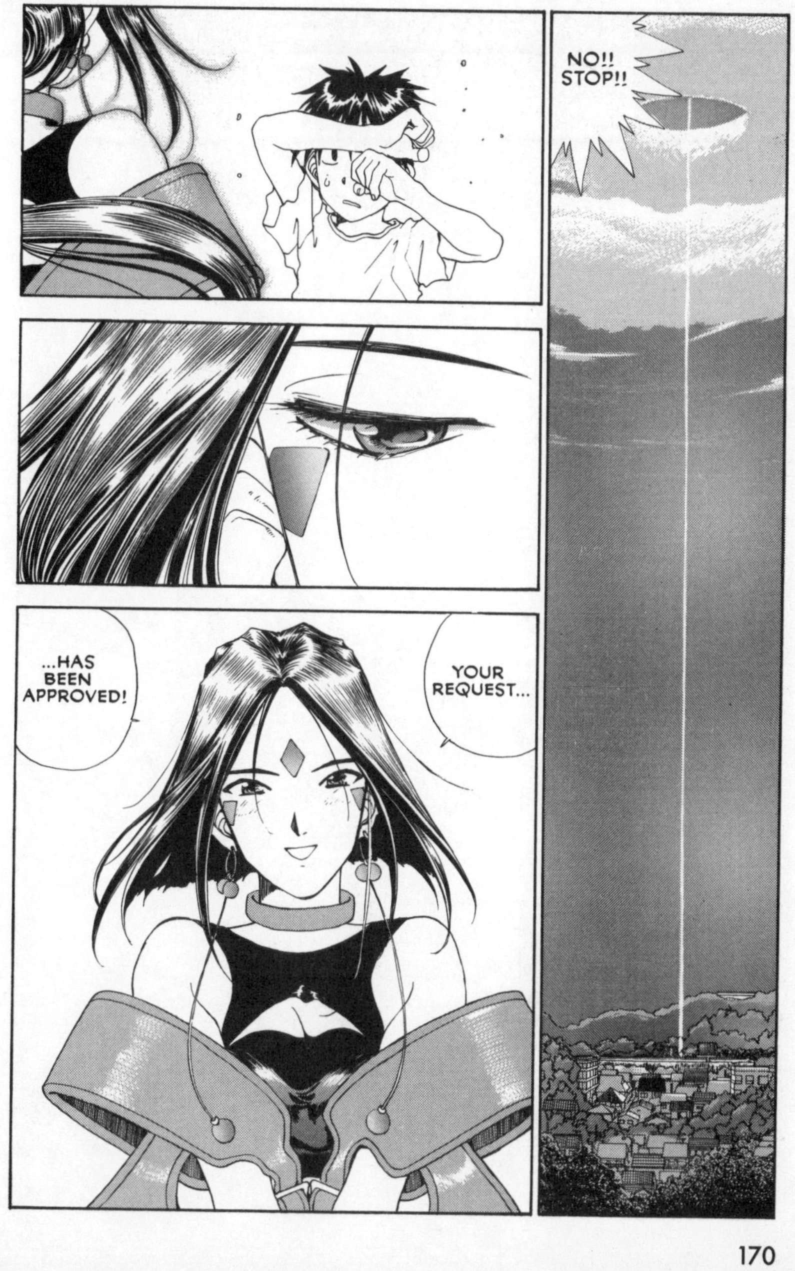
NO!! STOP!!
YOUR REQUEST...
...HAS BEEN APPROVED!

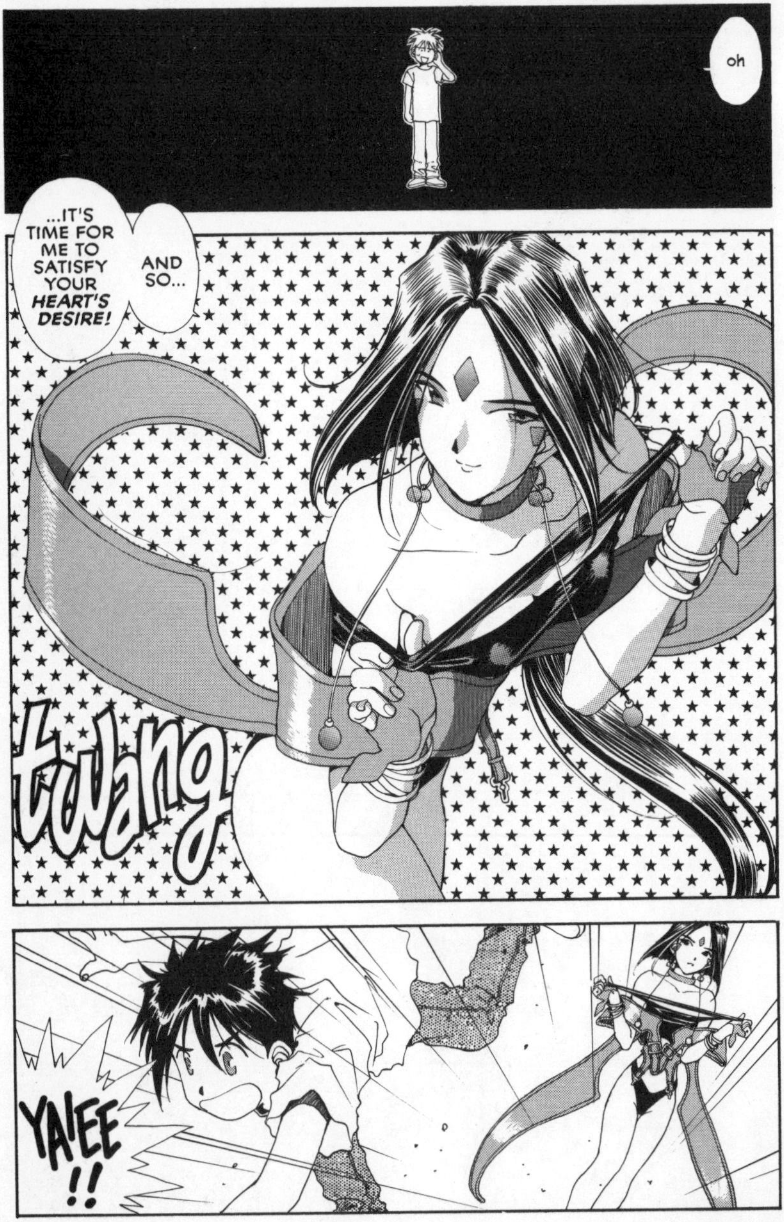

oh
AND SO...
...IT'S TIME FOR ME TO SATISFY YOUR HEART'S DESIRE!
twang
YAIEE !!

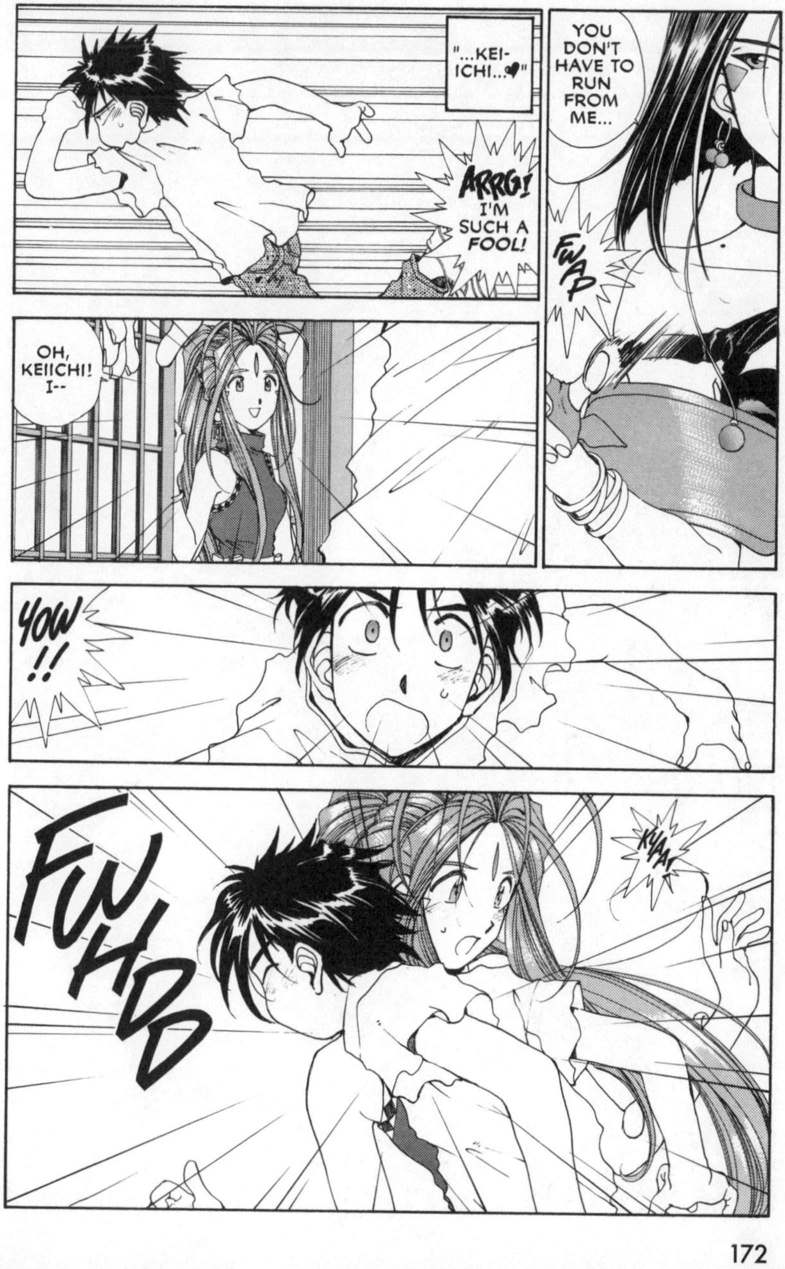
YOU DON'T HAVE TO RUN FROM ME...
FWAP
"...KEI-ICHI...♥"
ARRG! I'M SUCH A FOOL!
OH, KEIICHI! I--
YOW!!
KYAA
FUHDD

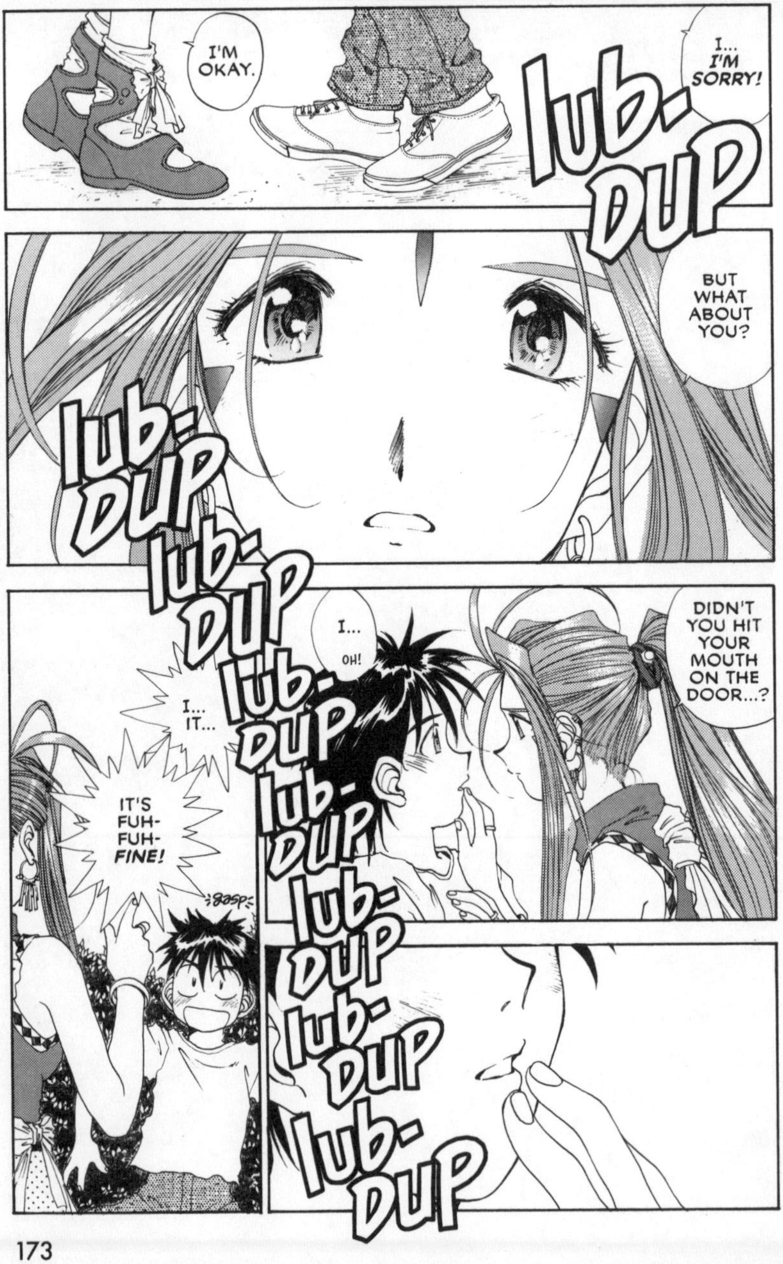
I... I'M SORRY!
lub-DUP
I'M OKAY.
BUT WHAT ABOUT YOU?
lub-DUP lub-DUP lub-DUP lub-DUP lub-DUP lub-DUP lub-DUP
DIDN'T YOU HIT YOUR MOUTH ON THE DOOR...?
I... OH!
I... IT...
IT'S FUH-FUH-FINE!
gasp

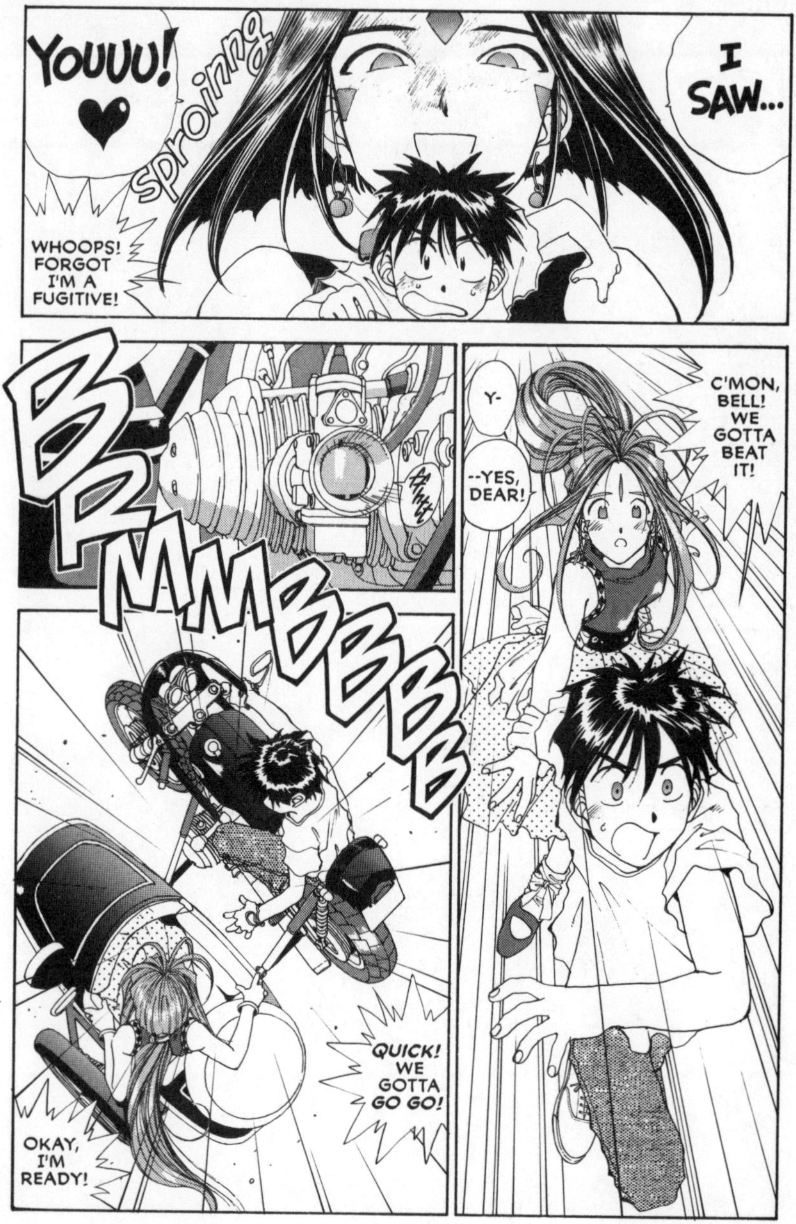
I SAW...
YOUUU! ♥
sproinng
WHOOPS! FORGOT I'M A FUGITIVE!
C'MON, BELL! WE GOTTA BEAT IT!
Y-
--YES, DEAR!
BRMMBBBB
QUICK! WE GOTTA GO GO!
OKAY, I'M READY!

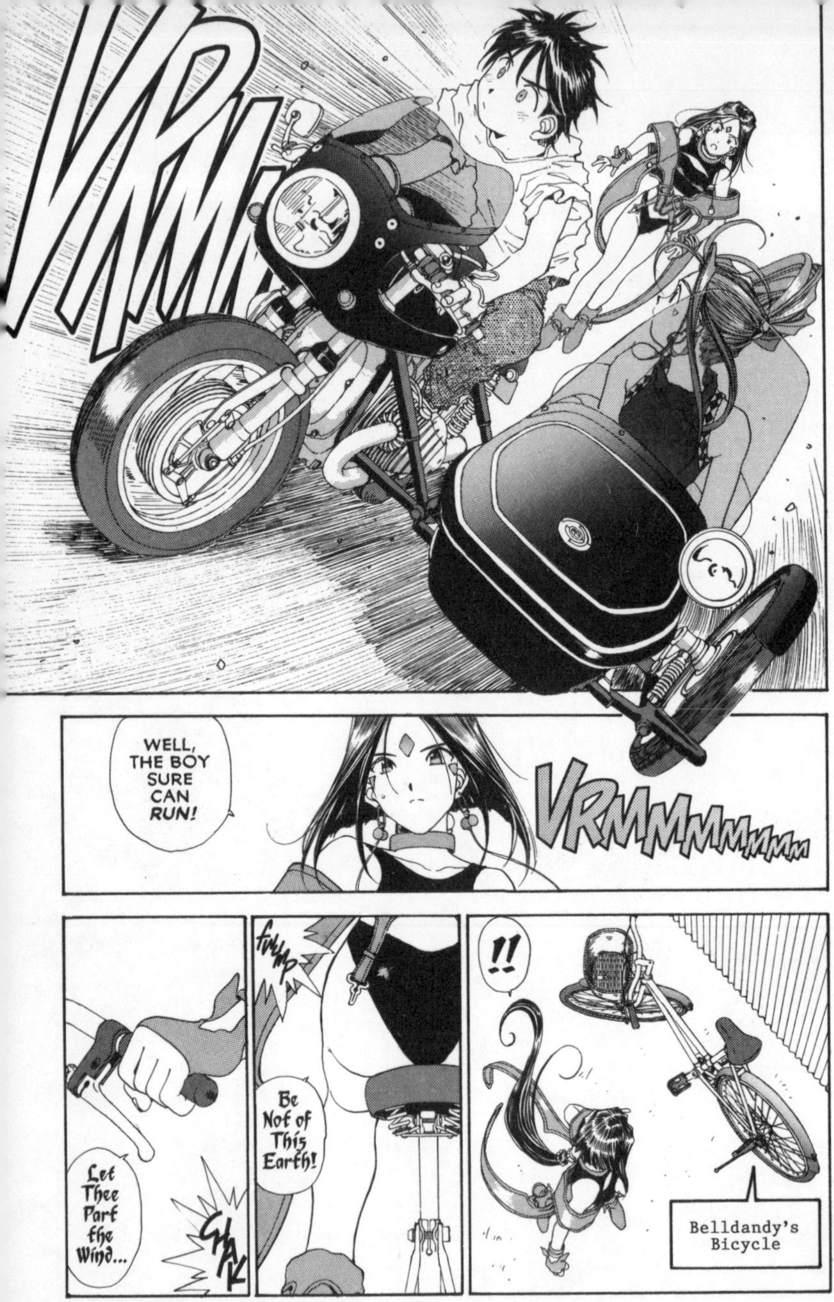
VRMM
WELL, THE BOY SURE CAN *RUN!*
VRMMMMMMMM
!!
Belldandy's Bicycle
FWUMP
Be Not of This Earth!
Let Thee Part the Wind...
CHAK

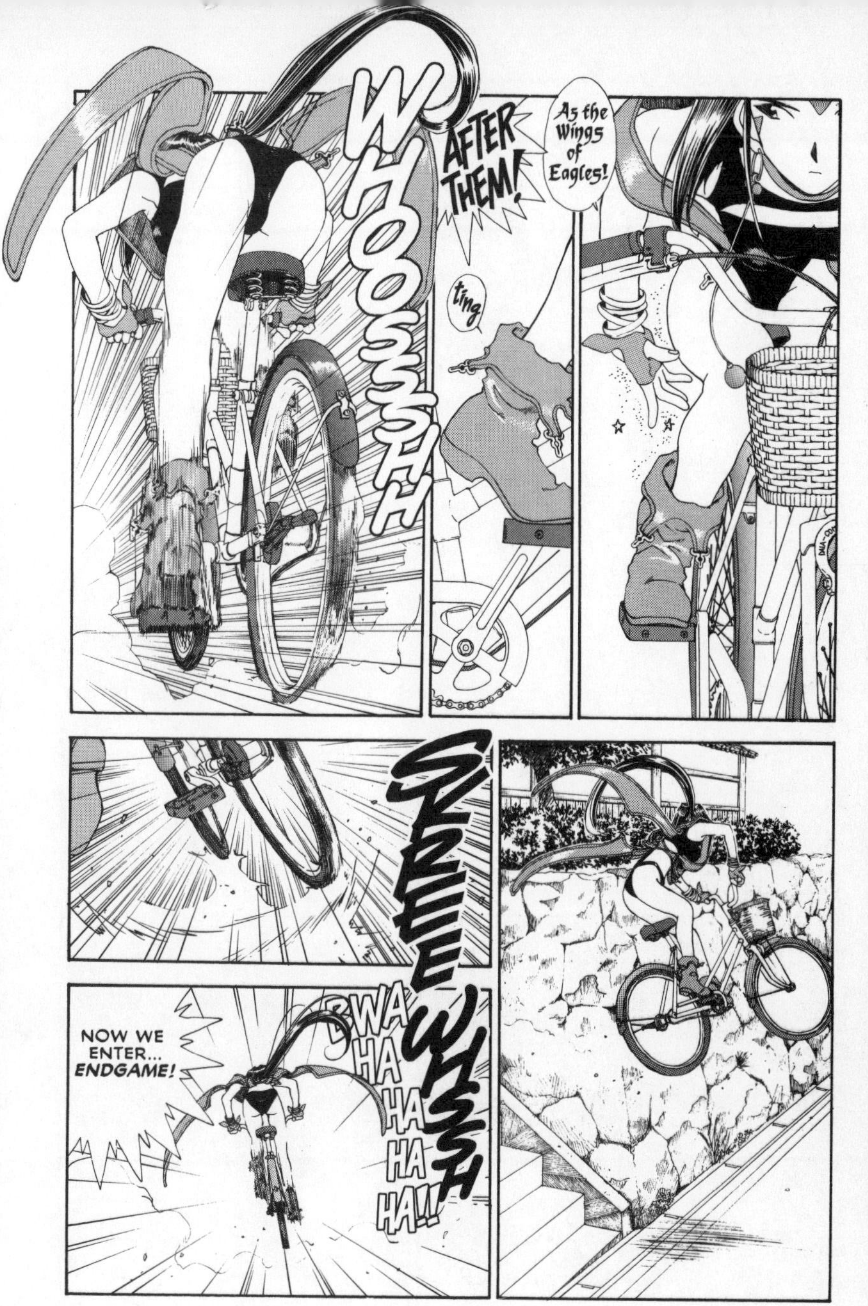

As the Wings of Eagles!
AFTER THEM!
ting
WHOOSSHH
SKREEE
WHISSH
NOW WE ENTER... ENDGAME!
BWA HA HA HA HA!!

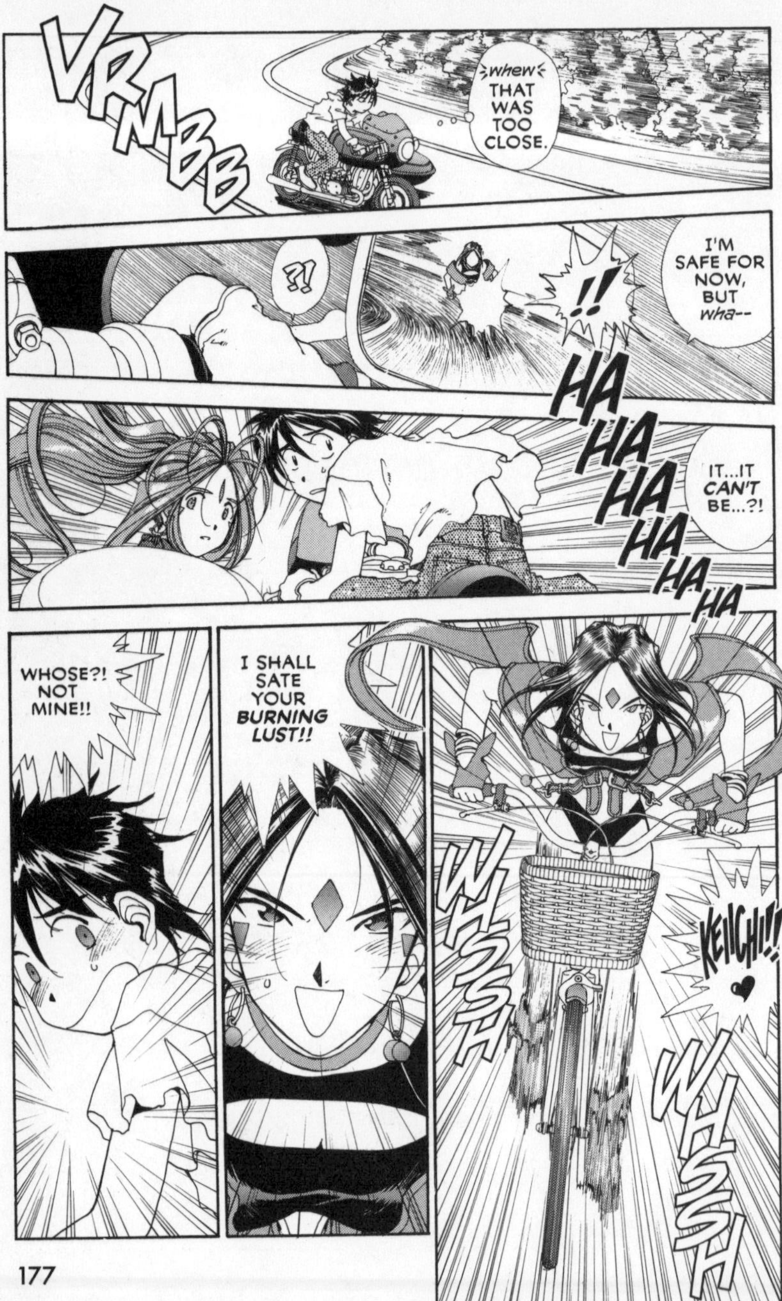
VRMBB
whew THAT WAS TOO CLOSE.
I'M SAFE FOR NOW, BUT *wha--*
!!
?!
IT...IT *CAN'T* BE...?!
HA HA HA HA HA HA
KEIICHI!! ♥
WHSSH
WHSSH
I SHALL SATE YOUR ***BURNING LUST!!***
WHOSE?! NOT MINE!!

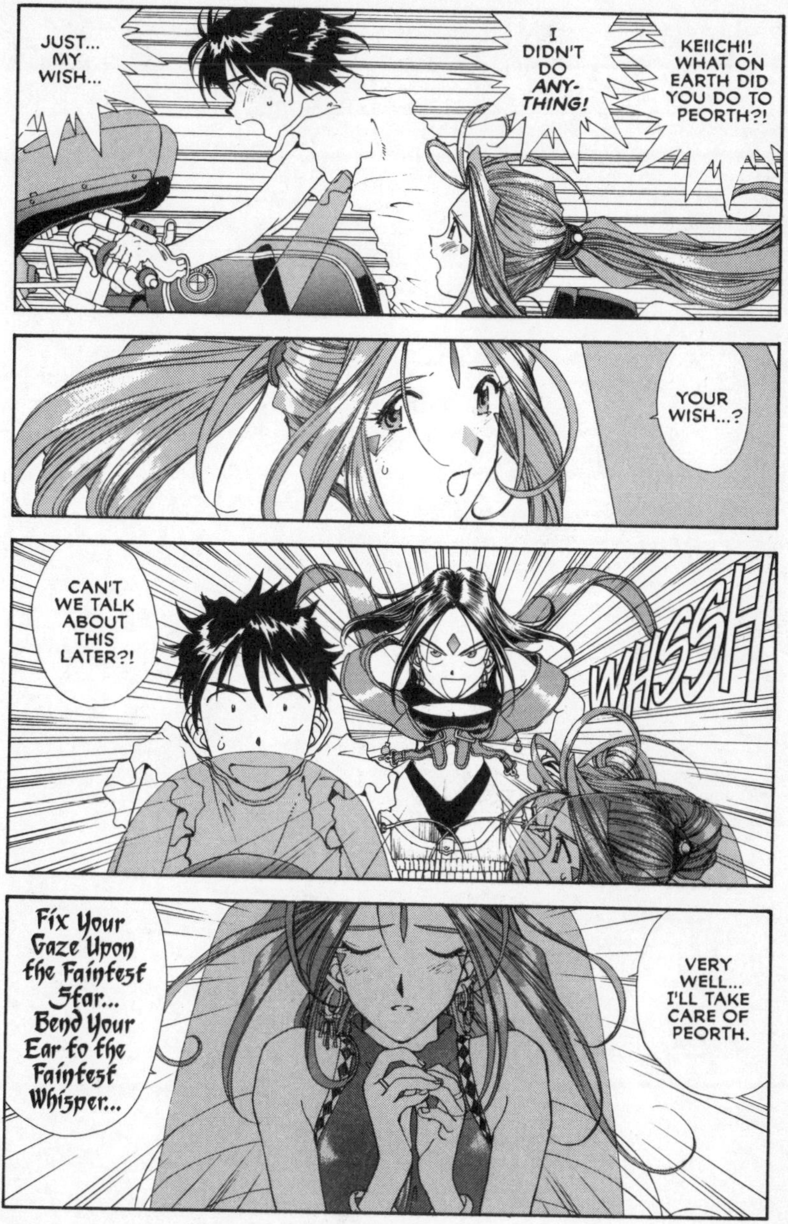
KEIICHI! WHAT ON EARTH DID YOU DO TO PEORTH?!
I DIDN'T DO ANY-THING!
JUST... MY WISH...
YOUR WISH...?
WHSSH
CAN'T WE TALK ABOUT THIS LATER?!
VERY WELL... I'LL TAKE CARE OF PEORTH.
Fix Your Gaze Upon the Faintest Star... Bend Your Ear to the Faintest Whisper...

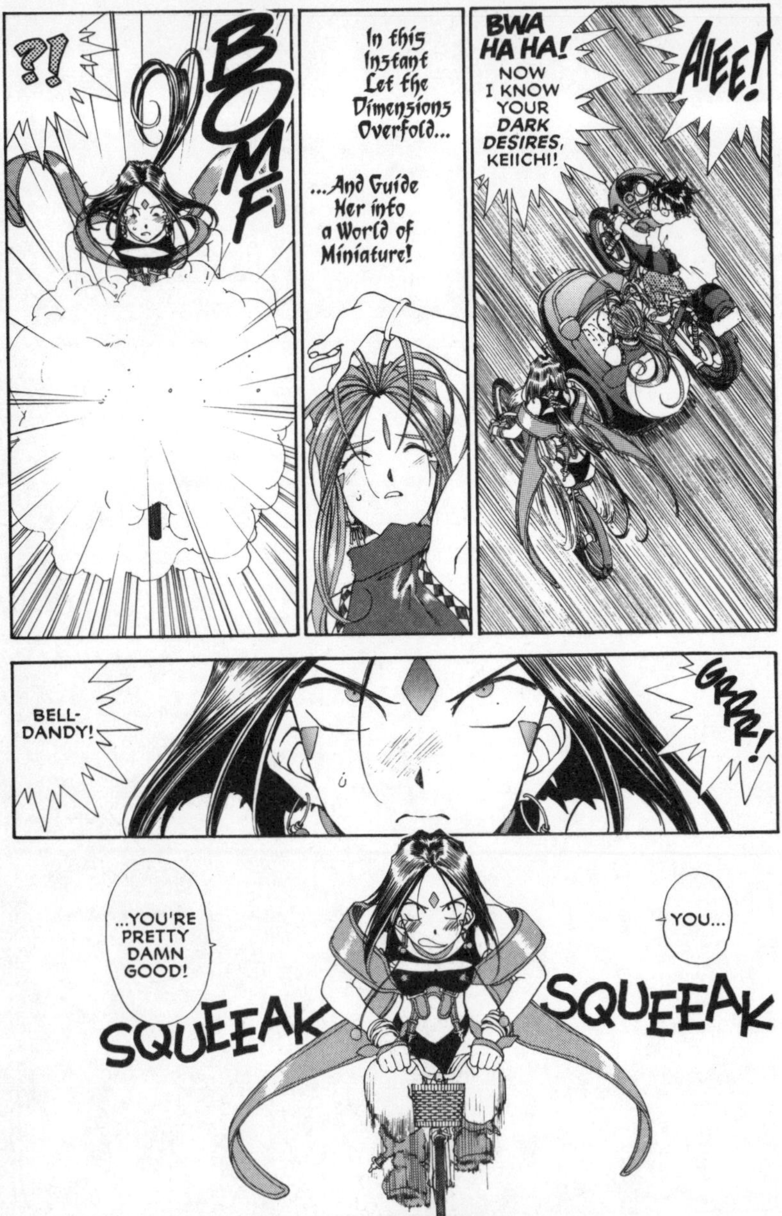
AIEE!
BWA HA HA! NOW I KNOW YOUR DARK DESIRES, KEIICHI!
In this Instant Let the Dimensions Overfold...
...And Guide Her into a World of Miniature!
BOMF
?!
GRRR!
BELL-DANDY!
YOU...
...YOU'RE PRETTY DAMN GOOD!
SQUEEEAK
SQUEEEAK

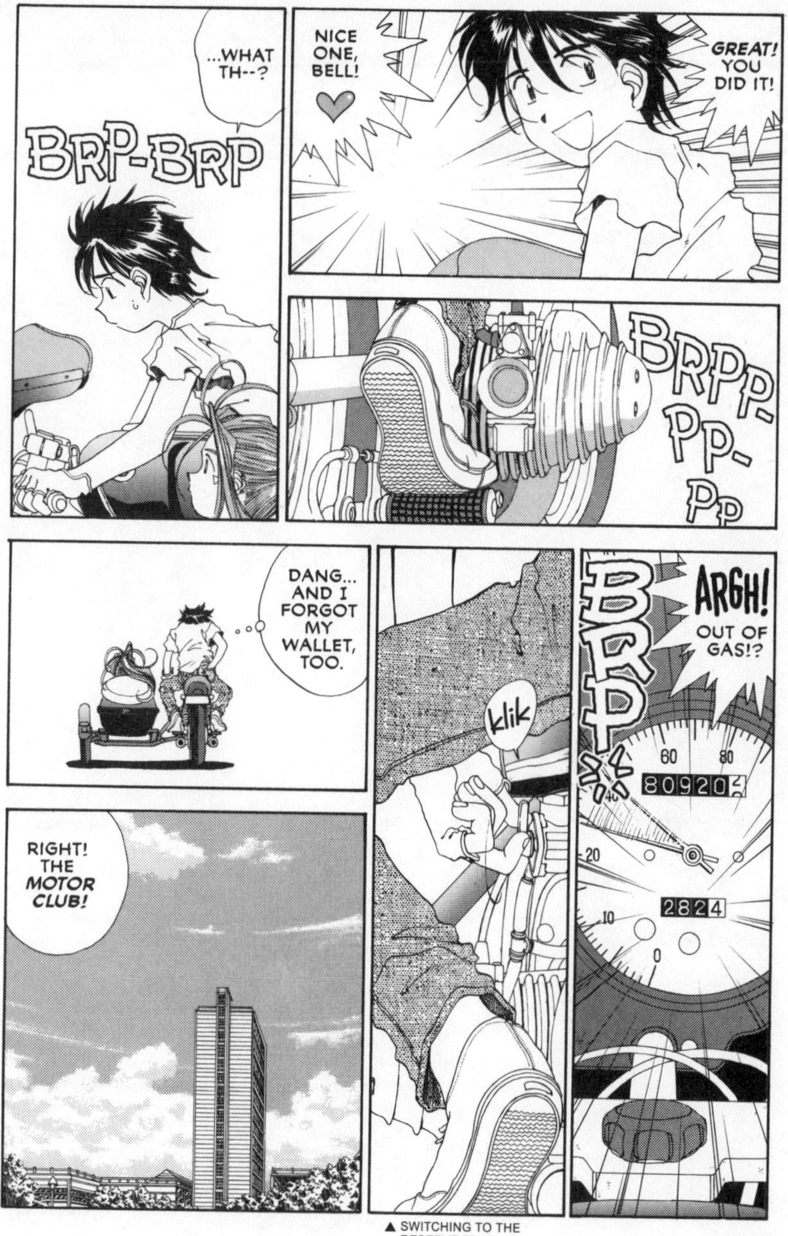
GREAT! YOU DID IT!
NICE ONE, BELL!
BRPPP-PP-PP
...WHAT TH--?
BRP-BRP
BRP
ARGH!
OUT OF GAS!?
60
80
80920
20
2824
10
0
klik
DANG... AND I FORGOT MY WALLET, TOO.
RIGHT! THE MOTOR CLUB!

▲ SWITCHING TO THE RESERVE TANK.

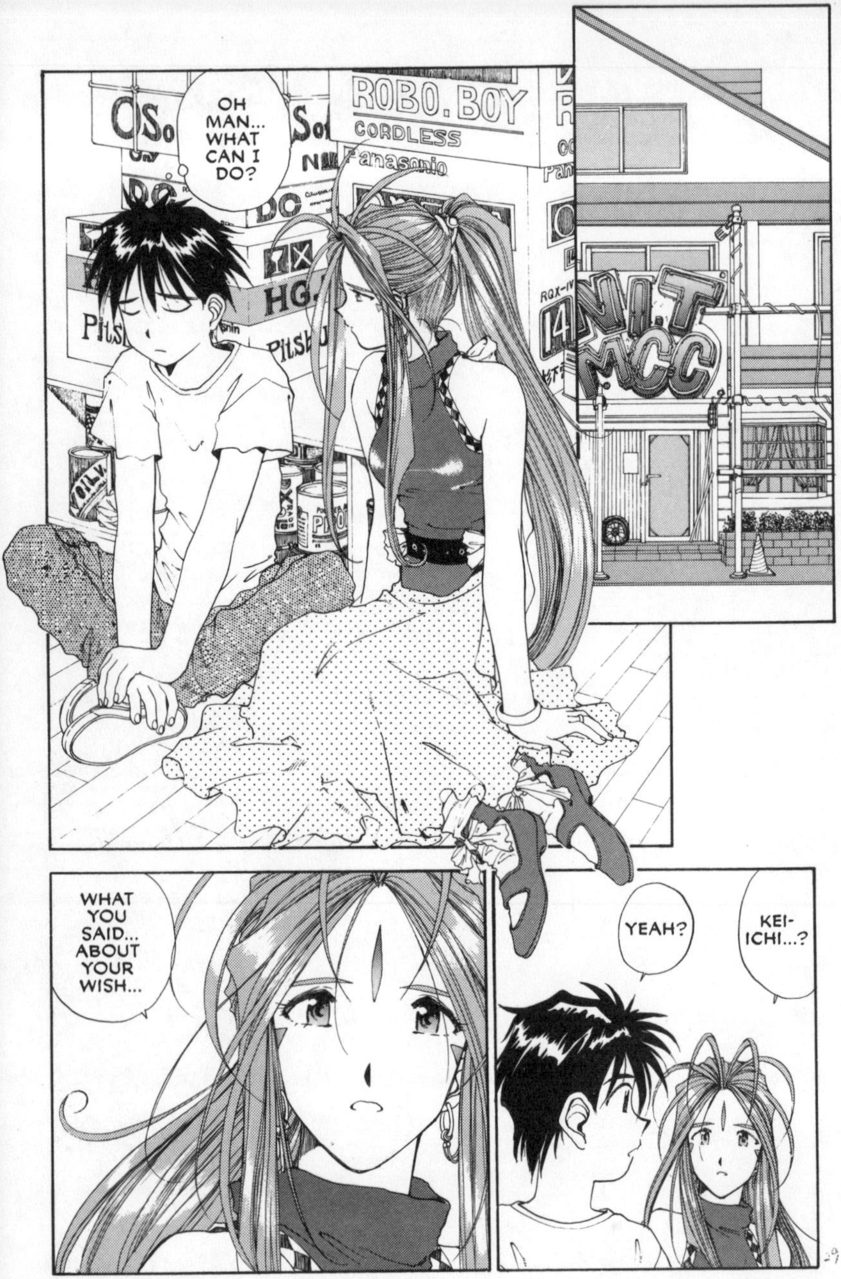
N.I.T
MCC
ROBO.BOY
CORDLESS
OH MAN... WHAT CAN I DO?
KEI-ICHI...?
YEAH?
WHAT YOU SAID... ABOUT YOUR WISH...

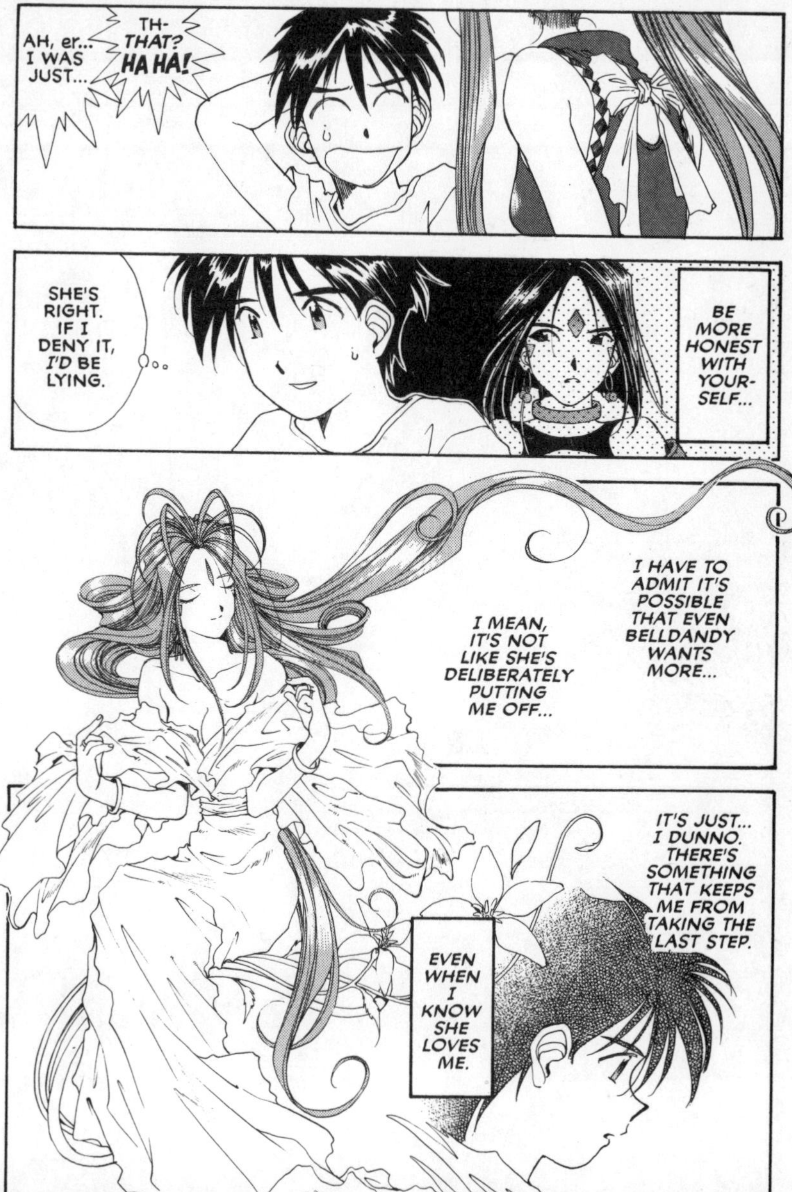
TH- THAT? HA HA!
AH, er... I WAS JUST...
BE MORE HONEST WITH YOURSELF...
SHE'S RIGHT. IF I DENY IT, I'D BE LYING.
I HAVE TO ADMIT IT'S POSSIBLE THAT EVEN BELLDANDY WANTS MORE...
I MEAN, IT'S NOT LIKE SHE'S DELIBERATELY PUTTING ME OFF...
IT'S JUST... I DUNNO. THERE'S SOMETHING THAT KEEPS ME FROM TAKING THE LAST STEP.
EVEN WHEN I KNOW SHE LOVES ME.

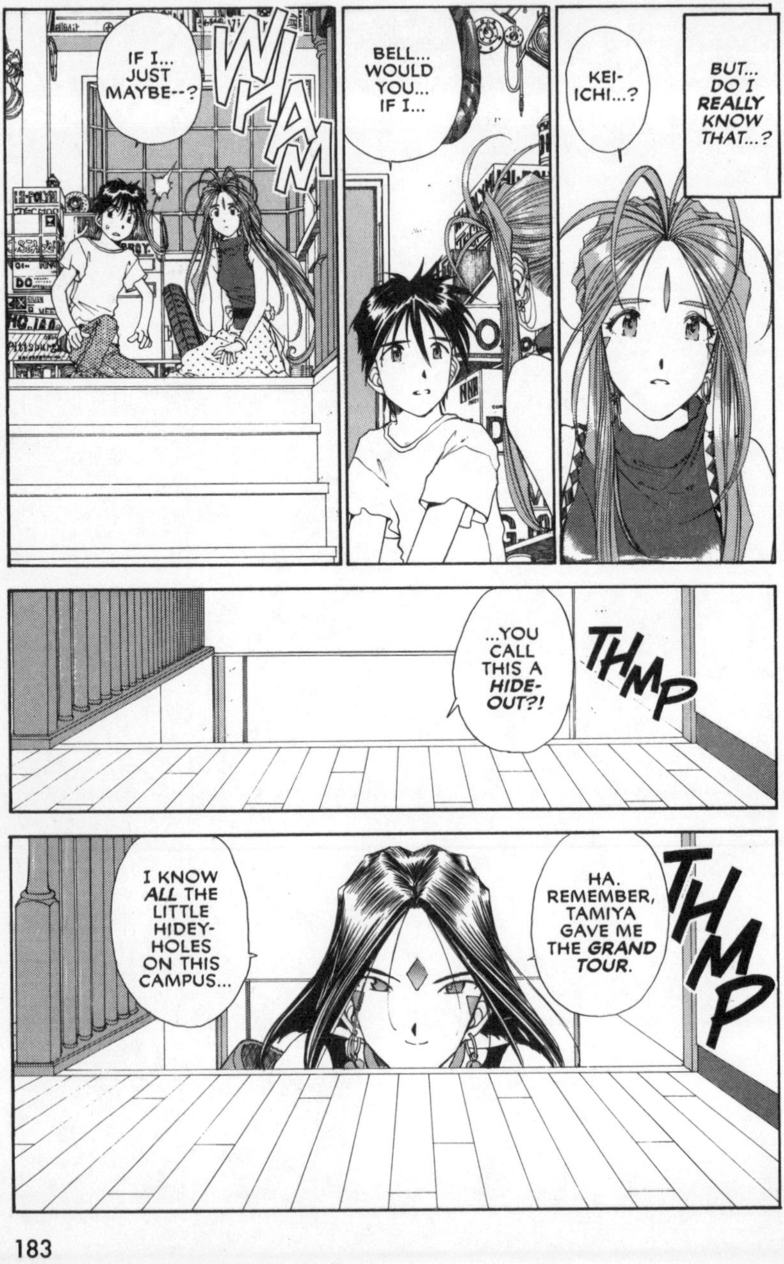

BUT... DO I REALLY KNOW THAT...?
KEI-ICHI...?
BELL... WOULD YOU... IF I...
WHAM
IF I... JUST MAYBE--?
THMP
...YOU CALL THIS A HIDE-OUT?!
THMP
HA. REMEMBER, TAMIYA GAVE ME THE GRAND TOUR.
I KNOW ALL THE LITTLE HIDEY-HOLES ON THIS CAMPUS...

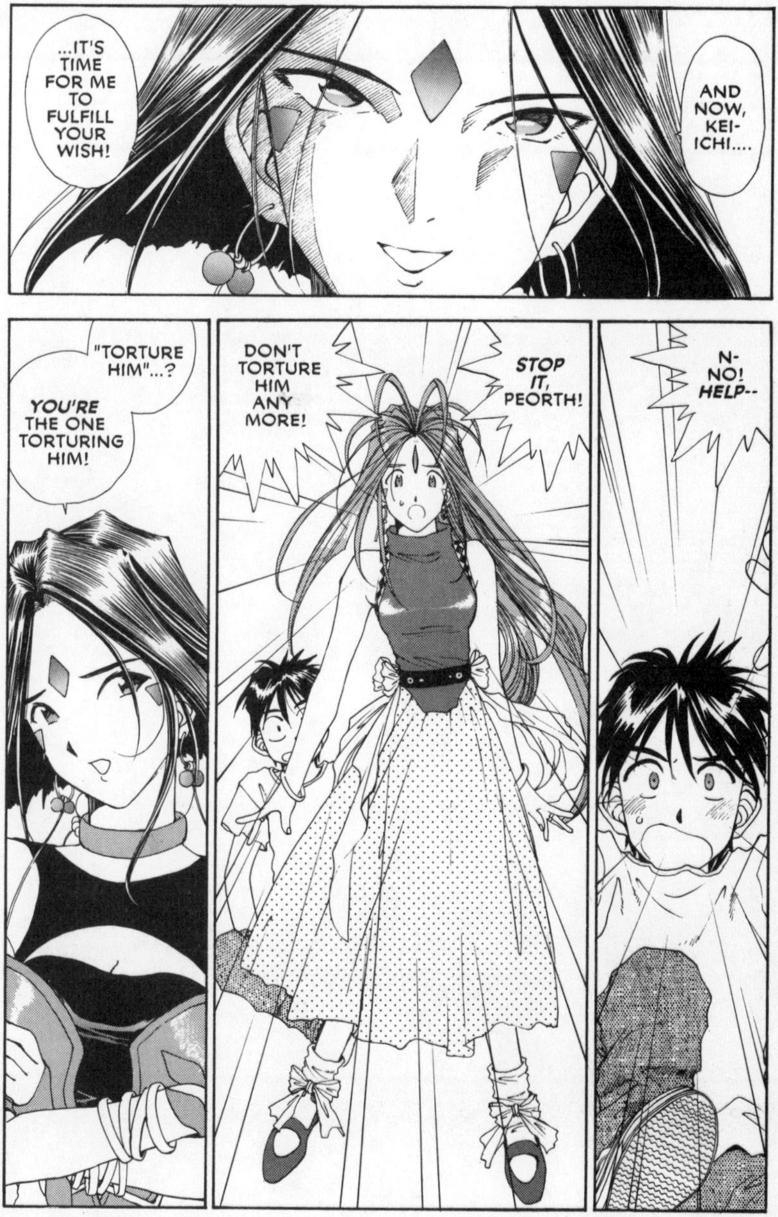
AND NOW, KEI-ICHI....
...IT'S TIME FOR ME TO FULFILL YOUR WISH!
N-NO! *HELP--*
STOP IT, PEORTH!
DON'T TORTURE HIM ANY MORE!
"TORTURE HIM"...?
YOU'RE THE ONE TORTURING HIM!

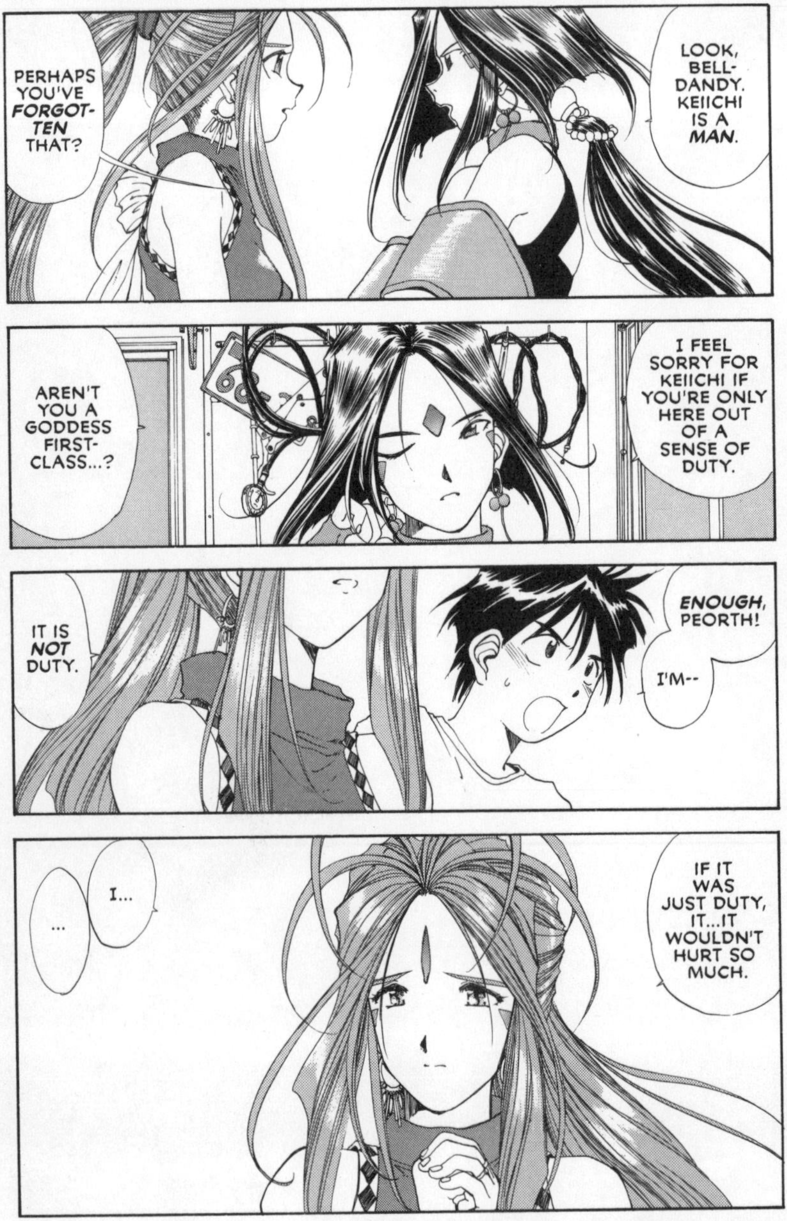

LOOK, BELL-DANDY. KEIICHI IS A *MAN*.
PERHAPS YOU'VE *FORGOT-TEN* THAT?
I FEEL SORRY FOR KEIICHI IF YOU'RE ONLY HERE OUT OF A SENSE OF DUTY.
AREN'T YOU A GODDESS FIRST-CLASS...?
ENOUGH, PEORTH!
I'M--
IT IS *NOT* DUTY.
IF IT WAS JUST DUTY, IT...IT WOULDN'T HURT SO MUCH.
I...
...

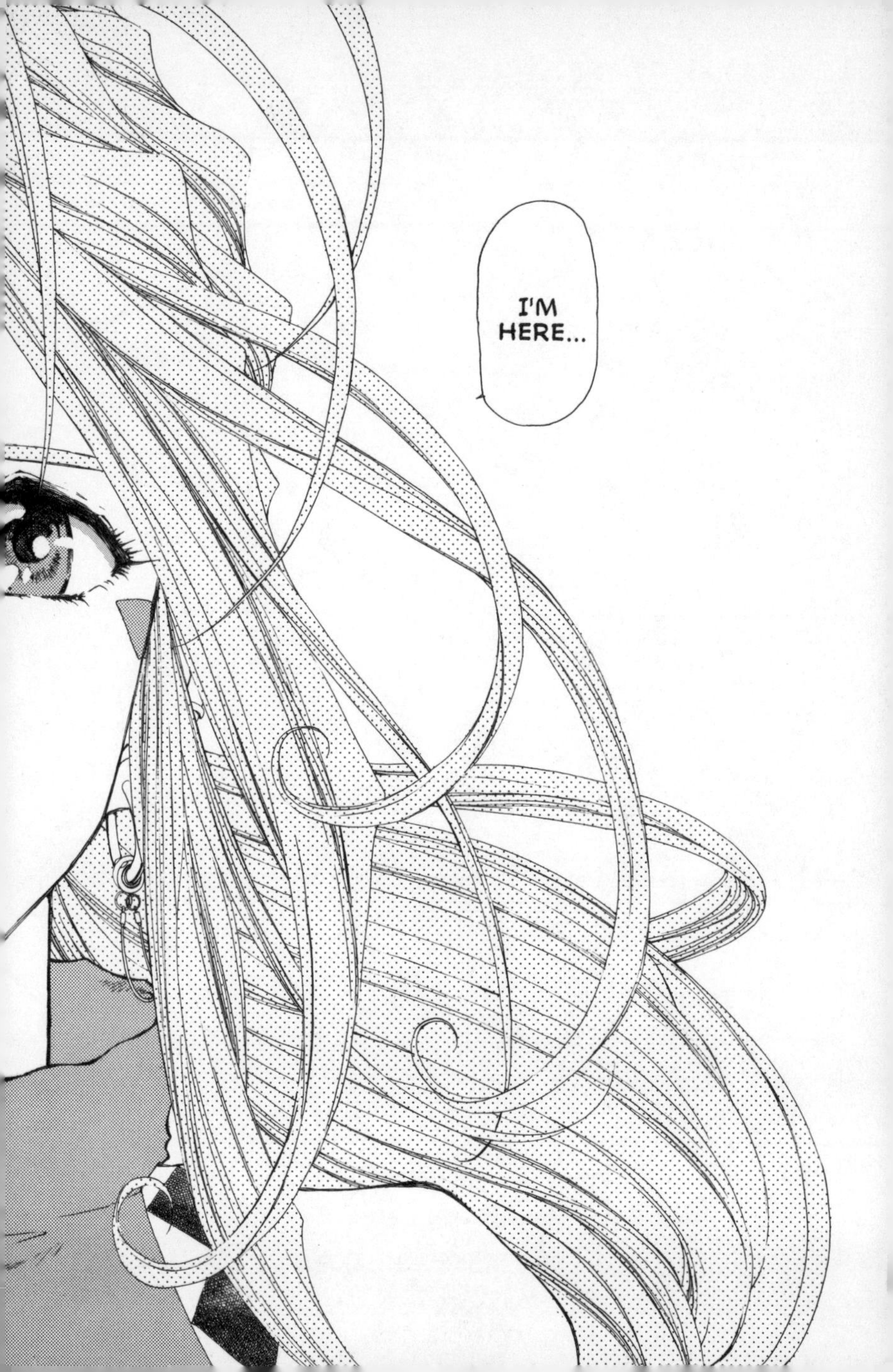
I'M HERE...

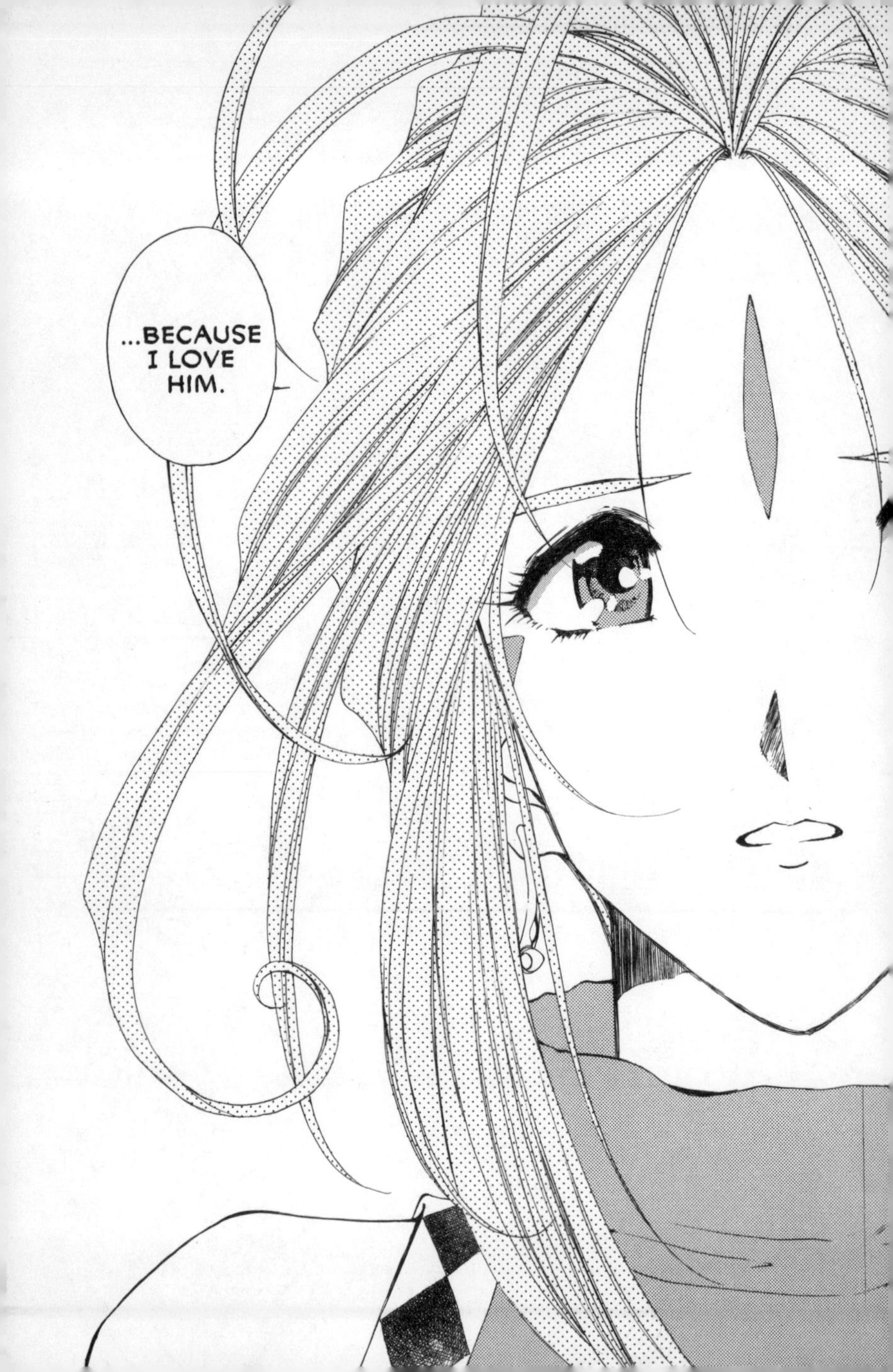
...BECAUSE I LOVE HIM.

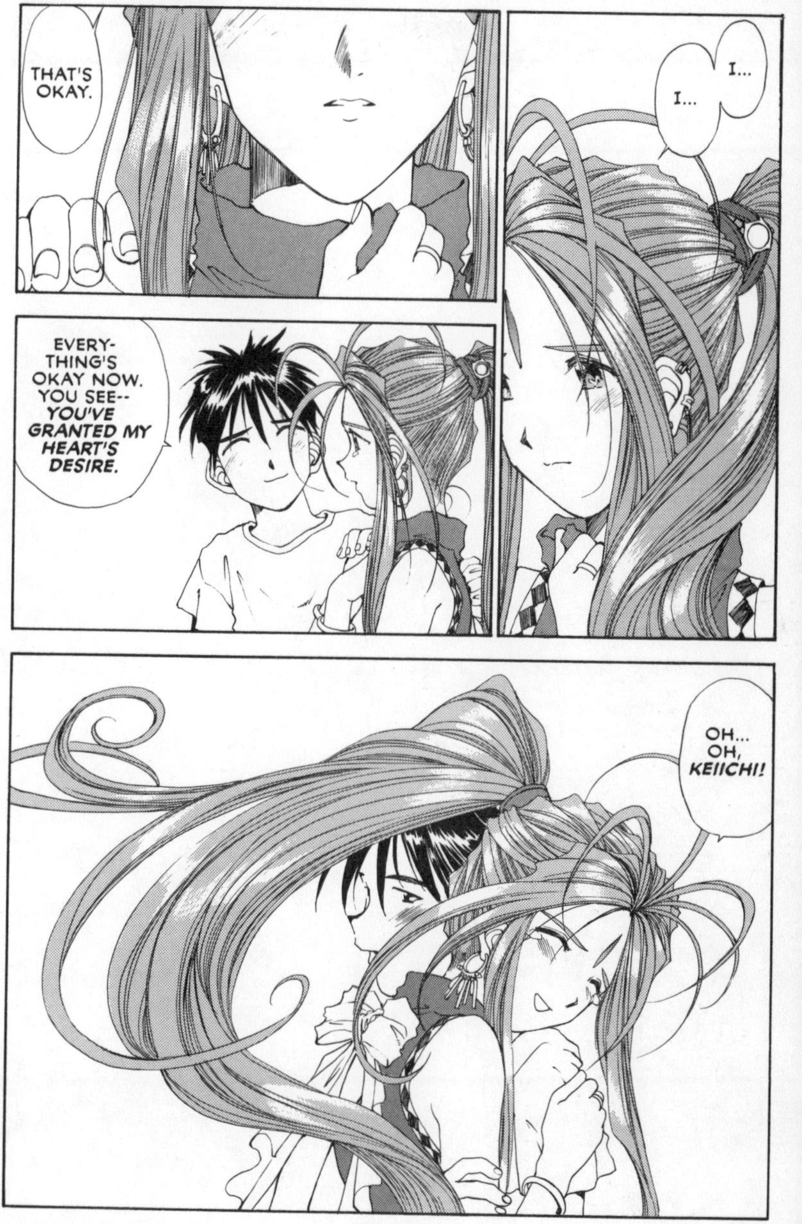

I... I...
THAT'S OKAY.
EVERY-THING'S OKAY NOW. YOU SEE-- *YOU'VE GRANTED MY HEART'S DESIRE.*
OH... OH, *KEIICHI!*

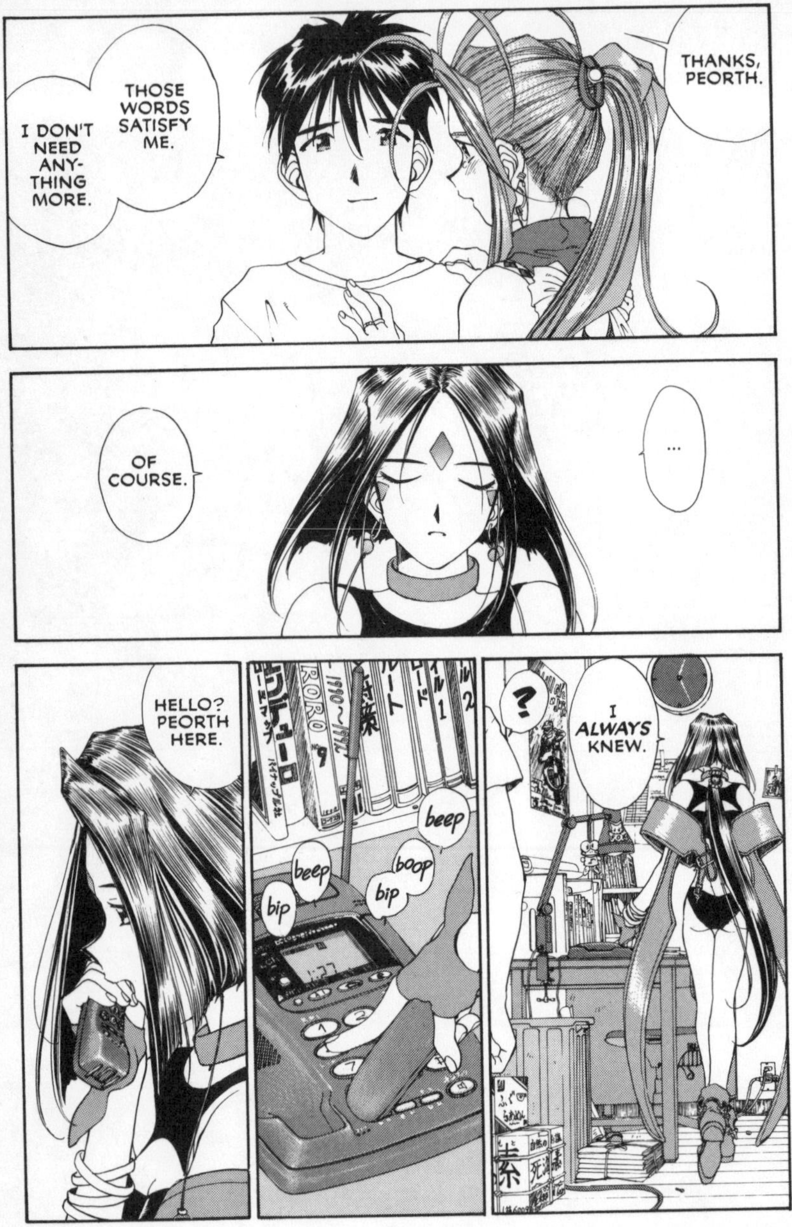
THANKS, PEORTH.
THOSE WORDS SATISFY ME.
I DON'T NEED ANYTHING MORE.
...
OF COURSE.
?
I ALWAYS KNEW.
beep
boop
beep
bip
bip
HELLO? PEORTH HERE.

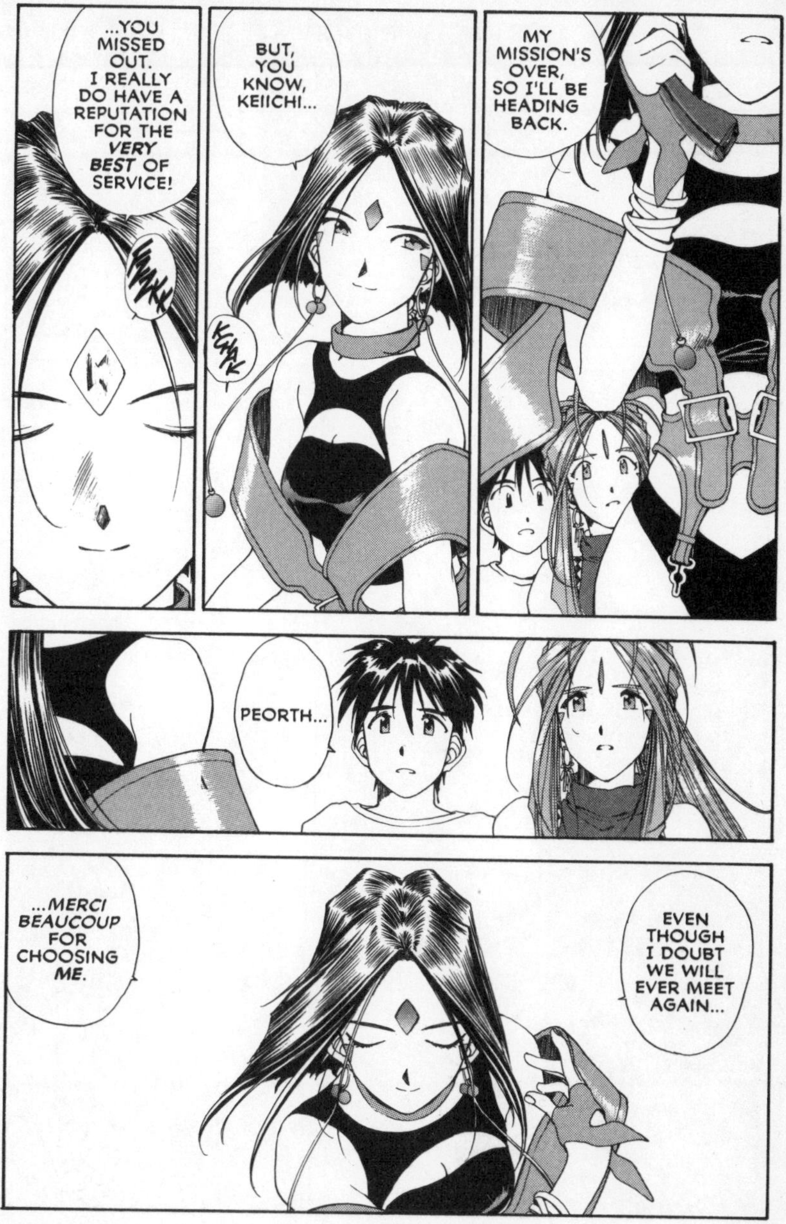
MY MISSION'S OVER, SO I'LL BE HEADING BACK.
BUT, YOU KNOW, KEIICHI...
...YOU MISSED OUT. I REALLY DO HAVE A REPUTATION FOR THE *VERY BEST* OF SERVICE!
PEORTH...
EVEN THOUGH I DOUBT WE WILL EVER MEET AGAIN...
...*MERCI BEAUCOUP* FOR CHOOSING *ME*.

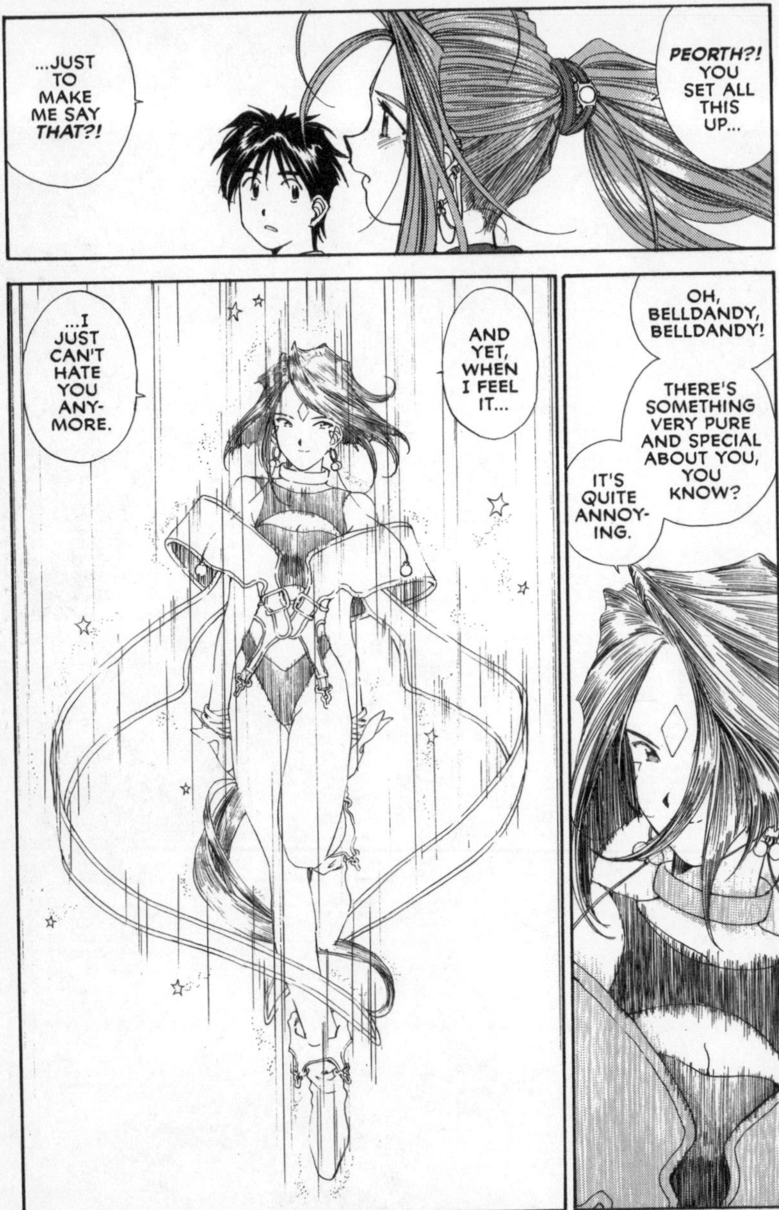
PEORTH?! YOU SET ALL THIS UP...
...JUST TO MAKE ME SAY THAT?!
OH, BELLDANDY, BELLDANDY!
THERE'S SOMETHING VERY PURE AND SPECIAL ABOUT YOU, YOU KNOW?
IT'S QUITE ANNOY-ING.
AND YET, WHEN I FEEL IT...
...I JUST CAN'T HATE YOU ANY-MORE.

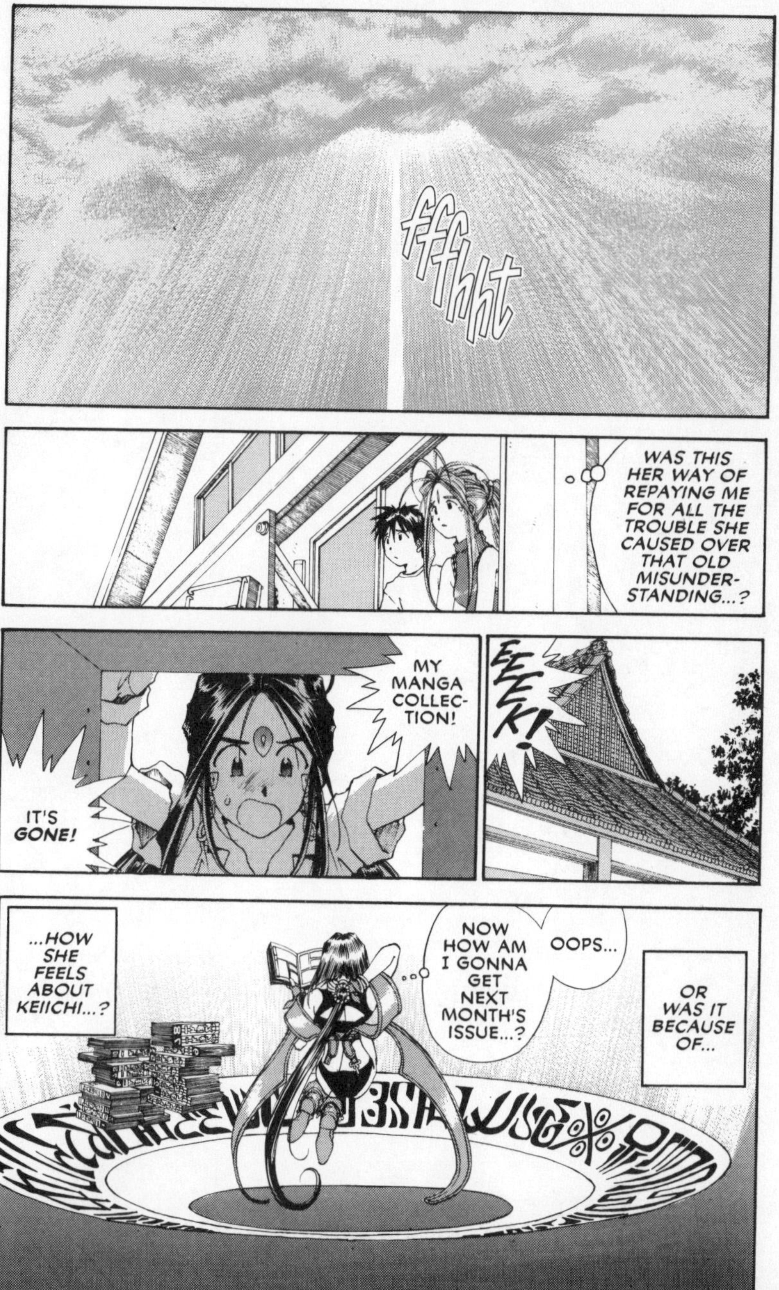
fffhht
WAS THIS HER WAY OF REPAYING ME FOR ALL THE TROUBLE SHE CAUSED OVER THAT OLD MISUNDER-STANDING...?
EEEK!
MY MANGA COLLEC-TION!
IT'S GONE!
OR WAS IT BECAUSE OF...
OOPS...
NOW HOW AM I GONNA GET NEXT MONTH'S ISSUE...?
...HOW SHE FEELS ABOUT KEIICHI...?

THE ADVENTURES OF THE MINI-GODDESSES

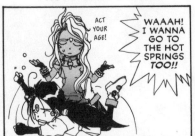

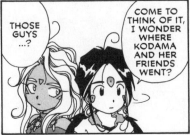

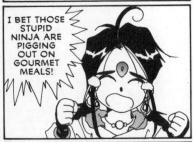

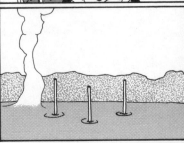

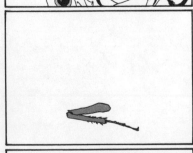

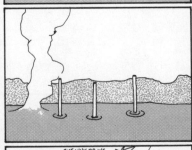

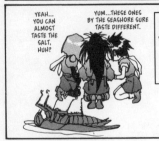

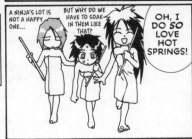

◇ A NINJA'S LOT IS NOT A HAPPY ONE ◇

COME TO THINK OF IT, I WONDER WHERE KODAMA AND HER FRIENDS WENT?
THOSE GUYS ...?
OH, I DO SO LOVE HOT SPRINGS!
BUT WHY DO WE HAVE TO SOAK IN THEM LIKE THAT?
A NINJA'S LOT IS NOT A HAPPY ONE...

◇ A NINJA'S LOT IS DEFINITELY NOT A HAPPY ONE ◇

WAAAH! I WANNA GO TO THE HOT SPRINGS TOO!!
ACT YOUR AGE!
I BET THOSE STUPID NINJA ARE PIGGING OUT ON GOURMET MEALS!
SKULD, DEAR... WOULD YOU LIKE SOME, TOO?
YUM...THESE ONES BY THE SEASHORE SURE TASTE DIFFERENT.
YEAH... YOU CAN ALMOST TASTE THE SALT, HUH?

THE ADVENTURES OF THE MINI-GODDESSES

MORISATO, YOU MAY HAVE BREASTS, BUT YOU'RE STILL A GUY!

(Might as well dig your grave right now!!)

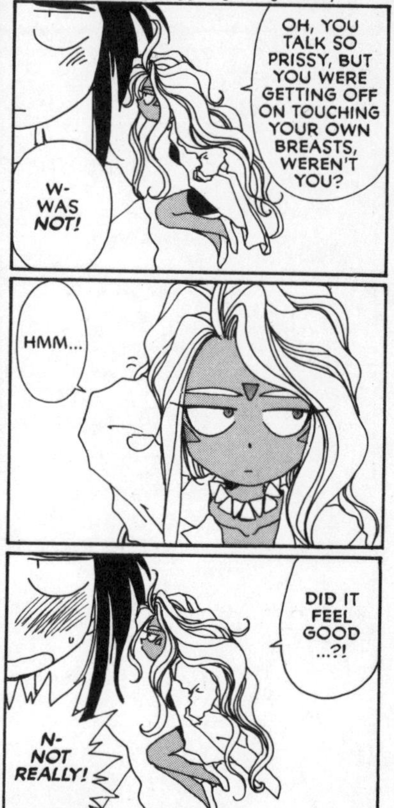
OH, YOU TALK SO PRISSY, BUT YOU WERE GETTING OFF ON TOUCHING YOUR OWN BREASTS, WEREN'T YOU?
W-WAS NOT!
HMM...
DID IT FEEL GOOD ...?!
N-NOT REALLY!
SO YOU WERE DOING IT, THEN?
HEY, YOU DON'T HAVE TO CRY...
...!

OH MY MANGA-KA! (SPECIAL ROAD-TRIP EDITION)

BATTLE! THE CHALLENGE OF THE FAKE FOOD SAMPLES!

AN ALMOST-TRUE STORY STARRING "KIKUKO INOGASHIRA" (PSEUDONYM— BELLDANDY'S VOICE ACTRESS)

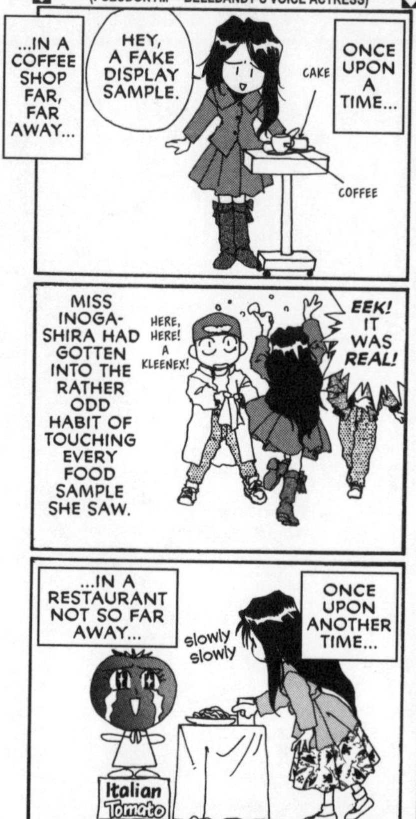
ONCE UPON A TIME...
CAKE
HEY, A FAKE DISPLAY SAMPLE.
...IN A COFFEE SHOP FAR, FAR AWAY...
COFFEE
EEK! IT WAS REAL!
HERE, HERE! A KLEENEX!
MISS INOGASHIRA HAD GOTTEN INTO THE RATHER ODD HABIT OF TOUCHING EVERY FOOD SAMPLE SHE SAW.
ONCE UPON ANOTHER TIME...
slowly slowly
...IN A RESTAURANT NOT SO FAR AWAY...
Italian Tomato
EEK! IT WAS REAL AGAIN!!
HERE Y'GO!
FIGHT ON, MISS INOGASHIRA! A WORLD OF REAL FOOD SAMPLES AWAITS YOU!

Any similarity with any person living or dead is purely coincidental! Honest! I swear!

EDITOR
Carl Gustav Horn

DESIGNER
Scott Cook

PUBLISHER
Mike Richardson

English-language version
produced by Dark Horse Comics

OH MY GODDESS! Vol. 12
©2009 Kosuke Fujishima. All rights reserved. First published in
Japan in 1995 by Kodansha, Ltd., Tokyo. Publication rights for this English edition arranged through Kodansha Ltd. This English-language edition
©2009 by Dark Horse Comics, Inc. All other material ©2009 by Dark Horse
Comics, Inc. All rights reserved. No portion of this publication may be repro-
duced, in any form or by any means, without the express written permission of
the copyright holders. Names, characters, places, and incidents featured in this
publication are either the product of the author's imagination or are used ficti-
tiously. Any resemblance to actual persons (living or dead), events, institutions,
or locales, without satiric intent, is coincidental. Dark Horse Manga™ is
a trademark of Dark Horse Comics, Inc. All rights reserved.

Published by Dark Horse Manga
A division of Dark Horse Comics, Inc.
10956 SE Main Street
Milwaukie, OR 97222
darkhorse.com

To find a comics shop in your area,
call the Comic Shop Locator Service
toll-free at 1-888-266-4226

First edition: July 2009
ISBN 978-1-59582-322-9

1 3 5 7 9 10 8 6 4 2

Printed in Canada

MIKE RICHARDSON president and publisher **NEIL HANKERSON** executive vice president
TOM WEDDLE chief financial officer **RANDY STRADLEY** vice president of publishing **MICHAEL MARTENS**
vice president of business development **ANITA NELSON** vice president of marketing, sales, and licensing
DAVID SCROGGY vice president of product development **DALE LAFOUNTAIN** vice president of information
technology **DARLENE VOGEL** director of purchasing **KEN LIZZI** general counsel **DAVEY ESTRADA** editorial
director **SCOTT ALLIE** senior managing editor **CHRIS WARNER** senior books editor, Dark Horse Books
DIANA SCHUTZ executive editor **CARY GRAZZINI** director of design and production
LIA RIBACCHI art director **CARA NIECE** director of scheduling

letters to the
ENCHANTRESS

10956 SE Main Street, Milwaukie, Oregon 97222
omg@darkhorse.com • darkhorse.com

NOTE: Full addresses and e-mail addresses will not be printed, unless you ask! All fan artwork, letters, and e-mails submitted become the property of Dark Horse Comics.

Dear Tohma-san,

I am writing this letter to you in hopes it reaches you from far away and is translated enough so that its meaning still stays intact, so please regard me kindly. I wanted to be able to write you in regard to your book *Oh My Goddess! First End*. Your book and your writing were wonderful! Thank you! Thank you! Thank you so much for continuing with the *Oh My Goddess!* storyline! I wanted to keep this letter short since I know you to be a very busy person, and continuing this letter with compliments and praises would probably eventually bore you. So beyond writing to tell you what a beautiful story you wrote, I am writing in hopes that you will be further encouraged to continue writing the *Oh My Goddess!* storyline in novel form. You are one of the most qualified to be able to write such a story since you have such a strong connection with the overall story and characters of *Oh My Goddess!* I'm begging you to please continue and keep the stories and world alive. I thank you for your time and patience in this letter. Thank you again Tohma-san. Have a beautiful day.

Respectfully,
Michael McGee
Conyers, GA

I very much agree that Yumi Tohma's long involvement with the character of Urd created a great opportunity for her to express the *Oh My Goddess!* story in her own way. Sometimes you can tell that a voice actor thinks carefully about the people they portray; you can see this also, for example, in Megumi Hayashibara and Yuko Miyamura's essays on Rei Ayanami and Asuka Langley Soryu. Don't worry, she's still "Soryu" in Dark Horse's *Neon Genesis Evangelion: The Shinji Ikari Raising Project*—whoops, wrong manga (Or is it? As I like to point out, *Oh My Goddess!* was giving Anno props before *Evangelion*. Before *Nadia*, even).

Dear Enchantress,

OK, I've never done this before, so forgive me if I sound a little weird. First off, it was all thanks to *Ah! My Goddess* that I got into anime and manga in the first place, and ever since, I haven't been able to go into a bookstore without looking for the manga section. The way that Keiichi is a spineless wonder is one of the reasons I started to read it, because I could sort of relate to him back then, while the other reason is the funny stunts Urd, Skuld and Peorth pull off during their stay there. I also love the way Belldandy is so kind and loving, and even if someone tried to break them up, she would stay by Keiichi's side, no matter what. And if I never saw *Ah! My Goddess*, I don't think I would've ever become a *Eureka 7*, or *.Hack//* fan either, and met all these kinds of people, including some friends that I don't think I would've ever met had I not been into this stuff. In a way, had I not seen this or even heard of it, I don't think I would've even known about you. But, since I did, I can say that I am glad that I saw it, and hope to see more keep on coming. Thank you guys. But if I may, I have a few questions of my own to ask you. First off, is there going to be another A!MG movie, who is YOUR favorite character, and if you could, which character might you bring back into the manga?

Sincerely,
Joseph Marin
AKA Nirvash Destroyer

No, you don't sound weird, but what's this "Ah! My Goddess" you keep referring to? *Naaaaan chatte*—just kidding. If you wrote in here, you know it's all the same series!

I think you point out that one of the best things about anime and manga is how it allows you to meet new people, because you've got an immediate common interest. This is true regardless of race, nationality or religion; I've met Iranian, Syrian, Chilean, Mexican, French, Dutch, and Potawatomi fans (she used her dividend from the tribe's casino to go to anime cons). And why not? No matter where we are in the world, we all face in one common direction: towards Japan.

I haven't heard anything specific about a new *Oh My Goddess!* movie, although, considering the enduring popularity of the manga, it can hardly be ruled out (think how long it took for there to be an *OMG!* TV series!).

As editor (much like a mother), it is my duty to like all characters equally. I will say, however, that one of my favorite things for characters to do in *Oh My Goddess!* is

gearhead stuff—races, working on bikes, and so forth. It may be because that's something you can do in the real world (unlike, say, summoning air elementals or calling down lightning ^_^). It's also a place, of course, where the enthusiasm of the artist himself shines through. As you all know, we switch off between old and new volumes of *OMG!* each two months, so coming up next will be a new one, vol. 33—and it happens to center on Chihiro, her high-school friends, motorcycle construction, and, of course, a race. Belldandy is known for her beautiful costumes (as she can conjure them out of thin air), but she has a special beauty just in mechanic's overalls.

I don't mean that in a mecha-fetish way; it's more like the philosophy of life you see in her concern for performance, workmanship, and engineering. Belldandy wants to take care of creation, to see that things work well and come to be, whether they're people or machines (in the case of Sora or Skuld, she taught both lessons at the same time). She uses her power to help, instead of insisting she be feared and worshiped for that power. One of the things that's so appealing about the goddess sisters is that they're down to earth in behavior as well as fact. Even though they *are* goddesses, they don't expect people to bow down before them (when Urd invites you to lick her sneakers, it's just for the sake of karaoke). Sayoko Mishima's jealousy of Belldandy (which becomes near-catastrophic in vol. 14) is ironic because she *does* expect to be worshiped, as the goddesses don't.

As for bringing a character back into the manga, I'd like to see more Megumi, please.

Creator Kosuke Fujishima in 1995!

His message to fans in the original Japanese *Oh My Goddess!* Vol. 12:

Hey, everybody, have you locked yourself inside the house? Sit in your house all day, and you too will become a manga-ka! Let's head outside and scream at the top of our lungs! Let's howl at the blue skies and kick the clouds around! WHOAAAAAAA!!! But please be sure to read my manga. WHOAAAAAAA!!!

P.S. I think I just sprained my crotch.

Kosuke Fujishima's Oh My Goddess!

Dark Horse is proud to re-present *Oh My Goddess!* in the much-requested, affordable, Japanese-reading, right-to-left format, complete with color sections, informative bonus notes, and your letters!

$10.95 each!

AVAILABLE AT YOUR LOCAL COMICS SHOP OR BOOKSTORE
*To find a comics shop in your area, call 1-888-266-4226

For more information or to order direct:
•On the web: darkhorse.com •E-mail: mailorder@darkhorse.com
•Phone: 1-800-862-0052 Mon.–Fri. 9 AM to 5 PM Pacific Time.

STOP! This is the back of the book!

This manga collection is translated into English, but arranged in right-to-left reading format to maintain the artwork's visual orientation as originally drawn and published in Japan. If you've never read comics this way before, take a look at the diagram below to give yourself an idea of how to go about it. Basically, you'll be starting in the upper right-hand corner, and will read each word balloon and panel moving right to left. It may take a little getting used to, but you should get the hang of it very quickly. Have fun! If this is the millionth manga you've read this way, never mind. ^_^

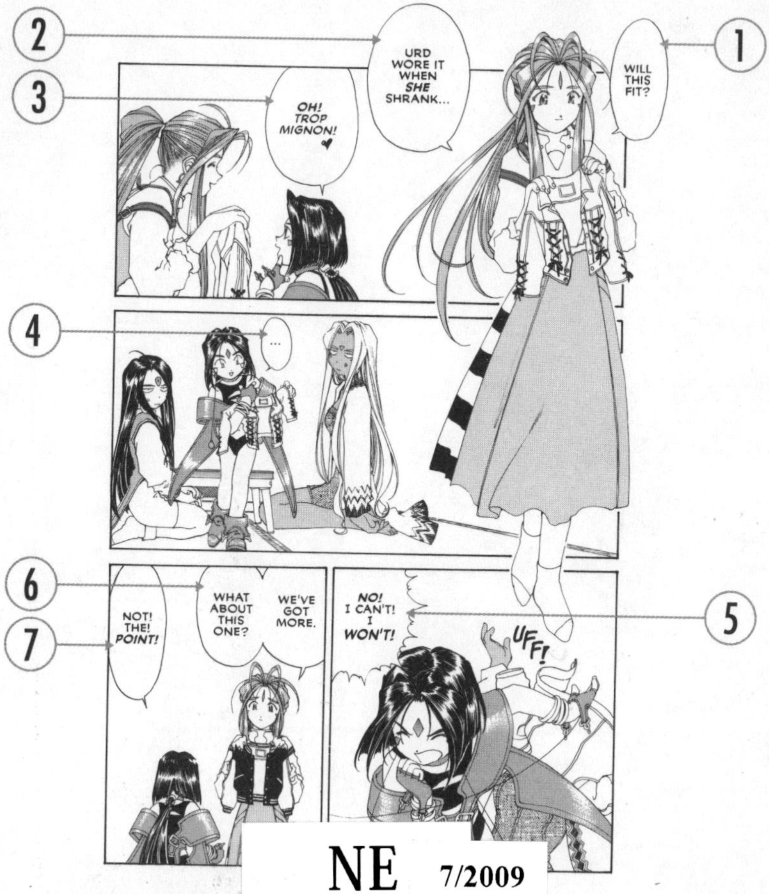
1
WILL THIS FIT?
2
URD WORE IT WHEN SHE SHRANK...
3
OH! TROP MIGNON!
4
...
5
NO! I CAN'T! I WON'T!
UFF!
6
WE'VE GOT MORE.
WHAT ABOUT THIS ONE?
7
NOT! THE! POINT!